The Origins of Faulkner's Art

The Origins of Faulkner's Art

by Judith L. Sensibar

UNIVERSITY OF TEXAS PRESS, AUSTIN

First Edition, 1984

Requests for permission to reproduce material from this work
should be sent to Permissions, University of Texas Press,
Box 7819, Austin, Texas 78712

LIBRARY OF CONGRESS CATALOGING IN PUBLICATION DATA
Sensibar, Judith L. (Judith Levin)
    The origins of Faulkner's art.

    Bibliography: p.
    Includes index.
    1. Faulkner, William, 1897–1962—Criticism and
interpretation.   2. Faulkner, William, 1897–1962—Poetic
works.   I. Title.
PS3511.A86Z9665   1984   813'.52   83-23382
ISBN 0-292-79020-1

Publication of this work has been made possible in part by a grant from
the Andrew W. Mellon Foundation.

TO DAVID, JESSE, AND NOAH

Contents

Illustrations

Acknowledgments

Texts—William Faulkner's manuscripts and typescripts—inform every aspect of this study. These and the study itself could not have been presented without the cooperation of Faulkner's executor, Jill Faulkner Summers. I want to thank her for her early and continuing interest in and support of this project, for giving me permission to quote and publish extensively from all of Faulkner's published and unpublished poetry, and for the unfailing courtesy and thoughtfulness with which she has answered questions concerning her father's interest in poetry and its place in his life.

My debt to those who have preceded me in criticism and in Faulkner studies is acknowledged as fully as possible in my notes and bibliography. A number of students of Faulkner encouraged or criticized my work at various stages. James B. Meriwether and Louis Daniel Brodsky offered invaluable assistance when I first began research on Faulkner's poetry. Professor Meriwether also gave generously of both his time and the resources at his command and I am grateful to him. My readers for the University of Texas Press—Linda W. Wagner and a still anonymous Faulkner scholar—offered balanced and thoughtful suggestions for small but significant changes in my manuscript. Later Thomas C. Moser asked to read it and provided sound advice for further revisions. He also took time to comment on a draft of my introduction to Faulkner's *Vision in Spring*. Thanks are due to those who agreed to read and criticize various versions of this book—Arthur F. Kinney, Joseph Blotner, Noel Polk, and Cleanth Brooks. In each instance I have benefited from their longer acquaintance with aspects of my subject. I am also grateful for Jill Spiller's efficient and tactful editing and David C. Hanson's help with the index. The staff of the University of Texas Press has been thorough and competent. Those who knew and loved William Faulkner gave unusually forthright interviews and I wish especially to thank author Joan Williams and script supervisor Meta Doherty Wilde for their time, thoughts, and memories.

From the beginning of my work on this book I was fortunate to have a small core of diverse, exacting, and sensitive readers. Of the friends and advisers who watched and sometimes guided its early progress my teachers at Chicago—Wayne C. Booth, James E. Miller, Jr., and John Paul Russo (now department of English chairperson, University of Miami)—deserve special thanks. I am grateful to Wayne Booth for his good humor and sustained enthusiasm, his open and challenging critical stance, and his insistence on clarity. Jim Miller's knowledge of the counter- and crosscurrents of Modernism and his early encouragement were essential. John Paul Russo's generous contributions in act and spirit extend beyond the bonds of either friendship or professional commitment. Others at the University of Chicago have read and rigorously questioned various chapters. Robert Ferguson, Ellen Keck, Janel Mueller, Jeffery Stern, and Bob von Hallberg all contributed from their particular areas of specialization, and discussions with Bert Cohler, Amy Kass, Robert Streeter, and Edward Wasiolek proved stimulating and helpful. Students in my Faulkner class at the University of Chicago Extension asked direct and penetrating questions that further clarified my thoughts.

Many libraries and librarians facilitated my research. Ellen Dunlap's high standards of professional integrity made her a valued friend as well as colleague. Other members of the staff at the Humanities Research Center (University of Texas at Austin), especially Cathy Henderson and John Kirkpatrick, were always helpful. Both Edmund Berkeley, Jr., of the Alderman Library (University of Virginia) and Thomas E. Verich at the University of Mississippi Library facilitated final preparation of this manuscript by their efficient handling of my requests and queries. I wish also to thank the staffs of the William B. Wisdom Faulkner Collection (Tulane University), the Berg Collection (New York Public Library), the Beinecke Library (Yale University), and the Memphis Public Library. Robert Rosenthal and Pat Swanson, both at Regenstein Library (University of Chicago), gave consistently sensible advice, which has served me well throughout.

A fellowship from the American Association of University Women (Jane Addams Fellow 1981–82) helped finance the first drafts of this manuscript. The final stages of research and last drafts were completed under a fellowship from the American Council of Learned Societies (Recent Recipients of the Ph.D., 1983–84). I am grateful to both organizations for their support.

Finally I wish to thank my friends—my Common Readers—who often helped me to see what I really wanted to say: Harold R. Balikov who first asked me to identify Pierrot, Barbara and David Cramer, Jeffrey Rubin-Dorsky, Jacqueline Kieff, Nancy Schaefer, Harvey Strauss. And David who read it all, again and again.

Grateful acknowledgment is made to the following for permission to reprint, reproduce, or quote from copyrighted material:

To Jill Faulkner Summers for permission to quote from, reproduce fragments of, and reprint from unpublished and published poetry by William Faulkner; for permission to quote from the "Elmer" papers by William Faulkner; for permission to reproduce three drawings from *The Marionettes*, the unpublished drawing appearing opposite the hand-lettered poem "A Song," and the drawing on Faulkner's letter to Maud Falkner postmarked 22 September 1925, all by William Faulkner. I am also grateful for the use of photographs of William Faulkner and Estelle Faulkner (my Figures 1, 4, and 15).

To Mary Hoover Aiken for permission to quote from *Turns and Movies and Other Tales in Verse* by Conrad Aiken, and to reprint the unpublished letter from Conrad Aiken to Joseph Blotner dated 16 May 1964. Material from *The Jig of Forslin* by Conrad Aiken has been reprinted courtesy of Branden Press, Inc., 21 Station Street, Brookline Village, Massachusetts 02147.

To Joseph Blotner for kindly providing photocopies of William Faulkner's letter to Maud Faulkner postmarked 22 September 1925 and of Conrad Aiken's letter to Joseph Blotner dated 16 May 1964, and for providing a revised version of the Faulkner genealogy from his *Faulkner: A Biography*.

To the Humanities Research Center, the University of Texas at Austin, for permission to reproduce fragments of variant lines of *Vision in Spring* and, on the versos, the holograph draft of the review of Conrad Aiken's *Turns and Movies*, both by William Faulkner (my Figure 8).

To the University of Mississippi Library for permission to reproduce the illustrated poem "Nocturne," and to quote from the "Elmer" papers, by William Faulkner.

To the University of Virginia Library for permission to reproduce three drawings from *The Marionettes*, the drawing on William Faulkner's undated letter to Alabama L. McLean postmarked 10 September 1925, and fragments from *The Lilacs* by William Faulkner.

To Professor Keen Butterworth and to the *Mississippi Quarterly* for permission to quote from Keen Butterworth, "A Census of Manuscripts and Typescripts of William Faulkner's Poetry," *Mississippi Quarterly* 26, no. 3 (1973): 333–359.

To Professor Joseph Killorin and to Yale University Press for permission to quote from Joseph Killorin, ed., *Selected Letters of Conrad Aiken.*

To Liveright Publishing Corporation for permission to quote from *Soldiers' Pay* by William Faulkner.

To Random House, Inc., for permission to quote from the following copyrighted works by William Faulkner: *Absalom, Absalom!*, *Flags in the Dust*, *Light in August*, *The Marble Faun and A Green Bough*, *Sanctuary*, and *The Sound and the Fury*. To Random House Inc., also for permission to quote from copyrighted material in Joseph Blotner, *Faulkner: A Biography*; Joseph Blotner, ed., *Selected Letters of William Faulkner*; and *Poems by Algernon Charles Swinburne* (Modern Library).

Memory believes before knowing remembers. Believes longer than recollects, longer than knowing even wonders. Knows remembers believes . . . —William Faulkner, *Light in August,* 1932

Introduction

William Faulkner the novelist was once William Faulkner the poet. For six, perhaps eight years (1916? to 1924) Faulkner wrote poetry almost exclusively. But these poems, his most transparently auto-biographical work, have been virtually ignored. No comprehensive study has been attempted and no one has shown how important Faulkner's poetic apprenticeship is to his fiction. My purpose here is to begin to fill the void.

I am especially interested in what Walter Jackson Bate calls the elementary psychological import of Faulkner's poem sequences. I ask not only what these poems mean, but what it meant to Faulkner to be a poet. My answers present a portrait of the young writer at a time in his career when the boundaries between fantasy and reality were noticeably shaky.

Faulkner completed many poems but, because some have been lost or destroyed, we will never know the exact number. Keen Butterworth's 1973 bibliography of Faulkner's published and unpublished poetry contains more than two hundred poems and poem fragments, excluding numerous alternate versions.[1] Since then other poems, including three complete and handbound poem sequences (*The Lilacs*, *Vision in Spring*, and *Helen: A Courtship*), have been recovered.[2] The addition of these sequences as well as other poems and sequence fragments owned by private collectors suggest a substantial body of work.

As my focus here is the relation of Faulkner's poetry to his novels, specifically those published before 1937, I have limited myself to those poems that most clearly illuminate this issue, particularly three major poem sequences Faulkner wrote before he began his first novel: *The Marble Faun* (ca. 1920, revised ca. 1923 to 1924), *The Lilacs* (January 1920), and *Vision in Spring* (1921, possibly revised 1923 and renamed *Orpheus, and Other Poems*). In their context, I also discuss Faulkner's 1920 dream-play, *The Marionettes* (December? 1920). Together these four works demarcate the essence—aesthetic and psychological—of Faulkner's self-designed poetic apprenticeship.

Because Faulkner's poems are apprenticeship writings, their interest attaches more to the process than the product of composition. What did Faulkner teach himself from writing poems, in which he imitated the great and not so great? How did he apply what he learned? What insights can the answers give to Faulkner's fiction? The answers reveal the artist in the process of developing formal structures, techniques, and thematic concerns that, in his novels, will support what Helen Vendler has called "new forms for consciousness."

Faulkner's critics have given short shrift to his years as a poet.³ Although Cleanth Brooks, Michael Millgate, Carvel Collins, Joseph Blotner, and more recent scholars like Hugh Kenner, John T. Irwin, David Minter, and Arthur F. Kinney assert that Faulkner's poetry and his novels are related, they have not explored the implications of their assertion. Faulkner's poetry has been dismissed, in Brooks's words, as the work "of a young romantic, whose imagination was filled with tales of derring-do, of knights errant and their lovely ladies; with landscapes in which fauns and nymphs danced to the music of the pipes of Pan; and with the search for an infinite beauty and a love too ethereal for this earth."⁴ As these scholars have studied only samples of Faulkner's poems, they have not noted that Faulkner generally wrote his poetry to be read in sequences rather than as discrete or separate lyrics. Their comments on specific poems, therefore, are often misleading because the poems have been separated from their context in a specific sequence.

Besides ignoring this important formal aspect of Faulkner's poetry—one that suggests that, from the beginning and even in poetry, his intentions leaned toward sustained and experimental forms of narrative—critics have not tried to view his poetry as a comprehensive body of work. They have, for the most part, disregarded the circumstances under which Faulkner wrote his poems, taking only passing note of the ways in which literary and familial influences acted both to hinder and encourage him. My intent in concentrating on Faulkner's years as a poet is to show that behind the poet's mask he conducted intriguing and useful exercises of imagination. The nature and interrelationship of these experiments reveal how his poetry, when placed in the context of his life, provides new insights concerning the formal style and thematic concerns of his novels, especially those novels that directly followed his long apprenticeship to poetry.

In reading the hundreds of surviving poems and poem fragments, two organizing principles emerged. The first concerned the identity of the most insistent voice or mask Faulkner favored; the second, the large formal structures with which he consistently experimented. It was my discovery of the latter—the notion of the poem sequence, particularly as Conrad Aiken had developed and explored it in his series of "symphonic" sequences written between 1915 and 1921—that helped determine and confirm the identity of Faulkner's favorite mask in all its manifestations.[5] Faulkner's subject, like Aiken's, is the quintessential masker himself, Pierrot, the darling of the Symbolists and early Modernists alike whose "vacillations between two dramatic and psychological 'types'"—amoral Harlequin and Hamlet—explain both the great attraction and the severe limitations of his appeal as a poetic persona.[6]

In his poetry Faulkner often, but not always, calls him by his rightful name. Nonetheless, Pierrot's character, even when disguised, informs and animates the protagonists of much of Faulkner's apprenticeship work. In the first sequence he started—a cycle of pastoral eclogues—he calls his *pierrotique* protagonist the Marble Faun.[7] In *The Lilacs*, Faulkner's first completed extant sequence, this figure appears variously as an airman in pursuit of a nympholeptic vision ("a white woman, a white wanton"); as an adolescent boy held in "snare" by the commanding "caress" of a Miss Havisham–like woman; and as a young man lamenting the loss of a love never actually possessed, the heart of "a dead dancer." The sleeping, drink-sodden Pierrot and his libidinous Shade are central to *The Marionettes*. In *Vision in Spring*, the sequence in which Faulkner ascertains the limitations of his mask, Pierrot becomes most like one of the fictional protagonists.

Besides its protean qualities, what drew Faulkner to Pierrot? The nineteenth- and twentieth-century variants of this mask, as Robert F. Storey explains, may trace their lineage at least as far as the Pedrolino characters in seventeenth-century commedia dell'arte.[8] But we are here concerned with Faulkner's Pierrot, a mask generated in part by his reading of Arthur Symons's *The Symbolist Movement in Literature* and early Modernist adaptations of the Laforguian Pierrot mask.[9] The poets most directly molding the cast of Faulkner's *pierrotique* mask were Mallarmé, Verlaine, and Laforgue via Symons and his own, slightly older contemporaries, Conrad Aiken and T. S. Eliot. Of all the Modernist poets, Faulkner appears to have read Aiken and Eliot most carefully. For it is their poems and masks he plagiarizes shamelessly as he composes his own poem sequences.[10]

Storey's explanation of Laforgue's appeal to Eliot and Wallace Stevens is applicable to Aiken and Faulkner as well. These young poets' major aesthetic preoccupations mirrored Laforgue's. Like him, they were indeed artists of masks but also poets whose subject was always themselves: "The worm that gnaws at Pierrot's white breast is consciousness being conscious of itself." Laforgue's Pierrot is an obsessive voyeur who prefers to look rather than act. Thus he constantly assumes "a stylized pose of total, deathlike, amused passivity." This Pierrot's sexual orientation was compatible to both Eliot and Faulkner. "The enemy is woman or instinct which must be resisted at all costs." The Pierrot mask was that of "a poet in love with dreams," not with real women.[11] Pierrot's excessive use of alcohol as an anodyne for psychic pain and escape into dreams of sadistic acts or nympholeptic visions had, as we shall see in Faulkner's art and life, a very direct personal appeal.

Yet another aspect of Laforgue's Pierrot made him a perfect persona for Faulkner. His impostures, his narcissism, his protean, androgynous character attracted the young poet who often appeared to imagine himself as an actor in his own dramas—dramas that were, in their essence, dream visions. Faulkner was drawn to the mask of Pierrot as he was drawn to the uniform of a World War I Canadian Royal Air Force officer. And these two costumes—one assumed in writing, the other in life—give graphic evidence of the ambivalence of Faulkner's self-expectations and idealizations during his apprenticeship years.

Faulkner, like Eliot and Stevens, discards the Pierrot mask, but only to reinvent Pierrot-like figures for the cast of Yoknapatawpha. Following his progress and observing how he gradually transforms Pierrot from poetic mask into vital aspects of the characters who inhabit the horrific cosmos of his fictional world, I show how experimenting with Pierrot's many voices in the formal context of the poem sequence taught Faulkner ways of discarding the mask while retaining in his writing the qualities that made it so imaginatively compelling. When he gave up his *pierrotique* persona Faulkner did not abandon either its language—the language of dream—or its character. Rather he began to make these dreams intelligible. The protean poet-dreamer resurfaces in his tragic and comic fictional protagonists. These characters' tragic flaws or grotesquely comic qualities are firmly rooted in Faulkner's *pierrotique* mask.

While Pierrot provided Faulkner with a basic character type possessed of multiple and often contradictory voices, the poem sequence offered a formal structure in which Faulkner could explore multilinear, noncausal, episodic, narrative modes of presentation. Sequences proved extremely effective forms within which to split, multiply, and then counterpoint Pierrot's voices through an increasingly complicated and sophisticated style.

What, then, is a poem sequence and why did Faulkner choose to compose in sequences rather than to write either long narrative poems or discrete lyrics? What, if any, is the relation between the forms of Faulkner's poem sequences and the formal aspects of his fiction? And was he, from the first, inventing and experimenting with stylistic devices also found in his novels—novels he did not begin to write until 1925?

As I read his completed but unpublished books of poetry, books he hand-lettered and bound himself, and as I studied his typescripts of sequentially grouped poems in the Faulkner collections at the University of Virginia, the University of Texas at Austin, the University of South Carolina, Tulane University, the University of Mississippi, and in private collections, it became apparent that even as a poet, Faulkner was experimenting with stylistic devices and thematic arrangements akin to the organization we associate with his and other elliptical Modernist novels. Such novels are condensed, like much lyric poetry, in the sense that the reader must supply narrative connections. They are also highly organized. Joyce's *Ulysses*, Virginia Woolf's *Mrs. Dalloway*, and Faulkner's *The Sound and the Fury* are paradigms of this kind of ellipsis and condensation.

While only one of Faulkner's poem sequences, *The Marble Faun*, has a recognizably linear narrative structure, the poems in his three others—*The Lilacs*, *Vision in Spring*, and, much later, *Helen: A Courtship*—are organized tonally and stylistically so that each poem in the sequence leads logically into the next.[12] Moreover, a complete sense of formal closure is not experienced until the reader has reached the end of the sequence. This does not mean that each poem cannot also be read as a discrete unit; Faulkner is careful to make his separate poems formally complete. But when they are read in sequence, we note that as each poem closes it opens out thematically, resulting in a much richer reading as one poem leads into and enlarges the meaning of the next and the whole sequence.

It has been observed that poetic closure is experienced when tensions created in a poem are released.[13] In a poem sequence release does not occur until the final poem. (Compare, for example, the lyrics in Eliot's 1917 volume with his *Four Quartets*.) Barbara Herrnstein Smith notes that in a single poem the poet uses various devices to prevent closure and sustain tension throughout the poem while simultaneously promising that the poem will end. Through analogy and repetition—tonal, structural, and thematic—the poet trains us to anticipate final closure. The same is true, on a larger scale, for the poem sequence.

Faulkner's adherence to formal closure coupled with what appears to be a deliberate avoidance of thematic closure is evident in both his discrete poems and in his poem sequences. This stylistic quality is a distinguishing and often problematic feature of Faulkner's novels, especially those I discuss in the context of his poetry.[14] How and to what purpose does Faulkner learn and develop this method of creating, maintaining, and sustaining dramatic tension so that it extends far beyond our actual reading experience? Looking at his novels in the light of his poetic apprenticeship and of the poetry embedded in them suggests some interesting answers.

Faulkner's sequences, like his novels, are variously constructed. Sometimes, as we read through them, our growing sense of a poet striving for more space cannot be explained adequately by the mere presence of varieties of sequential organization, multiple themes, and points of view. Technical devices Faulkner uses are also directed toward developing and layering the material with which he is working in ways that generally do not concern writers of discrete lyrics.

Poets have been writing sequences for centuries: Spenser's *Shepheardes Calender*, Sidney's *Astrophel and Stella*, Blake's *Songs of Innocence* and *Songs of Experience*, Meredith's *Modern Love*, Housman's *A Shropshire Lad*, and Eliot's *Four Quartets* are examples. But while much has been written about these poems, the genre itself has not been treated explicitly.[15] My analysis of *The Lilacs* and *Vision in Spring* suggests some criteria for defining or analyzing the sequence genre, but it is not a vigorous examination of it. My primary subject here is the growth of Faulkner's mind. The pivotal surviving work of his years as a poet is a previously unpublished and virtually unnoticed bound typescript called *Vision in Spring*.[16] It both marks and describes Faulkner's transformation from mediocre poet and dreamer to potentially brilliant novelist. The story of that transformation, of how he became what he wanted to be, of the internal and external struggle this involved, is my subject. Therefore, my chief concerns are the ever-deepening moral and aesthetic preoccupations of his poetry. I ask not only what the poems mean but what it meant to Faulkner to be a poet—what public and private place did poetry have in his perception of himself as an artist and as a human being? In answering these questions I show how Faulkner's lifelong concern with poetry, coupled with his abandoned desire to be a poet, shapes the form, the language, and the moral preoccupations of his major novels.

Through his apprenticeship to poetry, Faulkner began to teach himself "authentic and fluent speech."[17] Faulkner was, as he said with studied melodrama, a "failed poet"; but verse was not a dead end for him; rather it was a valuable and enduring beginning. For the essence of the poet's mask proved the source of the novelist's imaginative vision.

PART ONE

The Marble Faun and The Marionettes: Early Pierrotique Voices

. . . With half closed eyes I see
Peace and quiet liquidly
Steeping the walls and cloaking them
With warmth and silence soaking them;
. . . .
They sorrow not that they are dumb:
For they would not a god become.

—William Faulkner, *The Marble Faun* XVII (ca. 1924)

With *Soldiers' Pay* and *Mosquitoes* I wrote for the sake of writing because it was fun. . . . *Sartoris*. . . opened up a gold mine of other people, so I created a cosmos of my own. I can move these people around like God, not only in space but in time too.

—William Faulkner, interview, 1956

CHAPTER I

Apollonian Vision: *The Marble Faun*
(1918? to 1924)

In early December 1918 William Faulkner, whose name was then spelled "Falkner," returned to Mississippi from serving in World War I.[1] But, unlike the wounded soldier Donald Mahon in his first novel, *Soldiers' Pay*, Faulkner's tour of duty amounted only to a five-month training program in the Canadian Royal Air Force. He never saw action and probably never flew a plane.[2]

However, when he limped off the train in his home town of Oxford, Cadet Faulkner wore an overseas officer's cap, a Sam Browne belt, and flier's insignia on his unearned officer's uniform and he walked slowly, leaning on a cane.[3] The effect of his costume was immediate and gratifying. Bystanders ignored the other returning soldiers to cheer the apparently maimed officer and hero. His fellow enlistees looked on enviously. This hoax did not end at the station. Nor had it begun there. During the spring of 1918, before enlisting in the RAF, Canada (hereafter RAF), Faulkner and his mentor Phil Stone invented a fictional genealogy, which is preserved in his RAF certificate of service. There he lists his birthdate as 25 September 1897; his birthplace as Finchley, Middlesex, England; his religion as Church of England; and the person to be informed in case of casualty as Mrs. Maud *Faulkner*, Oxford, Mississippi. In listing his mother rather than his father he changes the spelling of her name and suggests by the form that she is no longer married.[4]

When Faulkner's honorary second lieutenant's pips arrived he wore the entire costume around Oxford and memorialized his imposture in a series of "official portraits" (Figure 1).[5] In them he looks tall, cocky, and authoritative. Actually he was only 5'5" tall, while his wounded brother Jack, his father, and his grandfather were all six-footers. Throughout the years 1918 through 1925, Faulkner, the spelling he used with the publication of his own version of "L'Après-midi d'un faune" in the August 1919 *New Republic*, assumed all or parts of his war hero imposture as it suited his needs. Furthermore, he alternated between it and a second character, a poet who had assumed the mask of Pierrot. Faulkner's poet dress was either so outrageously dandified or so slovenly that his peers at the University of Mississippi began calling him Count No 'Count.

Faulkner's role playing seems at odds with the difficult task he set himself after his arrival home: to write *The Marble Faun*, a cycle of pastoral eclogues; a series of shorter poems, some of which he included in his first completed poem sequence *The Lilacs*; and a Symbolist dream-play, *The Marionettes*. But understanding of these works and their relation to and significance for Faulkner's later prose fiction is hampered unless they are read in the context of the identities Faulkner assumed when he wrote them. Faulkner became aware of the implications of his poses as warrior and aesthete. He later parodied both in *Soldiers' Pay*[6] and in his first Yoknapatawpha novel, *Flags in the Dust*.[7] Only when he converted the fantasies behind his need for such impostures into fiction, as he did first in these early works and later in his five finest novels, did he establish his unique voice.

Faulkner spent the years 1918 through 1924 writing poetry. He also, at intervals throughout these years, revived his wounded war hero imposture. There seems to be a close connection between Faulkner's extended apprenticeship to poetry and his role playing in real life. Six, possibly eight years was a long time to write in a language he could not master. One wonders if there is a relationship between Faulkner's long apprenticeship to poetry and his concurrent commitment in life to the "masks" of poet and wounded warrior. Faulkner's later assertion that he was a "failed poet" suggests as much. On the surface it might appear to be a typical Faulknerian joke to tease the press. But it contains a germ of truth, as it acknowledges and accepts the failure of his youthful, impossibly idealistic desires.

Although pretending to be a wounded war hero gave him gratification in his everyday life, it made a large and fertile area of his fantasy life unavailable for conversion to an artistic form; thus that nagging question of identity—so central and so imaginatively pursued in Faulkner's mature work—hindered him in these early years. The poets and novelists Faulkner chose as models also aided and impeded his growth. He could imitate, paraphrase, and plagiarize them, but he could not, at first, make them serve the needs of his own voice. The beginnings of Faulkner's transformation from poet to novelist, so apparent in his 1921 sequence *Vision in Spring*, reached completion in his Yoknapatawpha novels. There Faulkner draws upon both sequence structure and his early poetic visions to generate emblematic scenes and the language that characterizes them.

In about two years by Faulkner's own dating, starting the April following his return from military service, the twenty-two-year-old writer completed the two most ambitious projects of the first stage of his apprenticeship to poetry: a pastoral cycle of nineteen eclogues, *The Marble Faun*, which imitates a poetic genre dating at least from the third century B.C., and a one-act dream-play, *The Marionettes*, which derives in part from the Symbolist movement of the late nineteenth century.[8] Between these two larger efforts Faulkner published a series of thirteen short, thematically unrelated poems in the University of Mississippi student newspaper and yearbook.[9] Many of these are adaptations, imitations, or free translations of famous Symbolist poems. He reprinted some of these in *The Lilacs*, a poem sequence completed in 1920. It is within the framework of *The Marble Faun* and *The Marionettes* that Faulkner's intentions concerning *The Lilacs*—a more diffused sequence—can be clarified.

During the two, possibly three, years from beginning *The Marble Faun* to completing *The Marionettes*, Faulkner moves imaginatively from an idyllic Arcadian landscape inhabited by mythical figures and statues to a decadent magic garden peopled with stylized, erotic, cruel characters from commedia dell'arte. The parts played by his family in the conception of *The Marble Faun* and *The Marionettes* are significant, emanating primarily from two of Faulkner's most colorful and articulate relatives: his mother, Maud Butler Falkner, a painter; and his paternal great-grandfather, Colonel William Clark Falkner, the author of several novels and a mock-epic poem, who died almost eight years before his namesake's birth.[10] Maud Falkner's influence is most apparent in Faulkner's 1921 sequence, *Vision in Spring*, but the Colonel is a different matter. Recognition and understanding of Faulkner's ambivalent attitude toward the Colonel and his works, particularly his military and financial exploits and his writing career, explain in part the impetus behind the elaborate role playing Faulkner indulged in during this period. As previous critics have noted, emulation of the Colonel began early. Even at nine years of age, Faulkner identified with him, telling his teacher and classmates, "I want to be a writer like my great-grandaddy."[11]

Living male relatives and two male friends who were Faulkner's early mentors figure in Faulkner's aesthetic and moral development, but, as others have shown, their ultimate influence was relatively insignificant. Faulkner quickly discarded them as, at a much earlier age, he had dismissed his weak, ineffectual father and had chosen instead to idealize, emulate, hate, and love a long-dead "father" whose successes had achieved legendary status. This identification

Royal Flying Corps

FIGURE 1. William Falkner/Faulkner posing in his various Canadian Royal Air Force (RAF) outfits. Note that the handwriting on the photograph of Faulkner in his overseas officer's cap is Faulkner's mother's (Jill Faulkner Summers, interview, 16 May 1983). The writing is identical to Faulkner's in *The Marionettes* (ca. 1920). Faulkner had it taken while he was in Canada. Stamped on the verso is "Post Card / Made in Canada / Place Stamp Here." For other photographs from this period, see Blotner, *Faulkner*, pp. 200, 225, and Jack Cofield, *William Faulkner: The Cofield Collection* (Oxford, Miss.: Yoknapatawpha Press, 1978), pp. 53, 55, 56. Photographs courtesy of Jill Faulkner Summers.

works both for and against him as a writer. At first Faulkner's ideal-ization of the Colonel was a stumbling block. But once he grasped its imaginative potential he transformed it to an unending wellspring for his vast fictional world: the history and people of Yoknapatawpha.

Neither Faulkner's writing nor his impostures as wounded officer, British aesthete, and penniless poet during the years 1918 through 1925 can be fully understood unless each is viewed in the context of the other. But the focus here is primarily on the works with the life as it informs them. It begins with the literary heritage of *The Marble Faun*, Faulkner's first long poem.

The Literary Ancestry: Keats and Hawthorne

At twenty-two, Faulkner had read the major novelists of the past three centuries, as well as Shakespeare, the Romantics, the Symbol-ists, Swinburne, the Georgians (especially Housman), Yeats, and, fi-nally, Eliot, Aiken, and other Modernists. Which of these writers did Faulkner choose to emulate in *The Marble Faun* and to which as-pects of their art was he most attracted? What did he question or re-ject? Faulkner's tastes were eclectic, and he drew upon both an American and a European heritage, most obviously upon Haw-thorne, Keats, and Tennyson. Hawthorne influences both Faulkner's intention and the direction of the plot in *The Marble Faun*; Keats, the intention and the mode; and Tennyson, much of the cycle's ton-al color. Tennyson's *The Princess* is echoed throughout Faulkner's cycle. As others have observed, the Symbolist poets' influence is pervasive.[12] By comparing Faulkner's treatment of influences in this cycle to his use of them in the works immediately preceding and in his later prose fiction we learn something about *The Marble Faun*'s place in Faulkner's imaginative development.

As he learns to control his influences, he can use them not only to recall, echo, or attempt to emulate the past but also to question it. Those influences that Faulkner has transformed reveal his appren-tice work's elemental psychological import.[13] Faulkner's later use of such literary influences, often for humorous or ironic purposes, en-abled him to question and transform the past. But such humor and irony also had a private autobiographical function: it permitted him, either consciously or unconsciously, to comment on his own earlier self, the young poet who wrote *The Marble Faun*.

Why did Faulkner choose the eclogue for what was essentially a medium-length poem? Quite possibly he took his cue from other fa-mous writers: Vergil, Spenser, Pope, and especially Keats, the poet who influenced Faulkner throughout his career. Keats's explanation for his first great test of invention, *Endymion*, is equally applicable to Faulkner's *The Marble Faun*: "a long Poem is a test of Invention which I take to be the Polar Star of Poetry, as Fancy is the Sails, and Imagination the Rudder. Did our great Poets ever write short pieces? I mean in the shape of Tales . . ."[14]

Like Keats, Faulkner imposed a time scheme for his "tale" that is controlled, as in most pastorals, by the rhythms of the seasons in large units and by the cyclical movement of the days and nights in smaller units.[15] He also set a rigid production schedule for himself, following in the steps of other famous writers.[16] That Faulkner carefully dated the sequence following its epilogue, "April, May, June, 1919," was exceptional in that he was generally careless about dating poetry. Furthermore, he did not publish *The Marble Faun* until 1924. By the 1919 dating, Faulkner appears to be saying, this is how I want to be perceived at this particular stage in my life; he is shaping his own life story for posterity much as he later shapes the lives of his fictional characters. This bit of fictive dating as well as his impostures of this period, the photographs and the fanciful genealogy he added to *The Marble Faun*, were all ways of imposing a fictional screen over his private life. Faulkner's choice of April, May, and June 1919 suggests a further identification with Keats: these were the months during which the poet wrote his great odes in 1819. In the body of the poem, Faulkner's fear of and desire for fame is expressed in his tortured vision of the impotent artist transparently masked by the character of the *pierrotique* Marble Faun.

Also, like Keats, Faulkner charged himself with constructing a poetic narrative. Its subject matter bears striking similarities to Keats's first trial of invention. The tale, like Endymion's, is of a quest: Endymion's for ideal love and the ability to find a mode for its expression, the Faun's for a poetic voice and the personal freedom to permit its expression. But Endymion's quest ends in success and the Marble Faun's in failure. In terms of its conventions, Faulkner's cycle, while possessing allegorical tendencies or aspects, is not as strictly allegorical as Keats's. But its narrator and central subject, the Marble Faun, is, like Endymion, the young poet disguised. In both poems, the god Pan plays a central role as a symbol of the imagination.[17]

Faulkner's Faun, a statue carved by another artist, feels "imprisoned" by his "cast." He can only see nature as it exists in his walled garden and is reflected in its man-made pool and fountain. The Faun's garden is "nature methodized." Its linear poplar trees and hyacinths are planted in rows, purple asters and phlox are confined to their appropriate beds, and a natural spring has been channeled. Although his garden is beautifully ordered, the Faun is "sad." His view is restricted. His marble form condemns him to the role of passive perceiver. He says he is a "prisoner" and contrasts his lot to that of Pan, who is free to roam the world and create songs so powerful that they hold nature in thrall. Thus Pan is like the Faun's maker, who sculpted him "in marble bonds" and confined him to "enthralled impotence" in his formal garden setting.[18]

In contrast to Keats's 4,000 lines, Faulkner's maiden poem is only 810 iambic tetrameter lines. By choosing, like Keats, an ancient poetic mode with a traditional subject and title for his first long poem, Faulkner was simultaneously identifying with and challenging the great poets of the past.[19] Adopting the title of Hawthorne's last completed novel for his poem, Faulkner dares the reader to measure his own novice poem against the last completed work of a great literary ancestor.[20] The challenge is neither casual nor coincidental. Throughout the cycle, both thematic and metaphorical parallels occur between Faulkner's eclogues and Hawthorne's novel. The most specific thematic parallel is the treatment of the young artist's uneasy relationship to the artistic achievement of the past. In Hawthorne's novel it is explicit; in Faulkner's poem it is implicit. But Hawthorne remains ambivalent about the artist's relation to his or her past. The main figures in his novel, three young American artists, seek inspiration in their European past. That Hawthorne sympathizes with but sees the inherent dangers in dependence on this past for inspiration is apparent in his authorial intrusions and in the quality of the art his characters produce. Explaining why American artists congregate in Rome, Hawthorne as the narrator says:

> In every other clime they are isolated strangers; in this land of art, they are free citizens. . . . They shiver at the remembrance of their lonely studios in the unsympathizing cities of their native land. For the sake of such brotherhood as they can find, more than for any good that they get from galleries, they linger year after year in Italy, while their originality dies out of them, or is polished away as a barbarism.[21]

Of his three artists, Hilda is an avowed copyist who paints reproductions of the great masters. The sculptor, Kenyon, produces original work, but his best one, a bust of Cleopatra, is a reworking of a historical figure.[22] The other painter, Miriam, the novel's heroine, tries to escape the influence of her past. "Is the past so indestructible, the future so unmitigable?" she asks. But when she paints her own portrait, she creates a double imitation: instead of an original, she produces a portrait of the painting Hilda is currently reproducing.[23] Miriam's recognition of her own "plagiarism," her own dependence on the past, is a moment of illumination. The experience makes it possible for her to accept the stifling influence of the past on the present.[24] But having had her illumination, Miriam renounces both her femininity and her art by condemning herself to a solitary life of "toil, sacrifice, prayer and penitence."[25] Her realization saves her soul in the Christian sense, but condemns her, literally and metaphorically, to a barren existence. The subtitle of Hawthorne's last novel could have been *The Death of the Artist*.

Faulkner found Hawthorne's resolution both challenging and untenable. Thus he rejected it and attempted to offer an alternative as he explored the same theme. The cycle might be read as Faulkner's reworking not only of Hawthorne's disturbing conclusion but also of the conception underlying many myths and fairy tales: to name one's fear is to conquer it. Faulkner does this in *The Marble Faun* both by his oblique attack on Hawthorne's pessimistic prophecy regarding the future of the young American artist and by his attempt to offer another vision in its stead.

Faulkner borrows Hawthorne's symbol of the Marble Faun in order to transform it. Both fauns are marble statues and represent completed works of art; both are contrasted to a mirror image. But Hawthorne's mirror image is human and very fallible, the opposite of the statue that he describes as a perfect work of art. Faulkner makes Pan the ideal image and his statue a mere imitation. Hawthorne suggests that ancient artists could create ideal images, but Faulkner argues that such ideals exist only in imagination. Gods—like Pan—can be imagined but cannot be translated to concrete forms. Hawthorne opts nostalgically for an idealized past; Faulkner insists on grappling with the present.

In one important way Faulkner's sequence succeeds where Hawthorne's novel wavers. Although the poem lacks thematic resolution and concludes with the Faun still circumscribed by artistic achievements of the past, the poet/Faun has a moment of imaginative transcendence not available to Hawthorne's heroine. It occurs when he at last defines the source of his paralysis and states his wish to be a poet. Read biographically, then, Faulkner's *Marble Faun* becomes a kind of artistic manifesto: by simultaneously utilizing and challenging themes and language of past artists Faulkner can describe his present impotence and express his wish to be a poet.

How and where do Faulkner and Hawthorne differ? In Hawthorne's novel, the faun is split: his two halves constitute art and life. The statue, Praxiteles' Marble Faun, is, according to the narrator, the paradigm of superlative artistic achievement.[26] Kenyon first notes its physical similarity to Hilda and Miriam's companion, a "simple" Italian count named Donatello.[27] His apparent innocence, lack of sophistication, and physical appearance all combine to make Donatello the statue's mirror image. In the course of the novel, Donatello moves from a state of innocence to one of knowledge and guilt. The transforming agent is, ironically, Miriam, with whom he falls in love. Although Miriam corrupts Donatello unwittingly, she pays a heavy price: the forfeiture of her wish to be an artist.

For Hawthorne, then, the statue represents an ideal that only an artist of the Golden Age could have envisioned and executed. In contrast, Donatello, the statue's living mirror image, is a corrupted, tarnished version of the original. His corruption is effected just as the perfection of Praxiteles' marble statue was effected: by an artist.

In contrast to Hawthorne's narrator, Faulkner's Marble Faun sees his timeless existence as a terrible fate. It is one source of his thralldom and impotence. Faulkner's Faun, although contained within one character is also split: his form is the completed work of art while his voice is the aspiring poet's. His Faun represents both the present and the past: achieved artistic creation and artistic creation striving for expression. The statue, another artist's creative production, is only a poor copy of the original imaginative creation, the god Pan. It is to Pan that the Faun constantly compares himself, dwelling on Pan's power to bend the world to his will with his song and to move about and experience it. The Faun can dream, but he cannot use his imagination to mold his dreams into art. He remains "forever mute and impotent" (*TMF* X, p. 36), imprisoned in both his dreams and in a shape created by another artist.

The conventions of eclogue predetermine to a great extent the form and tone of the Faun's lament. That the structure and theme mirror one another offers a vivid portrayal of Faulkner's artistic dilemma at that time in his life and is a superb example of how a young writer's early works can illuminate his mature writings. The theme of a person so imprisoned in his fantasies that he fails to live a creative life and ultimately destroys himself and others recurs throughout Faulkner's novels. Through the Faun Faulkner is seeking to separate himself from the dreamer so that he may become the poet.[28] The same conflict will serve as a source of much of the tension in *The Sound and the Fury*, *Light in August*, and *Absalom, Absalom!*

How does Faulkner portray the young artist's struggle between obeisance to the past and commitment to life in the present in his poem? Idealization of the past is found only in his cycle's imitation of his predecessors' forms and language. The Marble Faun does not idealize the past. Quite the contrary, he feels imprisoned by a mold carved out for him by another artist. The prologue states his predicament. He is imprisoned in "dream" and "marble bonds."[29] When the Faun laments his fate he contrasts himself to a snake. When he dreams of being free he imagines himself as a snake (*TMF* II, p. 16). Like Adam before the Fall, he inhabits a perfect garden, but, like Adam, he may not taste of the fruit around him (*TMF*, prologue, p. 12). He longs to be both Pan and the snake; the artist and the sensualist. The snake also symbolizes knowledge of good and evil, which the Faun claims he lacks: "I dream . . . For things I know, yet cannot know," (*TMF*, prologue, p. 12). Both Pan and the serpent also control language—a power the Faun deeply desires. Like Adam, the Faun wants to explore not only his garden but the whole world, to roam the earth and try out his imaginative powers; in short, to taste of the forbidden fruit (*TMF*, prologue, p. 12).

The Faun's dilemma is the poet's, thinly disguised. In these eclogues Faulkner will try to give his conflict between dreaming and acting a communicable shape by transmuting it into art. It is the young poet as well as the Marble Faun who cries:

> Why am I sad? I?
> Why am I not content? The sky
> Warms me and yet I cannot break
> My marble bonds. (*TMF*, prologue, p. 12)

While Faulkner's language here is awkward and melodramatic, the thoughts expressed are revealing, particularly in the context of what the poet/Faun says about himself and his relation to the world. He feels his creativity limited to dreams and fantasies of becoming someone more powerful than himself: the snake, and Pan. While he writes the first drafts of *The Marble Faun*, Faulkner, as he pretends to be a wounded war hero, is also reenacting the life of his great-grandfather and his actually wounded brother Jack. For reasons inexplicable to himself ("for things I know, yet cannot know"), he does not feel free to transform his dreams and fantasies about his familial past into successful "songs." By contrasting himself to the snake in the prologue, he reinforces the reference to himself as an Adamic figure in Eden.

Faulkner's Thralldom to the "Horns of Elfland"

In the first and second eclogues of *The Marble Faun*, the Faun describes what he would do if he could assume Pan's powers and become a real poet, not a mere imitator or impostor. "Free," he would "fly" and "leap" and "whirl" like Pan about the world (*TMF* I, p. 13). He would leave his ordered and perfect garden for the wilds: mountains, abysses, and waterfalls. Unbonded he would tread in Pan's footsteps and participate in the mysteries of original artistic creation.

But when Faulkner tries to imagine the Faun's freedom, his language begins to imitate Tennyson, specifically the interlude concluding Part III of *The Princess*. In this interlude the poet makes an important distinction between mere fancy (the horns of Elfland) and true creative power (the poet's bugle cry).

> The splendor falls on castle walls
>   And snowy summits old in story;
> The long light shakes across the lakes,
>   And the wild cataract leaps in glory.
> Blow, bugle, blow, set the wild echoes flying,
> Blow, bugle; answer, echoes, dying, dying, dying.
>
> O, hark, O, hear! how thin and clear,
>   And thinner, clearer, farther going!
> O, sweet and far from cliff and scar
>   The horns of Elfland faintly blowing!
> Blow, let us hear the purple glens replying,
> Blow, bugle; answer, echoes, dying, dying, dying.
>
> O love, they die in yon rich sky,
>   They faint on hill or field or river;
> Our echoes roll from soul to soul,
>   And grow for ever and for ever.
> Blow, bugle, blow, set the wild echoes flying,
> And answer, echoes, answer, dying, dying, dying.[30]

Faulkner will echo other poets in these eclogues, but none more cleverly or with greater effect: lines from this interlude appear throughout Faulkner's sequence, acting as a unifying device. Furthermore, understanding their function here greatly enriches their meaning in a later fictional work, *Light in August*. There, Faulkner has "farmed" Tennyson's lines, which resurface as a leitmotiv in the Reverend Hightower's recurrent fantasy.[31] His passive immersion in Tennyson's poetry symbolizes Hightower's impotent thralldom to a private, solipsistic dreamworld.

Echoes of Tennyson's song appear at seven different points in the eclogues. Faulkner's first Tennysonian image comes from the song's opening lines, describing sunset reflecting on the castle walls. Faulkner changes the time of day: "As the tumbling sunlight falls / Spouting down the craggy walls" (*TMF* I, p. 14). By the sixth eclogue Faulkner has begun to describe sunset: "Evening turns and sunlight falls / In flecks between the leafèd walls" (*TMF* VI, p. 26).

In the seventh, continuing his description of the sunset he describes the light as:

. . . The crimson falls
Upon the solemn ivied walls;
The horns of sunset slowly sound
Between the waiting sky and ground;
. . . .
Now the vesper song of bells
Beneath the evening flows and swells,
And the twilight's silver throat
Slowly repeats each resonant note:
The dying day gives those who sorrow
A boon no king can give: a morrow. (*TMF* VII, p. 28)

This last couplet is repeated with two variations as the closing couplet of the eighth eclogue and in the cycle's final lines. In the eleventh eclogue, Faulkner invokes Tennyson to describe Pan's voice, the true poet's song:

Clear and sad sounds Pan's thin strain,
Dims in mystery, grows again;
Mirrors the light limbs falling, dying,
Soothes night voices calling, crying,
. . . .
And flames the shadows' subtleties
Through endless labyrinthine walls
Of sounding corridors and halls . . . (*TMF* XI, p. 38)

In the sixteenth eclogue, the Faun suddenly rejects the passionate human experiences he has clamored for and, as he complains about the hideous noises humans make as they dance and sing, he misreads Tennyson's description of his poet's music. The Faun calls the noise an "unclean heated thing / Debauching the unarmed spring" (*TMF* XVI, p. 46). Such debauchery has destroyed his "dreams of peace" and the order in his garden: "the hyacinths, straight row on row" (*TMF* XVI, p. 47). Even invoking Tennyson's music fails to keep the Faun's nightmares at bay (*TMF* XVI, p. 47). These nightmare images mock the Faun with Tennyson's song, making us question whether the Faun really does wish to experience "things I know, yet cannot know" (*TMF* I, p. 12). Here he seems to wish to settle for the horns of Elfland rather than to rise to the challenge of his imagination's bugle cry.

In the seventeenth eclogue the Faun states his wish to be as powerful as Pan—to be, in fact, "a god." Shifting from the conditional to the present tense he then experiences a brief transcendental moment:

> . . . I am sun-steeped, until I
> Am all sun, and liquidly
> I leave my pedestal and flow
> Quietly along each row,
> Breathing in their fragrant breath
> And that of the earth beneath. (*TMF* XVII, pp. 48–49)

Apollonian vision belongs momentarily to the Faun: he is "all sun." He is also, momentarily, a sensate and sensual being: "liquidly" and "flow" recall the snake image of earlier eclogues. His first act is to enjoy the earth's smells. Now that he is no longer another's immortal work of art but his own, Faulkner's Faun says, "Time may now unheeded pass: / *I am the life* that warms the grass" (*TMF* XVII, p. 49, emphasis added).

He cannot sustain this state for long. By the eclogue's third and final strophe, the Faun has permanently abandoned his quest "for things I know, yet cannot know" in favor of eternal sleep:

> . . . Pan's understanding eyes
> Quietly bless me from the skies,
> Giving me, who knew his sorrow,
> The gift of sleep to be my morrow. (*TMF* XVII, p. 49)

The Faun's childlike dependence on Pan mirrors Faulkner's dependence on Tennyson, whose language he invokes at key points in his cycle. While it soothes, it also inhibits or restrains him from achieving a successful thematic resolution. The Faun does not, ultimately, free himself from his dreamlike, volitionless, and emotionally anesthetized state. As long as he clings to Tennyson's language he remains in the form imposed on him by another artist.

By the time Faulkner returns to Tennyson, when writing *Light in August* (1932), he is able, in Lipking's terms, to farm the older poet and harvest his own imaginative material. No Marble Faun but the Reverend Gail Hightower, a poet of sorts and a self-appointed outcast, gently eases himself into impotent fantasies with Tennyson's language. In inventing Hightower, Faulkner weaves Tennyson's poem into his own creative vision, as he simultaneously offers an autobiographical comment on the young poet who wrote *The Marble Faun*. In *The Marble Faun*, Faulkner's imitation of Tennyson illustrates the wide gap between his intention and performance. But in the character of the Reverend Hightower, Faulkner manifests awareness of his earlier deficiency. Hightower is hopelessly tangled in a web of fantasied glory based upon his dead grandfather, a Civil War soldier shot while raiding a chicken coop. Hightower uses Tennyson's language to transform his grandfather's antiheroic exploits into heroic acts. These fantasies, like the young Faulkner's, are built with someone else's language. Here is Hightower's vision of his grandfather:

> He can remember how when he was young, after he first came to Jefferson from the seminary, how that fading copper light would seem almost audible, like a dying yellow fall of trumpets dying into an interval of silence and waiting, out of which they would presently come. Already, even before the falling horns had ceased, it would seem to him that he could hear the beginning thunder not yet louder than a whisper, a rumor, in the air. . . .
> You can see it, hear it: the shouts, the shots, the shouting of triumph and terror, the drumming hooves, . . . you can feel, hear in the darkness horses pulled short up, plunging; clashes of arms; whispers overloud, hard breathing, the voices still triumphant; behind them the rest of the troops galloping past toward the rallying bugles.[32]

Hightower is "that son who grew to manhood among phantoms, and side by side with a ghost" (*LIA*, p. 449). He too dwells in a "fairyland." Because he does, he has about him "the smell of people who no longer live in life."[33] When he is not escaping reality through fantasy he escapes by reading Tennyson, and the swift change in the rhythm of his thinking as he begins to read—from short declarative sentences to long ambiguous ones—records this.

> One wall of the study is lined with books. He pauses before them, seeking, until he finds the one which he wants. It is Tennyson. It is dogeared. He has had it ever since the seminary. He sits beneath the lamp and opens it. It does not take long. Soon the fine galloping language, the gutless swooning full of sapless trees and dehydrated lusts begins to swim smooth and swift and peaceful. It is better than praying without having to bother to think aloud. It is like listening in a cathedral to a eunuch chanting in a language which he does not even need to not understand. (*LIA*, p. 301)

When Faulkner links Hightower's sexual and spiritual impotence to his explicit desire not to communicate—"to not understand"—he also comments autobiographically on the young Faulkner caught up in the rhythms of Tennyson. But Faulkner, unlike Hightower, was trying to break the "bonds" that chained his imagination to the past.

When Hightower gives up his grandfather fantasy, he also discards Tennyson:

> He moves like a man with a purpose now, who for twentyfive years has been doing nothing at all between the time to wake and the time to sleep again. Neither is the book which he now chooses the Tennyson: this time he also chooses food for a man. It is *Henry IV* and he goes out into the back yard. . . . (*LIA*, p. 383)

Hightower, as Faulkner ironically suggests by his choice of *Henry IV*, will not sustain his resolve to give up dreaming of and living in the past. Unlike Faulkner, he fails to translate and transform his vision into art and thereby live. His final vision, a wheel in which he sees his life revolving, is of stasis. The wheel spins, fading, "without progress" (*LIA*, p. 466). It is also in part the vision of his grandfather's army unit in which he sought refuge for so long: "And I know that for fifty years I have not even been clay: I have been a single instant of darkness in which a horse galloped and a gun crashed" (*LIA*, p. 465). Hightower, like many of the characters in Faulkner's novels, is chained to a mythical past dominated by a grandfather whose great stature, partly mythologized and partly real, possesses him and constricts his life.[34]

Comparing Faulkner's use of Tennyson in *The Marble Faun* and *Light in August* we gain access to this fantasy material as it appeared in an earlier, more psychologically transparent form. Such a view yields insight into the immense power literary and familial voices from the past held for him. We then understand why Faulkner made them central to his mature imaginative vision and why characters like Hightower are always doomed to failure. In his unacknowledged dialogue with Keats, Hawthorne, and Tennyson in *The Marble Faun*, Faulkner has addressed the relation of the would-be artist to his subject: the question of how to be a poet.

CHAPTER II

Virginity's Burden: *The Marble Faun* and *The Marionettes*

The Marble Faun's prologue and first eclogue establish his desire to be Pan, desire expressed in part through both imitating and questioning famous poets. He continues to do both in the next poems as he explores aspects of pastoral convention.[1] In the second eclogue, the Faun identifies the source of Pan's creativity: viewing his own image. Falsely, the Faun equates looking in a mirror with knowing oneself. Thus, according to the Faun, seeing his image reflected in a woodland pool triggers Pan's song. While this sylvan "hushed" pool is Pan's source of poetic inspiration, the Faun also identifies it with abstinence and withdrawal from the world. The pool offers the solace of "sleep within its cool / Virginity" (*TMF* II, p. 17). Immediately correspondences are set up between artistic inspiration and sexual abstinence.

A mirror image in a pool becomes central to the meaning of *The Marionettes*, where Faulkner reveals his new understanding of the Faun's error.[2] No longer ambiguous, as in *The Marble Faun*, the pool in Faulkner's dream-play reflects and magnifies its female protagonist's death-creating narcissism. Thus it serves as the very antithesis of creative inspiration. Other apparently pastoral poolside scenes—where the pool represents an oasis, a place where dreams are realized—reappear throughout Faulkner's poetry and in early novels like *Soldiers' Pay* and *Mosquitoes*. But beneath the glassy beauty of each scene lurk these questions: Who am I and how can I know anything? Faulkner, moving from his poet's Pierrot mask to his fictional voices, binds this pastoral image more and more tightly to the darker epistemological issues and themes inherent in the Narcissus myth. He does not effect a complete transformation of this conventional pastoral setting until he writes *Sanctuary* (1931), where he completely subverts the image to create an atmosphere of silent terror that serves as an analogue for the entire novel. In *Sanctuary*, mirror images, rather than serving as sources of poetic inspiration or as retreats from worldly desires, reflect either external reality—a grotesque antipastoral, a viciously fragmented world—or characters' hidden and forbidden desires. A good example is Faulkner's use of mirrors to reveal Horace's desire for his step-daughter.

In *Sanctuary*, Faulkner thwarts traditional expectations by invoking elements of pastoral tradition to show the irrelevance of that ordered Golden Age to the irrational world of Popeye, Temple Drake, and Horace Benbow. Their world is not merely upside down; it lacks causality; nature seems perverted and vision deliberately fragmented.

> The spring welled up at the root of a beech tree and flowed away upon a bottom of whorled and waved sand. It was surrounded by a thick growth of cane and brier, of cypress and gum in which broken sunlight lay sourceless. Somewhere, hidden and secret yet nearby, a bird sang three notes and ceased.
>
> In the spring the drinking man leaned his face to the broken and myriad reflection of his own drinking. When he rose up he saw among them the shattered reflection of Popeye's straw hat, though he had heard no sound.[3]

Reading *The Marble Faun* gives added dimension to Horace's role in *Sanctuary* and Quentin's in *The Sound and the Fury*. They and the Marble Faun have much in common. Sons of dangerously powerful mothers, their voices are those of creatures "given to much talk and not much else."[4] They are all, at heart, hopeless *pierrotistes*, whose failure and moral culpability are prefigured in the mirror visions through which they constantly think they see reality. The Marble Faun, Horace, and Quentin Compson are also would-be artists. Noel Polk interestingly suggests that Faulkner's "guiding principle" in revising *Sanctuary* was "the felt need to get outside Horace Benbow's cloyingly introspective, narcissistic personality."[5] Had Faulkner's Faun and his Pierrots from *The Marionettes* and other poems and poem sequences been considered in the analysis, a different conclusion might have been reached. As early as 1920 to 1921, Faulkner, wearing the mask of Pierrot, was already, in both *The Marble Faun* and *The Marionettes*, waging and beginning to win his battle to control this kind of character. In the novels Faulkner wrote between 1925 and 1936 he displays his victory prize: an apparently infinite capacity to invent a fascinating array of fictional figures like Darl, Horace, and Quentin, who are often, in essence, Pierrots or Marble Fauns. Neither more nor less realized characters, they are brilliant variations on Faulkner's earliest persona.

Although, in the first eclogues of his poem, the Faun describes the pleasures Pan enjoys, contrasts his own "unseeking impotence" to the god's powers of action and song (*TMF* III, pp. 18, 19), and resigns himself to statuedom, he nevertheless retains his powers of observation. Although his eyes are "shackled" by his physical confinement, his desire to perceive and record remains, suggesting that, despite the obvious limitations of his position, Faulkner as Faun cannot really imagine what it would be like not to want to be a poet.

Acts of observing and recording (that is, trying to know while remaining physically passive) continue to preoccupy the Faun throughout this early sequence. To speak, to see, to sing are the fourth eclogue's dominant verbs, and they clash against verbs describing the Faun's actual condition, his stasis and impotence. Here the image beckoning to the Faun becomes sexualized. The eternal feminine, disguised as trees (poplars, beeches, and aspens), lures the Faun, tempting him with "curving shivering hands" or "fluttering hands." As a statue, he is safe from erotic movements or touch and can continue to dream.

Faulkner makes the theme of sexual temptation—specifically luring virgins from Adamic gardens—more explicit in *The Marionettes*. This theme, like that of looking versus acting, is central to Faulkner's fictional world (remember Horace and Little Belle, Caddy Compson and her daughter Quentin, or even Dewey Dell) and its genesis is worth watching. Who is tempted and who does the tempting? How, if at all, is anyone's perception changed by such an experience?

Temptation in his Symbolist dream-play *The Marionettes*, though more specifically sexual than in *The Marble Faun*, is safe to express, because being merely a dream within a fantasy it is twice removed from reality. Pierrot's dream is about the exploits of his "shade," his heroic ideal.[6] As Pan calls to the Marble Faun, so Pierrot's Shade calls to Marietta. Unlike his inventor, the Shade succeeds in love and art: he "hypnotizes" and seduces the virgin with his song.

Noel Polk rightly observes that Marietta's "narcissistic" character is suggestive of Narcissa Benbow, "perhaps the coldest, most aloof, and most destructive of Faulkner's women" (*TM*, p. xvi). Marietta's relation to Temple Drake is, however, even more intriguing. Like that "virgin" she presents somewhat questionable, if not tarnished goods: "My bed is heavy and hot with something that fills me with strange desires. Why am I filled with desire for vague, unnamed things because a singing voice disturbed my dreams?" (*TM*, p. 10). Pierrot's Shade gives her what she wants as he calls her to sexual initiation:

You are a trembling pool,
  Love!

A breathless shivering pool,
And I am the flame that only you can quench.
. . . .

Let me drown myself between your breast points,
  Beloved! (*TM*, pp. 20–21)

The doubling and transforming quality of this image coupled with the pain associated with penetration—breast points/corn cob—all presage a bad end for Marietta's adventure, or Pierrot's dream. Consummation of desire results in Pierrot's Shade's disappearance and the revelation of Marietta's true colors. Marietta's end prefigures Temple Drake's in the Luxembourg Gardens. Totally enmeshed in her own image in the garden pool she seems—like the Symbolist playwrights her language slavishly echoes—paralyzed by her own verbal concoctions. Reverberations of Wilde's *Salomé* and Mallarmé's *Hérodiade* appear in her concluding speech.[7] Marietta seems obsessed by metaphors of cannibalism and death. Her final solution, like the Faun's, is total withdrawal. But because she is human, her refusal to act is a choice. And she chooses, like so many Faulkner characters, to die. Although he makes no comment on her choice in this play, Faulkner portrays it in the concluding drawing he made for *The Marionettes* (Figure 2). In the summer of 1921 Faulkner provides further interpretation in a poem called "Pierrot, Sitting Beside The Body of Colombine, suddenly Sees Himself in a Mirror."[8] The subject here is not so much his lover's death as Pierrot's tenuous grasp of his own reality. Although he sits beside the dead Colombine, his thoughts are on his own extinction: engulfed in darkness "like water" and watching "his hands / Dissolve from his knees and the crumpled wrists of his jacket," he sees "his face in the mirror before him / Slowly extinguished."[9] In the final strophe Pierrot's mirrored image is "like a dead match" while the body of Colombine seems "to him / The symbol of his own life: a broken gesture in tinsel."

The setting for Pierrot's dream in *The Marionettes*, a walled formal garden containing a pool and a fountain, establishes its close kinship with *The Marble Faun*. Linguistic parallels between the Faun's and Marietta's opening laments coupled with a similar setting are too deliberate not to confirm that Marietta, like her dreamer/creator, is also an elaboration of the Faun figure. Although it has been argued that "Pierrot and Marietta . . . are two sides of the same narcissistic coin, sterile and moribund in their selfish insistence on living exclusively for their own satisfaction" (*TM*, p. xxx), Faulk-

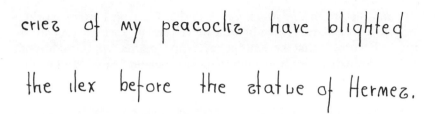

cries of my peacocks have blighted

the ilex before the statue of Hermes.

Curtain

FIGURE 2. Faulkner's drawing of Pierrot standing beside a dead girl and watching himself in a mirror. From *The Marionettes*. Courtesy of Jill Faulkner Summers and the William Faulkner Collections (Acc. No. 6271aj), University of Virginia Library.

ner's main point in *The Marionettes* is that Pierrot's fantasy world is enclosed, solipsistic. It is not that he is selfish. Rather he is so terrified of women that he cannot, even in dreams, *imagine* anyone "living exclusively for his or her own satisfaction." Sex, though compelling, is no fun for any of the marionettes.

Imagination and Mirror Images in Art and Life

The explicit sexuality of *The Marionettes* and its explicit denial in *The Marble Faun* contrast sharply. The similarity in setting and language between the two works suggests that in *The Marionettes* Faulkner is entering another level of the two essentially autobiographical concerns first raised in *The Marble Faun*: whether to be a poet or a dreamer and whether to be active or passive in personal relationships. How do Faulkner's love experiences inform his portrayals of sexuality, especially in his early writing, where authorial presence is so often thinly disguised?

In December 1918, when Faulkner returned to Oxford, Estelle Oldham Franklin, the woman he wanted to marry, was living in Honolulu with her husband, Cornell. She had wed him in April 1918, shortly before Faulkner enlisted. Manuscript evidence suggests that Faulkner worked on his poems for *The Marble Faun* during that winter and spring, and continued to do so during and after Estelle's first visit home in June 1919. (The University of Texas typescript of an earlier version of *The Marble Faun* containing twelve eclogues has some poems dated "April 1920.")[10] Certainly Faulkner, dating the final published copy as he did, wished the sequence finished before Estelle's return. She arrived in Oxford without her husband but with their four-month-old daughter Victoria, nicknamed Cho-Cho.[11]

Inscriptions Faulkner wrote in several books and his own poems suggest that he was deeply affected by Estelle's visit. When she returned to her husband in September 1919, she took Faulkner's copy of Swinburne. It contained his RAF faked title: "W. Faulkner / Royal Air Force / Cadet Wing / S of A / Borden." On its flyleaf he also wrote a dedication, which she felt impelled to remove. Its passionate tone was incriminating. It is possible that she also carried with her Faulkner's similarly inscribed copy of Ralph Hodgson's *Poems*. Its grandiose inscription read: "W. Faulkner R.F.C. / 2 Squadron 43rd. Wing / Royal Flying Corps."[12] Like the Swinburne, the Hodgson is missing the front endpaper. It also contains a holograph fragment of Pierrot's Shade's love song introduced and then commented upon by the Marble Faun, indicating the two once shared the same poem.

Although Estelle did not return to Oxford again until May 1921, perhaps five months after *The Marionettes* was completed, the play is filled with her presence. Faulkner hand-lettered and illustrated all extant copies. His drawings of the female lead sharply contradict the text, which states that Marietta has golden hair (*TM*, p. 44). Faulkner draws her as a skinny but bosomy flapper, her dark hair cut in a bob (Figure 3). She looks remarkably similar to the photographs of the young Estelle, who had dark red hair (Figure 4). But as we shall see in chapter 4, Faulkner began combining and splitting these female images—the dark and the light—at a very early age. Whether he sent Estelle a copy of his play or saved it to give her on her return a year and a half later is not clear, but one copy was hers and it was significantly dedicated thus:

TO "CHO-CHO,"
A TINY FLOWER OF THE FLAME, THE
ETERNAL GESTURE CHRYSTALLIZED;
THIS, A SHADOWY FUMBLING IN
WINDY DARKNESS, IS MOST RE-
SPECTFULLY TENDERED.[13]

The important figure here is not the baby Cho-Cho, but "the flame," her mother. Faulkner celebrates not so much the child as the the sex act itself, "the eternal gesture," of which Cho-Cho is the "flower." Juxtaposed to this act is another creative act: his play *The Marionettes*, a poor substitute. Faulkner persists in using this phrase, "shadowy fumbling in windy darkness," in early criticism and other dedications of poems to characterize love, his own poetry, and, in his fiction, bad art (see *Mosquitoes*). The flame also continues to figure in his poetry and prose as a symbol of female sexual power and of death.[14]

After Estelle returned to her husband in September 1919, Faulkner attempted to conform externally to his community's and family's expectations by enrolling at the University of Mississippi. His academic performance was unimpressive. Furthermore, his arrogance, his championing of French poets, and the grotesque personas he adopted antagonized students and professors alike. He registered again in September 1920, but failed to attend any classes and withdrew in November of that year. However, he continued to use his connections at the university to further his apprenticeship.

In part, *The Marionettes* represents Faulkner's thinly disguised attempt to come to terms with his own sexuality and with Estelle's marriage and motherhood. When Estelle announced her engagement

FIGURE 3. Faulkner's drawings of Marietta, Pierrot's Shade, and other characters from *The Marionettes* (ca. 1920). Courtesy of Jill Faulkner Summers and the William Faulkner Collections (Acc. No. 6271aj), University of Virginia Library.

to Franklin in March 1918, Faulkner promptly left town, assumed another identity, and enlisted in the RAF (July 1918). On his return, he adopted the imposture of wounded war hero and added two other roles: poet and artist. Although *The Marble Faun* is a sequence in which human beings and their relationships are curiously absent, *The Marionettes* and many of the poems written just before it importantly feature human relations. In this strange play the author manipulates his characters rather than playing a character who is manipulated. Stage directions indicate that the characters are consciously patterned after puppets; their movements and costumes are

FIGURE 4. Photograph of Estelle Oldham Faulkner (then Franklin) holding her son, Malcolm Franklin (ca. 1927). Courtesy of Jill Faulkner Summers.

highly stylized. But one has only to recall Popeye's and Temple Drake's stylized appearances and motions to recognize the incipient power of this early vision. Like their fictional offspring, Faulkner's first marionettes possess recognizably human forms whose actions Faulkner controls.

The similarity of the settings in *The Marionettes* and *The Marble Faun*, as well as the similarity of Pierrot's physical state to the Faun's (both are immobilized and "dreaming"), suggest that (like Popeye's) the Faun's lamented "impotence" may also be sexual. Using language to connect Pierrot's malaise with the Faun's, Faulkner hints that he (as author) is not capable of fuller imaginative exploration until he has experienced, absorbed, and integrated his feelings about Estelle as wife and mother. The objectives and results of leaving the protected garden in *The Marble Faun* and *The Marionettes* support such a hypothesis. However, Faulkner's ideas about the consequences of such a daring move changed during the months that lapsed between beginning *The Marble Faun* and writing *The Marionettes*. What does the garden represent; why are such virginal creatures, the Marble Faun and Marietta, tempted to leave; and when they choose to leave, what role does choice play in their decisions? These questions are important, for they recur in various forms throughout Faulkner's fiction.

The Marble Faun has no real choice. He is a statue and thus is physically unable to escape from the sheltered garden. So he settles for dreaming and sleep; that is, for noninvolvement in the real world. In *The Marionettes* Pierrot abrogates choice by choosing to be drunk while Marietta (Pierrot's dream image), like the Faun, wants to leave her Adamic garden in order to "know" and to be free. Pierrot's ambivalence is revealed through his two dream characters. Thus, although he endows Marietta with volition, he has her claim that she lacks free will because she has been hypnotized by Pierrot's Shade. In retaining his subject but transferring his fictional voice from a persona-statue to these marionettelike characters, Faulkner permits himself an imaginative latitude denied in *The Marble Faun*. In *The Marionettes* the deeper implications of this subject matter begin to surface.

CHAPTER III

Women and Language:
The Marble Faun's Bonds

Near the middle of *The Marble Faun* the unarticulated yet powerful agents of the Faun's imprisonment seriously retard his poem's progress. These are his fantasies of women and his still unassimilated awe of voices from the past. As a result his attempt to imagine himself outside his garden is a dismal poetic failure, the weakest part of this poem sequence. But because *The Marble Faun* is a maiden work, its weaknesses are, in some ways, of more interest than its successes. They help to explain the poet's progress toward inventing his own voice.

The Faun claims in the fifth eclogue that his prison keeper is Nature, who "holds all the pausing earth in thrall" (*TMF* V, p. 23). The Faun's overawed reaction to his jailer tells something about Nature's meaning for the Faun's creator. In her presence he feels impotent, which dramatically affects his voice in the sixth eclogue, where he shifts into awkward, archaic language, paraphrasing snippets of Tennyson, Eliot, and the Symbolists in the attempt to give life to his own verse. Describing the Faun's imagined journey through the world, Faulkner notes a wood, a road, a brook, a glade, and a dell where the Faun rests beneath a giant rock. These conventionally imaged landscapes appear flat despite a series of strained metaphors: "resilient poplar trees," "startled sunlight," "birches springing suddenly erect." These over-lively adjectives only highlight their author's dilemma. The Faun himself appears as passive perceiver in a stock pastoral world: nymphs bathe in yet another "silver languid pool," where figures meet their Swinburnian "inverted selves," their mirror images.

Despite some deliberately showy turns of phrase the quality of Faulkner's lines remains insistently imitative as he continues to lean on the language of other poets. Eliot's "Portrait of a Lady" wafts through the second strophe as Faulkner personifies summer ("around his head are lilac stalks") and "Prufrock" echoes where Faulkner describes the nymphs combing their hair ("And they kneel languorously there / To comb and braid their short-blown hair" [*TMF* IV,

p. 26]). Moreover, throughout the eclogue, Faulkner apes such popular Symbolist devices as synesthesia.[1] In the seventh eclogue—another on the Faun's imaginary journey—Faulkner continues to invoke *The Princess*, while in the eighth he achieves some formal successes that establish unity by reiterating and elaborating on the Faun's original lament (*TMF*, prologue, p. 20). As in Faulkner's fiction there is a steady accretion of images but, owing presumably to the dangerous subject matter, Faulkner's thematic intentions remain vague.

Having asserted Nature's power Faulkner continues his oblique approach to anything remotely female throughout these eclogues. He seems to be afraid to imagine a total woman or to represent women directly. Instead, he hides within the Romantic convention of portraying all nature as feminine and apportioning female physical characteristics, in unthreatening segments, to the trees, grass, and the swans' reflections. While such an approach fails here (and a more direct approach in *The Marionettes* is no more credible), precisely the same device works beautifully later in Faulkner's portrayal of Joe Christmas's or Horace Benbow's hopelessly distorted perceptions of women. Joe, for example, sees Bobbie as "two big knuckled hands lying on the edge of the counter" (*LIA*, p. 168), a "monstrous hand" (*LIA*, p. 200), "dead and pale as a piece of cooking meat" (*LIA*, p. 202). Alternatively this kind of fragmentation in the opening pages of *Sanctuary* suggests a global dislocation. The difference between the poet and the novelist is that the novelist knows Joe and Horace are hostile and terrified. The poet still cannot acknowledge the Faun's terror and hostility.

Sources of Nature's power are specified in the ninth eclogue, where Faulkner expands upon earlier images of the moon and world. Transforming both into essentially negative female figures—two old women, one mad and the other a hag—he permits them to "caress" the Faun. These metaphors contrast sharply with the fragmented virginal ones that described ephemeral Nature *on* the earth. Both earth and moon—sources of great dark and light—are all-powerful: "For old earth dumb and strong and sad" (*TMF* X, p. 36). They control the universe. As the moon caresses the Faun, she seems (prefiguring Joe's images of Bobbie and Joanna Burden) to imprison his mind and body with her powerful hands and feet:

> The ringèd moon sits eerily
> Like a mad woman in the sky,
> Dropping flat hands to caress

Plunging white hands in the glade
Elbow deep in leafy shade
. . . .

Her hands also caress me:
My keen heart also does she dare;
While turning always through the skies
Her white feet mirrored in my eyes
Weave a snare about my brain
Unbreakable by surge or strain,
For the moon is mad, for she is old . . . (*TMF* IX, p. 33)

In *The Marionettes*, the moon becomes Pierrot's Shade's foster-mother, aiding him in "hypnotizing" Marietta so that she follows him out of her garden. Rather than an imprisoning, the moon is a liberating force, a good mother who gives Pierrot the woman he claims to desire but later deserts: "Plunge your fingers in her hair, / Spin and weave moon madness there" (*TM*, p. 27). (Can she be good because she, like Pierrot's Shade, is Pierrot's idealized image?)

In 1921, when Faulkner wrote one of the love poems in *Vision in Spring*, he invoked the same image of imprisonment to describe a man who drives himself mad by his desire for an unattainable woman. Knowing the image's connotations in *The Marble Faun* and *The Marionettes* makes it apparent why the woman in *Vision in Spring* is unattainable: from her birth in Faulkner's earliest poetry she has been the Faun/Pierrot's mother. The implications this has for determining intention in Faulkner's fiction are significant, and will be discussed further in part III.

The Faun's Choice: To Be a Poet or Remain a Child

Although Faulkner has confused and complicated the syntax of the tenth eclogue of *The Marble Faun*, he does not obscure its intent: to stress the Faun's response to his imprisonment. He feels mute and blind, reflecting the author's feelings as he gropes his way through his first long poem. The Faun's union with Nature in her guise as the mad moon (*TMF* IX, p. 33) suggests that the caresses of powerful, older women, the moon and the earth, are a mixed blessing. They solace, but they also hurt him and threaten his sanity:

And my carven eyes embrace
The dark world's dumbly dreaming face,
For my crooked limbs have pressed
Her all-wise pain-softened breast

Until my hungry heart is full
Of aching bliss unbearable. (*TMF* X, p. 36)

The Faun simultaneously fears and longs for contact with these hypnotic dark and light mother figures. He wants desperately to hear the sounds of life, but only silence floods his head until it can hold no more. As he cries, he feels the silence "spill / Like water down my breast" (*TMF* X, p. 35). Like the Faun, the world also is bound "soundlessly in fold / On fold of blind calm rock." But unlike the Faun, the world contains Pan's instrument, his violin. The earth then, as an extension of Pan, is not bound to silence. Pan's music is described variously as ice, gold, sunsets, flame, dawn's burn, and ultimately as "Peace for living, peace for dead." It is the poet/Faun's wish that he contain within him, as does the earth, Pan's fingers: the ability to create music or poetry. The final strophe of the eclogue suggests, however, that the earth's ability to sing is an illusion:

For old earth dumb and strong and sad
With life so willy-nilly clad,
And mute and impotent like me
Who marble bound must ever be . . . (*TMF* X, p. 36)

Life on earth is indeed likened to a veneer or a suit of clothes, recalling Faulkner's role playing in the borrowed officer's uniform and his arrogant posturing as poet-aesthete. Is he suggesting that when he masquerades in real life, aping other poets or his great-grandfather and his war-wounded brother, his borrowed garments make him feel mute and impotent?

The salutary effects of this insight are felt near the middle of the next eclogue (*TMF* XI, p. 38) where Faulkner (through Pan's song) introduces another dreamer, Philomel, and makes an analogy between her and the Faun. Both can only imitate and dream. This analogy acts as a distancing device and the results are apparent immediately. Now Faulkner, echoing Tennyson's song about Fancy versus the Imagination, successfully describes the powers of Pan's voice, the voice of the Imagination:

Clear and sad sounds Pan's thin strain,
Dims in mystery, grows again;
Mirrors the light limbs falling, dying,
Soothes night voices calling, crying,
Stills the winds' far seeking tone
Where fallow springs have died and grown;
Hushes the nightbirds' jewelled cries
And flames the shadows' subtleties

Through endless labyrinthine walls
Of sounding corridors and halls
Where sound and silence soundless keep
Their slumbrous noon. Sweet be their sleep. (*TMF* XI, p. 38)

As the Faun continues his imagined journey, the next eclogues pick up speed despite the lapses that occur as the poet daubs his language with some of the gaudiest Symbolist images. The sky draws a veil of gold and purple across the Faun's face; azure veils fall from the sky; the earth's "breast" is "sharp and burning"; and on it the Faun is impaled "as I plunge panting down to rest" (*TMF* XII, p. 39).

The loosening that occurred as a result of the poet's insight in the tenth eclogue and the introduction of Philomel continues as the Faun drops out completely (*TMF* XIII). Now Faulkner's language becomes lyrical. Even the heavy overlay of Keats does not distract:

Vineyards struggle up the hill
Toward the sky, dusty and still,
Thick with heavy purple grapes
And golden bursting fruits whose shapes
Are full and hot with sun. (*TMF* XIII, p. 41)

In contrast to the purple veils in the previous eclogue, the shadows shifting from green to purple here create an integrated and believable image. The image contrasts sharply with the Faun's earlier fumbling and self-conscious language. There his ear was so caught up in memories of Swinburne or Verlaine or Mallarmé that he could write only a flimsy and forced imitation rather than a vision received by his own mind's eye.

As night falls (*TMF* XIV) and the moon appears, the Faun's pain returns as he describes "the solemn staring mad / Moon" whose light he likens to "prying fingers." She "stares blandly" at the Faun, who is "sudden blind and chill." Her presence calls a halt to his imaginary wandering. Beneath a frosty hill he cries out "in stiff pain / Unheeded." The mad female moon, prying and staring, is ultimately unresponsive to his grief and pain. But the Faun is a would-be poet, so despite her stare and the earth's coldness he continues trying to articulate the source of his sadness:

The silent world blazes and dies,
And leaves slip down and cover me
With sorrow and desire to be—
While the world waits, cold and sere—
Like it, dead with the dying year. (*TMF* XIV, p. 43)

With his mother prying at and spying on him, this is as far as he dares go. He still cannot state his wish: to be a poet like "the great god Pan."

As winter falls its snows solace him with frigid blanketing silence (*TMF* XIV, XV, p. 45). No longer tormented by his mother's pitiless stares or by images seen but not felt, the Faun experiences momentary relief. His eyes are no longer "shackled to the skies." Freed from his visions, he is also relieved of the pressure that comes from longing to articulate them, to translate them into new forms, to make poetry of them: he is freed from his ambition to become a poet. This "peace" is an illusion, and so offers only a brief respite, for the Faun *is* an aspiring poet and his eyes can remain veiled for only two eclogues.

The next eclogue (*TMF* XVI) is a welcome surprise. It functions as a strong catalyst in this cycle and reverberates in Faulkner's later poem sequences and in his fiction. That he is attempting something new here is immediately clear, for he interrupts the sequence's predictable diurnal progress. We see the Faun as a dreaming observer at a summer's night garden dance. He asks why he cannot always use sleep and dreams as anodynes for the pain caused by his physical and emotional imprisonment and impotence. But as soon as the Faun opts for insentience, his unconscious abruptly wrenches him away:

> But now we, who would dream at night,
> Are awakened by the light
> Of paper lanterns, in whose glow
> Fantastically to and fro
> Pass, in a loud extravagance
> And reft of grace, yet called a dance,
> Dancers in a blatant crowd
> To brass horns horrible and loud. (*TMF* XVI, p. 46)

His dreams appear to shatter as a terrible noise—human noise—shocks him awake. In apparent contradiction to all he longs for, the Faun finds the noise and activity abhorrent.

These human dancers, whom the Faun describes as "unclean" and debauched, will continue to intrude on Faulkner's *pierrotique* mask in other sequences like *The Lilacs* and *Vision in Spring*. The eclogue is important for this reason and because when it is compared to its fictional analogue in *Soldiers' Pay*, Faulkner's first novel, its elemental psychological import clarifies the fictional scene it generates. The scene occurs in *Soldiers' Pay*, chapter 5, sections 8–15.[2] There, at a summer's night dance that is tense with unarticulated and unexpressed desires, the narrator enters the consciousness of George Farr, a bystander who watches and lusts for one of the dancers. She is Cecily, a young girl who slept with Farr once and has since ignored him. The plot in this instance resembles *The Marionettes* with a role reversal: girl deserts boy.

Farr's jealousy mounts as he watches Cecily dancing with different men throughout the evening. Faulkner uses both the voice of an unidentified narrator and interior monologue to counterpoint the dreamlike quality of the scene to its seamy underlayer of lust and passion. Dancers move but seem masked and unreal:

> His face, under a layer of powder, was shaved and pallid, sophisticated, and he and his blonde briefly skirted partner slid and poised and drifted like a dream. The negro cornetist stayed his sweating crew and the assault arrested withdrew, leaving the walls of silence peopled by the unconquered defenders of talk. (*SP*, p. 190)

Shy young men are

> standing or sitting near the steps, managing in some way to create the illusion of being both participants and spectators at the same time. They were all of a kind: there was a kinship like an odor among them, a belligerent self-effacement. Wallflowers. Wallflowers. (*SP*, p. 191)

Rivers, another watcher and, like Farr, one of Cecily's rejected suitors, is portrayed in a highly stylized scene in which sex is simultaneously suggested and denied:

> . . . couples strolled in, awaiting the music, talk and laughter and *movement distorted by a lax transparency of curtains inside the house.* Along the balustrade of the veranda *red eyes of cigarettes glowed; a girl stooping ostrich-like drew up her stocking and light from a window found her young shapeless leg.* The negro cornetist, having learned in his thirty years a century of *the white man's* lust, blinked his dispassionate eye, leading his crew in a *fresh assault.* Couples erupted in, clasped and danced; *vague blurs locked together* on the lawn beyond the light. (*SP*, p. 192, emphasis added)

George Farr continues to watch impotently. Forbidden to claim her, he stares with unshackled eyes like the Marble Faun. Drawing on phrases from Pierrot's and Colombine's fatal dance in *Vision in Spring* and from *The Marble Faun*, Faulkner describes how he

> . . . glowered at her, watching *her slim body cut by a masculine arm,* watching her head beside another head, seeing her limbs beneath her silver dress anticipating her partner's limbs, *seeing the luminous plane of her arm across his black shoulders and her fan drooping*

[35]

from her arched wrist like a *willow at evening*. He heard the rhythmic troubling obscenities of saxophones, he saw vague shapes in the darkness. . . . (*SP*, p. 195, emphasis added)

By 1925, when the novelist wrote this, he could see the humor in this situation and comment that George Farr was "wallowing in all the passionate despair of spring and youth and jealousy, getting of them an exquisite bliss" (*SP*, p. 195). As narrator, he can ironically describe the contradictory sensations Farr's ungratified lust provokes. In the novel Faulkner seems to be making fun both of George Farr and his own earlier work. Farr, like the Faun, has read his Swinburne and Mallarmé. Later in the evening Farr, like drunken Pierrot in *The Marionettes*, seeks to drown his pain in alcohol. Liquor gives him "a sweet, inner fire, a courage" (*SP*, p. 195), and he lets loose with an ornate burst of fin de siècle language that is clearly meant as parody:

> The music beat on among youthful leaves, into the darkness, beneath the gold and mute cacophony of stars. The light from the veranda mounting was lost, the house loomed huge against the sky: a rock against which waves of trees broke, and breaking were forever arrested; . . . The sky . . . had seen . . . her—her taut body prone and naked as a narrow pool sweetly dividing: two silver streams from a single source. . . . (*SP*, p. 196)

In 1925, Faulkner can create George Farr from his own discarded poetic persona. Farr, like the Faun or Pierrot, is a voyeur. But unlike the Faun Farr is neither reluctant nor disapproving. Thus he differs from the Faun in this uncharacteristic sixteenth eclogue. As he describes his nightmare orgy of sex and sound his language is simultaneously puritanical and salacious.

> The blaring beats on gustily
> From every side. Must I see
> Always this unclean heated thing
> Debauching the unarmèd spring
> While my back I cannot turn,
> Nor may I shut these eyes that burn? (*TMF* XVI, p. 46)

Ironically, this orgy, like everything else in the eclogues, issues from the Faun's own imagination. The Faun is reporting *his* nightmare vision, a vision that will flee with the "clean" light of day (*TMF* XVI, p. 47). Because his vision is self-induced, it can only be dispelled from within. This is why the Faun next attempts a return to the mood of the cycle's prologue by invoking the image of the orderly Adamic garden.

> Once there was peace
> Calm handed where the roses blow,
> And hyacinths, straight row on row;
> And hushed among the trees. (*TMF* XVI, p. 47)

The poem's formal movement toward closure—invoking the past by recreating the garden as it appeared in the prologue—contrasts vividly with the Faun's nightmare vision. Here theme and structure are at odds as they are in many of Faulkner's novels.[3] Whether the poet intends this remains unclear. Certainly the inconsistencies of this eclogue, internally and in the context of the sequence, reveal their author's conflicting impulses. Thus, although he invokes the past to do so, the Faun fails to reestablish order. His garden becomes overwhelmed by noisy and sensual human dancers, causing him to cry out,

> Has my poor marble heart forgot
> This surging noise in dreams of peace
> That it once thought could never cease
> Nor pale? Still the blaring falls
> Crashing between my garden walls
> Gustily about my ears
> And my eyes, uncooled by tears,
> Are drawn as my stone heart is drawn,
> Until the east bleeds in the dawn
> And the clean face of day
> Drives them slinkingly away. (*TMF* XVI, p. 47)

The Faun/poet's language betrays his ambivalence toward his nightmare vision. Despite his claim to detest its uncleanness and ugliness, he twice uses the adverb "gustily" to describe the phallic horns that sound these dancers' music. Although disgusted, the Faun is drawn toward this "unclean heated thing"; but because it makes him uncomfortable, he must define its cause—his vision—as evil and deny any affinity with it. To divorce oneself from one's imagination, to condemn it, to deny responsibility for it or kinship with it can have severe consequences, especially for a would-be artist like the Marble Faun. But why is such an intensely charged emotional situation inserted in a cycle of pastoral poems characterized by ennui and sadness?

The first question to consider is whether withdrawal from life is desirable. The Faun characterizes the world to which he withdraws as "grey" or neutral. In it is peace, peace composed of order and silence: "hyacinths, straight row on row / And hushed among the

[37]

trees." Earlier in the cycle, the Faun has rejected both in favor of song and experience. The second issue is whether the world of the dancers—"blatant, debauched, reft of grace"—is really revolting to the Faun. If it is so disgusting, why is he mesmerized by it? "My ears / And my eyes, uncooled by tears, are drawn as my stone heart is drawn."

Eighteen months later in *The Marionettes* Faulkner dramatizes similar arguments as he explores how Marietta's sexual initiation affects her self-knowledge. In the opening scene Pierrot's song has not yet "hypnotized" Marietta into venturing from her garden. When the play ends, both her perception of herself and the world have been profoundly changed by her seduction: her imagination now has more latitude in which to wander. Her language shifts from breathy and self-conscious naïveté to a style that is rich, heavy, and coated with allusions. Metaphors hang like great, obscene jewels from her sentences: "a white island in a sea of amethyst, then a wind . . . streaked the sea with lapis lazuli" (*TM*, p. 52). Her language is, however, morbid: "my breasts, like twin moons that have been dead for a thousand years" (*TM*, p. 53); "The leaves are dead like hands that have held love" (*TM*, p. 47). For Marietta, sexuality and passion breed visions of death and decay in which she revels. In contrast, the Faun disclaims any interest in or any connection with his visions, censuring them as immoral or "unclean." If Marietta is an extension and elaboration of the Faun, the ambivalence in the Faun's argument reveals an area of Faulkner's conflict, one he has begun to address by the time he writes *The Marionettes*. In *The Marble Faun*, Faulkner wanted to give his imagination free play. But he was afraid of the "mad" moon's prying fingers, and could only give free rein there, very briefly, in the realm of nightmares. The nightmares are just an eclogue's duration, and are censured by "the clean light" of day.

Another look at the biography suggests reasons for the advances present in *The Marionettes*. Between beginning *The Marble Faun* (1918?) and January 1920, being enrolled in the university gave Faulkner acceptable status. As a student, he was free to pursue his own profession—becoming a writer—without being subjected to constant and considerable external pressures to conform. Although his wounded-officer pose won his community's approval, his *pierrotique* figures drew its ire. He also, like Pierrot's Shade, like the numerous failed heroes in his novels, and like his father and grandfather before him, lost himself and assumed other identities through the excessive use of alcohol.[4] During the summer of 1919 that Estelle Franklin and her baby daughter spent in Oxford, Faulkner presumably began to come to an understanding of the nature of his love for her. Clearly she did not discourage his devotion, accepting presents, poetry, and other written affirmations of his love. The artistic results were the single poems; a completed sequence, *The Lilacs*; and his Verlaine translations, which come after the first drafts of *The Marble Faun* and before *The Marionettes*. In a very short time Faulkner moved from poetry to a mixture of poetry and prose; from an ancient, highly imitative and structured form to the freer structure of a Symbolist dream-play; from a single narrative persona, a mythical marble statue, to more recognizably human characters who are free to make choices.

That the Faun's nightmare has acted as another psychic freeing device within this cycle is apparent from the eclogues that follow. At last the Faun states what he really wants: to be a god like Pan. He then experiences a brief moment of relief and transcendence brought on by his confession. He captures, for a few lines, the lost unity of man and nature that the pastoral tradition so often laments, and in doing so he looses his marble bonds and the form molded for him by another artist. Admitting that he aspires to godhood, not only so he can sing but also so he can be free from the restrictions and deceptions imposed by time and space, he moves toward formal closure of the sequence as he reluctantly accepts the impossibility of knowing the answer to the question he first asked in the cycle's prologue (*TMF* XVII, p. 48). He contrasts his desire to know despite his marbleness with the total absence of such desire in the stone walls of his garden: "*They sorrow not that they are dumb: / For they would not a god become*" (*TMF* XVII, p. 48, emphasis added).

Confessing to aspire to godlike knowledge and power brings the Faun further release signaled by a suggestive time-lapse of ellipsis. Nature no longer threatens him. Fearless, the Faun now merges with the sun and loses himself in the life about him. Final release occurs as the Faun transforms his experience into poetry:

. . . I am sun-steeped, until I
Am all sun, and liquidly
I leave my pedestal and flow
Quietly along each row,
Breathing in their fragrant breath
And that of the earth beneath.
Time may now unheeded pass:
I am the life that warms the grass— (*TMF* XVII, pp. 48–49)

Infused with Apollo's light, the Faun escapes his marble bonds, his prison. His imagination, freed of time, space, and others' voices, at last "flows" with nature and receives new life from the fusion. In so doing he renews nature, giving it life and warmth. The Marble Faun thus becomes, for an instant, the poet.

Following the opening lines of the third strophe, however, the Faun characteristically undercuts his freedom by asking, "Or does the earth warm me?" He partially recovers himself by saying the answer is not important. What counts is his achievement:

> Or does the earth warm me? I know
> Not, nor do I care to know.
> I am with the flowers one,
> Now that is my bondage done . . . (*TMF* XVII, p. 49)

Strangely enough, Pan's gift is not the freedom to feel with all his senses and sing, but oblivion:

> For Pan's understanding eyes
> Quietly bless me from the skies,
> Giving me, who knew his sorrow,
> The gift of sleep to be my morrow. (*TMF* XVII, p. 49)

The Faun's reward is precisely the resolution he previously rejected: sleep and dreams. Both preclude the possibility of maintaining the state of total awareness described in the first two strophes of the eclogue. In welcoming Pan's gift, the Faun negates the thematic resolution of his quest. Throughout the cycle's epilogue, the Faun emphasizes his terrible incapacity to express what he feels: "And yet my marble heart is cold. . . . Who marble bound must ever be. . . . My heart is full, yet sheds no tears . . . I would be sad with changing year, / Instead a sad, bound prisoner, . . . My heart knows only winter snow." The conclusion is depressed and unresolved. The Faun's frigid imprisonment contrasts the more sharply to the warmth of the May day, the actual season and time that are the setting of this final poem. He claims this vision of Nature calls out to him, but he—a "sad, bound prisoner"—cannot respond (*TMF*, epilogue, p. 51). The Faun's inability to weep or to be sad reflects Faulkner's inability to write a successful poem in the poetic mode and form he chose for his first large-scale "test of invention." Because the epilogue recalls, in both its form and language, the prologue, the cycle is technically completed or closed, but there is no thematic resolution to the Faun's dilemma. He is still constricted by Pan's suspect "gift" and his ambivalent relation to Nature. Failure itself, however, once again holds great interest because of the remarkable success that Faulkner later has with this kind of ending for the conclusions to his best novels.

CHAPTER IV

Ancestral Echoes

In 1918 William Faulkner announced the official commencement of his life as a poet by renaming himself, choosing a new mother country, and discarding his father. He also claimed military honors he had not earned: by his account he was an officer-pilot who had sustained two serious war wounds. I began discussion of Faulkner's earliest books—*The Marble Faun* and *The Marionettes*—by describing the first recorded "scene" in Faulkner's new life in Oxford, a scene the twenty-two-year-old poet created, directed, and acted. During the years he wrote poetry exclusively (1916? to 1924), and to a lesser extent throughout his life, Faulkner continued to replay the roles of poet and warrior. As poet, he consistently assumed in his writing the mask of Pierrot, the impostor par excellence of literary convention.[1] As warrior Faulkner posed for a series of formal portraits in his officer's uniform and claimed imaginary wounds (Figure 1). As with pathological impostors, costume was all-important. These poses of the poet Pierrot and his antithesis, the man of action, are significant, for they deeply affect the nature and course of Faulkner's creative development as well as the content and moral thrust of his mature fiction.

The real origins of this homecoming scene predate Faulkner's birth. The wounded officer pose Faulkner assumed both replayed his famous great-grandfather's homecomings from the Mexican and Civil wars and anticipated and eclipsed his wounded brother Jack's return from the battlefields of France in March 1919. Faulkner's poses thus displaced two important men. In perpetrating this hoax and in changing the spelling of his last name to accord with the original spelling of his great-grandfather's name, Faulkner imposed a basic element of his fantasy life on reality: his identification with and assumption of the role of a familial and societal ideal. This ideal was a composite made up of Colonel William Clark Falkner and his time—the ante- and postbellum South. This kind of war hero and particular historical period were central to Faulkner's childhood fantasies.[2] Many of Faulkner's grown relatives and fellow townsmen shared his fantasy—a fact that made his first pose so easily accepted.[3]

Upon returning from military service, Faulkner's actions mirror his great-grandfather's, who wrote a long narrative poem called *The Siege of Monterey* (1851) after his return from the Mexican War. Colonel Falkner also claimed to have a war wound, a claim not supported by his military discharge papers. Here, however, the similarity ends. The Colonel's poem, based loosely on his love life and war experiences, is melodramatic and sometimes bawdy and self-mocking. Although it draws heavily on popular conventions, it has little literary merit.

After writing this poem and a novel in the same year, the Colonel abandoned literature for the law.[4] Twenty years later, with his financial success assured, he turned again to writing. But he wrote for amusement. Unlike his namesake, the Colonel was primarily a man of action. And, although he included fraudulent elements in his early war record, the Colonel did fight heroically, if briefly, in the Civil War. Furthermore, as a man of action, he claimed only to "play" at writing while aggressively pursuing his real work, amassing a modest fortune.[5] His great-grandson "played" at being a war hero while pursuing his real work, writing.

When he assumed the identities of poet and soldier, Faulkner altered the spelling of his last name, symbolically rejecting both his father, the ineffective, alcoholic Murry, and the name associated with all his great-grandfather's accomplishments. He renounced the name, the values, and the achievements associated with the three previous generations of Falkners in order to begin the family again. The paradoxical duality in Faulkner's behavior—simultaneously adopting and rejecting the heroism of his great-grandfather and brother—suggests the depth of his conflict about his own choice of vocation.[6]

To pose as a heroic or famous figure is not unusual for a young artist. Biographers have documented many such incidents.[7] Bate's account of Keats donning a laurel wreath is an excellent example because it shows the difference between an artist for whom imposture is merely an episode and Faulkner for whom such deception was, in periods of stress, common. Keats's momentary assumption of "Apollo's glories" was followed immediately by feelings of guilt, shame, and self-revulsion.[8] He never repeated his behavior. Faulkner not only repeated it, he shamelessly reenacted his soldier pose and even preserved it for posterity with photographs (Figure 1). Later he added other characters and elaborated on the first. Clearly one of the best writers of our century was not simply an impostor.[9] But the elaborateness, repetitiousness, and sheer quantity of these episodes coupled with the repetition and constant reworking in all his major novels of the theme of the characters who ultimately commit suicide or allow themselves to be killed because, despite an infinite capacity for chameleonlike behavior, they do not know who they are, begs for comment.[10]

In some ways Faulkner's behavior resembles that of pathological impostors. Like them he appeared to feel no guilt about his activities.[11] In contrast to Keats, who was embarrassed by his pretense, Faulkner never admitted that his posing was a sham. In fact, when directly challenged on another aspect of it, his plagiarizing Hawthorne's title for *The Marble Faun*, he vehemently denied knowing of that novel.

Furthermore, Faulkner's childhood was marked by traumatic experiences and a family constellation similar to those described in the case histories of impostors. It suggests that while at an early age Faulkner consciously chose to become a writer, his choice was marked by a unique conflict: in choosing to write, he also chose not to become an impostor, a person whose only creative achievement is ephemeral impersonation.[12] The evidence of the rejected choice remains: in his long years as a poet using other poets' voices and in these episodes of imposture that, in later life, appear related to and are ultimately replaced by his increasingly severe drinking binges.[13]

But by the autumn of 1920, Faulkner's ambivalence, so evident in his poses and in the impotent yearnings of his *pierrotique* mask the Marble Faun, moves tentatively toward resolution as he gains the distance needed to begin to give it an artistic rather than a neurotic form. It is apparent that a shift is occurring as in his life his impostures vary, moving between the idealized image of his great-grandfather and a more realistic self-image: the poet-outcast. The beginnings of resolution and a concomitant developmental leap in creative expression mark his next major piece of writing, *The Marionettes*. There, in the characters of the drunken would-be Pan figures of Pierrot, Pierrot's Shade, and the elaborately costumed virgin/femme fatale Marietta, Faulkner begins to explore the darker implications of difficulties merely hinted at in *The Marble Faun*. Faulkner's probings are tentative, and full translation does not occur until he writes *Flags in the Dust* in 1927, "THE book, of which those other things," said Faulkner, referring to his poems and two earlier novels, "were but foals. I believe that at last I have learned to control the stuff and fix it on something like rational truth."[14] By 1927 Faulkner had completed the work necessary to achieve a creative identity separate from his youthful idealized images: the warrior and the poet Pierrot. In doing so he at last gained full control of his fantasy material.

The clearest proof of his control is textual. In *Flags in the Dust*, Faulkner has begun to hold his great-grandfather up for critical and disinterested examination. In brilliant convoluted sentences, he separates the myth from the reality and then depicts the demise of a Southern family whose lives are dominated and made impotent by their idealized visions of the past. These visions manifest themselves in an unseen presence: the great-grandfather's ghost.[15] In *Flags* Faulkner also divests himself of his Pierrot mask, transforming it to create Sartoris's great-grandsons, the failed twins Bayard and John. These brothers are Faulkner's first successfully tragic *pierrotique* figures.

Why did Colonel Falkner hover in the lives of the Falkner clan much as the fictional Colonels Sartoris, Benbow, and Sutpen ruled their descendants? The Falkner history offers clues. That history of four generations of fathers and sons became the forcing bed for all of William Faulkner's fictional grandfathers, fathers, and sons (see genealogy, Figure 5). Part fact and part myth, it is a history in which intense and thinly disguised father-son rivalry remains the one stable component from generation to generation. Dr. Phyllis Greenacre notes that in the typical pathological impostor "ego defects derived from very strong pregenital fixations cause a thin but dramatic enactment of the oedipal conflict which is constantly reenacted in each imposture."[16] When Faulkner the poet pretended to be his great-grandfather or his own wounded brother, he was acting out those conflicts. But when, as a novelist, he wrote about the terrible antagonisms dominating the lives of his fictional fathers and sons—the Sartorises, the Benbows, the Sutpens—he had succeeded in mastering these same conflicts. He could now, as he said, fix them on "something like rational truth," translating them into the essential concerns of his art.

My account of the Falkner clan, drawn from Blotner, concentrates on the incidents in these men's lives that best illustrate the anger and jealousy that characterize four generations of Falkner father-son relations. The first incident may be apocryphal but, as it was told by the Colonel, it is his perception of his relationship with his father and later with his adopted father. Its validity, as a measure of his attitude toward father figures, is thus unquestionably accurate.

At fourteen, after a bitter quarrel in which he almost killed his younger brother, the Colonel was beaten so severely by his father that he ran away from home in Tennessee to his maternal aunt and her husband, John Wesley Thompson, in Pontotoc, Mississippi. Colonel Falkner's description of his arrival gives a sense of the boy's state of mind as he tried to track down his self-chosen "father," a man remarkably like the father he had abandoned in Tennessee.

> He came from Memphis on foot, to meet his uncle here. He was a poor, sick, ragged, barefoot penniless boy. His cup of sorrow was filled to the brim when he learned that his uncle had left for Aberdeen the day before. He sat down on the hotel steps and wept bitterly, as though his heart would break.

Contemporaries claimed that when the Colonel spoke of this childhood episode "he became so affected that utterance failed him, and he had to pause until his emotions had subsided."[17]

The first clear indication of any tension between foster-father and son occurred when the Colonel was about twenty. Thompson apparently refused to allow William to clerk with him, so Falkner trained instead at a rival firm.[18] His legal training came in handy because the Colonel, like his uncle and like a fictional counterpart (Colonel Sartoris), was jailed several times on murder charges. He also seems to have had difficulty dealing with authority figures, as his clouded service records in both the Mexican and Civil wars indicate.[19]

Although his relationship with his uncle was uneasy, when the Colonel's first wife died, leaving a baby boy, Colonel Falkner gave the child, John Wesley Thompson Falkner, to the Thompsons to raise as their own. When he remarried shortly thereafter, he did not ask to have his son returned. The official account of this transaction states that Thompson's terms for taking his namesake were that he could keep him, and that the Colonel would provide for his financial support.[20] He didn't. Meanwhile he continued to compete with his foster-father and was defeated by him in an election for the state legislature in 1855.[21]

Years later, the Colonel countenanced the murder of his son Henry, the oldest child of his second marriage. Acting on protocol, the cuckold who shot him said to the Colonel, "I hate to have to tell you this, but I had to kill Henry." The Colonel answered, "That's alright. I'm afraid I would have had to do it myself anyway."[22] While this story may also be apocryphal, its persistence suggests the public's awareness of the Colonel's great dislike for Henry. Thus, the Colonel disposed of both his sons. He abandoned the first to his own foster-father with whom he had a tense and rivalrous relationship and appears to have applauded the second's killer.

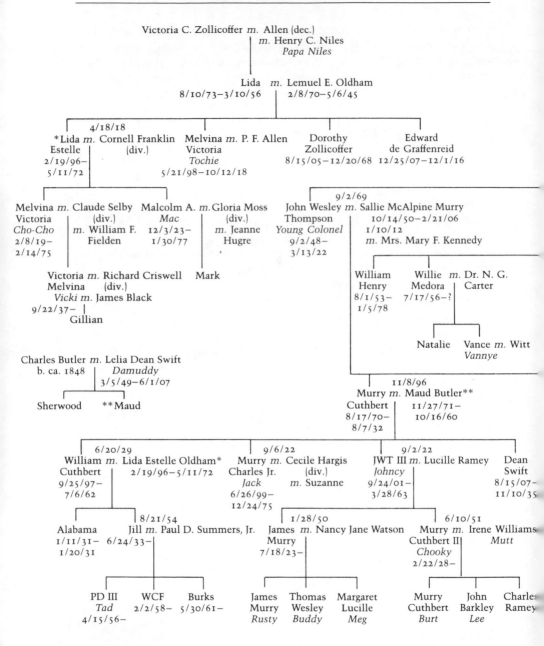

Victoria C. Zollicoffer *m.* Allen (dec.)
m. Henry C. Niles
Papa Niles

Lida *m.* Lemuel E. Oldham
8/10/73–3/10/56   2/8/70–5/6/45

4/18/18
*Lida *m.* Cornell Franklin   Melvina *m.* P. F. Allen   Dorothy   Edward
Estelle   (div.)   Victoria   Zollicoffer   de Graffenreid
2/19/96–   *Tochie*   8/15/05–12/20/68   12/25/07–12/1/16
5/11/72   5/21/98–10/12/18

9/2/69
Melvina *m.* Claude Selby   Malcolm A. *m.* Gloria Moss   John Wesley *m.* Sallie McAlpine Murry
Victoria   (div.)   *Mac*   (div.)   Thompson   10/14/50–2/21/06
Cho-Cho   *m.* William F.   12/3/23–   *m.* Jeanne   *Young Colonel*   1/10/12
2/8/19–   Fielden   1/30/77   Hugre   9/2/48–   *m.* Mrs. Mary F. Kennedy
2/14/75   3/13/22

William   Willie *m.* Dr. N. G.
Henry   Medora   Carter
Victoria *m.* Richard Criswell   Mark   8/1/53–   7/17/56–?
Melvina   (div.)   1/5/78
Vicki m. James Black
9/22/37– |
Gillian   Natalie   Vance *m.* Witt
                                                    Vannye

Charles Butler *m.* Lelia Dean Swift
b. ca. 1848   *Damuddy*
3/5/49–6/1/07   11/8/96
Murry *m.* Maud Butler**
Sherwood   **Maud   Cuthbert   11/27/71–
8/17/70–   10/16/60
8/7/32

6/20/29   9/6/22   9/2/22
William *m.* Lida Estelle Oldham*   Murry *m.* Cecile Hargis   JWT III *m.* Lucille Ramey   Dean
Cuthbert   2/19/96–5/11/72   Charles Jr.   (div.)   *Johncy*   Swift
9/25/97–   *Jack*   *m.* Suzanne   9/24/01–   8/15/07–
7/6/62   6/26/99–   3/28/63   11/10/35
                         12/24/75

8/21/54   1/28/50   6/10/51
Alabama   Jill *m.* Paul D. Summers, Jr.   James *m.* Nancy Jane Watson   Murry *m.* Irene Williams
1/11/31–   6/24/33–   Murry   Cuthbert II| *Mutt*
1/20/31   7/18/23–   *Chooky*
                                           2/22/28–

PD III   WCF   Burks   James   Thomas   Margaret   Murry   John   Charles
Tad   2/2/58–   5/30/61–   Murry   Wesley   Lucille   Cuthbert   Barkley   Ramey
4/15/56–   *Rusty*   *Buddy*   *Meg*   *Burt*   *Lee*

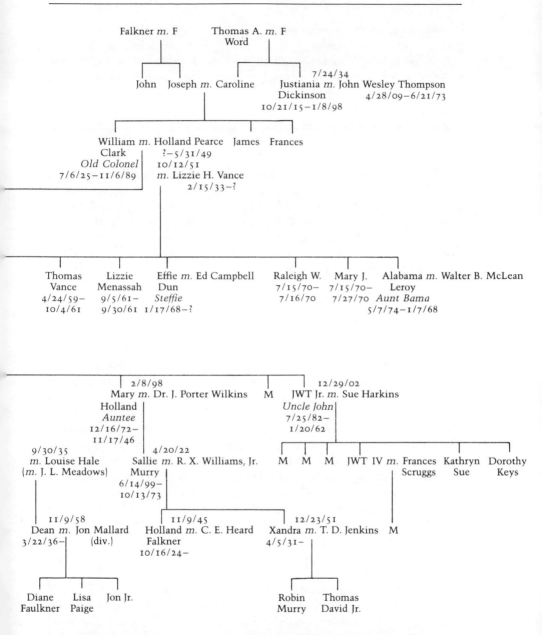

FIGURE 5. William Faulkner's paternal genealogy (adapted from new genealogy in Joseph Blotner, *Faulkner: A Biography*, revised and condensed 1984 edition). Courtesy of Joseph Blotner and Random House, Inc.

John Wesley Thompson Falkner (J.W.T.) became a lawyer like his father and foster-grandfather.[23] Although Thompson had refused his foster-son the privilege of practicing with him, he granted it to his foster-grandson. Such kind treatment apparently did not make up for J.W.T.'s real father's rejection, and in turn J.W.T. Falkner's treatment of his eldest son, Murry Cuthbert, William Faulkner's father, was more cruel although subtler than his own clear rejection had been.

With behavior characteristic of Falkner fathers toward their sons, J.W.T. Falkner never made life easy for his eldest son. Murry, whose passion was the family's railroad, had worked his way up from fireman to auditor and treasurer by the time his own first son William was one year old.[24] But J.W.T. retained financial control of the operation and kept its workings to himself. In September 1901 he told Murry the railroad was for sale. By June it was gone. J.W.T. had literally sold it out from under his son. There was not even an employment contract for Murry under the terms of the sale. Not only had his father arbitrarily stripped Murry of his profession, but he substituted in its stead the operation of a much less prestigious means of transportation, a livery stable. Financially the sale appears illogical. While on 24 June 1902 the Falkner estate received as cash payment for their railroad $75,000, the railroad's earnings for that year were almost $35,000. In his memoir, William's brother, John Falkner, claims that prior to the final sale Murry tried unsuccessfully to borrow enough money to buy the railroad from his father.

As if trying to buy his grandson's approval, J.W.T. at the same time gave William his first horse, a Shetland pony. But a pony could not replace Faulkner's ruined father. Murry's response to his demotion was passive and self-destructive. He drifted from job to job, each one supplied by his father, and he drank copiously. Regular family trips to a nearby sanatorium, where William observed his father being "dried out," were integral to Faulkner's childhood. Murry's depression, deepened by his heavy drinking, made him unavailable to his eldest son when, that same September, his wife gave birth to John, their third child.

John's birth was misfortunately timed: the day before William's fifth birthday. Four days later William contracted scarlet fever and nearly died. He recovered only to learn of another loss and displacement. Because his father had lost his job, the family was now forced to move from Ripley, the Colonel's hometown, to Oxford, where J.W.T. lived. Their new house, supplied by J.W.T., was the one in which their father had grown up and which J.W.T. had discarded when he had built his mansion, appropriately called "The Big Place." It is difficult to believe Murry's father's actions contained no conscious element of malice. Joseph Blotner describes the situation:

> Murry Falkner . . . had suffered through two years of college before he was allowed to go to work full time for the railroad. He had advanced from one job to another until he had reached a responsible position. He was 32 years old, with a wife and three small children to support, and now his job was . . . taken away from him. . . . He was an inarticulate man who was not very adept at personal relationships. . . . He was . . . a dutiful son, . . . too dutiful to attempt revolt, and certainly too proud to implore.[25]

The life of the Murry Falkners was that of an upper-middle-class, sixth-generation Southern family, dominated by the whims of Murry's father, the rich and successful offspring of the mythically proportioned Colonel Falkner. Murry Falkner's life could serve as a paradigm for Erik Erikson's comments about the third generation descendants of powerful men:

> The grandfather's picture hangs over the fireplace, a little bulb eternally lighting the rosiness of the cheeks in his generally powerful and contented countenance. His "individualistic" ways in business, his almost primeval power over the fate of his children, are known but not questioned; rather they are overcompensated for by a sensitive show of respect, scrupulousness, and thrift. *The grandsons know that in order to find an identity of their own they have to break out of the mansion,* so to speak, and join the mad striving which has engulfed the neighborhood. . . . *these men, of the once highest strata, join those from the very lowest ones in being the truly disinherited in American life; from where they are there is no admission to free competition, unless they have the strength to start all over.* (emphasis added)[26]

Although Murry may have fantasized about joining "the mad striving" by participating in westward expansion, in reality he moved right into his own father's discarded mansion and read penny Westerns. Murry did not have the strength "to start all over" and what little effort he made in that direction was stifled by his wife, Maud, who vetoed his plan to move to Texas and become a rancher. She was given support by her mother, Leila Butler, by this time a permanent member of the household. According to Blotner, Murry Falkner never forgave his wife for denying him the chance to go West once his father had sold the railroad.[27]

Although Murry Falkner neither implored nor revolted, his anger found an outlet that teetered on the brink of Southern respectability, alcohol. When well fortified with liquor, he would rain down verbal abuse on his family. But he did not attack the person primarily responsible for his condition, his powerful father who lived across the street. Rather he focused his ire on weaker opponents like his eldest son, William, who looked most like Maud and whom he nicknamed "Snake-Lips."[28]

What resemblances are there between this family history and that of impostors described in psychoanalytic literature? Where does William Faulkner diverge from the classic pattern, making it not simply his innate genius that accounts for his success in resisting a life confined to role playing? The most obvious similarity between William's history and that of pathological impostors centers on his relationship with his parents and their response to his father's destruction by his own father. The sale of the railroad and his parents' reaction to it drastically shaped and colored William's childhood. His father became a confirmed alcoholic and his family continued, until William was in his twenties, to move to increasingly less distinguished homes as the Falkner fortunes dwindled and Murry's jobs, always in one of J.W.T.'s many ventures, became less lucrative.

A traumatic incident in which a young boy (William was four in 1901) sees his father succumb to either psychic or physical defeat is often a precipitating event in the childhoods of pathological impostors.[29] The trauma lies not so much in the destruction itself as in the parents' inadequate response to it, which leaves the child defenseless, making him think that his unconscious fantasies of killing his father and marrying his mother will indeed be realized. But no recorded history of a confirmed impostor so literally repeats and reenacts the myth of Oedipus in reverse, and nowhere does a real father actually do in his own son as J.W.T. did Murry Falkner. And nowhere does the son watch it happen.

Even so, events alone are probably insufficient and it is doubtful that a single incident could explain a lifetime of disease. If the parents' response is healthy, the child's suffering should be minimal. But if the parents' response leaves the child emotionally unprotected, so that his father's real devaluation is permitted to feed his illusion that he can possess his mother, the child may resort to imposture to defend against the terror he feels at having his fantasy realized. The situation is made worse if the mother actively aids in the father's destruction. William's mother contributed to her husband's sense of defeat by refusing to allow Murry to act on his initial reaction: to physically separate himself (as the Colonel had done) from his father. Maud not only vetoed her husband's last bid for economic and emotional independence, she also did not suggest compromise. And she humiliated him in front of his children by taking them along on trips to the sanatorium.

With Murry's failure, the close family members with whom William could positively identify became limited to his mother and' grandfather. Both were very threatening possibilities, as identifying with either would mean siding with them against his father. William had seen them destroy his own father. Would it not seem that he, as the eldest son, would be their next victim? The alternative, which he seems to have chosen, was to replace his ruined real father with an imaginary ideal father who, though small like William, was more powerful than either his father or his grandfather and was safely dead. William's great-grandfather, Colonel William Clark Falkner, was an obvious and unthreatening choice.

One could speculate endlessly about why Faulkner would make this choice rather than succumb to the life of an impostor. Available evidence suggests that he did so not only because he was a highly gifted person but because there were mitigating factors in his mother's behavior that would have discouraged him from a fraudulent existence. While she demeaned her husband, she did offer another father figure, the Colonel, as a *kind* of ideal. Her idealization encompassed his physical appearance as well as his financial successes—so much so that between William's thirteenth and sixteenth years she had her son wear a back brace so he would stand as straight as the Colonel.[30]

But Maud Falkner's attitude toward the Colonel and toward her son was, luckily for William, not unequivocally adulatory. She saw neither as a paragon of virtue. Thus she admonished one of her grandsons, "You've got a back like the Colonel's but you've got to be a better man than he was." In 1925 when she read her son's first novel, she thought it a disgrace and wrote Faulkner in New Orleans that the best thing he could do under the circumstances was leave the country.[31]

Similarly, because she did not send any of her four sons to school until they were eight, Maud Falkner could be considered an indulgent and overly protective mother like those of typical impostors. But before concluding that, one must consider that she didn't keep them home to fool around. All the boys were accomplished readers, spellers, and mathematicians so that when they did enter school they entered at their appropriate grade levels. Most likely she kept them home because she felt she could do a better job. Furthermore, teaching them gave this woman, whose artistic ambitions had been frustrated by her own father's desertion and her mother's financial needs, some creative outlet. She could attend to something more rewarding than housework and tea parties, parties like those her son would parody in novels like *Flags in the Dust* and *Sanctuary*. Maud was furious at her husband's failure to emulate the old Colonel. But she did not think her sons' success lay in her spoiling them. Nor, perhaps, was she capable of doing so.

Maud Falkner was, essentially, a witty but distant and cold person. Faulkner's early perception of his mother's controlling, seductive, and icy character is preserved in his earliest recorded memory. Writing from Paris in 1925 to his mother's chief familial rival for his affections, his paternal great-aunt Alabama, Faulkner says of his aunt's sister's daughter:

> I will be awfully glad to see Vannye again. The last time I remember seeing her was when I was 3, I suppose. I had gone to spend the night with Aunt Willie (in Ripley) and I was suddenly taken with one of those spells of loneliness and nameless sorrow that children suffer, for what or because of what they do not know. And Vannye and Natalie [her sister] brought me home, with a kerosene lamp. I remember how Vannye's hair looked in the light—like honey. Vannye was impersonal; quite aloof: she was holding the lamp. Natalie was quick and dark. She was touching me. She must have carried me.[32]

Faulkner's introductory sentence coupled with this recalled scene suggests that his memory is a screen memory and that the scene depicts not so much his young aunts or his mother as his *two* earliest mothers, the composite for which he quests throughout his fictional career and actual life.[33] He looks forward to being with Vannye (his real mother), who is his leader—she holds the light. Her honey-colored hair looks inviting and seductive although she acts aloof and impersonal. But it is his other mother, the quick, dark Natalie (Caroline "Callie" Barr, his black nurse who cared for and lived with him from his birth until her death in 1940), who touches him and carries him. She offers him warmth and protection from "loneliness" and "sorrow."[34]

My reading of this screen memory would be mere speculation were it not corroborated by Faulkner's fictional reweavings of it in *The Sound and the Fury* (1929) and in *Light in August* (1932). In the earlier novel Quentin, remembering his one actual sexual experience, describes his partner, named Natalie, as a "dirty girl." Even so he hugs her and "dances sitting down" with her. When Caddy surprises them and Natalie runs off, Quentin rolls in the "mud" and embraces Caddy, smearing her with mud so that they both "stink" (*TSATF*, pp. 166–172). Quentin is reminded of Natalie by another dark "sister," a little Italian child whom he picks up and whom he describes ambivalently as having "dirty hands" (*TSATF*, p. 163) that are "damp and hot, like worms" (*TSATF*, p. 157), but a "serene" expression and eyes that are "black and unwinking and friendly" (*TSATF*, p. 162). Although she wears a "filthy dress" (*TSATF*, p. 165) and her hair is like "patent leather," Quentin is deeply attracted to this other Natalie whose looks he continually experiences as "black, and secret and friendly" (*TSATF*, pp. 168, 172). (It is no accident that Faulkner has Quentin note that both Natalie and the Italian child, like Faulkner's nurse Callie Barr, are socially beneath him.) Ultimately these past and present dark sisters mingle in Quentin's consciousness with his memories of trying to merge with his real sister, the fair and untouchable Caddy, whose loss he associates with the "unbearable" scent of "honeysuckle" (*TSATF*, pp. 165–166).

In *Light in August* Faulkner drew upon the actual scene as well as the language and attendant emotions of his screen memory to create Joe Christmas's first meeting with the spinster, Joanna Burden. She enters her dark kitchen into which Joe Christmas has snuck to seek warmth and food. Like Vannye in Faulkner's memory, she carries "a candle, holding it high, so that its light fell on her face: a face quiet, grave, utterly unalarmed. . . . 'If it is just food you want, you will find that,' she said in a voice calm, a little deep, quite cold" (*LIA*, p. 218). Like Vannye, she offers material but not emotional warmth. Joe immediately divides her into two women: the "day" woman who speaks "with speech that told nothing" (*LIA*, p. 219) and the "night" woman whom he will continually rape but never see until the night he murders her. Joe never feels he possesses either woman (*LIA*, p. 221). Joanna has "a dual personality": she looks "in the lifted candle," with her offer of food, to promise "physical security and adultery if not pleasure." But her intelligence, her presence, and her physical strength terrify Joe and make him feel "as if I was the woman and she was the man" (*LIA*, pp. 221–222).[35]

Faulkner maintained close relations with his mother throughout her life. As long as he lived in Oxford and whenever he returned, he stopped by her house every morning to have coffee and talk.[36] She initiated and encouraged his early love of reading, his art work, and his poetry. And, as has been pointed out, he dedicated *The Marble Faun* to her. In it, the would-be poet/Faun obsessively laments his "enthralled impotence." Such closeness created severe tensions between Faulkner and Estelle when they finally did marry in 1929. Indeed it is questionable whether Faulkner ever sustained a compatible relationship with his wife.

A typical instance of Faulkner's playing his mother off against Estelle occurs in a letter written to Maud from Hollywood (dated "Easter 1943"). It begins, "Dear Moms." After talking about the advantages of working for Howard Hawks and saying "I want you to let Estelle read this letter and tell her what you remember about Hawks," he continues in the next sentence with an apparent non sequitur:

> At times she thinks I'm here just having fun, which troubles me. I dislike to be where I domt [*sic*] want to be, earning money so my loved ones can be comfortable, and to have some of those loved ones refuse to be grateful that I am earning the money.[37]

While he treated his two mothers, Callie Barr and Maud Falkner, with love and deference, his relations with both men whom he chose as early mentors were prickly at best. His apparent need to denigrate Phil Stone and Sherwood Anderson, like his impostures, appears to be a symbolic destruction of men who acted briefly as good father figures.

The highly imitative poetry of Faulkner's youth represented to some degree the work of Faulkner the poet-impostor, a public identity he discarded completely after 1925.[38] When he was writing this early poetry he came closest to living out his impostures. The unusual length of his apprenticeship to poetry is explicable if the poetry is considered in some respects to be the work of a poseur. And Faulkner's first two novels, *Soldiers' Pay* and *Mosquitoes*, while not imitative like his poetry, draw their main characters and settings from the counterfeit worlds of the would-be soldier and would-be artist. In these novels, where he simultaneously satirizes aspects of his impostures and people who have only borrowed identities, Faulkner comments on his own attitude toward assumed lives. His ironic handling of fictional impostors suggests a new distancing and objectivity about his own poses. However, when in these novels he attempts to portray the tragic results of assuming a false identity, he is less successful, producing melodrama rather than tragedy.

This flaw, so obvious in his early fiction, shows signs of being corrected in Faulkner's third novel, *Flags in the Dust*. Its setting was modeled on Oxford and its surrounding territory. And it is the first novel that draws directly on Faulkner's own family experiences and mythology rather than on the experiences of his soldier and poet impostures. In writing it, Faulkner said he first realized that "by sub-limating the actual to the apocryphal, I would have complete liberty to use whatever talent I might have to its absolute top. It opened up a goldmine of other people so I created a cosmos of my own." The original version of *Flags* was judged a failure. In 1931 Faulkner, ac-knowledging his continuing sense of instability—that his greatness even as an artist is an illusion—describes an early session with Ben Wasson who, he said, told him

> . . . the trouble is . . . that you had about six books in here. You were trying to write them all at once. He showed me what he meant, what he had done [to edit the manuscript] and I realized for the first time that I had done better than I knew and the long work I had to create opened before me and I contemplated those shady but ingenious shapes by reason of whose labor the impulses of my own ego in this actual world without stability, with a lot of humbleness, and I specu-lated on time and death and wondered if I had invented the [teeming] world to which I should give life or if it had invented me, giving me an illusion of quickness.[39]

Faulkner and Wasson were correct. *Flags in the Dust* contained his third novel *Sartoris* plus the seeds of the five great novels that were to follow it. These novels, set like *Flags* in Faulkner's own physical and emotional past, mark the high point of his creative achievement and bring to fruition Faulkner's thematic concern with the moral implications of imposture. In them, particularly in *The Sound and the Fury*, *Light in August*, and *Absalom, Absalom!*, he successfully portrays the tragedies of men and women whose commitment to the dead and concomitant inability to perceive reality condemn them to rage, passivity, and impotence. They live only in the past and live through others. Their fanatic devotion to private, untranslatable dreams causes other peoples' spiritual and physical destruction. But worst of all, they never know who they are.[40] Seeking inspiration in the myths and realities of his own history rather than in experiences grafted on by pretending to be what he wasn't, Faulkner could, as he wrote his fiction, abandon his role as an impostor in real life. As he portrays characters who fail to establish identities separate from oth-ers in fantasied and glorified pasts, he both develops a metaphorical device that vividly portrays this struggle and produces his greatest artistic achievement. Faulkner had learned much about the language of transformation from those Swinburne poems that are concerned with and are thus constructed of a series of transformations (see chapter VI). American writers Faulkner read and found fascinating—

novelists like Melville, Hawthorne, and James—had also invented fictions whose forms and themes were deeply concerned with the implications of a transforming perception of reality. In Faulkner's own novels such language is constantly associated with characters who are unable to determine who they are and thereby separate themselves from their inherited pasts. Their struggle to arrive at definitions and their tragic failure are made manifest as these men and women compulsively resort to a series of personas: they imagine themselves and are even seen by others as being alternately male/female, black/white, pregnant/sterile, Satan/Christ, child/adult. Thus, at perhaps the richest period in his career (1928 to 1936), Faulkner's handling of the notion of the impostor in his writing becomes a highly sophisticated and finely integrated aspect of his art.

PART TWO

Steps toward Modernism: *The Lilacs* (January 1920)

Hard task to analyze a soul in which
Not only general habits and desires
But each most obvious and particular thought,
Not in a mystical and idle sense
But in the words of reason deeply weighed,
Hath no beginning.

—William Wordsworth, *The Prelude*, part II

CHAPTER V

Lyric or Narrative?
Countermanding Forces

What is poetry? In 1957, Faulkner gave this vague, powerful, and unequivocal response.

Question: Mr. Faulkner, would you give your definition of poetry?

Answer: It's some moving, passionate moment of the human condition distilled to its absolute essence. . . . there's no room at all for trash. It's got to be absolutely impeccable, absolutely perfect.[1]

But the time when Faulkner the poet sought a method of distilling that moving, passionate moment to his own satisfaction had come thirty-seven years earlier. In the rambling narrative of an early draft of the opening poem in *The Lilacs*, his first completed poem sequence, the problem Faulkner faced was as much temperamental as aesthetic (Figure 6). Coupled with his desire to "distill" was his antithetical need to tell a tale. Stray strands of narrative play through the rather loose and episodic structures of *The Marble Faun* and *The Marionettes*. A writer with such antithetical preoccupations would have to invent a narrative structure that defied traditional expectations. Probably it would depict and concentrate on interior rather than exterior action: a voice's response to events, not the events themselves, would be the focus. There would perhaps even be more than one voice. The structure of the poem or, likely, the series of poems would be elliptical, having as connectors not plot but a metaphorically and thematically controlled form. In short, such a structure would have about it many qualities more like poetry than prose. But to tell a story, to be able, as he later said, "to move these people around . . . not only in space but in time too" and to show characters "compelled to make choices between good and evil sooner or later, because moral conscience demands that from him in order that he can live with himself tomorrow," his poetry would also have to form a narrative. This narrative's movement would be dynamic rather than "the slow and deliberate unfolding that characterizes the typical Victorian long poem."[2]

Faulkner's discarded drafts of this sequence's first poem provide evidence of the kinds of technical and aesthetic choices he made as he composed (Figure 6). In 1920, as he wished to write poetry rather than fiction, he excised much narration from later versions of "The Lilacs." Similarly, he excised a counterpoint narrative tale from "A Dead Dancer," another Modernist poem he wrote for this volume (Figure 7). Still, Faulkner's need for more space and more voices remained, but rather than writing a long narrative poem in the manner of previous generations of poets, he chose the poem sequence.

Faulkner apparently did not keep a journal or write any letters about his work during these early years, so there is no extrinsic proof that in December 1919 when he assembled *The Lilacs* he made a conscious decision to write in sequence form. It is known, though, that by April 1920, the dating on the earliest extant version of *The Marble Faun*, he had adopted the form completely. It is also known from the opening and closing poems in *The Lilacs* that Faulkner was familiar with the poetry of one of the form's chief American adherents, Conrad Aiken. Between 1916 and 1921 Aiken wrote a series of poem sequences that he called "symphonies" to indicate the thematic and tonal texture of interconnecting links of the poems. In his prefaces to these sequences and in reviews in *Poetry* and *The Dial* (1917 to 1919), Aiken discussed the advantages and disadvantages of writing poetry in this mode.[3] Faulkner's own review (1921) of Aiken's early sequence, *Turns and Movies and Other Tales in Verse* (1916) shows that he was both familiar with and sympathetic toward Aiken's experiments with poetic form and with much of Aiken's criticism.

It seems reasonable to surmise that Faulkner, wanting desperately to be a poet but needing a different kind of space than that provided by the discrete lyric, should find the poem sequence an accommodating form, a form that would give him an opportunity to explore the multilinear, noncausal, episodic narrative modes of presentation that would become closely identified with his fictional voice. Since he was also in an imitative phase of his development it seems natural that he chose to model his sequences after those of Aiken, whose writing on the subject was both engaging and articulate. In *The Lilacs*, Faulkner indicates his debt to Aiken in two of its thirteen poems, but Aiken's sequences do not become a significant formal consideration until a year later when Faulkner writes *Vision in Spring*.[4]

What differentiates *The Lilacs* from the works that bracket it? Do these differences tell anything about the directions in which Faulkner was heading? The structure of *The Lilacs* seems less obvious and ultimately more complex though perhaps less successful than the simpler narrative structures of either *The Marble Faun* or *The Marionettes*. The book's physical condition contributes to the difficulty of grasping and defining its form: four of its short lyrics exist only in fragments. However, it is clear that, as in most sequences, the plot or action is interior and is subordinate to a thematic concern that is approached from many points of view and by apparently different *pierrotique* voices that ultimately appear to merge. Echoes and repetitions running between the various poems, all concentrating upon a single theme, help connect the voices.

In contrast to *The Marble Faun* and *The Marionettes*, voices in *The Lilacs* are human. They alternate between a series of first- and third-person narrators who descant upon the ways in which women and time appear to control their lives. In transforming his voice from statues, gods, or marionettes to human beings, Faulkner's *pierrotique* mask, less shielded by conventions associated with these inhuman forms, becomes slightly less opaque. But in dropping these conventions, Faulkner assumes others, simultaneously abetting and hindering successful reading of this sequence. However, writing *The Lilacs* helped him determine what he did and did not want to do in *Vision in Spring*.

Like his great-grandfather's, William Faulkner's first completed book was handmade and self-published. The Colonel's first publication, a convicted murderer's "true confession" pamphlet, was a commercial success. Andrew J. McCannon, its subject, chose the Colonel to write, publish, and sell the story of his life. Falkner timed publication to coincide with McCannon's hanging. According to Colonel Matthew G. Galloway (*Jackson* [Mississippi] *Clarion*, 28 November 1889), "The demand was so great for the books at $1.00 apiece that every hour or two, Falkner had to go to his hotel to deposit his money."[5] Faulkner's first effort was a single copy, not for sale, and not intended to be. Rather, he gave it to his friend and earliest mentor, the lawyer and classical scholar Phil Stone. This booklet was badly burnt when a fire razed Stone's home in 1942, but what remains of Faulkner's dedication reads:

(   ), Phil Stone
(   ) book is
(   ) affectionately dedicated:
(   ) quand il fait Sombre.'

(   ) Jan. 1 1920.[6]

The booklet, bound in red velvet, is a gaudy tour de force.[7] Stylis-

It was a morning in late May
[take?] a white woman
A white woman at the edge of a [brake?]
A morning whiteness mirrored in a lake

Yes — said James — you are right
One should not die better [than?]   al right
And for no cause or reason in the world
tis right enough for you to talk
Of [struck through]
Of [struck through]
Of going into the sky to [shelter?]
The [kiss?] of [death?], you did not know the [kiss?]
Of home and children and the [serene?]
Of living, and the [work?] and joy that was our [heritage?] . . . .
[struck through]
Yet it could not be [because?]

We had been
[Raiding?] our [mountains?], you of [seen?]
the place? then you know
How we hang [that?] [assault?] the Sun, and [comes?]
to see the [incandescent?] [inhale?] of the [flame?]
And you doubtless [turns?]
The search light gleams that cross and [across?] the [mind?]
the [ratchet?] of [engines?] and the [roughing?] [unfolding?] of [arches?]
[illegible]

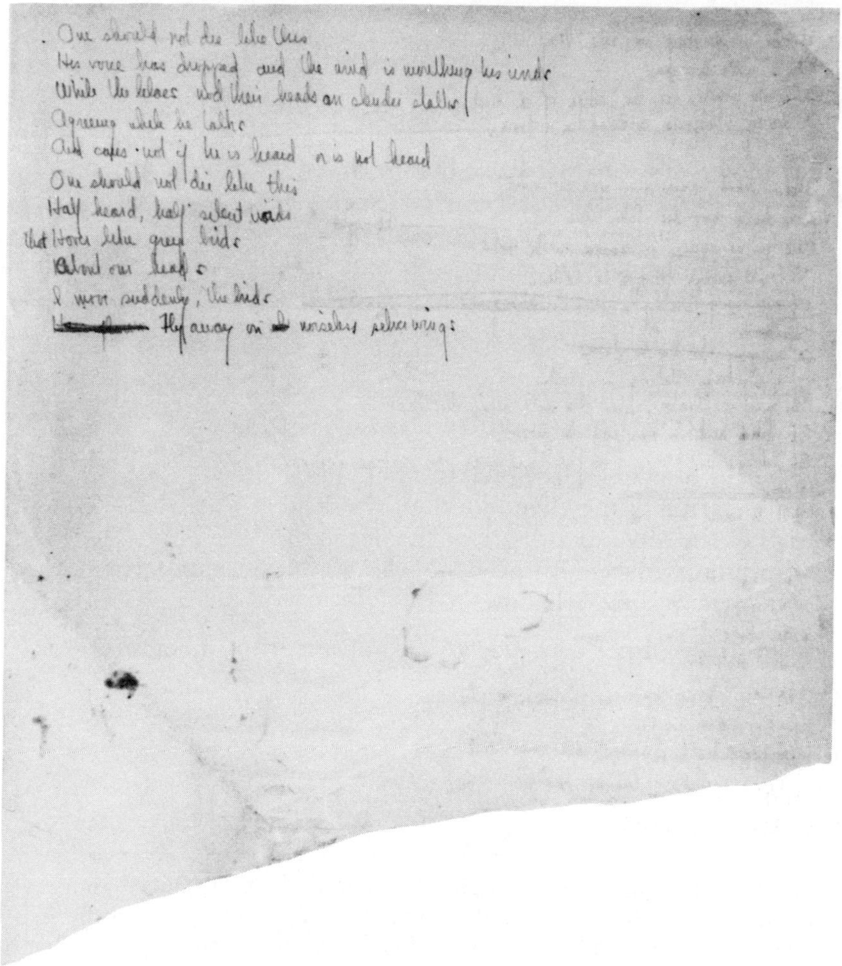
One should not die like this
His voice has dropped and the wind is mouthing his words
While the lilacs nod their heads on slender stalks
Agreeing while he talks
And cares not if he is heard or is not heard
One should not die like this
Half heard, half silent words
that Hover like grey birds
About our heads
I more suddenly, the birds
Fly away on ~~the~~ noiseless silver wings:

FIGURE 6. Photocopy of manuscript fragments of variant verses from Faulkner's poem "The Lilacs." Permission to reprint here courtesy of the William Faulkner Collections (Acc. No. 9817b), University of Virginia Library, and Jill Faulkner Summers.

The hurdy gurdy in the street below] all versions
Weaves the song across the silent street] 2 back and forth across [the gr(?)]owing shadows]4
Like gold threads in a time worn tapestry]2 [Like gold threads(?)] in a dim old tapes-[try(?)]]4
And we that she had loved at different times
Sit in the back wash of self consciousness] 2 So we sit here in the [back wash of self(?)] consciousness]4
Dreaming dreams beyond the ebb and flow]2 Dreaming dreams beyond [the ebb and flow(?)]]4
Of Life—Visions, flawless children of the kiss]2 Of Life and Death, w[(?)]]]4
While each one whispers to himself—I was the last]2 [While each one whis(?)]pers to him[self—I was the last(?)]]]4

She dances now for apocryphal lovers
To pale staring of the alive mouth of the dead.]2 There are whisper-ing[s of the alive mouths(?)] of the dead]4
A wind that whispers in the shadows]2 About her now, a wind that [whispers in the(?)] shadows]4

[The following lines conclude "A Dead Dancer" number 4.]

Of pale asphodels, and [lilacs(?)]
   wreathed about (   )
While her song, (   )
   sil[ence(?)]
Still loops [and coils(?)]

FIGURE 7. The University of Virginia version of "A Dead Dancer" (num-ber 2) has eleven lines in its final strophe that were excluded from the Crane/Freudenberg collation, as they do not appear in either UVa number 1 or number 3. However, some of these lines either correspond to or are variants of lines appearing in all three strophes of "A Dead Dancer" num-ber 4. A collation of UVa number 2 with "A Dead Dancer" number 4 ap-pears above. The concluding lines of number 4 are also printed above, as these are different from those completing either UVa numbers 1, 2, or 3. Note that two of its three concluding lines may be variants of the open-ing lines of the three UVa versions of the poem. Poem fragments, courtesy of Jill Faulkner Summers and the William Faulkner Collections (Acc. No. 9817b), University of Virginia Library.

tically eclectic, it displays an array of poetic techniques and voices from across the centuries. Faulkner had published four of its poems the previous summer and fall in the campus weekly newspaper, *The Mississippian*. One of these was his own (now published) version of Mallarmé's "L'Après-midi d'un faune." Another was his adaptation of Swinburne's "Sapphics," which was included in his Modern Library copy of Swinburne's *Poems*, one of the books he had taken with him to Canada on his RAF tour. "Cathay" and "After Fifty Years" were the other two. The titles of the poems—there is no table of contents—give some idea of Faulkner's wide-ranging reading and of his current literary interests. He subsequently published four other poems that appeared first in *The Lilacs* in slightly altered forms. These were the title poem (*A Green Bough* I, 1933), "To a Co-ed" (*Ole Miss* 34 [1919–1920]), "O Atthis" (*A Green Bough* XVII, 1933), and his tribute to Villon, "Une Ballade des Femmes Perdues" (*The Mississippian*, 28 January 1920). Of the five remaining poems, one has been published posthumously. The other four poems are almost completely destroyed. There are several versions of the posthumously published poem, "A Dead Dancer," the longest and most innovative of the five. Drafts are located in the Faulkner collections at the University of Virginia and at the University of Texas at Austin, while three other versions are owned privately.[8] Although *The Lilacs* booklet is badly damaged and several poems are partially or almost completely obliterated, one can, with the aid of extant versions of all but the four badly burnt poems, draw a fairly complete picture of Faulkner's intentions in choosing his lyrics and in organizing them as he did in this sequence.

That he meant the book to be read as a sequential if circular progression is indicated not only by the contents and formal arrangement of its poems but also by its physical layout. Faulkner framed his poems with two drawings, visual manifestations of the sequence's central concern: Woman. The book's frontispiece is a watercolor of a sparsely draped female and the endpiece is a small line drawing of a mummylike epicene nude. With one exception, all the poems share this concern: Woman—especially Woman as perverse and fatal temptress. Surviving words and phrases of *The Lilacs*'s four badly burnt poems give a fairly good sense of each poem's subject and tone, supporting this assertion.[9] The common subject matter, counterpoint mode of verbal repetition, and variety of poetic discourse suggest that Faulkner conceived *The Lilacs* as a single organic unit, rather than simply a miscellaneous collection of thematically independent lyrics united only by their single authorship and time of composition. Faulkner arranged *The Lilacs* to present the reader with a dynamically unified whole that develops and expands upon a theme and then moves to a conclusion. The sequence begins and closes with Faulkner's most modern poems, "The Lilacs" and "A Dead Dancer," which he wrote in free verse with occasional rhyming lines. They share a common theme: love, betrayal, and death.

What techniques did Faulkner use to weave *The Lilacs*'s apparently disparate parts into a unified whole? In what ways—formal and thematic—does this sequence both prefigure and illuminate the preoccupations of Faulkner's fictional voice? A survey of its poems reveals *The Lilacs*'s formal structure while a close examination of his most imitative poems—his versions of "Sapphics" and "L'Après-midi d'un faune," and "A Dead Dancer"—discloses his thematic concerns. Looked at both overall and in this kind of detail, *The Lilacs* reveals the direction and means of Faulkner's imaginative growth during the months immediately preceding and following his brief 1918 foray into Canadian military life.

Critics have called the title poem "The Lilacs" Faulkner's "Waste Land" poem—a reference to its Eliotic echoes.[10] Although Eliot's voice is present, it is his Harvard roommate, Conrad Aiken, who emerges as the dominant influence in both "The Lilacs" and "A Dead Dancer." In their word choice, experimentation with narrative voice, and thematic presentation, these two poems bear many striking similarities to poems Aiken published between 1916 and 1920. Furthermore, Eliot's cool irony and attendant sense of distance from his poetic persona are absent in both Faulkner poems. In fact, there is no intentional humor in either "The Lilacs" or "A Dead Dancer."

Faulkner opens his sequence with "The Lilacs."[11] Both its internal structure and its role in structuring the sequence foreshadow Faulkner's fictional techniques. Margaret Yonce suggests that in its experimentation with point of view, "The Lilacs" anticipates structural aspects of *The Sound and the Fury*, and notes that its plot line, such as it is, resembles Bayard Sartoris's fantasies about his brother's death in *Flags in the Dust* (1927).[12] "The Lilacs" introduces the central themes with which the sequence as a whole concerns itself and sets out the recurring metaphors that invoke those themes. Faulkner suggests the first of these by juxtaposing a lyrical pastoral title to the grotesque physical and mental condition of the poem's speaker, a war casualty. This persona, a wounded pilot, appears in the first strophe to be speaking for three people:

And we sit, we three,
In diffident contentedness

Lest we let each other [guess(?)]
How pleased we are
Together here, watching [the young moon(?)][13]

The second strophe appears to contradict the first. Here other characters comment on the "we" as if he were only one person: "Last spring—Poor chap, his mind / . . . doctors say . . . hoping rest will bring—." The strophe concludes as the principal narrator reasserts that he is "we." Echoing *The Marble Faun* as he describes the others at an English garden party beneath the lilacs, he says, "Their voices come to us like tangled rooks. / We sit in silent amity." At the beginning of the third strophe, and as if to contradict the closing lines of the second strophe, the principal narrator attempts to assert his oneness by shifting into the first person. In doing so he moves from the tea party into his memory of the war zone over Mannheim where he was shot down by German fighter planes while chasing a mirage: "A white woman, a white wanton . . . / A rising whiteness mirrored in a lake." He pursues this mirrored image until a German bullet hits his "breast": "I thought that I could find her when I liked, / But now I wonder if I found her, after all." The poem then becomes the maimed pilot's lament on his life-in-death existence. At this point the pilot's fragmentation asserts itself through an interior dialogue. As he muses, this nymph-chasing flyer reveals himself as an incurable romantic, a *pierrotiste*, who would have preferred to have been a Greek hero shot "with an Etruscan dart." He views his war experience and close touch with death as both pointless and unglamorous; his preference is for a mythical Golden Age where, once dead, he could transform like a character in Greek mythology into "a tall wreathed column" or "an ilex on an isle in purple seas" (fourth strophe). The last strophe echoes the first, returning the reader and the poem's persona to the present, reuniting yet asserting the separateness of the "we" and "I" narrators:

We sit in silent amity.
I shiver, for the sun [is gone(?)]
And the air is cooler [where we three(?)]
Are sitting.

The persona's pursuit of an imagined idealized woman punished by death, his desire to return to a golden pastoral age, and his total immersion in the intensely private realm of uninterpreted dream are major themes introduced in this sequence's title poem, a poem phrased in an idiom that is a peculiar admixture of early Modernist and Georgian tones.

[67]

"The Lilacs" is followed by two poems, "Cathay" and "To a Co-ed," that are more traditional in form and tone. "Cathay" is the only poem in the sequence whose subject is something other than women.[14] The subject of "To a Co-ed"—woman idealized—is treated ironically. Like "The Lilacs," "Cathay" is a dreamscape. The poem itself is a rather prosaic and abstract rendering of the second recurrent theme in *The Lilacs*: fame, decay, and death. It also functions in the sequence as a means of indirectly contrasting and then commenting upon two ways of thinking about what a person's own death means to him and how one man's dying pales to insignificance when placed within the all-embracing structure of the universe.

As Faulkner juxtaposes the moods of these two poems by placing them sequentially, the intriguing formal qualities of *The Lilacs* begin to emerge. To conclude his sequence Faulkner returns to the theme of death, uniting it with images of fame and unreciprocated love. In this way he uses sequential form to change and develop his subject so that at the end of *The Lilacs* we have a much fuller sense than we would have from reading only its initial poem of the poet's vision of the intimate relation between love, artistic achievement or fame, and death. Furthermore, there is a progression: the final poem records its persona's response to a dancer's death and his observations about the meaning of her death to others *besides* himself.

An abrupt tonal shift occurs in "To a Co-ed," *The Lilacs*'s third poem.[15] Cast in sonnet form, the poem's tone tentatively recalls some of Shakespeare's sonnets, particularly "Shall I compare thee to a summer's day?" and "What is your substance, whereof are you made?" The poet explains here that "The dawn herself could not more beauty wear / Than you 'midst other women crowned in grace." Faulkner continues this vein of strained hyperbole as he compares the co-ed to famous literary and mythological beauties: Venus, Helen, and Beatrice. The poem's colloquial and contemporary title is at odds with the classical allusions and archaic language of its contents. Faulkner's ear was exceedingly keen, and in "To a Co-ed," which appeared subsequently in the University of Mississippi yearbook (*The Ole Miss* 34 [1919–1920], p. 174), he may have been toying with his untutored undergraduate audience as he tossed off lines like "Than you does Venus seem less heavenly fair." Stone would have noticed and been amused by the odd juxtaposition. Faulkner's point in including it in *The Lilacs* may have been to share a private joke with one of his few well-read friends in Oxford. It may also be the earliest example of a famous Faulknerian device: the grotesque effect achieved by this kind of tonal shift.

With "O Atthis" (*TL* V) Faulkner continues to develop his image of woman as a compelling and fatal temptress.[16] In making the temptress Atthis, Sappho's bisexual lover who deserted her for a man, he introduces an idea that he enlarges in the next poem, "Sapphics." This kind of woman, epicene yet dangerously subversive and erotic *because* of her androgyny, prefigures early Faulkner women like Cecily Saunders in *Soldiers' Pay* and her most fully realized incarnation, Temple Drake in *Sanctuary*. In "O Atthis" (derived probably from Pound's "O Atthis," first published in *Poetry*, September 1916) Faulkner suggests the poet's death or blinding or both—depending on the version—as he "plunges" upon his beloved. In *The Lilacs* version the poet cries,

O Atthis

For a moment, an eon
I pause, blind[?]
Drawn down
Consumed
In the blaze of the son[g(?)]
That burns on thy [lips(?)]

O Atthis

In the version published in *A Green Bough* the poet is

... plunging
above the narrow precipice of thy breast.

In both cases sexual union with the androgynous and thus twinned beloved results in disaster.[17] In contrast to Faulkner's ironic use of classical allusions in "To a Co-ed" and in conformity with their use in "The Lilacs," "O Atthis" celebrates the perfection of the past. Thus the poem enlarges upon this theme as it appeared in "The Lilacs" and counterpoints "To a Co-ed."

The voices in the next five poems in *The Lilacs* continue to develop and expand upon the sequence's central theme: that women, though lovely and initially desirable, are inevitably unfaithful, inaccessible, and even physically threatening. Faulkner continues to tease out and pursue this theme throughout his poetic apprenticeship. Part of the aesthetic problem inherent in his somewhat limited and rigid response to women is apparent in this first sequence. Real or mythical, his women are such caricatures of literary types that they cannot bear the weight and stress of any ordinary human emotion. They wilt under its real heat. The threatening implications of their androgyny, implications he treats so successfully in his fiction, are merely hinted at here.

Extant phrases suggest that the tone of the sixth poem is similar to previous poems in this sequence and in *The Marble Faun*. Tired truisms like "beseeching hands, young breasts, sighs and tears" fail to evoke an image of a provocatively interesting and alive woman.

In the two and perhaps three subsequent poems (*TL* VII through IX)—IX is too burnt to discuss in any detail—Faulkner attempts to develop a portrait of his idealized and unattainable woman, envisioned as a nymph pursued by her eternally disappointed lover. Faulkner introduced this theme in *The Lilacs*'s opening poem where the mortal lover chased a nymph mirage, thereby condemning himself to a living death. But instead of drawing on the poetry of his near contemporaries (Eliot, Aiken, and perhaps Pound), in these poems he shifts to the poetry of two fin de siècle poets, Mallarmé and Swinburne, who, despite the great differences in their poetic styles, share similar aesthetics.[18]

The Lilacs's seventh poem, called, after Mallarmé's famous eclogue, "L'Apres Midi d'un Faune" [*sic*], is an adaptation of and therefore implicitly a comment on the original.[19] In it, Faulkner expands his other major theme: the agony of being forced to choose between the desire for mortal love and the ambition to create immortal art. Faulkner had touched upon this theme in both *The Marble Faun* and *The Marionettes*. He elaborates on it in this and other poems in *The Lilacs*.

Like Mallarmé's, Faulkner's poem is a dramatic monologue whose surface structure is controlled by a formal rhyme scheme; but that scheme, basically alternately rhyming iambic lines, is not as strict as Mallarmé's Alexandrine rhymed hexameter couplets. Faulkner's primary interest, as in "The Lilacs," is the poem's interior structure, the content of the faun's mind. His poem is much shorter than Mallarmé's—40 lines as opposed to 110—because Faulkner chose to concentrate on only one chase episode of the several recounted in the original. Recalling the chase in *The Lilacs*'s initial poem, here, too, the chaser pursues an illusion:

> I follow through the singing trees
> Her streaming clouded hair and face
> And lascivious dreaming knees.

The only lascivious part of the poem is that adjective. Faulkner wrote a chaste and tame variation on Mallarmé's celebrated erotic vision. There is no interweaving of the faun's narrative of his experience the previous day and his gloss on that narrative. Faulkner's poem occurs in the present. But, as in the original, the faun's vision, an illusion, is rudely shattered by intrusions from the real world. In Faulkner's poem, the intrusion is an unspecified sound "like some great deep bell stroke." This recalls the noises in the nightmare vision of *The Marble Faun*.

In Mallarmé's eclogue, the illusion is also self-generated, but Mallarmé's is explicitly sexual. His faun experiences an erotic sensation that arises from fantasizing about the nymphs.[20] Eroticism is absent in Faulkner's adaptation. Thus, he ignores a central purpose of Mallarmé's poem: to show that although the faun's fantasy was an illusion, he distinguishes it as such. Mallarmé's faun also realizes that illusions are powerful agents capable of generating real and deeply felt emotions. Such emotions, if listened to objectively and carefully perceived, may be used, as in Mallarmé's faun's case, to make poetry and music. Faulkner, unable still to be a disinterested observer of his own emotions, excludes this daring suggestion from his poem.

In "Naiads' Song" (*The Mississippian*, 4 February 1920), Faulkner invokes other scenes or episodes from Mallarmé's "L'Après-midi d'un faune." He reinterprets and purifies the moment in Mallarmé's eclogue when the faun surprises two nymphs sleeping in each other's arms. In the next poem in this sequence the persona resembles Mallarmé's faun. Faulkner's deep and abiding interest in this poem becomes transmuted in his fiction.

A unique and remarkable feature of Mallarmé's eclogue is his experimentation with point of view; specifically, his technique of using typological indicators to signal shifts in point of view and time. In the three poems that use "L'Après-midi" as their imaginative starting point, Faulkner makes no attempt to experiment with point of view. Although it is clear from *The Lilacs* that he is aware of the visual and tonal effects of the arrangement of a poem upon a page, he never uses typological indicators in his poetry to signal time shifts. Yet it is exactly these two features that characterize the formal structure of Faulkner's first great novel: extreme experimentation with point of view and typographical indicators to signal shifts in time and point of view.[21] Thus, by the summer of 1918 or early summer of 1919 Faulkner was already greatly intrigued with a poet whose poetic techniques clearly foreshadow the innovative, novelistic techniques Faulkner used ten years later in *The Sound and the Fury* (1929). It was Mallarmé's depiction of the dynamic and elliptical progression of his faun's inner consciousness that most intrigued Faulkner. But he could not assimilate and transform Mallarmé's poem for his own use until more than ten years after his initial encounter.

The eighth poem of *The Lilacs*, "Une Ballade des Femmes Perdues," is a pastiche of other poets' poems.[22] Its title and theme are derived from Villon's "Ballade des dames du temps jadis," and its epigraph from the poem's refrain, "Mais où sont les neiges d'antan?" He was actually borrowing twice, as Swinburne had used the refrain as his epigraph for "Felise," his endless ballad on ended love.[23]

Like Villon's, Faulkner's poetic persona calls for poetic inspiration upon his memories of a series of women who become the subject of his lyric. But in contrast to Villon's or Swinburne's, Faulkner's women are nonspecific and undifferentiated. Both Villon's and Swinburne's poems are addressed to flesh and blood women (Swinburne's are heavy on the blood), but Faulkner's alliterative "Gay little ghosts of loves in silver sandals" are literary concoctions. Faulkner's persona in this poem summons his ladies into his daydreams by playing on a musical instrument, which, as in Mallarmé's poem, serves as a symbol for his imagination: "They dance with quick feet on my lute strings." Like Mallarmé's faun's nymphs, the ladies' embraces are a dream: "They brush my lips with little ghostly kisses." Although the poem's subject—discarded women—is ostensibly derived from Villon with a little help from Swinburne, the tone created continues in the same vein as Faulkner's own "L'Apres Midi d'un Faune." In his "Ballade," Faulkner, like Mallarmé, attempts to evoke a mood that cannot be adequately described in language:

Stealing away
. . . . .

Like windflowers from some blown garden of dreams
To their love nights among the roses . . .

He echoes both Mallarmé's "la faute ideale de roses" (line 7) and his later image, locating the imagined double rape scene in "ce massif . . . De roses" (lines 73–74).[24] These phrases, ineffective though they are, show Faulkner gingerly exploring the phonological and syntactical innovations of Mallarmé's "L'Après-midi."

Faulkner's ballade ends on a note that is at odds with Villon's original, Swinburne's spin-off from Villon, and Mallarmé's "L'Après-midi"—in short, all operative influences. As if to countermand the reality of his own youth, Faulkner insists that his poetic persona is infinitely old and worn out:

I am old, and alone
And the star dust from their wings

Has dimmed my eyes
I sing in the green dusk
Of lost ladies—Si vraiment charmant, charmant.[25]

Faulkner later published "L'Apres Midi d'un Faune" in the university's campus newspaper (28 January 1920). And while its publication was not solely responsible for his being blackballed from the campus literary society, it helped. It also provoked a series of parodies, which *The Mississippian* printed throughout the winter and spring of 1920. There Faulkner was referred to as Count No 'Count.[26]

Faulkner's peers can hardly be blamed for making fun of his poetry and his affected dress. One wonders whether, on Faulkner's part, the provocation wasn't at some level deliberate. It was certainly an effective way of further allying himself with the poets he admired, like Swinburne, Mallarmé, and Verlaine. They too perceived of the poet as a social outcast.[27]

The ninth poem in *The Lilacs*, "Bathing," is almost completely destroyed, but by looking at the remaining words and phrases of its rhyming couplets in the context of this poem sequence and in the wider context of the bathing scenes in Faulkner's novels and short stories, it can be presumed to describe the narrator's voyeuristic pleasure in spying on someone, in this instance a "sprite," bathing in a moonlit pool.[28] Structurally and thematically, "Bathing" acts as a transition to the next two poems in the sequence. Its subject looks back, connecting it thematically to the two previous poems, but its highly formal structure looks forward to the two poems that follow, "After Fifty Years" and "Sapphics," the most traditional poems in *The Lilacs* sequence.

Like the speaker of "Une Ballade des Femmes Perdues" the subject of "After Fifty Years" (*TL* X) is old and isolated.[29] Although the speaker has become a third-person narrator, two phrases in this sonnet's first line echo the final strophe of the previous poem, connecting the voices. Their subjects enlarge and complement each other. The old woman in "After Fifty Years" has a memory that is also peopled with "shades" and her house is filled with "echoes" that "deceive / No one save her." As the previous speaker's eyes were dimmed by fantasies, so her loveless fingers are described as "blind." Both the speaker of the previous poem and the main subject of "After Fifty Years" live exclusively in their private dreamworlds.

Faulkner constructs an old woman's world of echoes and mirror images that works within the sonnet and beyond it, binding the poem into the sequence and enlarging the meaning of both. "She rose in dreams from other dreams that lent / Her softness as she stood, crowned with soft hair" (lines 9–11).[30] The first image describes how she sees herself in her mirror, recalling the pilot's private, deadly vision in *The Lilacs*'s first poem: "A white wanton at the edge of a brake / A rising whiteness mirrored in a lake." The second repeats and enlarges upon an image that appeared earlier in "After Fifty Years" where, describing the old woman's powers of attraction, the poet says, "A crown she could have had to bind each tress / Of hair, and her sweet arms the Witches' Gold."

"After Fifty Years" uses repetition and echoing to reintroduce and then rework the theme of the Lamia-like fatal temptress. And just as in his novels where Faulkner tells the same story many times, each time from a different character's point of view, so here in his first completed poem sequence he employs a similar technique as he elaborates on an earlier image of another temptress. But here he presents it from a different angle. As in the novels, where his technique of building a rich and complex fictional fabric succeeds in producing a multidimensional fictional world, a world of infinite variety and nuance, so here the image gains a complexity only hinted at in "The Lilacs." In both poems, the woman is presented as a double image. In the first, the pilot narrator (and the reader understood) sees her standing at the edge of a thicket and then sees her image reflected in a lake. In the sonnet the impersonal narrator and the old woman herself (and the reader understood) see the woman independently but also see her examining her image reflected in mirrors. The assumption in both poems is that if something is seen both independent of and reflected in a mirror it must be real. This assumption derives from the folk belief that ghosts, spirits, and, by extension, illusions of any sort cannot be reflected in mirrors or cast a shadow. But as readers we also know—in the first poem from the seer himself and in this poem from its impersonal narrator—that these are false and illusory reflections, that they are only extensions of both characters' vividly imagined dreams, "for *there* she rose in dreams from other dreams."

By introducing the image operating in the first poem of *The Lilacs* sequence, then reiterating and playing upon it in the tenth, Faulkner suggests antithetical perceptions of reality. Furthermore, by drawing upon the myth of Narcissus, he hints at why both the pilot and the old woman can be deceived. Both the pilot and the old woman are trapped into a death-in-life existence by their fantasies imaged here as their reflections or projections of themselves. (As if to emphasize this point, Faulkner uses the word "mirror" both literally and figuratively in both poems.) So Narcissus too loved, was trapped by, and then drowned in his own image. Like Narcissus, the characters in both poems reject the love of real people in favor of pursuing an illusion that is in its essence self-reflexive. The full meaning of this image in *The Lilacs* sequence is now clarified: neither a mirror nor water can be depended upon to give back a true reflection to a person who insists on living in a private and sterile dreamworld, and such self-reflexive fantasies lead to emotional and physical paralysis.

The old woman (reflected in her mirror) resembles Dickens's Miss Havisham in *Great Expectations*. Like Miss Havisham, she deceives no one but herself. Nonetheless, she still tries "to weave with blind bent fingers, nets that cannot hold." The second quatrain says that at one time all men "hovered like white birds for her caress." The narrator's earlier denial of the old woman's powers seems contradicted by the evidence he presents in the final sestet; it is not clear whether this is the first instance of an unreliable narrator in the Faulkner canon or whether it is supposed to be understood that her powers to deceive, like Miss Havisham's powers over Pip, are ultimately useless. For like Miss Havisham and *The Marble Faun*'s moon-mad mother, she can "blind and snare" a young and inexperienced boy:

> And with his bound heart and his young eyes bent
> And blind, he feels her presence like shed scent,
> Holding him body and life within its snare.[31]

Faulkner shows the child's imprisonment by transferring to him the adjectives "bound" and "blind," which he used to characterize the old woman who is the child's captor. Faulkner succeeds in concretizing abstract language by showing the words on the page "bound" within the sonnet form actually doing what they mean.

In Faulkner's portrait of an elderly temptress, her terrible power is sharply focused and illuminated by the condensed synesthetic image in the sonnet's final lines, "he feels her presence like shed scent." Casting forward to *The Sound and the Fury* one recognizes in this early sonnet the germ for a central metaphor for enthrallment in Faulkner's first great novel. There, other innocent boys, Benjy and Quentin, are emotionally bound to their sister Caddy and literally *feel* her physical presence in olfactory synesthetic images. To Benjy, Caddy's presence smells and feels like leaves, "like trees and like when she says we were asleep" (*TSATF*, p. 5). To Quentin

> her face looked at the sky it was low so low that all smells and
> sounds of night seemed to have been crowded down like under a slack
> tent especially the honeysuckle it had got into my breathing it was on

her face and throat like paint her blood pounded against my hand I was leaning on my other arm it began to jerk and jump and I had to pant to get any air at all out of that thick grey honeysuckle (*TSATF*, p. 188)

Benjy's obsession with Caddy leads to his castration while Quentin's leads to suicide.

Faulkner later develops the mirror imagery of this poem as well, making its meaning more explicit in the poem "Pierrot, Sitting Beside The Body of Colombine, suddenly Sees Himself in a Mirror" (see pp. 231–232). In *The Sound and the Fury* Quentin forces the reader to connect sex, sin, and loss through a series of associations that culminate in his mirror vision of Caddy on her wedding day: "*In the mirror she was running before I knew what it was. That quick, her train caught up over her arm she ran out of the mirror like a cloud . . .*" (*TSATF*, p. 100). In *Sanctuary* a mirror records for Horace the futility of his obsession with his step-daughter Little Belle: "and then I saw her face in the mirror. There was a mirror behind her and another behind me, and she was watching herself in the one behind me, forgetting about the other one in which I could see her face, see her watching the back of my head with pure dissimulation" (*Sanctuary*, pp. 14–15). For Horace this nymphet *is* a mirror image of all the unattainable women in his life, in particular his sister Narcissa and his wife, Belle. These are just two of numerous examples of an inventive and powerful expression of an idea, image, and theme that Faulkner discovered during his long and difficult apprenticeship to poetry.

CHAPTER VI

Sex and Death in *The Lilacs*: Swinburne, Mallarmé, and Aiken

Of his relationship with G. E. Moore, I. A. Richards remarked, "It is reasonable, is it not, to expect that a deep influence may take years—even decades—before producing its full effect. And the effect produced may often be very unlike what might be thought likely."[1] Richards's remark is an appropriate introduction to *The Lilacs*'s seemingly most derivative poems. Here, as Faulkner completes his sequence, he begins to experiment more radically with content, style, and point of view. The voice that will direct and inform his mature novels speaks faintly from beneath the imitative surfaces of these lyrics. Besides their stylistic innovations, both Swinburne's "Sapphics" and Mallarmé's "L'Après-midi d'un faune" suggest a legitimate means of access to questions about the relation of creativity to sexuality. Faulkner's deepening interest in this issue, spurred on by his work with Aiken's poetry and criticism, will result in an even more direct treatment in his 1921 sequence, *Vision in Spring*.

Writing about Swinburne in 1925, Faulkner acknowledged his debt: "Whatever it was that I found . . . , it completely satisfied me and filled my inner life. . . . I cannot tell to this day exactly to what depth he stirred me, just how deeply the footprints of his passage are left on my mind."[2] In other parts of this essay, Faulkner appears to be confining Swinburne's influence to his own adolescence, but evidence from Faulkner's fiction and from his life indicates that Swinburne's footsteps sank permanently into Faulkner's consciousness.[3] His long association with Swinburne significantly transformed his voice. Both resonances and dissonances with that poet proved continually provocative. Faulkner's version of "Sapphics" in this early sequence reveals both what drew him to Swinburne and what disturbed him.

Faulkner never wrote or said anything about the influence of Mallarmé or other Symbolists. Textual and biographical evidence shows their continuing presence in his work and life. Besides the poems in *The Lilacs* and *The Marble Faun*, his Verlaine translations and his Symbolist dream-play are indicative. Less obvious because subsumed are the stylistic techniques Faulkner learned from the Symbolists and incorporated into his novelistic vision. He continued to read Verlaine, Mallarmé, Baudelaire, Laforgue, and Swinburne long after he had stopped writing poetry for publication. He also read and recited their poetry to and with his daughter, Jill Faulkner Summers, throughout his lifetime. He taught her much of Swinburne's poetry. She says throughout his life her father kept his Modern Library edition on his bedside table. Of his books—some two hundred remaining in his daughter's library—the Swinburne is the most worn.[4] Faulkner was more circumspect about Conrad Aiken. In fact, he never acknowledged his influence, but in reviewing Aiken's *Turns and Movies* (1916) in 1921, Faulkner praised him and indicated that he had read most of what Aiken had written. Aiken's stamp on Faulkner's work appears first in this sequence. While these and other poets' voices overlap and intertwine in *The Lilacs*, they are easiest to locate and most significantly affect Faulkner's intention in "L'Apres Midi" and the final poems, "Sapphics" and "A Dead Dancer."

"Sapphics": Faulkner's Troubled Dialogue with Swinburne

"Sapphics" (*TL* XI), Faulkner's second lesbian poem, continues his dialogue with poets he admires, a dialogue that forms a continuous subtext throughout much of Faulkner's apprenticeship poetry.[5] Although this dialogue is halting and fragmented, it provides numerous clues about the state and progress of Faulkner's imaginative vision. "Sapphics," ultimately derived as was "O Atthis" from a Sapphic fragment, advances the sequence by enlarging upon thematic material suggested earlier. But, whereas in "O Atthis" the poet praised the Sapphic tradition by choosing to die in Atthis' annihilating embrace, he now questions that tradition. Cleanth Brooks observes that Faulkner imitates Swinburne's use of the Sapphic strophe and that his "Sapphics" is an intentional glossing and reworking of Swinburne's great lyric from *Poems and Ballads*, First Series (1866). He also asserts that Faulkner's intention was Swinburne's: "Faulkner's opening phrase, 'So it is,' implies that the speaker here has just put down Swinburne's poem and is stating his general agreement with it."[6] But that is debatable. As Swinburne "consciously imitated Sappho's 'Ode to Aphrodite' only to advance an alternative vision," so Faulkner recalls Swinburne in order to offer a radical reinterpretation of the meaning of Sappho's life and songs.[7]

In her own "Ode to Aphrodite," Sappho tells of calling the goddess to come and assuage her grief at being deserted by her Lesbian maiden, Anactòria. The ode thanks Aphrodite for speaking comforting words that mitigate her grief at losing Anactòria's love. In Swinburne's poem, he, not Sappho, is the speaker and visionary. Swinburne's Sappho rejects Aphrodite's words of comfort and invents new forms of song to express her grief. Her songs are not meant to assuage. Rather, they memorialize the grief of mortals. They recognize that human suffering, because it is human, cannot be salved and forgotten in Lethe's waters. Swinburne's Sappho spurns Aphrodite's language of comfort for she has mortal needs. Aphrodite, an immortal, can never know or understand the unmitigable pain of human suffering. Sappho's denial of Lethe's powers and her celebration of human beings' ability to feel grief and pain at loss of love is so powerful that even the goddess Aphrodite flees its awful beauty while the songs of the nine other Muses are silenced:

Newly fledged, her visible song, a marvel,
Made of perfect sound and exceeding passion,
Sweetly shapen, terrible, full of thunders,
    Clothed with the wind's wings.

Then rejoiced she, laughing with love, and scattered
Roses, awful roses of holy blossom;
Then the Loves thronged sadly with hidden faces
    Round Aphrodite,

Then the Muses, stricken at heart, were silent;
Yea, the gods waxed pale; such a song was that song.
All reluctant, all with a fresh repulsion,
    Fled from before her.[8]

Faulkner's lyric, like Swinburne's, and in keeping with his own first poem in *The Lilacs* sequence, is the poem's narrator's waking vision. But unlike Swinburne's it does not lead to revelation. Rather, it is a negative statement. Faulkner's poem's structure imitates Swinburne's, but Faulkner's is shorter, having six to Swinburne's twenty Sapphic strophes. Such condensation is possible because Faulkner, as he does in his adaptation of Mallarmé's "L'Après-midi d'un faune," chooses to tell only part of the story. He omits the strophes that describe the effect of Sappho's "visible song" on the gods and on mortals. He also makes another change, one that casts an oddly judgmental light on the figure Swinburne uses to symbolize the new poetry: Sappho's chosen form of sexuality, homoerotic love. In "Sapphics," "lesbian lovers are Swinburne's figure for the new life and speech which Sappho brings to the world."⁹ Faulkner's poem reverses the beliefs expressed in Swinburne's lyric. One can see the differences between Swinburne's and Faulkner's attitudes toward the Lesbian women by comparing the last three strophes of Swinburne's poem with the final two strophes of Faulkner's adaptation.

Swinburne:

All withdrew long since, and the land was barren,
Full of fruitless women and music only.
Now perchance, when the winds are assuaged at sunset,
    Lulled at the dewfall,

By the grey sea-side, unassuaged, unheard of,
Unbeloved, unseen in the ebb of twilight,
Ghosts of outcast women return lamenting,
    Purged not in Lethe.

Clothed about with flame and with tears, and singing
Songs that move the heart of the shaken heaven,
Songs that break the heart of the earth with pity,
    Hearing, to hear them.

Faulkner:

She sees not the Lesbians kissing mouth
To mouth across lute strings, drunken with singing,
Nor the white feet of the Oceanides
    Shining and unsandalled.

Before her go cryings and lamentations
Of barren women, a thunder of wings,
While ghosts of outcast Lethean women, lamenting,
    Stiffen the twilight.

Swinburne's point in the first two lines is that although the Lesbian women did not bear children, they were nevertheless creative and productive: they wrote great poetry in which they spoke and sung of their unassuaged pain in words that could "move the heart of the shaken heaven." Furthermore, while nature, "the winds," can be lulled into a state of forgetfulness by the gods' songs and inventions, even the ghosts of the Lesbians cannot be soothed by things of the gods' making. The implication of Swinburne's poem also seems to be that the Lesbians have rejected the fruits of heterosexual passion so that they may bear a different kind of fruit: songs. Their land is "barren" but, paradoxically, "*full* of fruitless women and *music* only." Swinburne further implies that this was a necessary and positive choice: one cannot bear both children and poems.

Faulkner takes his second-to-last strophe—a description of the Lesbians kissing—from a strophe in Swinburne's poem. It reports Aphrodite's and Sappho's feelings and actions at the moment the goddess fled from Sappho's "visible song." In Swinburne's poem, Sappho turns away from the sorrowing Aphrodite so that she "Saw not how the bosom of Aphrodite / Shook with weeping, . . ." In doing so she turns toward her own

> . . . visible song, a marvel,
> Made of perfect sound and exceeding passion,
> Sweetly shapen, terrible, full of thunders, . . .

and sees the reflectors of her own new language and song. It is these she *chooses* above Aphrodite's forms of love and song:

> Saw the Lesbians kissing across their smitten
> Lutes with lips more sweet than the sound of lute-strings,
> Mouth to mouth and hand upon hand, her chosen,
>   Fairer than all men . . .

Faulkner deletes Sappho from his lyric and limits his subject to Aphrodite's rejection of the Lesbian women. Thus, although he inserts Swinburne's image of the Lesbians for the first time in his second-to-last strophe, he changes the subject, making Aphrodite turn away and fail to see the Lesbians: "She looks not back . . . / She sees not the Lesbians kissing mouth / To mouth." Ignoring them, she spurns their sensuality and their singing that has made them "drunken." By then calling them "Lethean women" Faulkner suggests precisely the opposite viewpoint from that stated in Swinburne's lyric: his Lesbians *can* forget.

Like Swinburne, Faulkner also uses "outcast" to describe the Lesbian women, but they are outcast not as in Swinburne because they are mortals and they have been "cast out" by their lovers as Sappho was by Anactòria, but because they have succumbed to the lures of homoerotic love and are, therefore, "barren." Faulkner says their songs are merely "the cryings and lamentations of barren women." His Lesbians are not

> Clothed about with flame and with tears, and singing
> Songs that move the heart of the shaken heaven,
> Songs that break the heart of the earth with pity,
>   Hearing, to hear them.[10]

It is curious that Faulkner, who was translating, imitating, and adapting the poems of older poets as a means of finding his own path to "original song," should ignore the strophes that celebrated Sappho's great poetic achievement. Faulkner's adaptation implies that Sappho's sexual proclivities excluded her from Aphrodite's favor and that rather than singing, she and her women were condemned to "barrenness, cryings, and lamentations." It is of course possible that Faulkner missed the import of Swinburne's "Sapphics." But the accuracy with which he has condensed its opening strophes into the first three strophes of his own version indicates he has made a careful study of the language as well as the meter of Swinburne's poem.

The Moral Stance: Faulkner Questions Vision in Swinburne and Mallarmé

Why did Faulkner advance a diametrically opposed version of "Sapphics"? In two earlier poems, "The Lilacs" and "After Fifty Years," he has condemned other forms of love that are blatantly narcissistic. We find more information relevant to answering this question in Faulkner's treatment of sexual love in "L'Apres Midi d'un Faune." Faulkner excluded from his version the scene that is the specific source of Mallarmé's faun's erotic feelings. In Mallarmé's poem the faun creates music and initiates a fantasy in which he surprises and then attempts to rape two intertwined nymphs:

> J'accours; quand, à mes pieds, s'entrejoignment (meurtries
> De la langueur goûtée à ce mal d'être deux)
> De dormeuses parmi leurs seuls bras hasardeux;
> Je les ravis . . .

This poem, although in a different way than "Sapphics" and in search of a different effect on its audience, is also about homoeroticism and the creative imagination. The faun's music making triggers a homoerotic fantasy, which he then tells. The final product of the faun's fantasy is a unique work of art, a poem that gives his fantasy coherence and form, making it available to others. The faun's (poet's) act is equivalent to what Sappho does with her grief in Swinburne's "Sapphics." She makes a new kind of poem. What Mallarmé and Swinburne are celebrating is a positive narcissism coupled with an acceptance of the myriad forms of sexuality—homosexual fantasies in particular—from which they, as mature poets, derive imaginative inspiration. Faulkner, in contrast, appears threatened by the underlying emotional currents in these poems. Although they attract and fascinate him he feels compelled to purify them. He reacts much as the Marble Faun responded to his nightmare (*TMF* XVI):

while claiming them as his, he censors them as he adapts them to his conscious needs in *The Lilacs*.

Both "Sapphics" and "L'Après-midi" interested Faulkner in part because they speak in new ways about the connections between creativity and sexuality. Although "L'Après-midi" may not be a poem about poets, it concerns the making of poetry, and Faulkner responded to it because it fired his own imagination.[11] However, in adapting these two poems, he either excludes or condemns homoerotic elements and ignores the connections Swinburne and Mallarmé make between homoerotic fantasies and the creative imagination. His censorship also forces him to omit their other common subject, the origins of new forms of poetry. This seems odd, for like Swinburne, or Swinburne in the guise of Sappho, Faulkner was seeking a radically new way of speaking to encompass and communicate his own unique poetic vision. In fact, new song is the object of the Marble Faun's quest.

Clearly the resonances and dissonances Swinburne provoked have sent Faulkner's imagination into turmoil. His conscious morality makes him reject Swinburne's solution even as he is emotionally drawn to it. Not until he gives up his identity as poet, removing himself as a persona in his texts, will he deal directly with this issue. In Faulkner's fiction sexual love is generally destructive but the most passionate and most fatal love of all is the love of twins (the Sartoris brothers), brothers (Bon and Henry), or siblings (Quentin and Caddy). Death always results from homosexual and/or incestuous love. As novelist, Faulkner's morality does not alter, but by separating himself from his poet persona and punishing his fictional offenders he gives himself the freedom to explore this deeply attractive theme in all of its ramifications.

In making his version of "Sapphics" about Aphrodite rather than Sappho, Faulkner also passes over another crucial issue raised by Swinburne's poem: man's attitude toward fate: "For who shall change with prayers or thanksgivings / The mystery of the cruelty of things?"[12] Sappho knows that the only way to deal with fate is to speak of it truthfully and to thereby memorialize it. Aphrodite, because she is a goddess and, therefore, an embodiment or instrument of fate, does not experience fate as mortals do and, therefore, cannot speak the truth. Faulkner's omission here is remarkable as Swinburne's conception of how man should deal with fate foreshadows a point of view expressed in his own later novels.

Many of Faulkner's fictional characters assert, as does Swinburne's Sappho, an unchanging and uncompromising belief in certain moral values. For them such belief stands as an image of permanence in an otherwise unremittingly chaotic, irrational world. Characters, like Dilsey in *The Sound and the Fury*, have, as Sappho does, moments of total vision: "I seed de beginnin, en now I sees de endin" (*TSATF*, p. 371). Their all-encompassing vision allows them to "endure" and to memorialize the past but not succumb to it. They see both the beginning and the ending; their vision stretches to the "boundaries" of perception. Characters like Dilsey, or Lena Grove in *Light in August*, are constantly juxtaposed to people like Quentin Compson or the Reverend Hightower, characters who have succumbed and who live in sterile fantasies of a past that never was. Responding to Swinburne's "Sapphics" provided Faulkner a way into subjects that will matter deeply to him throughout his career.

Faulkner's statements about other writers' significance to him are, with the exception of Sherwood Anderson and Algernon Swinburne, brief and often misleading. He wrote essays on both Anderson and Swinburne in the early spring of 1925 when he was living in New Orleans, writing a series of humorous "letters" with Sherwood Anderson, working on his first novel, *Soldiers' Pay*, and contributing a series of prose sketches and short stories to the New Orleans *Times-Picayune* and the *Double Dealer*.[13] In the essay "Verse Old and Nascent: A Pilgrimage," he tries to explain Swinburne's meaning for him in the context of his own moral and creative development.[14] The essay offers clues about Faulkner's feelings toward Swinburne and may serve to explain why he treated "Sapphics" as he did when he adapted it in 1919.

> *At the age of sixteen, I discovered Swinburne. Or rather, Swinburne discovered me*, springing from some tortured undergrowth of my adolescence, like a highwayman, making me his slave. My mental life at that period was so completely and smoothly veneered with surface insincerity—obviously necessary to me at that time, to support intact my personal integrity—that *I can not tell to this day exactly to what depth he stirred me, just how deeply the footprints of his passage are left in my mind. It seems to me now that I found him nothing but a flexible vessel into which I might put my own vague emotional shapes without breaking them. It was years later that I found in him much more than bright and bitter sound, more than a satisfying tinsel of blood and death and gold and the inevitable sea.* True I dipped into Shelley and Keats—who doesn't, at that age?—but they did not move me. . . .
> I do not mean . . . that I ever found anything sexual in Swinburne:

there is no sex in Swinburne. The mathematician, surely; and eroticism just as there is eroticism in form and color and movement wherever found. But not that tortured sex in—say—D. H. Lawrence. . . .
    *Whatever it was that I found in Swinburne, it completely satisfied
    me and filled my inner life.* I cannot understand now how I could
have regarded the others with such dull complacency. Surely, if one be
moved at all by Swinburne he must inevitably find in Swinburne's
forerunners some kinship. Perhaps it is that Swinburne, having taken
his heritage and elaborated it to the despair of any would-be poet, has
coarsened it to tickle the dullest of palates as well as the most dis-
criminating, as used water can be drunk by both hogs and gods. . . .
(emphasis added) [15]

In tapes of question and answer sessions Faulkner held with University of Virginia students shortly before his death, he pays passing
homage to Dickens, Hawthorne, and other writers to whom he and
most twentieth-century novelists owe a debt, but Swinburne is the
only writer Faulkner ever speaks of with such passion and intensity.

What is it then that Faulkner divines in Swinburne's poetry? What
attracts him so immediately and intensely? Partly it was Swinburne's cadences: "He liked it just for the sound, you read the first
few lines and you're gone," said Jill Faulkner Summers about the
Swinburne poems her father had memorized and then taught her. [16]

But beyond the immediate attraction lies an intuitive identification with certain aspects of Swinburne's mode of perception.
Whether Faulkner's identification at this deeper level was ever conscious is impossible to know. Faulkner's attempts to define the quality of Swinburne's attraction for him in this 1925 essay suggest that
his unconscious understanding of the nature of his identification, at
least at that time, was acute. His description of Swinburne's poetry
as "a flexible vessel into which I might put my own vague emotional
shapes without breaking them" prefigures the way in which Swinburne ultimately serves Faulkner. But this does not occur until three
years later, in 1928, when he writes *The Sound and the Fury.* Then,
having successfully internalized Swinburne's influence, he actually
uses the older poet's constructs in precisely this manner.

In describing Swinburne's effect upon him, Faulkner says that he
doesn't know "to what depth he stirred me, just how deeply the
footprints of his passage are left in my mind." Then he states that he
cannot define the qualities that drew him to Swinburne, but "whatever it was . . . it completely satisfied me and filled my inner life."
Swinburne is at once the container and contents of Faulkner's creative emotional life. Faulkner describes here an immensely rich and

fluid relationship. He fills and is filled by the older poet's language, but he does not find Swinburne's deep impact either threatening or overpowering. Rather, his experience is one of totally joyful and accepting identification with Swinburne's mode of perception. In this essay, Faulkner makes it appear that his immersion in Swinburne occurred prior to 1919, but his writing and inclusion of "Sapphics" in *The Lilacs* (1920) and other more subtle indications of Swinburne's influence in that and later sequences suggest that it was during 1918 to 1920 that Faulkner fell under the older poet's sway.

Faulkner describes his feelings about Swinburne in terms of an idealized parent-child relationship. The child—Faulkner—is completely satisfied in his identification with and internalization of his parent—Swinburne. And because he is, he does not feel that his thoughts or actions are either fettered or inhibited by his parent. Rather, this influence stimulates him to think and act independently, to create his "own vague emotional shapes," the poetry of his apprenticeship.

The manner in which Faulkner seeks to characterize Swinburne's influence illustrates how similarly these two men's minds worked on the problem of simultaneous presentation of multiple ways of seeing and feeling. Thus Swinburne's effect on Faulkner's language is exemplified in the mode of expression Faulkner uses to try to define that effect. To articulate Swinburne's impact on his mental life, Faulkner slips into Swinburne's multifaceted mode of describing perception: the constant return to and repetition of the impossible union in antithesis.[17] The result is constantly paired antithetical images such as spring/winter, day/night, life/death. The first line of "A Ballad of François Villon" is an example: "Bird of the bitter bright grey golden morn." Faulkner and his daughter played a game that drew attention to the antithetical structure of this and other Swinburne poems. One of them would begin by reciting a line from a poem and the other would respond with the next line and so on until either one missed or the poem was completed. The person giving the last line correctly would then start the next poem. A poem they played with often was

If you were queen of pleasure,
  And I were king of pain,
We'd hunt down love together,
Pluck out his flying-feather,
And teach his feet a measure,
  And find his mouth a rein;

If you were queen of pleasure,
   And I were king of pain.[18]

In "A Match" each word in the pair is the limit of its counterpart.[19] Another example, also a favorite of Faulkner's, is a chorus from *Atalanta in Calydon*. Its structure depends on an amassing of antithetical pairs:

Before the beginning of years,
   There came to the making of man
Time, with a gift of tears;
   Grief, with a glass that ran;
Pleasure, with pain for leaven;
   Summer, with flowers that fell . . .[20]

Most of the poems like this from *Poems and Ballads* are reprinted in Faulkner's copy of Swinburne's *Poems*. Faulkner used their titles and subjects for some of his own poems and stories, including "Hermaphroditus," "Sapphics," "An Interlude," and "A Vision of Spring in Winter."

In his novels Faulkner's long and intimate association with Swinburne bears fruit. Like Swinburne's poems the novels attempt to transcend the limitations of space and time, which is what Faulkner wanted the long sentences that abound in his fiction to accomplish. He once explained that he was

. . . trying to put the whole history of the human heart on the head of a pin, you might say. Also to me, no man is himself, he is the sum of his past. There is no such thing as was because the past is. It is a part of every man, every woman, and every moment. . . . And so a man, a character in a story at any moment of action is not just himself as he is then, he is all that made him and the long sentence is an attempt to get his past and possibly his future into the instant in which he does something.[21]

The purpose of such a sentence is to make the reader experience multiple points of view within its physical boundary and thus to transcend the limitations of space and time. Long sentences are Faulkner's hallmark; they help create the unique language he invented to describe his constantly transforming fictional world peopled by characters who continuously envision themselves as the sum of infinite boundaries. Embedded in these sentences is Faulkner's language of transformation and antithesis, which forces the reader to see and experience his men and women as simultaneously living/dead, moving/static, young/old, male/female, black/white, loving/hating, etc. Thus Rosa Coldfield says of her life with Sutpen, "I found only that dream-state in which you run without moving from a terror in which you cannot believe, toward a safety in which you have no faith."[22] Or, with intentional self-irony Faulkner has Joe Christmas describe his fate as "a printed sentence, fullborn and already dead" (*LIA*, p. 98). As Temple Drake tells Horace what she thought when she was waiting to be raped, she says,

> So I'd hold my eyes shut and say Now I am. I am now. I'd look at my legs and I'd think how much I had done for them. I'd think about how many dances I had taken them to—crazy, like that. . . . now they'd gotten me into this. So I'd think about praying to be changed into a boy. . . . Then I'd think maybe I couldn't tell it and I'd get ready to look. Then I'd think maybe it was too soon to look; that if I looked too soon I'd spoil it and then it wouldn't, sure enough. . . . I hadn't breathed in a long time. So I thought I was dead. . . . Then I said That won't do. I ought to be a man. So I was an old man, with a long white beard. (*Sanctuary*, pp. 210, 212, 213)

In *As I Lay Dying*, the young boy Vardaman strikes out at the horses of the man he believes has killed his mother. He then sees the horses "wheeling in a long lunge, the buggy wheeling onto two wheels and motionless like it is nailed to the ground and the horses motionless like they are nailed by the hind feet to the center of a whirling plate."[23] Synesthesia, a metaphorical device used extensively by Swinburne and Faulkner, is a superb means for presenting this point of view.

The difference between Swinburne's and Faulkner's use of boundary lines lies in the resolutions they or their characters reach when they have experienced their moment of vision as a result of being placed or placing themselves at such a point. For Swinburne's personas, such an experience leads to a moment of illumination and consolation, as in the opening stanzas of "Sapphics":

> All the night sleep came not upon my eyelids,
> Shed not dew, nor shook nor unclosed a feather,
> Yet with lips shut close and with eyes of iron
> Stood and beheld me.
>
> Then to me so lying awake a vision
> Came without sleep over the seas and touched me,
> Softly touched mine eyelids and lips; and I too,
> Full of the vision . . .[24]

Here the Swinburnian mask is acutely aware of both the objective world and the free-flowing realm of his unconscious; the attendant vision is a positive though often painful experience. But it is also an inward-turning vision with little applicability beyond the almost mesmerizing linguistic constructs of Swinburne's poetic world. It is on this count that Faulkner ultimately rejects Swinburne's vision.

It is all very well to urge a reader to experience "a state of mind where everything is at last possible,"[25] but the problem with this is that at some point the reader must, as Faulkner's characters do (though often with great reluctance and poor judgment), *act*. That is, even fictional characters, to be relevant as Faulkner wanted his to be, must deal with the world. If they are lucky, they can also live in the worlds of their imaginations, but they cannot cloister themselves there. To say this is not to argue that Swinburne is flawed. Rather it is to try to locate the point at which Faulkner's poetic vision diverges from Swinburne's. Faulkner presents his characters for our view and has them experiencing life from a Swinburnian perspective, but he does not necessarily equate such vision with illumination. In Faulkner's fictional world, acute perception such as that accorded the Swinburnian hero is as often a source of moral confusion as it is a kind of momentary clarity or illumination. The boy in the poem "After Fifty Years" may feel the old temptress's presence "like shed scent." But rather than being freed by his acute poetic sensibility—this transforming perception that occurs when imagination is operating at the boundary lines—he is trapped by it. Or a man like the Reverend Hightower, because he is equipped with a mind that works in transformations, at last experiences his moment of illumination only to reject it and be destroyed by it (*LIA*, pp. 466–467).

It might be argued that this difference exists because Swinburne is an accomplished poet and Faulkner, ultimately, a novelist. But the presence of this difference in Faulkner's early poetry as well as in his mature novels, coupled with the muted but definite Swinburnian aura in Faulkner's fictional style, suggests that it is rather the authors' differing points of view about where this kind of perception can lead. Both see it as essential to their own creative vision, but when Faulkner endows one of his fictional characters with such powers of vision he is as likely to use them to obscure or avoid or reject the truth as to illuminate reality and then act according to the dictates of his vision. In "The Lilacs," "Une Ballade des Femmes Perdues," "After Fifty Years," and "Sapphics," characters with a Swinburnian mode of perception are portrayed negatively. Because they have withdrawn from any form of action, they are somehow not in life. They merely exist. They resemble their fictional descendants like Hightower or Ellen Coldfield, "who even while alive had moved but without life . . . who now had an air of tranquil and unwitting desolation, not as if she had either outlived the others or had died first, but as if she had never lived at all" (*Absalom, Absalom!*, pp. 13–14).

In the early poems of *The Lilacs* Faulkner adopts Swinburne's method of vision and its accompanying devices of transformation and synesthesia, but he employs them to create life-denying figures like the wounded pilot, the old woman and her boy captive, or the aged dream-bound Don Juan in "Ballade." These characters are not fully developed because the formal structures they inhabit discourage such complexity; however, they are forerunners of the tragic figures who populate Faulkner's fictional world. Such men and women, like Hightower, Sutpen, Quentin Compson, or even Jefferson County's self-styled "poetess laureate" Miss Rosa Coldfield, have no place in the scheme of a poet like Swinburne, who "practices a severe aestheticism whose purpose is to empty the reader of the worlds he possesses."[26] Because Faulkner's vision is essentially tragic, he turns, even in this early poem sequence, to the task of creating characters who see like Swinburne's poetic personas and may be momentarily transformed, but who ultimately must choose or not choose to act. For Faulkner's poetic personas and his fictional characters, perception at the boundary line does not lead to the conclusion that "everything is at last possible."[27] Faulkner, as poet and novelist, rejects the Swinburne who insists upon the positive visionary quality of perception at the boundary point and whose purpose is to empty the reader of the actual world. Faulkner's intuitive tragic vision, his insistence that characters must take responsibility for choosing "not to live in life," forces him to part company with Swinburne.

Closure in *The Lilacs*: "A Dead Dancer"

Faulkner begins and concludes *The Lilacs* with free verse poems, framing his more traditionally structured lyrics within a Modernist form.[28] Death, the subject of both, is appropriately closural. Thematically "A Dead Dancer" enlarges upon *The Lilacs*'s introductory poem. The lyric's *pierrotique* voice is still a man's, but he, unlike the wounded pilot, is very much alive. His lover, however, has died and the poem describes the speaker's response to a death that is actual rather than psychic. There are other reversals and parallels. Both the dancer and the "wanton" look and act remarkably alike although one is human and the other a phantom, suggesting that neither speaker distinguishes between fantasy and reality. The poems' conclusions echo, reinforce, and extend each other: any desire for and pursuit of sexual fulfillment ends, invariably, in death. Faulkner uses the archetypal dream of sexual release to connect the meanings of the opening and closing poems in his sequence: to fly, whether it be in a plane or on one's feet, means to court disaster.

Both the awkwardness and the ingenuity of "A Dead Dancer" are traceable, in part, to its literary influences. Examination of four successive drafts of the poem reveals Aiken's sturdy presence. But even more valuable, the drafts show the author at work attempting to surmount narrative problems presented by the verse he was imitating. This record of Faulkner's editing, even though it may not be complete, provides a graphic example of how the poet, as he wrote, first imitated and then diverged from his source. In the successive drafts, he erases the crudest of his borrowings as he polishes and refines his own variation of a garnering of image clusters, phrases, episodes, even line lengths lifted from Aiken's poetry. Some of these remain. Faulkner retains Aiken's customary technique of describing the effects of music upon the mind in terms of the psychoanalytic theory of free association. Faulkner also retains throughout each draft Aiken's use of musical devices—in this poem the refrain—to impose form upon the free verse structure. Faulkner further develops musical structures when he uses music as a metaphor for "the image stream of the mind" in *Vision in Spring*. There musical analogues figure largely in his progress toward his fictional voice.

Like the voices in "The Lilacs," the speaker in "A Dead Dancer" plays a role in the poem. He shares its stage, "a dusky silence," with the spirit of a young girl: "She who danced [on slender(?)] gilded feet." Meanwhile the narrator sits among other men who were her lovers "in the [backwash of self(?)] consciousness, / Dreaming dreams beyond [the ebb and flow(?)] / Of Life and Death, while [each one whis-(?)]pers to himself[—I was the last(?)]." The narrator portrays himself as a somewhat guilt-ridden survivor: "Is it relief we feel?" The poem is in part a memorial to the dead girl but it is also an attempt at using interior monologue to capture the moods and feelings of her admirers. Physically together but spiritually alone they are like the pilot in "The Lilacs" as they "sit in diffident guttering silence." Their minds play over images of "yesterday" recalled by the music of a "hurdy gurdy in the street below." Each man, as he muses, "whispers to himself—I was the last" of those "that she had [loved at different times(?)]." The poem hints strongly that women who cause men to feel jealousy and unfulfilled desire may be best off dead. Once more Faulkner writes about an absent but powerful woman.

Discussion of "A Dead Dancer" is, for the most part, based on the two published collations of various extant versions.[29] The University of Virginia owns three drafts of the poem (hereafter referred to as number 1, number 2, and number 3) while *The Lilacs* version (hereafter number 4) is privately owned (Figure 7). Numbers 2 and 4 appear to be later versions than numbers 3 and 1. Number 4 bears the closest resemblance to number 2, and number 4 appears to be the most finished version of "A Dead Dancer." In numbers 2 and 4 interest is centered on the narrator's memories of the dead dancer and his attempt to explain how he feels about her death. Like numbers 1 and 3, 2 and 4 begin with an image of the dancer's mourners— "We that she had loved at different times"—but in contrast to 1 and 3, numbers 2 and 4 end with images of the dancer herself: "There are now whisperings of (   ) the dead / About her now" (number 4) and "She dances now for apocryphal lovers" (number 2). In contrast, the final strophe of number 1 drifts into a parallel but unconnected narrative about a pair of lovers; and each strophe in number 3 is simply a series of images, strung tentatively together with music heard by the narrator. The latter version, showing no attempt at thematic or narrative development, seems the most diffuse of all the drafts despite the fact that it is closest in length to the compact *Lilacs* version. (Number 3 has 26 lines and number 4 has 27 lines, while numbers 1 and 2 are 36 plus 4 canceled lines and 39 plus 4 canceled lines, respectively.)

In the second strophe of all four versions, the speaker juxtaposes the dance and music of his worldly dead dancer to the dancing and music of "girls too young to be self conscious / Dancing gravely in a twilit garden" (numbers 1, 2, 3). Number 4 indicates improvement where the speaker describes his virgins merely as "little girls in white dresses," a more subtle image that shows rather than tells of their innocence. But why introduce the image of little girls at all? The speaker's mind moves from his worldly dead dancer to young virgins because he sees women as a bitter mix of impossible evil and equally impossible good. Faulkner's fiction also contains many such women. Or, rather, Faulkner's fictional men perceive their women like this, too. Caddy Compson, Faulkner's "heart's darling," is a benign example and Temple Drake and Narcissa Benbow, the villainesses of *Sanctuary*, are dangerous ones. Temple's name alone marks a brilliantly concise instance of antithetical imaging. Faulkner extends the metaphor to her appearance. An "elongated and leggy infant," she looks virginal and "doll-like." But tacked onto her flat, curveless body and long, "golden," skinny legs (note the "slender gilded legs" in "A Dead Dancer" numbers 1, 2, and 3) is a mop of "tight red curls like dots of resin" and a "mouth painted into a savage and perfect bow . . . cut carefully from purple paper and pasted there" ("like bits of torn colored paper . . . Whispering colored paper" ["ADD," numbers 1 and 3]).[30] When Faulkner transforms his dancer into a fictional character like Temple Drake, the specific nature of her power, just vaguely expressed in this poem, manifests itself. While he may not have used his dead dancer as a conscious centering image for *Sanctuary*, its resonances there are integral to the power of Temple's evil. From the moment her blond legs flash into Gowan's car to her final dancing spree precipitating Red's death, Temple's dancing, her whirling and dashing about the Old Frenchman place, causes men to kill and die: "She dances now for apocryphal lovers / To pale starings of the alive mouths of the dead" ("ADD," number 2), and "There are whisperings (   ) of the dead / About her now, a wind that (   )" ("ADD," number 4). The bevy of jealous suitors sitting at dusk in "A Dead Dancer," each one claiming "I was the last," prefigure Temple's assorted would-be lovers sitting in the dusk and later dark on the porch at Lee Goodwin's. Faulkner's virginal/worldly dead dancer also replicates a fantasy of illicit sex in child's clothing that figured persistently in his real world. In her memoir, *A Loving Gentleman*, Meta Wilde writes that Faulkner fantasized her as "a girl-child." She was twenty-nine and Faulkner thirty-nine. She writes:

> Although he made love to me as a man to a woman, there were times when he saw me as being far younger than I was. . . . he would edit out . . . my birthdays, my marriage, my work—and behave toward me as if I were just out of high school. . . . I was confounded by his need to turn me into a sweet, tremulous girl. . . . I was troubled by his choice of gift [of a child's hair ribbon]. The idealization of me as a girl far too young for him was to last a number of years and appear in some of his letters to me. I never protested. My acceptance of his vision of me as a maiden nourished his fantasy.[31]

Its meaning and relevance to his novelistic vision become clearer as Faulkner builds upon it in *Vision in Spring*.

One of the most important differences between numbers 2 and 4 of "A Dead Dancer," one that shows both how and why number 4 is a refinement of all three of the other versions, is found in the lines in number 2 recounting a parallel but thematically unrelated account of two disaffected lovers. The lines relating this story contain Faulkner's most extensive borrowings from one of Aiken's 1917 poem sequences, *Nocturne of Remembered Spring*.[32] As noted above, these lines, only slightly altered, had appeared first in the final strophe of number 1. Apparently Faulkner then tried to save this vignette and force a connection by moving it into the center of number 2. But it still did not work—two narratives were more than he could handle. So in number 4 he discarded the second lovers' story so as to focus his poem on the dead dancer and the speaker's feelings about her and her other lovers.

Clearly number 2 is a more finished and tightly wrought poem than number 3, but number 4, *The Lilacs* version, is the most compact of all. Faulkner removed the story of the disenchanted lovers, distributed lines from the second and third strophes of number 2 into all four strophes of number 4, and then added five additional lines as number 4's third and final strophe. The first two of these five lines also appear in number 2, third strophe, but the last three lines are unique to this version. In them the narrator describes the dancer being enveloped in death's music, a music that calls up visual images very similar to those in the death scene imagined by the dying pilot of "The Lilacs."

Although "A Dead Dancer" is full of image clusters culled from Aiken's early poem sequences, Faulkner found more in Aiken than pleasing images. That poet's novelistic concept of poetic structure had a profound and lasting effect on Faulkner's work. Aiken's first novel was not published until 1927, but his poetry created a narrative designed to capture man's interior life in its totality. (His was not a poetry of short or even long lyric cries or moments.) Aiken described his theories of poetry in the introductions to his "symphonic" poem sequences and in reviews of his own and others' poetry published between 1916 and 1921 in *Poetry, The New Republic,* and *The Dial.* In his preface to *The Jig of Forslin, A Symphony* (1916), which I quote because Faulkner read and wrote about it,[33] Aiken said *Forslin* was an amalgam of almost all existing poetic methods and tones:

> . . . it has been guided entirely by the central theme. This theme is the process of vicarious wish fulfillment by which civilized man enriches his . . . life and obtains emotional balance. *It is an exploration of his emotional and mental hinterland, his fairyland of impossible illusions and dreams*: ranging on the one extreme, from the desire for a complete tyranny of body over mind, to the desire, on the other

extreme, for complete tyranny of mind over body . . .
> As far as possible, the attempt has been made to relate these typi-
> cal dreams, or vicarious adventures, not discretely, but in flux. (em-
> phasis added)[34]

The Lilacs also explores many of its voices' emotional and mental
hinterlands, wilds that are often fraught with danger, the danger of
losing touch with the concrete world. Faulkner, too, is interested not
in discreteness but in flux.

Aiken explains the structure of *Forslin*: "As far as the technique of
the verse is concerned,—the harmony and counterpoint, if I may use
the terms in a general sense,—it has been governed as much, always,
by the consideration of the whole as of the part."[35] Aiken's technique—a sequential, symphonic structure in which the separate
poems are considered as parts of a larger whole—suggested new possibilities for poetic structures, possibilities to which Faulkner was
sympathetic, for they answered his current needs. The interior monologues and the "free rhythms and rhymeless verse" of the first and
semifinal poems of *The Lilacs* introduce a variety of movement
much as Aiken's "cacophonies and irregularities" created contrasts
in *Forslin*. Faulkner's poems are much shorter than Aiken's. They
can be read as discrete units but their effect is greater when they are
read as episodes. These parts or episodes, taken together, provide the
"harmony and counterpoint" that permit mood and movement to
fluctuate throughout the sequence.

The form and content of "A Dead Dancer" illustrate the two reasons Aiken's verse interested Faulkner: his verse cadences—very
different from Swinburne's but equally intriguing—and the artistic, emotional, and intellectual concerns shaping those cadences.
Aiken, like the Symbolists and others, wanted to derive new poetic
forms from music. He also had a corresponding desire, not shared
with the Symbolists, to create a narrative. But he wanted to use narrative in a revolutionary way. Spurred by his reading in Freudian and
other psychological theory, he wished "to present a state of mind or
interior monologue by means of a long poem in broken form and
with episodic treatment." To realize this ambition, he chose to write
poem sequences rather than narrative poems. His interest in Freudian theory also accounts for the inclusion of psychological terminol-
ogy in his poetry and criticism.[36] A key word for Aiken and one that
crops up in Faulkner's "A Dead Dancer" is "consciousness."

Aiken's attitude toward love between men and women, although
less harsh than Eliot's, was one Faulkner understood. In most of
Aiken's early poetry, the hero experiences a moment of brief passion

for his adored one. Both lover and beloved are elevated to godlike status. Then poof! the hero becomes bored and disillusioned. In his disappointment, he deserts her and resumes a never-ending quest for ideal love. Sometimes, as a variation on the theme, both lovers become disillusioned but try unsuccessfully to pretend undying passion. It is this motif that Faulkner imitated in the lovers' tale he excised from his final version of "A Dead Dancer." Similar images from Faulkner's lovers' section are found in Aiken's "Episode in Gray" in *Nocturne* (pp. 65–75). Other images and themes in "A Dead Dancer" seem to have their origins in "Sonata in Pathos," a four-part poem from that same book (pp. 39–47). Faulkner has also borrowed images from Aiken's *The Jig of Forslin, A Symphony* (1916), from *Turns and Movies* (1916), and from other poems in *Nocturne*. The specific lines from "Episode" that Faulkner drew upon appear in the third, fourth, and fifth sections of Aiken's poem.[37]

In the two earlier versions of Faulkner's poem (University of Virginia, numbers 1 and 3), Aiken's voice dominates the thought, structure, and language. In comparing successive renditions, Faulkner's method of progressively excising more and more of what was originally an obvious imitation of Aiken as he wrote his way through the various drafts of his poem is evident. In number 4, *The Lilacs* version, Faulkner has removed the second lovers' story as well as several phrases from other parts of the poem. Examples are words from the first strophe of number 3 like "inflammable objectiveness" or in number 2 the concept of repression in the canceled phrase "we are withholding."

Among the images Faulkner did retain for *The Lilacs* version are some that illustrate what he was learning as he imitated. Faulkner collects the image of music weaving a pattern of memories "tapping softly at the doors of consciousness" from Aiken's *The Jig of Forslin*.[38] In number 4 Faulkner has dropped the "arc" of the lamp, or "arc-light" as Aiken calls it earlier in *Forslin* ("A man stepped out in the purple of an arc-light" [p. 18] or "Mark how the arc-lamp dims and starts and sputters" [p. 39]). He has then condensed Aiken's original image in his own first strophe by transforming Aiken's noun "gutters" into a gerund. Thus the opening lines of number 4 read:

> We, that she had loved [at different(?)] times
> Sit at dusk in diffident gutt[ering silence,(?)] a ring
> Of ill-trimmed lamps . . .

Other key images Faulkner borrows from Aiken and adapts to his own needs describe the music that "loops and coils" through the narrator's mind and through the night air. Aiken had written a poem called "Melody in a Restaurant" in a section from *The House of Dust* (1920), which Faulkner had read by February 1921.

> The cigarette-smoke loops and slides above us,
> Dipping and swirling as the waiter passes;
> . . . .
> A thousand dreams revolve and fall and flow.[39]

Faulkner also adopts Aiken's continual association of music, memory, and rain in the lines from number 2, second strophe, beginning "Delicate as the rain on running feet," which he amends in number 4 so that the hurdy-gurdy music is

> [The gold th(?)]reads in a dim old tapes[try(?)]
> [Delicate as(?)] the rain on running [feet(?)]
> Go tapping at the [doors of consciousness(?)]
> With the minute insist[ence of the rain(?)]
> Then fall spreading throu[gh the stillness(?)] of the street
> Into the silence again.

Echoes of "A Dead Dancer" in *Light in August*

These and other images do make their way into later Faulkner poems, but what is their further relation to Faulkner's fictional voice? Another image Faulkner borrowed from Aiken, used first in "A Dead Dancer" and then retained and expanded upon for later use, was Aiken's idiosyncratic "gravely," associated with virgins ("of girls / Dancing gravely in a twilit garden" ["ADD"]). Aiken's lines appear in another of his "symphonies," *Senlin: A Biography* (1918): "White unicorns come gravely down to the water. / In the lilac dusk they come, they are white and stately."[40] The unicorns are creations of Senlin's imaginary world, a world like that of *The Lilacs* in which "maidens spread their white palms to the starlight" and "The stars hang over the sea like polished glass" (pp. 15–16). According to myth, only virgins can catch unicorns. In adapting this image in "A Dead Dancer" Faulkner makes a substitution: white-robed virgins for white unicorns. The virgins appear in all versions and are called forth by hurdy-gurdy music, music that is also associated with the worldly dead dancer.

In several novels, Faulkner uses "grave" or "gravely" as a code word to introduce several especially beautiful women: Narcissa Benbow (*Sanctuary*), Caddie Compson (*The Sound and the Fury*), and Lena Grove (*Light in August*). While Narcissa is always dressed in white, Caddie and Lena have about them an aura of moral virginity or integrity that makes the fact that they are technically "fallen women" seem irrelevant. Paradoxically, Narcissa's prudish yet voyeuristic response to sex makes her the least virginal.

Within the first eighteen pages of *Light in August* Faulkner uses "grave" twice. In the face of Mrs. Armstid's silent accusation and her rigid moral stance, Lena's "voice is quite grave now, quite quiet" (*LIA*, p. 14) and her "lowered face is grave, quiet" (*LIA*, p. 18). Near the novel's conclusion, when Lena confronts her runaway lover with his lie about marrying her, she is described as holding Lucas with the look in "her grave face which had either nothing in it, or everything, all knowledge. . . . held him neither with rods or cords but with something against which his lying blew trivial as leaves or trash" (*LIA*, p. 409).[41] The narrator may equivocate, but we know Lena's look holds Lucas because it contains all knowledge. Here Faulkner has salvaged, refined, and given new life to an image borrowed from one of the earlier drafts of "A Dead Dancer," the one in number 2 that describes the emotional ties binding the two lovers:

> . . . they cannot part
> Because of something vague and thin as air
> Intangible, yet strong as steel that binds
> Them heart to heart.

But there is even more of "A Dead Dancer" that makes its way into the metaphorical structure of *Light in August*: the image in lines 3–6, which Faulkner reworked in each successive draft. In *The Lilacs*, it conveys the mourners' collective apprehension about displaying their real feelings concerning the dancer's death, as they have not had time to mask them with conventional responses (numbers on the left refer to verses, numbers on the right to versions):

> 3. Like so many ill trimmed lamps, for we dare not meet]1
>   Of ill trimmed lamps for as yet we dare]2
>   Of ill trimmed lamps, for we dare not meet]3
>   Of ill-trimmed la(   )4
>
> 4. Each others eyes, we are not ready yet]1
>   Not meet each other naked in the dark]2
>   Each other[s eyes (canceled)], we are not ready yet]3
>   Each other naked (   )4
>
> 5. For the—I knew her when—the vanity of regret]1,3
>   omit]2,4
>
> 6. An inflammable objectiveness]1,3
>   omit]2,4

7. —Or is it relief we feel?]1,3
   —For is it relief we feel?]2
   —Is it relief we feel?]4

8. As yet one cannot say]1,2,3,4[42]

In the manuscript of number 2, Faulkner has reworked the fourth
line four times. Besides constantly shifting the adjectives and adverbs modifying "meet each other" and "dark" he has also included a
series of variant interceding clauses. In his fourth and final attempt
he simply deletes this second clause:

line 3. Of ill trimmed lamps for as yet we dare
4*a*. Not meet each other in the dark a princely darkness dark, we
       are not ready yet (line canceled)
4*b*. Not meet each other in the dark (word canceled) naked dark.
       We are witholding (line canceled)
4*c*. Not meet each other naked (word canceled) in the dark, we are
       not ready yet (line canceled)
4*d*. Not meet each other naked in the dark
5.   —For is it relief we feel?

The result of these arduous revisions is remarkable not for the vivid-
ness of the image but for the concept that Faulkner is trying to convey. It is obvious from the care with which Faulkner reworked these
lines that he recognized the enormous potential of an idea that he
could not convey in poetry. In *Light in August* Faulkner took the images and ideas he struggled over in these drafts of "A Dead Dancer"
and transformed them into metaphors that design and elucidate the
atmosphere surrounding Lena Grove. These metaphors inform her
relations with most of the men and women she meets and knows.
Thus in her confrontation with Mrs. Armstid in the novel's opening
chapter,

> The young woman does not answer at once. Mrs. Armstid does not
> rattle the stove now, though her back is still toward the younger
> woman. Then she turns. They look at one another, suddenly naked,
> watching one another: the young woman in the chair, with her neat
> hair and her inert hands upon her lap, the older one beside the stove,
> turning motionless too, with a savage screw of grey hair at the base of
> her skull and a face that might have been carved in sandstone. Then
> the younger one speaks. (*LIA*, p. 15)

Lena tells Mrs. Armstid the truth because her chief concern is her
child, not conventional morality. Nakedness, literal or metaphorical, does not frighten her. The same image pervades the scene where
Lena confronts her child's father, Lucas Burch. Lena's presence alone,

her "grave gaze," is enough to force him to be truthful as he is "stripped naked for the instant of verbiage and deceit" (*LIA*, p. 409). In each instance the metaphor indicates a moment of human exchange when all pretense is banished, and the armor of language—truisms, the "I knew her when," false emotion, "the vanity of regret" and "verbiage"—falls away so that the participants, willingly or not, experience a moment of truth.

The mourners in "A Dead Dancer" shy from such an experience, trying to "elude" it, to "withhold" themselves. The story Faulkner wants to tell is too large to fit the confines of "A Dead Dancer," and the rhythms of Faulkner's language are too expansive to find satisfaction in a lyric. He is interested in showing people reacting to one another, and poetry, for the most part, elucidates a single person's feelings.[43] Perhaps this is another reason Faulkner attempted a larger unit than a single lyric and settled on poem sequences as an alternative, more elliptical form.

In the final strophe of "A Dead Dancer" Faulkner brings the sequence in a full circle by having the narrator imagine a scene that is reminiscent of the wounded pilot's Greek isle in *The Lilacs*'s opening poem. Although this strophe contains lines that appeared in earlier versions of "A Dead Dancer," it has others that are unique. In the following extract burnt lines are reconstructed by referring to earlier versions and to L. D. Brodsky's reconstruction (the sources of the extrapolations are indicated).

There are whisperings of the [alive mouths(?)] of the dead	version 2
About her now, a wind that [whispers in the] shadows	version 2
[in the poppies(?)]	LDB
Of pale asphodels, and [lilacs(?)]	JLS
wreathed about [her head,]	LDB
While her song, a[s it falls spreading unto]	LDB
sil[ence,(?)]	version 1
Still loops [and coils(?)] [about her painted legs]	LDB, version 2

The asphodels strewn about the Elysian fields are appropriate flowers as they are imagined by a *pierrotique* voice whose response to his lover's death is essentially narcissistic or inward turning. Although the line is incomplete, "pale asphodels" probably deliberately echoes "pale lilacs," the mourning flowers in the sequence's first poem, just as "wreathed about" echoes the pilot's imagined transformation into "a tall wreathed column." There has been a progression from the dead pilot to the dead dancer, the difference being that the pilot leaves no memory behind and she leaves her dance and song as memorials. The pilot flew to capture an imaginary image whereas the dancer, as she flew/danced, created an artistic image, *which she shared with others*. The pilot is a failed artist for his vision remains private. The dancer is a successful artist. In this sequence, as in *The Marble Faun*, Faulkner continues working toward his own definition of what it means to be a poet.

The final poem in *The Lilacs* sequence is very short, possibly no longer than four lines. The visible end-line fragments are "[wh(?)]ipping hair / thin garments to the sun / Chicago." From them one can infer that the form and tone of the poem is similar to "A Dead Dancer" and that its subject is another woman. Facing the last poem is a small undetailed drawing of a nude woman enclosed in an octagonal design that could be an Indian arrowhead or a coffin. It is similar both in subject and placement to the final drawing for *The Marionettes*. Will Pierrot ever see beyond his mirror image and escape the prison of the self to love real women who live? [44]

The poems in this sequence elucidate the value of Faulkner's literary self-education through reading, imitation, and dialogue to the development of his fictional technique. Most important at this stage are Mallarmé, Swinburne, and Conrad Aiken. Aiken's continuing influence is apparent in Faulkner's next completed poem sequence, *Vision in Spring* (summer 1921). Like many of Aiken's, this is a musical sequence: every poem is either about music, has a title drawn from musical vocabulary, or is about a related art, like dance or theater. Almost every poem bears Aiken's mark. *Vision in Spring* reveals what Faulkner learned from forcing his own language and thought into Aiken's mold. More important, this sequence shows that Aiken's chief attraction for Faulkner lay in his use of large novelistic units of poetry held together not by traditional narrative structures (plot, for example) but by patterns of language emerging in a stream of interior monologue from the minds of the narrators.

PART THREE

"Abstract Three Dimensional Polyphonic Verse": *Vision in Spring* (Summer 1921)

It is rather difficult to quote an example from him, as he has written with certain musical forms in mind, and any division of his work corresponding to the accepted dimensions of a poem is as a single chord to a fugue. . . .

—William Faulkner on Conrad Aiken, 1921

Writing people are all so pathetically torn between a desire to make a figure in the world and a morbid interest in their personal egos— the deadly fruit of the grafting of Sigmund Freud. . . .

—William Faulkner, 1922

What immoderately delights him . . . and what sets him above— shall we say it firmly—all his American contemporaries, is his continuous preoccupation with the novel as *form*, his passionate concern with it, and a degree of success with it which would clearly have commanded the interest and respect of Henry James himself.

—Conrad Aiken on William Faulkner, 1939

CHAPTER VII

Aiken and Freud: New Shapes for Faulkner's Inner Voices

Continuing to be a stylist of extremes, Faulkner devoted much of 1920 to imitating Verlaine, Swinburne, Housman, and other poets of the 1890s. He published many of these imitations, along with a series of amusing Beardsleyesque drawings, in the university's main student publications, *The Mississippian* and the yearbook.[1] *The Marionettes*, his hand-lettered and finely illustrated Symbolist dream-play, brought this phase of his apprenticeship to an end.

In late 1920, having pushed his infatuation with the nineties to its limits in *The Marionettes*, Faulkner turned to criticism. Meanwhile his poetry took off in the direction indicated by *The Lilacs*'s framing poems. His first critical essay, a review of William A. Percy's *In April Once*, appeared in the 10 November issue of *The Mississippian*.[2] This and five subsequent reviews indicate that he was unimpressed with most contemporary verse. Concurrently, Faulkner was working on his third poem sequence, *Vision in Spring*. Continuing to explore the problem he had first confronted in *The Lilacs* in 1920—how to fuse contrapuntal lyrical voices with a narrative structure—he turned once more for guidance and inspiration to the poetry of Conrad Aiken. Faulkner had praised Aiken above all other contemporary poets in his second book review published in February 1921.[3] In *Vision*, Aiken's poetic style and critical thought assume a central role, directing and informing not only its imagery but also the sequence's formal and thematic structure. *Vision*, in its form and content, presages by four years the shape and style of Faulkner's first novel, *Soldiers' Pay*, and other novels to come. Under Conrad Aiken's unknowing tutelage, Faulkner here took on the aesthetic and formal issue whose resolution aided in leading him into another genre entirely and on to a new and enduring professional identity.

T. S. Eliot identified the issue for the poets of his generation when he wrote, "I do not think it is too sweeping to say that there was no poet, in either country, who could have been of use to a beginner in 1908. . . . The question was still: where do we go from Swinburne?"

and, he added in his 1946 tribute to Ezra Pound, "the answer appeared to be nowhere."[4] Faulkner attempted to counteract Swinburne's effects on his imagination through immersion in Aiken.[5] Thus *Vision in Spring* is valuable for several reasons: it records his extraordinary effort to come to terms with Swinburne and his dawning realization, arrived at in part from imitating Aiken's extended narrative lyrics and symphonic poem sequences, that to become a great writer he must give up his dream of being a poet. Its further lasting value to Faulkner was its form. The poem sequence, built of a series of interior monologues and dialogues that are connected, in part, by the voice of a third-person narrator, showed Faulkner the limitations of his poetic voice: limitations in poetry that became the major strengths of his fiction.

In *Vision in Spring* Aiken, although major, is not the only Modernist influence. Faulkner draws also, but to lesser extent, on T. S. Eliot's 1917 lyrics, *Prufrock and Other Observations*. *Vision* climaxes in a dramatic monologue called "Love Song," which parodies Eliot's "The Love Song of J. Alfred Prufrock," Faulkner's own masks the Marble Faun and Pierrot, and the *pierrotique* voices of Aiken's symphonies. The objects of this parody stand at the center of other issues Faulkner must resolve before he can claim to write in a voice uniquely his own. These issues are: Can he possibly move beyond the poets of the nineties whom he loves and, if he does, can he find solutions to his creative dilemma by turning to his contemporaries? Can he discover his own voice by blending Conrad Aiken's verse forms and filtered Freudian psychology with the *pierrotique* voices of Aiken, Eliot, and his own earlier poems?

Because *Vision in Spring* in part attempts to deal with these questions, it contains two story lines. Explicitly, *Vision* takes the reader on a vicarious journey into the multiple-layered dreamlife of Pierrot, central consciousness of the sequence. Doing so permits the author access to his own unconscious: through the mask of Pierrot he approaches the problem of freeing himself from Swinburne, whom he describes three years later as "springing from some tortured undergrowth of my adolescence, like a highwayman, making me his slave."[6]

Both Faulkner's general and specific dating ("adolescence" and "at the age of sixteen") and his metaphor recalling the wonderfully rhythmic and melodramatic poem "The Highwayman" identify a second story line: Can he escape from the *pierrotique* mask that has dogged his verse since he began *The Marble Faun*? For *Vision*'s Pierrot, like the Marble Faun and Pierrot of *The Marionettes* as well as

Aiken's and Eliot's personas, is borrowed in part from the Symbolists' favorite mask, "that eternal adolescent."[7]

Faulkner was not the only poet to choose Pierrot for the poet's voice. Eliot, Aiken, and Stevens, as they puzzled out "where to go from Swinburne," also had first to find a substitute persona for the mask of Pierrot.[8] In *Vision*'s climactic poem, where Faulkner parodies Eliot's and Aiken's early *pierrotique* narrators, he has begun his own search by an act of rejection. By implication, the Pierrot of "Love Song" is also a self-parody; "the author" has become "the chief object of the satire."[9] Throughout the sequence, "Love Song" excepted, Pierrot is a serious figure. But since *Vision* marks Pierrot's final undisguised appearance in Faulkner's writing, the sequence suggests that he satirized Pierrot as a means of discrediting him. Faulkner permits him entrance again in 1925 when writing his first novel, but there, transformed to the middle-aged adolescent, Januarius Jones, he is clearly an object of ridicule. Faulkner has divorced his private voice from all his fictional voices. He no longer speaks as Pierrot the poet.

In *Vision* Faulkner, as he imitated, learned the limits of both his imitators and himself. Having learned their limitations, he could free himself of the *pierrotique* mask, that paralyzing presence that had dictated his poet's voice since he began *The Marble Faun*. In abandoning Pierrot, Faulkner also gives up his idealization of himself as a poet.

The Poet's Lives: 1920 to 1921

Faulkner gave Phil Stone *The Lilacs* on New Year's Day, 1920. He did not complete *Vision in Spring* for another year and a half, although he may well have written a good part of it by February 1921. In the streets of Oxford, on campus, on the golf course, Faulkner continued to wear his specially ordered RAF officer's uniform and unearned overseas cap. And throughout 1920 to 1921 he continued to keep up his roles of wounded war hero, aesthete, and ragged, dirty bohemian.[10] That spring he posed for a series of photographs; but only in his officer's uniform and overseas cap, not his other guises.[11] The part of aesthete also required an appropriate costume. According to his brother John, usually an unreliable source, although on such matters as this it does not seem outrageous to trust him, Faulkner bought a very tailored, expensive sport coat at Halles, a fancy Memphis clothing store.[12] At Faulkner's mother's request, his cousin Sallie Murry sold her diamond ring to pay Faulkner's clothing bill, as it was far in excess of what his parents could afford.[13] Faulkner's father was furious.

The young poet was no more popular with his peers and professors at the university than he was with his father. Students and faculty were annoyed by his military costume, feigned limp, and extravagant and arrogant behavior.[14] One of the three campus literary groups, the Scribblers Society, blackballed him. Its members then parodied Faulkner's Symbolist imitations in *The Mississippian* and in the Oxford paper, *The Eagle*, on 10 and 11 February 1920.[15] Their ridicule continued in the yearbook where, under "Freshman Literary Class," he was listed as "Faulkner, Count William."

In the fall of 1920, Faulkner re-registered at the university but attended few classes.[16] He did, however, hand-letter, illustrate, and bind at least four copies of his play *The Marionettes*. The campus drama club, the Marionettes, welcomed Faulkner as a member, but failed to produce his play. On 5 November 1920 Faulkner terminated his formal education by withdrawing from the University of Mississippi, although he remained an active member of the Marionettes.[17] Content to confine his role playing to real life, he took charge of staging.

Despite his peers' parodies, Faulkner continued to publish his writing in *The Mississippian* through 15 December 1922.[18] And, as noted, he had branched out, for he now wrote reviews as well. Faulkner's move to criticism, like his next sequence, may in part have been influenced by Aiken, a prolific reviewer and commentator on the current literary scene, whose work Faulkner praised so highly in his second review. The book reviewed was ostensibly Aiken's second published volume of poems, *Turns and Movies and Other Tales in Verse* (1916).[19] In fact, Faulkner's essay was considerably more comprehensive: he wrote about Aiken's theory of "symphonic poetry" and indicated familiarity with at least two of Aiken's "symphonies," *The Jig of Forslin* (1916) and *The House of Dust* (1920). The critical terms Faulkner used here were at that time unique to Aiken's own criticism, suggesting that Faulkner had learned them from their author. Faulkner's review, like his 1925 comments on Swinburne, indicates why he liked the poet and which aspects of his technique interested him. Aiken's *Turns and Movies* and Faulkner's *Marionettes* share only one common bond: their characters are all actors. But the parallels to Aiken's poetry in Faulkner's symphonic poem sequence *Vision in Spring*, drafts of which were typed on the verso of a holograph draft of Faulkner's *Turns and Movies* book review, are immense (Figure 8).[20]

Faulkner completed *The Marionettes* by December of 1920.[21] Then, apparently dissatisfied with that formal structure but still trying to present his characters' dreamlives unfiltered through any kind of omniscient narrator, he returned to the quest theme. This time, taking direction from Aiken, he began writing a musical poem sequence.[22] The result, an eighty-eight-page typescript, *Vision in Spring*, was finished and bound by the summer of 1921.[23]

Faulkner's verse "symphony"—his longest—is both an amalgam of and advance upon his previous work. In his apprenticeship it stands as a record of his intellectual journey from the nineteenth-century world of Keats, Swinburne, Tennyson, and the Symbolists through the Modernist work of the early twentieth century. Its themes are familiar: like the Faun of *The Marble Faun* and Pierrot and Marietta of *The Marionettes*, *Vision*'s protean narrator Pierrot asks,

Who am I, . . . who am I
To stretch my soul out rigid across the sky?
Who am I to chip the silence with footsteps,
Then see the silence fill my steps again?[24]

Major themes are repeated with variations throughout what appear to be the sequence's four movements. As Aiken claimed to in his sequences, Faulkner attempts to manipulate words as a composer would musical phrases. Thus he plays upon important images, words, and phrases throughout. Aiken's symphonies also suggested compatible themes and new ways of handling narrative voice and multiple points of view. As in Aiken's sequences, nympholepsy, the plight of the *pierrotique* poet, and the mnemonic character of music figure prominently. Symbols of the quest for self through nympholeptic visions (shadows, mirrors, immersions into dreamscapes through water and music), a sense of loneliness and impotence, and accounts of unfulfilled, thwarted, or unfulfillable desire permeate Faulkner's *Vision*. Place, as in Aiken's symphonic poems, is intentionally vague and dreamlike. Like Aiken's fictional world, it is sometimes a barren and silhouetted cityscape that becomes at other times an unparticularized, surreal pastoral or seascape. Faulkner, like Aiken, uses place as a metaphor for elaborating Pierrot's feelings and perceptions. These, reflected in and filtered through Pierrot's inner voices, "the image-stream in the mind which we call consciousness,—these hold the stage." Faulkner has discarded the multiple narrators of *The Lilacs* and replaced them with what appears to be a single but multifaceted voice similar to those of Aiken's symphonies. Occasionally,

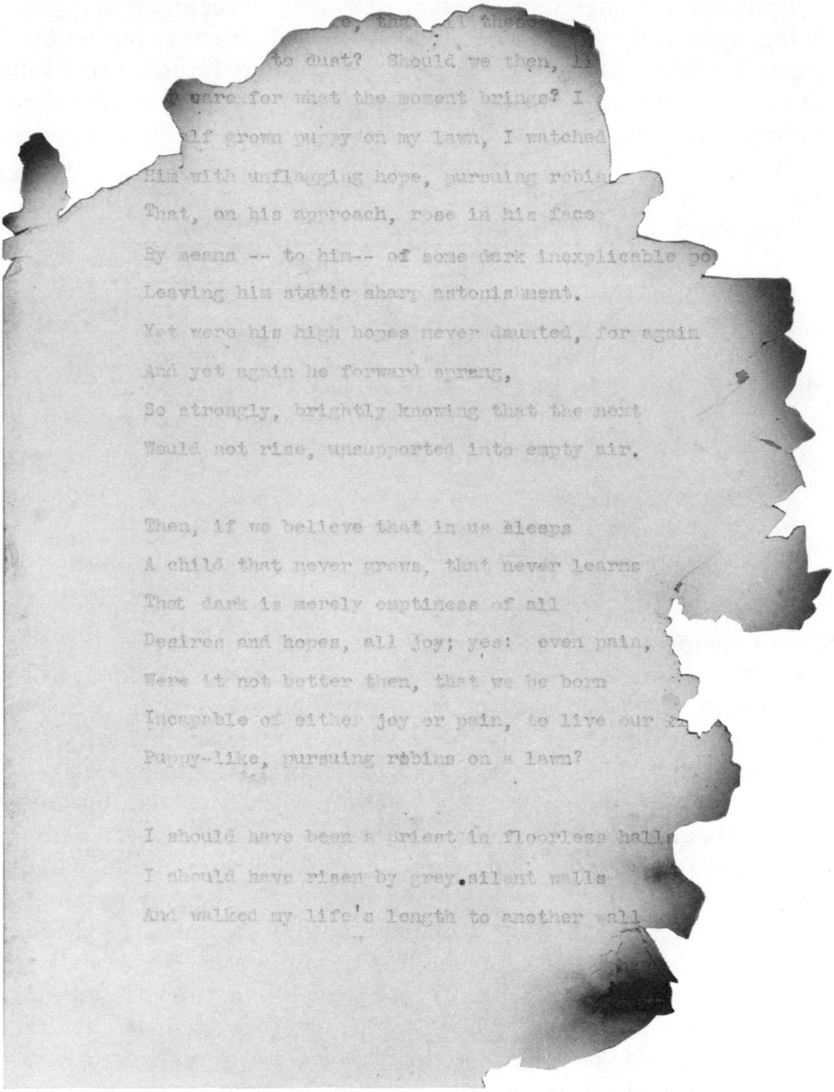

... to dust? Should we then, li...
... care for what the moment brings? I ...
... lf grown puppy on my lawn, I watched
Him with unflagging hope, pursuing robi...
That, on his approach, rose in his face
By means -- to him-- of some dark inexplicable po...
Leaving him static sharp astonishment.
Yet were his high hopes never daunted, for again
And yet again he forward sprang,
So strongly, brightly knowing that the next
Would not rise, unsupported into empty air.

Then, if we believe that in us sleeps
A child that never grows, that never learns
That dark is merely emptiness of all
Desires and hopes, all joy; yes: even pain,
Were it not better then, that we be born
Incapable of either joy or pain, to live our ...
Puppy-like, pursuing robins on a lawn?

I should have been a priest in floorless hall...
I should have risen by grey silent walls
And walked my life's length to another wall...

FIGURE 8. Fragments of variant verses of "Love Song" and Faulkner's review of Conrad Aiken's *Turns and Movies* written on the verso. The fragments are reprinted here courtesy of the Humanities Research Center, University of Texas at Austin, and Jill Faulkner Summers.

k: it matters not which on
ng to rest my eyes upon, and fr
scurrying thoughts. It is cold
th darkness, colder than I thought, fo
From sitting for so long there at the winde
My fire feels good, playing me with gold
In restless fugitive strokes. This lilac scent
Though, is too poignant, strong: I think
That I shall move them from the window in the sprin
Scents trouble me, I cannot sleep at night.
I do not notice it so much by day, for then
Then sparrows nest in them, and their bright intermitt
                    shadow
Is pleasant on the floor, across the rug.
At night though, there is naught to see, th
Rises with the twilight, fills my room.
It is only when we are too young, or old, th
That simple things like sounds and sights
And odors trouble us and send the child
slumbering within us, crowding close
And clinging to our hand, afraid of dark.

The child in us. Does one, then, never
Is one to think that living so, like th
Experiencing all emotion, strife and
Leads to nothing? That it were ju

In the fog of genius partly raised by contem...
in ... fifteen ... in ... over the sudden
sent rifts of blue — the poems of Conrad Aiken
entire part of yelping aesthetics, seems to bear ...
the others ... there are perhaps half a dozen exceptions
... sounds lost within a single depth of pencil ...
about them hastily with eyes closed and ... perfect
... less impenetrable ... of ... Russya...
hopelessly mired in the swamp of mediocrity ...
uninterestedly flung before darkness luridly engulfs them. ...
has ... realized that aesthetics is as much a science as ...
that there are certain definite scientific rules, which, where ...
will produce great art as surely as certain chemical ...
combined in the proper proportions, will produce certain ...
yet Aiken alone seems has made any attempt to ...
and beside him the British nightingales and Van...
... and arm ... form, the ... allag...
of ... sentimental Chicago propaganda...

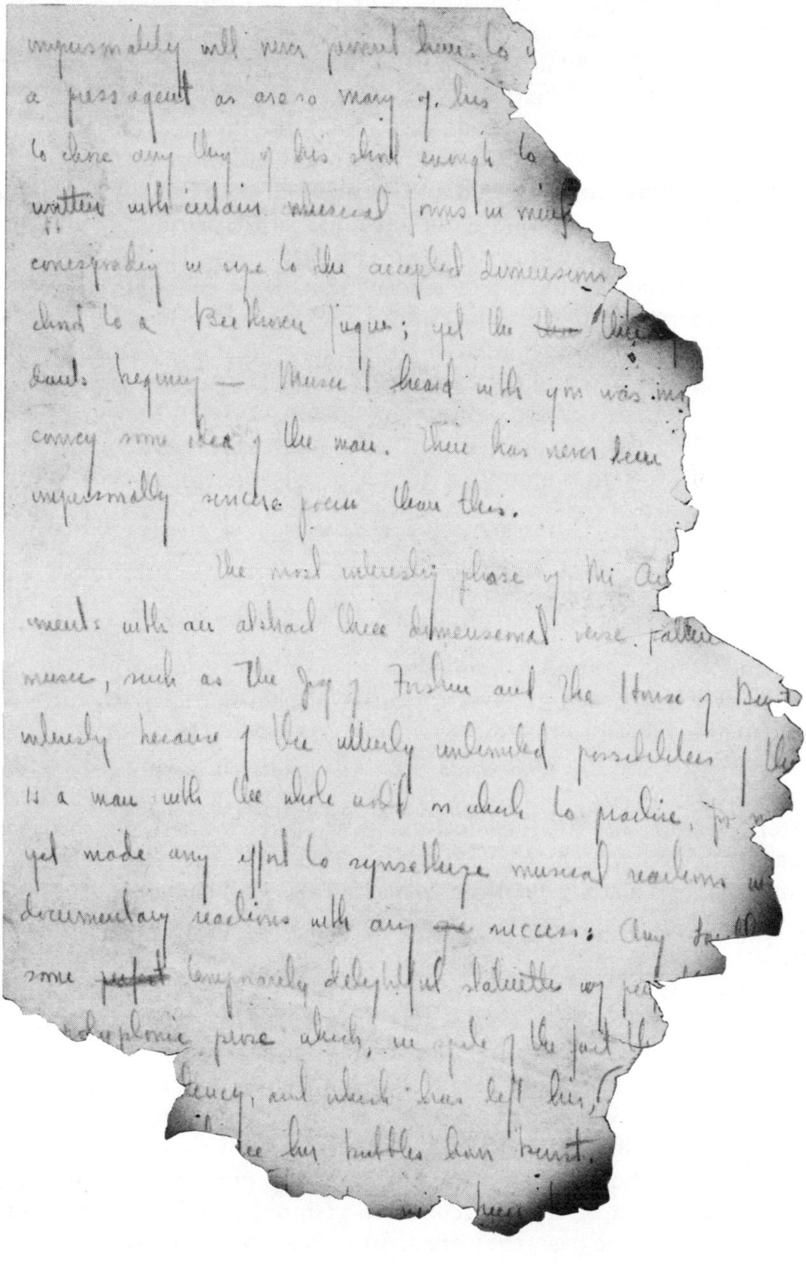

as in Aiken's sequences, an impersonal narrator intrudes upon the "I" to question or lecture.

Who is this "I" of *Vision*? He calls himself Pierrot, and in certain moods, particularly in parts of the third poem, "Nocturne," and the tenth, "The Dancer," he sounds very much like Pierrot of *The Marionettes*. But Faulkner has added a broader range of modulations to his voice and a contemporary echo to the metaphors of Pierrot's interior imaginings. In *Vision*, the Symbolist mask of the would-be poet, repeating phrases spoken previously by Faulkner's earlier narrators, alternates with a Pierrot of a distinctly Modernist cast. The tones of the first metaphor in these lines are shockingly familiar. Faulkner's new Pierrot is distinctly related to the *pierrotique* personas of the poems T. S. Eliot wrote between 1904 and 1911 "under the sign of Laforgue" and the narrators of Aiken's poems written between 1911 and 1920.[25] He muses on many of the same subjects and expresses himself in similar metaphors. In terms of superficial borrowing, many of his lines are simply variants of lines from Aiken's or Eliot's earlier poems.

Pierrot and the Quest Theme: Mythic Ideals

Faulkner found Conrad Aiken's theory and poetry most appealing at a time when his own personal quests were being met with intense opposition. His bid for fame as a poet in Oxford, Mississippi, was publicly ridiculed, and he had lost Estelle Oldham to Cornell Franklin.[26] On the subject of Estelle, Faulkner left no personal record, no letters or journals. But his fictional texts, his impassioned dedication in one copy of *The Marionettes* (which he gave to Estelle's baby daughter), and Estelle Faulkner's memories of these years recorded in interviews with Joseph Blotner after Faulkner's death together present a consistent picture. The author's quests for love and fame are unhappily related: pursuing one demands abandoning the other. Furthermore, both of his quests appear to be as frustrated at the time of *Vision*'s genesis as those of his early personas.

Faulkner's handling of the quest motif in *The Marble Faun*, *The Lilacs*, and *The Marionettes* is curiously idiosyncratic. His seekers, mostly first-person narrators, are static figures who confine their desires to the realm of dreams. *The Lilacs*'s narrators, though human, quest, like the Faun, in daydream and vision. Immobilized by their idealizations of the past, they are as lifeless as the Faun, for they cannot pursue their objectives. The maimed pilot, the old temptress lost in her own mirror image, Mallarmé's faun, the mourning lover in "A Dead Dancer": all lament imaginary and unattainable sexual partners.[27] In *The Marionettes*, Faulkner's text and accompanying illustrations highlighted the frozen, impotent, and narcissistic quality of his characters' quests. All try to fulfill their desires in tediously similar ways because their quests are for the same insurmountable, paralyzing goal: perfection in love and art.

Faulkner's continuous reworking of this theme suggests that his art mirrors his own dilemma. He, too, was searching for an ideal: the perfect form to contain and express what had to be the perfect imaginative vision. His choice of a *pierrotique* persona as the center of *The Marble Faun*, *The Marionettes*, and then his first completed poem sequence was, in this respect, brilliant. This mask is the poseur par excellence of literary convention: a figure "of adolescent despair . . . a painter-thinker . . . a failure of genius" who seeks through drink and drugs "the bliss of vegetable insentience."[28] The fin de siècle cartoonist Adolphe Willete perceptively claimed Pierrot's role playing to be the source of the clown's malaise:

> Now courting his muse (and a *cocotte*) by candlelight, now dancing drunkenly before three indulgent and weakly smiling moons, the *zanni* of Willete . . . has become a poet, an artist; but precisely because of his two talents, which never lend themselves to serious professions, the unfortunate Pierrot remains and will remain a malingerer, a whitefaced simpleton, a simple whiteface.[29]

Faulkner chose Pierrot, the paradigm Symbolist poet-*isolé* in part because he was in the air. Aside from Aiken, Eliot, and Wallace Stevens, numerous minor poets were turning out Pierrot poems. They proliferated in poetry publications as diverse as those of Harriet Monroe and W. S. Braithwaite.[30] But he also chose Pierrot because he was trying to maneuver toward a persona who would bring together and subsume diverse sources and problems. Finally, he chose Pierrot for personal reasons. Pierrot's paralyzing duality of vision, his doubleness, was something Faulkner recognized. It sprang from a dilemma almost eerily familiar: Pierrot was Faulkner's fictional representation of his own fragmented state. In pretending simultaneously to be the wounded war hero, the great airman, the British dandy, the poet-aesthete, and the filthy tramp, Faulkner too was playing forms of Pierrot. As both writer and illustrator of his own books, Faulkner also was attempting dual idealized roles: the artist (like his mother, Maud) and the poet-outcast.

The Decadents' Pierrot, reinterpreted by Aiken, becomes then a perfect emblem for this private tension. As Faulkner presents Pierrot in *The Marionettes*, one half of him, constricted by drink to the world of inaction, impotence, and dreams, mirrors a solution Faulkner actually tried: steeping himself in alcohol. Pierrot also suggests Faulkner's own father, Murry, who drank to escape his wife and father. The other half, Pierrot's Shade, the Rake, is a fictionalized ideal; a fantastically successful poet and lover, he wields his poetry as a soldier does his sword: for conquest. For Faulkner's Pierrot, the enemy is most often, and paradoxically, the ideal woman, whose perfection and/or filial relation makes her unattainable.

In *Vision*, Pierrot, his character enlarged, his voice range multiplied by Faulkner's reading of the Modernists and by his conscious and sophisticated use of the sequence as a narrative poetic form, continues the quest he began in *The Marble Faun*. The more personal, colloquial voice Faulkner gives him in many of *Vision*'s poems permits him insights not granted his marble statue or the drink-numbed figure of Faulkner's Symbolist play.

"A White Woman . . . a White Wanton": *Vision*'s "Lady"

Faulkner's reading of the Modernists and his growing facility with poetic technique cannot account completely for either the delicacy or the painful clarity of some of his insights in *Vision*. Faulkner made this booklet for Estelle Franklin and he gave it to her when she returned to Oxford during the summer of 1921 for her annual visit. She had brought her two-and-a-half-year-old daughter, Victoria ("Cho-Cho"), but, as usual, had left her husband, Cornell, in Honolulu. The visit marked Estelle's third extended stay in Oxford since her marriage in April 1918.[31] That Faulkner gave *Vision* to her is significant, because knowing that he chose to continue their relationship, despite or perhaps because of her marriage, is essential to understanding the preoccupations of *Vision in Spring*. Not only was Estelle still married to another man and thus safely unattainable, she was also mostly absent. Both facts made her an ideal recipient of and muse for the love poems Faulkner wrote in *Vision*.

The Form of "Formlessness": Aiken's Poetics

Throughout *Vision* there are identifiable echoes of numerous older poets, among them Housman, Milton, Keats, Yeats, and Swinburne. But it is his contemporaries, especially Conrad Aiken, who suggest to Faulkner the kinds of technical experiments that lead him from poetry into prose.[32] The fourteen poems constituting Faulkner's new sequence bear closest ties in form and tone to the poems he placed at the beginning and end of *The Lilacs*. *The Lilacs* was a cluster of poems held in tension or sequence, like the flowerets of their title, by a commonality of similar qualities. The poems in *Vision*, a series of associative episodes in which a single narrative voice multiplies himself as he explores his own "emotional and mental hinterland, his fairyland of impossible illusions and dreams," are Faulkner's first extended attempt to catch and portray his mask's mind in flux.[33]

Aiken's poetry and criticism fascinated Faulkner and drew his highest praise, in part because in both the poet subtly subsumed aspects of Freudian psychoanalytic theory. Freud influenced Aiken's ideas of character formation, motivation, and thought: his conscious intent was to translate many of the tenets of Freudian dynamics into lyrical utterances. Faulkner's stated attitude toward Freud ranged from hostile to merely uninterested.[34] He claimed he never read Freud. Whether or not he did is irrelevant, because his close reading of Aiken provided him with a useful guide to Freudian concepts and theory. Freud's language permeated Aiken's criticism and poetry during these years, providing Faulkner with a fictional rendering of applied Freudian theory, one with which he first experimented extensively in this poem sequence. Despite his denials of ever having read Freud, most critics assume from novels like *The Sound and the Fury*, *Sanctuary*, and *Light in August* that Faulkner's understanding of and empathy for the basic tenets of psychoanalytic theory were fairly sophisticated. Drafts of his early unfinished novel, *Elmer*, support this view (see chapter XII).

Conrad Aiken was an amusing and articulate explicator of his theories about poetry as well as the "new psychology." For his poetic sequences, *Forslin* and *The Charnel Rose*, he wrote prefaces explaining why he called his long poems "symphonies" and used other musical terms to describe smaller "movements" within his symphonies. He also explained the role of the "new psychology" in helping him to invent and depict the minds of characters like Forslin and Senlin.

Forslin is probably the first symphony Faulkner read and he refers to it in his 1921 review of Aiken's *Turns and Movies*. *Forslin* was described as "a novel of adventure in verse, based on the Freudian psychology, and containing poetry of unusual power and beauty."[35] Aiken endorsed this description. In the preface to *Forslin* he says, "This theme is the process of vicarious wish fulfillment by which civilized man enriches his circumscribed life and obtains emotional balance." Forslin, like all of Aiken's *pierrotique* masks, has clearly read *The Interpretation of Dreams*.[36] If Faulkner needed any sanction for his current occupation, he found it here.

The symphony itself is an exploration of Forslin's wide-ranging dreamscapes. Because the different poems or "movements" describe Forslin's "fairyland of impossible illusions and dreams" and because Forslin is not "a man but man . . . , opposite types of experience are here often found side by side, and it would be obviously false to force a connection."[37]

Aiken's reasons for drawing on the symphonic unit for his structure relate to his theme—Forslin's "dreams or vicarious adventures"—and to the way in which he wishes to present it—"not discretely but in flux." He also knows he must solve the purely practical problem of keeping the reader's attention throughout a long poem that is not a conventional narrative. Thus he breaks the poem into five main parts to allow for Forslin's broad ranges of experience and to keep the reader engaged. He describes his verse technique as "harmony and counterpoint" and says that "cacophonies and irregularities have often been deliberately employed as contrast."[38] Faulkner creates a similar structure for his symphony, *Vision in Spring*. Forslin is introduced—as *Vision's* Pierrot will be—by an impersonal narrator. Music is the propelling force. Carried by it, Forslin submerges into his dreamworld:

> In the mute evening the music sounded,
> Each voice of it, weaving gold or silver
> Seemed to open a separate door for him. (*Forslin*, p. i)

The metaphors are familiar, for we have already seen Faulkner borrowing them from Aiken to use in "The Lilacs" and "A Dead Dancer."

Once we enter Forslin's dreams, the impersonal narrator breaks in only occasionally, usually with an ironic comment. Throughout *Forslin's* five movements, themes are stated and restated with verbal and metric variations that are determined by the quality or aspect of Forslin's fantasy life being explored. The sudden juxtapositions of tone, mood, and place seem natural, for they mimic the sharp juxtapositions of tone, mood, and place in real dreaming. In his preface to *The Charnel Rose* (1915), Aiken had already described his method for developing thematic material. In language reminiscent of Swinburne and the Symbolists, Aiken wrote that nympholepsy, "that impulse which sends man from one dream, or ideal, to another, always disillusioned and therefore always inventing new fictions, is a theme upon which one might build wilfully a kind of absolute music . . . beginning with the lowest order of love, the merely carnal, the theme leads irregularly, with returns and anticipations as in music, through various phases of romantic or idealistic love, to several variants of erotic mysticism; finally ending in a mysticism apparently pure."[39] He also had explained why he called *The Charnel Rose* a symphony:

> . . . in some ways the analogy to a musical symphony is close. Symbols recur throughout like themes, sometimes unchanged, sometimes modified, but *always referring to a definite idea.* The attempt has been made to divest the successive emotions dealt with of all save the most typical or appropriate physical conditions, suggesting physical and temporal environment only so far as the mood naturally predicates it. *Emotions, perceptions,—the image-stream in the mind which we call consciousness,—these hold the stage.* (emphasis added)[40]

Aiken differs from his Symbolist precursors in that he wishes to retain in his poems the sense of a mind not only in ecstasy or despair but at work and at play. Even though he aims at "a mysticism apparently pure," his is hardly a mysticism of "le Beau," "l'Idéal," and "l'Absence." His is not "a mystical form of aestheticism."[41] For Aiken the Absolute was not the Beautiful but Being. For him poetry was life, it was not divorced from it. This dissimilarity, which Faulkner saw so clearly, marks the basic underlying difference between Aiken and the Symbolists and explains why Aiken was a logical progression from Swinburne. Faulkner saw in Aiken's symphonies a lyric/narrative bridge from the nineteenth into the twentieth century. In *Vision*, Faulkner remains intrigued with the Symbolist notion of the poet as the "musicienne de silence," but the poet of *Vision* is firmly lodged in a definably human consciousness.[42]

Aiken writes in "Counterpoint and Implication" for the June 1919 issue of *Poetry* that the symphonic form he evolved for *The Charnel Rose, Forslin*, and his later symphony, *The House of Dust* (Faulkner mentions the latter two in his Aiken review), was not "at the outset entirely conscious or clear." Rather, "it was partly the working of some complex which has always given me a strong bias towards an architectural structure in poetry analogous to that of music." What he was after, Aiken wrote, "was some way of getting at the contrapuntal effects in poetry—the effects of contrasting and conflicting tones and themes. . . . It seemed to me that by using a large medium [the sequence or symphonic unit], dividing it into several main parts, and subdividing these parts into short movements in various veins and forms, this was rendered possible."[43] Never dogmatic, Aiken is careful to say he is only making a loose analogy. He adds that if the themes "will permit rapid changes of tone . . . will not insist on a tone too static, it will be seen that there is no limit to the variety of effects obtainable."

Aiken's method makes it difficult for him to talk about tone and structure separately: "For such symphonic effects one employs what one might term emotion-mass with just as deliberate a regard for its position in the total design as one would employ a variation of form. One should regard this or that emotional theme as a musical unit having such-and-such a tone-quality, and use it only when that particular tone-quality is wanted." Emotions then are presented "not so much for their own sake or to persuade of a reality, as to employ such emotion or sense of reality . . . with the same cool detachment with which a composer employs notes or chords. . . . Such a poetry will not so much present an idea as use its resonance."[44] But resonances are not enough. Faulkner found in this poet, who was also his own best critic, a generous, funny, extremely intelligent man who was willing to experiment and take risks, who did not fear ridicule, and who shared many of Faulkner's aesthetic values. Like Faulkner, Aiken was trying to stretch the boundaries of poetic form and expression in order to introduce a new narrative technique and multiple points of view. Like Faulkner, he was torn between the lyric and the novel and no one, except perhaps Faulkner, knew it as well as he.

Aiken's Poetic Interpretation of Dreams

Equally valuable to Faulkner was Aiken's moral stance: his insistence on the validity of presenting multiple and sometimes contradictory viewpoints. Here was a poet who was not committed to a veneer of surface consistencies and who did not feel obliged to sit in judgment on his characters' fantasies. Rather, he wanted to suspend judgment so as to gain full access to his characters' lives, to explore his fictions in their totality, and to explore from within. How did Aiken combine a set of aesthetic values and verse techniques derived in part from the Symbolists with an outlook that was essentially humanistic and realistic, and how did Faulkner profit from Aiken's experiments?

Aiken dated his introduction to Freud's writing to around 1909 to 1910.[45] In 1913, when it was first published in English, he read *The Interpretation of Dreams*. His own imaginary dreamscapes, his symphonies in verse, followed swiftly: *Earth Triumphant, Part I* (1914), *The Charnel Rose* (1915), *Turns and Movies and Other Tales in*

Verse and *Earth Triumphant, Part II* (1916), *The Jig of Forslin* (1916), *The House of Dust* (1916 to 1917), *Nocturne of Remembered Spring* (1917), and *Senlin: A Biography* (1918). Sketching his intellectual and moral evolution, Aiken wrote: "I decided very early that Freud and his co-workers and rivals and followers, were making the most important contribution of the century to the understanding of man and his consciousness; accordingly I made it my business to learn as much from them as I could."[46]

Neither an uncritical nor ignorant convert, Aiken recognized that, like most geniuses, Freud was an excellent synthesizer as well as an original mind.[47] And, as early as 1917, in an essay reprinted in *Scepticisms*, Aiken argued with and suggested modifications in "the theory of Sigmund Freud, that poetry like the dream, is an outcome of suppression [*sic*], a release of complexes." The poet is not some Orphic deity writing in an ecstatic frenzy. Rather he is guided by some "selective . . . affective pleasure principle . . . *he exercises a rigid system of selection and suppression* on his material" (emphasis added). Both the poet and to a lesser extent his readers—the first creating, the latter experiencing the creation—operate from "some basic need . . . some deep hunger, whether erotic or not." From this hunger springs "the source of the power that sets in motion the delicate mechanism of poetic invention."[48]

Aiken consciously used insights gained from the new psychology to invent the structure for and to explore point of view in his symphonies. When the Four Seas Company with Aiken's approval (the same publishers to whom Faulkner submitted what was probably his revised manuscript of *Vision in Spring* in June 1923 and *The Marble Faun* in May 1924) wrote advance publicity for Aiken's *Forslin*, they emphasized its Freudian cast and its close formal connections to the novel. In *Forslin* "a wealth of startling and absorbing episode, . . . and a powerful Freudian motive that runs through the narrative, combine to make what we believe will be hailed not only the most interesting *poem* but also the most interesting *novel* of the season." Its reviewers spoke of *Forslin* in similar terms.[49]

Faulkner's Critical Response to Aiken's Poetry and Criticism

In reviewing Aiken's *Turns and Movies and Other Tales in Verse*, Faulkner studiously avoided any mention of his novelistic proclivities or his Freudian bias. But in *Vision in Spring*, in the fragments of revisions Faulkner made of poems in *Vision*, and in his earliest novels there are numerous indications that he was intrigued by Aiken's fictional rendering of Freud's revelations about the psyche.[50] (Faulkner's denial of having read Freud is not surprising; he also claimed he had never heard of Hawthorne's *The Marble Faun*.) Faulkner's bounding, histrionic prose in his essay on Aiken, published in *The Mississippian* in February 1921, suggests enormous enthusiasm for this poet and equally enormous disdain for " 'versifiers' writing inferior Keats or sobbing over the middle west." This "yelping pack" of adolescent bards is caught up in "thickets of Browningesque obscurity" and "mired in swamps of mediocrity." Such poets exercise no control over their material and have no specific goal in mind: these "British nightingales" are hopelessly in thrall to the ancients. He ticks off their names, attaching epithets to each: "Mr. Vachel Lindsay with his tin pan and iron spoon, Mr. Kreymborg with his lithographic water coloring, and Mr. Carl Sandburg with his sentimental Chicago propaganda are so many puppets fumbling in windy darkness." Faulkner next takes on Amy Lowell's poetry, which Aiken also had disparaged, condemning her experiments in "polyphonic prose which, in spite of the fact that she has created some delightful statuettes of perfectly blown glass, is merely literary flatulency." In brief, Lowell fails to communicate.

Sound without sense, inattention to formal verse structures, verbal pyrotechnics, color without shape, propagandistic messages, a slavish dependence on foreign influences, a kind of perpetual adolescence, and an inability to control their material: these are, according to Faulkner, the faults of all contemporary poets but Aiken. "Many . . . have realized that aesthetics is as much a science as chemistry, that there are certain definite scientific rules which, when properly applied, will produce great art . . . Mr. Aiken alone has made any effort to discover them and apply them intelligently. Nothing is ever accidental with him."[51] Faulkner goes on to explain Aiken's aesthetics and the theory informing the formal structures of his symphonic poems: "Mr. Aiken has a plastic mind, he uses variation, inversion, change of rhythm and such metrical tricks with skillful effect, and his clear impersonality will never permit him to write poor verse. He is never a press agent as are so many of his contemporaries [e.g., Sandburg]."[52] His description of Aiken's technique is based on what he has observed and on Aiken's prefaces to his symphonies. In speaking of Aiken's "plastic mind" and his "clear impersonality" he is applying Aiken's own critical term, defined in his 1916 essay, "The Impersonal Poet," to its originator.[53] Besides defining what he means by "the impersonal poet," Aiken suggests that such a poet's main source of strength lies in the creative use he makes of past and foreign influences in art and literature:

> We have become so accustomed to admiring poetry for one definite and perhaps idiosyncratic personality which shines through it, that an objective and impersonal poet, who endeavors to keep personality in the background, or to break up personality, for purposes of analysis [e.g., *Forslin*], is often thought unoriginal. I believe that just as art is becoming more and more international, or unnational, so on another plane the poet may become less idiosyncratic, more impersonal. He will understand himself, discount himself: . . . His point of view will not be single, or at rest, but multiple, and forever in motion. He will interpret things not merely seen from one personal angle, but as seen, impersonally, in relation.[54]

This less idiosyncratic, more impersonal poet will be attuned but not enslaved to past traditions; "what Shakespeare teaches him he will use," as well as other cultures:[55] "—it appears only natural that any one poet should derive the fruits of the labor of those who preceded him. As a matter of fact all poets have done this,—some more, some less. . . . Every successful poet is both originative and eclectic. . . . This does not mean that he will be lacking in essential character. His originality will consist in his mental outlook, rather than in his speech: and in artistic virtuosity. *Although he may invent no sharply new moods of his own, he must perfect the moods of others beyond the powers of those who themselves invented them*" (emphasis added).[56]

Aiken's theory of the impersonal poet suggested to Faulkner a means of escaping his double bind, which was thralldom to Swinburne and other poets of the nineties and to a literary, single-toned, and tediously derivative narrative voice: the ennervated, passive, narcissistic adolescent, Pierrot. In addition Aiken suggested that one could broaden the narrative range of poetry and give it new dimensions by using "roughly symphonic forms" and by transmuting Freud's explanations of man's unconscious into art. Faulkner acknowledges the validity of Aiken's theoretical concept, and comments on the integrity of *Turns and Movies* as a single unit. It is not, he says, a collection of discrete lyric episodes: "It is rather difficult to quote an example from him, as he has written with certain musical forms in mind, and any division of his work corresponding to the accepted dimensions of a poem is as a single chord to a fugue."[57] When Faulkner writes *Vision in Spring*, giving his own more narrative movements titles relating to either music or art, numbering them sequentially, then breaking the larger movements into smaller units with smaller roman numerals, he is adopting the symphonic structure Aiken had invented. He also is attempting to give new dimensions to the long poem.

Faulkner's critical remarks on Aiken constitute his second published review. In part, he is showing off his intellectual superiority by flinging a series of new theoretical terms at his ex-classmates from "Ole Miss." But Faulkner's posturing aside, it is clear that his comments refer to technical aspects of Aiken's poetry that fascinate him. Among the technical devices Aiken placed at Faulkner's disposal were polyphonic musical forms, which he had adapted to poetry. Aiken believed he had found "some way of getting at contrapuntal effects in poetry—the effects of contrasting and conflicting tones and themes, a kind of underlying simultaneity in dissimilarity." In writing of Aiken's attempt "to synthesize musical reactions with abstract documentary reactions" Faulkner is referring to the wide gamut of variations on themes that is available to the impersonal poet and that he then subjects to the discipline of his formal devices. In "Counterpoint and Implication," Aiken describes the possible range of tones: "not only can one use all the simpler poetic tones . . . ," but since one is using them as parts of a larger design, one can also obtain novel effects by placing them in juxtaposition as consecutive movements.[58] Casting forward, we note Aiken's continuing influence on Faulkner's technique. Describing how he wrote *The Sound and the Fury* Faulkner said,

> That began as a short story. . . . I found out I couldn't possibly tell that in a short story. And so I told the idiot's experience of that day, and that was incomprehensible . . . so I had to write another chapter. Then I decided to let Quentin tell his version of that same day, or that same occasion, so he told it. Then there had to be the counterpoint, which was the other brother, Jason . . . and then I had to write another section from the outside with an outsider, which was the writer, to tell what had happened on that particular day.[59]

In 1956, insisting to Jean Stein that *The Wild Palms* was "one story" Faulkner said,

> When I reached the end of what is now the first section of *The Wild Palms*, I realized suddenly that something was missing, it needed emphasis, something to lift it like counterpoint in music. So I wrote on "The Old Man" story until "The Wild Palms" story rose back to pitch. Then I stopped "The Old Man" story at what is now its first section, and took up "The Wild Palms" story until it began again to sag. Then I raised it to pitch again with another section of its antithe-

sis, which is the story of a man who got his love and spent the rest of the book fleeing from it.[60]

To a student at the University of Virginia in 1957 he explained the unusual and experimental structure of *Requiem for a Nun* by again invoking Aiken's criticism of the early 1920s: "The longer—I don't know what you would call those interludes, the prefaces, preambles, whatever they are—was necessary to give it the contrapuntal effect which comes in orchestration, that hard give-and-take of the dialogue was played against something that was a little mystical, made it sharper, more effective, in my opinion."[61] Faulkner's own explanations and the novels themselves make it clear that his fictional style developed in part from Aiken's own "musical structures" and filtering of Freud. Faulkner's concluding paragraph in his Aiken essay acknowledges his intense awareness of the value, scope, and validity of literary influences. He poses a question that he might well have been asking of himself: "where did he come from, and where is he going?" His answer, a prediction, applies ironically to himself but not to Aiken: "It is interesting to watch, for—say fifteen years— when the tide of aesthetic sterility which is slowly engulfing us has withdrawn, our first great poet will be left. Perhaps he is the man."[62]

The answer to where Faulkner was going when he wrote his own musical sequence *Vision in Spring* lies partly in the formal structure of this "symphony," his secret tribute to the poet he so much admired.

CHAPTER VIII

Sequence and Mask as Guiding Formal Principles

Faulkner's novels, like those of other great twentieth-century writers, do not conform to previously tried narrative forms. They are often characterized as "episodic and elliptical." According to one's critical approach, these episodes ultimately do or do not connect as they are seen to drive toward meaning or meaninglessness. Critics differ about the authorial intention informing these novels and debate persists over what is, in its subtlest and most wide ranging sense, the moral stance Faulkner's novels take.

In *Vision in Spring*, the early and intimate relation between form and intention in Faulkner's art becomes clear. He will retain this basic form—elaborating and embellishing upon it—in his novels. And although he will discard Pierrot as a persona, he retains his image as a source for character. Thus in the novels he transforms— splits, multiplies, and disguises—the figure who dominates his poetry. Pierrot's key position in Faulkner's novels suggests that a study of *Vision*'s form, as it is revealed through Pierrot's voices, can resolve questions of authorial intention in much of Faulkner's fiction.

A currently popular reading of Faulkner, which places him firmly in the high Modernist tradition, argues that he is a deconstructionist. Donald Kartiganer says, "My intention is not to deconstruct the novels—they perform this act admirably themselves—but to attend to the fragments, to describe their distinct voices" because "each novel is the sum of these voices trying to articulate the temporary magic of design."[1] He claims that Faulkner's novels *intentionally* do not, ultimately, make sense; that there is no overriding "principle of unity," even though all Faulkner's novels "struggle for a comprehensible design." For example, Kartiganer says that nowhere in *The Sound and the Fury* "do we see demonstrated the ability of the human imagination to render persuasively the order of things. Instead there is a sense of motion without meaning, voices in separate rooms talking to no one: the sound and the fury that fails to signify."[2]

Another critic, Arthur F. Kinney, who sees Faulkner's novelistic structures as "episodic and apparently unintegrated," has a different understanding:

> Although Faulkner is primarily concerned with studying one or more narrative consciousnesses in various and discrete episodes, as he studies Young Bayard's in *Flags in the Dust* both in isolation and alongside the somewhat analogous consciousness of a Horace Benbow, a Harry Mitchell, or a Byron Snopes, *still he does not openly integrate the units of his novels. The chapters of* Flags in the Dust *remain essentially disjunctive. Instead of providing connectives or transitions, Faulkner gives us central dramatic motifs and patterns of corresponding experiences which recur, correlating episodes and even taking on their own symbolic values. Elements scattered throughout a novel invite conflation or synchronization;* while Faulkner is repetitive, he is never redundant. (emphasis added)[3]

Because Kinney is unfamiliar with Faulkner's poems and does not know that Faulkner wrote much of his poetry in sequences, he cannot know that *Vision in Spring*'s structure is a skeleton or simplified form of the same narrative preoccupations he catalogs in his fine critical study of Faulkner's fiction. In *Vision*, Faulkner is following Aiken's example as he places his analogous consciousnesses all in one central figure rather than in separate characters. The consciousnesses, or voices, are sometimes interrupted and commented on by an impersonal narrator. The narrator's voice also appears to control the sequence's concluding vision. Faulkner's use of him for this purpose is, as we shall see in chapters IX to XI when we turn to the poem's text, analogous to Faulkner's use of particular characters at the conclusions of *Flags in the Dust, Light in August,* and *Sanctuary.*[4] *Vision in Spring* is neither a long narrative or dramatic poem nor prose fiction, and it lacks "the traditional arrangements of fiction as an understood subtext towards which the reader is always driving his impressions and judgments."[5] This is what makes *Vision* so difficult to read with any pleasure. Faulkner does not provide enough textual clues to make it possible to reach a satisfactory thematic resolution; the reader's "constitutive consciousness" has to make too many connections. In Faulkner's novels this is not the case. There, as Kinney observes, he can fairly ask the reader's "constitutive consciousness" rather than a narrative consciousness to be responsible for "meaning." If we read *Vision* with the style of Faulkner's mature novels as understood subtext and try, as Kinney suggests, to recognize how the voices do and do not fit together, how a poem (read episode) relates to the one before and after it as well as to the sequence (read novel) as a whole, "we discover *for ourselves* the configuration that makes each emblematic scene a part of the artistic whole."[6] *Vision* ends as it begins, with a vision in spring, a vision that, like the visions or scenes that conclude Faulkner's novels, is a synecdoche for the entire poem. But only by reading *Vision* while constantly connecting in our own minds the interrelations of the multiple visions presented within the text of any given poem can we arrive at an understanding of the patterns that constitute the structure and meaning of the whole sequence.

Vision in Spring is also difficult to read, because the "reconstitutive" quality of Faulkner's style is not yet fully functional. And the poem is difficult to attend to because the depression of its persona, Pierrot, can easily cast a soporific pall over most of its eighty-eight pages. But the sequence yields rich information about the genesis of Faulkner's mature style and the moral preoccupations that direct it. In reading *Vision in Spring*—looking forward to Faulkner's novels— it is apparent how Faulkner transposed what he learned from *Vision*. For example, emblematic scenes in *Vision* reappear in *Soldiers' Pay* where they are also emblematic scenes. Then, further transformed and refined, they reemerge in later novels like *Flags in the Dust, The Sound and the Fury, Light in August*, and even *Absalom, Absalom!*

Pierrot is the moral center of *Vision in Spring*. When we read this sequence in conjunction with the novels, we can trace Pierrot's transformations and understand why he remains in Faulkner's fiction, directing his intentions throughout his career. In his fictional guises Pierrot always represents specific forms of moral failure or weakness: failure to love, failure to create, failure to grow, and failure to choose. Pierrot has spoken in previous poems, but fragmenting his voices, as Faulkner did in *Vision*, was a necessary first step in mastering him. To parody him, even if only briefly, was the second step. To introduce an impersonal but not necessarily reliable narrator was the third.

Faulkner's subsequent fictional treatments of Pierrot are prefigured in *Vision*. He will reappear not only as parts of Januarius Jones, Donald Mahon, and Margaret Powers in *Soldiers' Pay* but also as parts of Gail Hightower and Joe Christmas in *Light in August* and Quentin Compson in *The Sound and the Fury* or Miss Rosa Coldfield or Sutpen in *Absalom, Absalom!* But we can only know this and comprehend its meaning in terms of Faulkner's intention if we know from reading Faulkner's poetry, especially the three sequences of 1919 to 1921 that culminate with *Vision in Spring*, how to recognize and weigh the import of the *pierrotique* elements in those and other Faulkner characters. Having done so, we can then understand Pierrot's place in Faulkner's canon.

Point of View: Pierrot's Vision as Controlling Metaphor

In *Vision in Spring* vision is a metaphorical, not a literal act: vision refers to what the inner eye or the imagination sees, not to what the eye sees. With this kind of vision as the chief mode of perception, the dominant narrative structural devices shift from calendar to conceptual time and from narrative sequence (description) of external events to the associative aspects of the persona's interior musings. While calendar time frames the sequence—Faulkner titles its opening and closing poems "Vision in Spring" and "April"—the time is static. Faulkner's emphasis, like Aiken's in *his* symphonies, is upon conceptual or interior chronology: "the image stream in the mind" of Pierrot.

Even in 1921 Faulkner was less dependent than Aiken on traditional narrative devices. Thus he did not, like Aiken, indicate breaks in his larger "more narrative movements" either in his table of contents or text. However, as in Aiken's symphonies, a four-part structure unified by recurring themes is discernible. *Vision*'s central intelligence, residing in Pierrot's multiple voices, repeats, varies, and reinterprets key metaphors and images throughout the poem. The sequence depends upon the melodies played, seen, heard, remembered, and imagined by Pierrot and an impersonal narrator. These melodies take the forms of monologues, soliloquies, and occasional interior and exterior dialogues, which, as they transform image to concept, create *Vision*'s structure and determine its style.[7]

Of *Vision*'s four sections, three are of almost equal length, with the fourth distinctly shorter. Having introduced his themes in *Vision*'s first movement, Faulkner uses the others to develop and counterpoint the themes through the multiple voices and visions of Pierrot. Pierrot's visions are occasionally interrupted by an impersonal third-person narrator, who in the first poem introduces Pierrot: "And at last, having followed a voice that cried within him . . . he stood, aghast" (p. 1). But not until *Vision*'s fourth movement does the narrator assert an identifiable and separate point of view, replacing Pierrot's and appearing to direct the final vision to its problematic resolution.

Vision's opening movement (poems I–III, pp. 1–29) invokes the first of Pierrot's dreamworlds, a nonspecific setting in which Pierrot, in the role of poet-*isolé*, introduces some of the major themes Faulkner will develop within its "polyphonic musical structure." Faulkner's experiment in "abstract three dimensional verse" begins with music. Bell tones lead to Pierrot's first vision—"a sudden vagueness of pain" that he claims is "my heart . . . that broke" (p. 1). His vision mourns the passing of time and the failure of his quests for love, fame, and a knowledge of his own identity: "Who am I . . . ?" (*VIS* III, p. 25). In these first twenty-eight pages Pierrot, occasionally helped by the impersonal narrator, delineates some facets of his own character, emerging from the third and longest poem of the movement, "Nocturne," as a composite of the Marble Faun, the two Pierrots of *The Marionettes*, and the voice(s) of *The Lilacs*. Like them, he appears to be a depressed, fragmented, will-less figure who lives primarily in a dreamlike world of nympholeptic fantasies. This frozen boy/man "spins and whirls," caged in his stark, moonlit world of icy peaks and deserts.[8] As he spins, "His bloodless hands are like two candle flames . . . / Beside the corpse of his face laid on his breast" (p. 11). To ensure that his readers will connect this deathlike Pierrot to the unnamed voice in *Vision*'s first two poems, Faulkner reintroduces phrases used earlier.

A scene shift in *Vision*'s second movement (poems IV–VIII, pp. 30–54) is signaled by its first poem's title, "After the Concert." Another voice describes how music is reexperienced "after the concert" and what visions attend this memory. Replacing the amorphous dreamscape of *Vision*'s first movement is an impressionistic but contemporary townlike landscape: a world of concerts, movies, lamplit streets. The voice of Faulkner's Modernist Pierrot informs much of *Vision*'s second movement; it imitates and echoes Aiken's *pierrotique* narrators, recalling the poetic persona heard briefly in *The Lilacs*. But this Pierrot sounds less forlorn: a more sociable and active creature, he speaks occasionally of "us" and "we" in contrast to the earlier Pierrot's solitary "I." He plays a sophisticated, slightly world-weary lover addressing a much younger, very naïve (read unthreatening) childlike woman:

> You are so young. And frankly you believe
> This world, this darkened street, this shadowed wall
> Are bright with beauty you passionately know
> Cannot fade nor cool nor die at all. (*VIS* V, p. 34)

In the eighth and closing poem of this second section, the Pierrot of *Vision*'s first movement returns. The "bells" of "vision" chime to reintroduce the first movement's major theme: the dangers of false vision. "Bells on golden wings"—false vision's seductive music—

confine Pierrot to a living death as they "echo his life away" (*VIS* VIII, p. 47).

Vision's third and climactic movement (poems IX–XII, pp. 55–82) begins with a "Love Song" in which Pierrot parodies the *pierrotique* voices of the two previous movements. The parodist asserts that "dream is death"—dream that reflects or mirrors but does not illuminate and give new meaning to old visions (p. 60). First in the guise of Pierrot the poet-*isolé* (poem X), then as a Modernist *pierrotique* figure (poem XI), and finally as the poet/musician Orpheus (poem XII), the combined Pierrot voices assert that questing after love is dangerous, depressing, and disappointing.

As the third movement concludes, all the *pierrotique* voices, the parodist excepted, are opting for a vision of a silent, frigid, isolated world where, as passive voyeurs, they can freely dream about the past: a womblike Aikenesque "sea in which I sink, yet cannot drown" (p. 81). The movement's concluding voice, Orpheus/Pierrot, like the other voices, has lost his ideal woman. As in the first two movements, Pierrot stands alone, but rather than simply daydreaming, he now sings about his lost love. Endowed with the godlike creative powers the Marble Faun wished for and with the mythic hero's stature, he claims to know the answer to the question Pierrot posed in *Vision*'s first movement.[9] He knows who he is. Orpheus then defines himself in seven different ways in nine short strophes. But his definitions are overblown and no more satisfactory than Pierrot's earlier nonanswers in "Nocturne" (*VIS* III, pp. 26, 27).

An abrupt scenic and tonal shift occurs in *Vision*'s fourth and final movement (poems XIII–XIV, pp. 83–88), where Faulkner banishes all Pierrot's voices. The impersonal narrator replacing him states that Pierrot's visions are dead: "There is no shortening-breasted nymph to shake / The thickets that stem up the lidless blaze" (*VIS* XIII, p. 83). The "lidless blaze" of the noonday sun has burned away Pierrot's Swinburnian dreams of "shortening-breasted nymphs."[10] The graveyard where Pierrot's false visions lie buried—real death—replaces the imagined death scenes of his previous visions. Setting and descriptive language anticipate the setting and metaphorical landscape in the concluding chapters of *Flags in the Dust*, Faulkner's first Yoknapatawpha novel. Faulkner's method of distancing the reader from his persona's dreamworlds anticipates, in a condensed and simplified form, the method he later uses to show Miss Jenny separating herself from her beloved but suicidal nephew, a *pierrotique* figure from *Flags*. In "April," *Vision*'s concluding poem, the impersonal narrator appears to be returning to the sequence's beginning. The time is still spring, but Faulkner's vision is new.

Typographical Clues to the Structure and Meaning of *Vision*

In comparing *Vision in Spring* to Faulkner's earlier booklets, a great difference in its physical layout is immediately apparent. It is hand-made, like *The Lilacs* and *The Marionettes*, but unlike them *Vision* looks as if it were meant to be published.[11] Faulkner did not decorate his text with anything that might detract from *Vision*'s language. Cold typescript replaces the ornate hand lettering of *The Lilacs* and *The Marionettes*. "Manuscript Edition. 1921." is typed on *Vision*'s title page, followed by a table of contents, then the opening poem. The contents page is unnumbered and the opening poem begins on page 1. The look is professional. *Vision*, as if to emphasize the abstract qualities of words, is barren of ornamentation. Gone are the lovely watercolor and the drawing that bracketed the text of *The Lilacs* or the sinuously graceful black-and-white drawings that formed a subtext for *The Marionettes*. The focus of *Vision*'s text is inward upon its language. Readers are meant to experience verbal images or *visions*. These images pass into the imagination through language, unadorned by visual aids.

Unlike *The Lilacs* or *The Marble Faun*, *Vision* carries in its title an abstract noun: vision. The singular suggests that the sequence derives from the "vision" of a central consciousness and that the series of poems reflects and counterpoints different aspects of "vision in spring." As in Aiken's symphonies, all the voices heard in Faulkner's poem—the third-person impersonal narrator excepted—arise from one dramatic center. The book's title also places it in time: the spring. Unlike the Marble Faun, *Vision*'s central intelligence experiences no diurnal progression. His body inhabits a wavering, indistinct present while his mind dwells in an emphatically vivid past. By claiming as his own the title of one of Swinburne's best lyrics, "A Vision of Spring in Winter," Faulkner suggests that this sequence, like *The Marble Faun*, is in some way a dialogue with or comment upon the echoed writer's poetic vision. Faulkner leaves out the final words of Swinburne's title and changes the preposition. He doesn't need the last phrase, for the "winter" of *Vision*'s persona (like that of the Marble Faun) lies within. Furthermore, the title is not, like Swinburne's, a vision *of* spring, which throws attention on the object, but a vision *in* spring, which keeps attention on the subject. Faulkner's title has, as well, internal reference. It recalls the vision poems in *The Lilacs* sequence and the Marble Faun's limited vision, suggesting that this new sequence may be a kind of thematic progression from these earlier sequences.[12]

With vision established as the sequence's general subject, Faulkner uses the table of contents to suggest the kinds of vision that concern his persona and to indicate that his visions are both related and ordered. Following a typographical format similar to those Aiken chose for his symphonies, Faulkner numbered each poem sequentially and titled all but four of his fourteen poems. Looked at together, the titles hint at one of *Vision*'s themes: the intimate relationship between vision and artistic creativity. The timeless arts— poetry and its related art, philosophy; the dance; music; and painting—appear in all titles but the first and last where time, always the frame of art, is asserted (Figure 9). The titles function, as they do in Aiken's symphonies, like program music titles, indicating the extra-musical idea Faulkner and Aiken will develop within the narrative form of the "verbal symphonic poem." But because they are writing poems, words take the place of musical notations as they expand and integrate their "verbal melodies."

Aiken and Faulkner were not alone in writing poems with titles of musical forms, but in the 1920s they were the only major writers attempting to adapt the more expansive narrative form of the symphonic poem to poetry. Poets like Eliot and Pound used musical forms as poetic analogues to create precisely the opposite effect: "DICHTEN-CONDENSARE," Pound proclaimed.[13] In keeping with Pound's ruling, their poetry was keyed—and then only tangentially— to the shorter, stricter lyric: cantos, rhapsodies, and preludes.[14]

Aiken once explained that "the idea of writing verbal symphonies occurred to me in connection with a passing passion for Strauss."[15] In his musical symphonic poems, Richard Strauss's emphasis was, like Aiken's, "on the statement of themes and their full development."[16] The symphonic poem then, as Liszt and Strauss had developed it in the nineteenth and early twentieth centuries, offered Aiken and Faulkner, whose lyrical inclinations were also narrative and dramatic, an ideal analogous structure. Like the novel the tone poem presented a wide-open form in which one could work out infinite thematic variations that lent drama and a kind of narrative to the total effect. The narrators of Aiken's and Faulkner's verbal symphonic poems contain within their consciousnesses the symphony's themes. The narrator's consciousness is thus the symphony's center or focus, and the theme or themes that dominate his consciousness become the "verbal symphony's" themes. How the themes are played

[Table of Contents]

FIGURE 9. Faulkner's table of contents to *Vision in Spring*. Bracketed material indicates my additions. Faulkner did not make any large divisions in his table of contents. Courtesy of Jill Faulkner Summers.

against and upon each other becomes the dramatic action of the poem.

In *Vision in Spring*, minor themes are subordinated to give metaphoric and tonal texture to the larger issue: whether vision is an acceptable substitute for more traditional forms of human, specifically masculine, action.[17] If it is, does it apply to all kinds of vision or only certain kinds? Finally, how does a writer, an artist, determine which kinds of vision are acceptable and which must be discouraged or ignored? Resolution of this last issue implies the making of important aesthetic and moral choices, and in *Vision in Spring* Faulkner finds his way to partial resolution. The voices in *Vision in Spring* are working toward definitions of true and false vision. But because as he writes this sequence Faulkner himself is not clear as to what constitutes true vision, the definitions and answers the voices suggest seem confusing and even contradictory.

The Music of Vision: Moral Choices and Authorial Intention

In most instances, Pierrot's visions are preceded by the sound of music, but does music inspire true poetic vision or is it somehow treacherous to the poet, leading him to imitate only other artists' voices or traditional definitions of a man of action? As Pierrot's voices try to differentiate between fruitful, active vision and unfruitful, passive vision, they also try to identify different kinds of music. Music, music played by others—a woman playing a piano (*VIS* XI, pp. 67–75, titled "Marriage" in another draft at the University of Virginia) or a woman talking (*VIS* VI, pp. 36–39)—interferes with true vision: it literally "breaks" Pierrot's heart. In the title poem Pierrot, standing "aghast," hears bell tones that he identifies as the sound of "my heart that broke." His heart broke because he did not "guard" it carefully from emotional commitment to another person: ". . . I disregarded / The pennies one should hoard if one would buy / Peace . . ." (*VIS* I, p. 2). One does not have to look as far as Horace Benbow (*Sanctuary*), Addie Bundren (*As I Lay Dying*), or Hightower (*Light in August*) for fictional exemplars of this voice. Echoing Pierrot's money metaphor, Margaret Powers in *Soldiers' Pay* muses: ". . . wondering why everything was as it was—iron beds, why you deliberately took certain people to break your intimacy, why these people died, why you yet took others. . . . Will my death be like this: fretting and exasperating? Am I cold by nature, or have I spent all my emotional coppers, that I don't seem to feel things like others?" (*SP*, p. 39). Mrs. Powers is fascinated, repelled, and terrified by the emotional commitment of a love affair and marriage with a somewhat mature and complete human being like Joe Gilligan. By *Soldiers' Pay*, a person who cannot love at all or who can love only the dead or the dying—a Marble Faun, as Faulkner's imagery implies—is portrayed as tragically misguided, with clearly false vision.[18] Throughout most of *Vision in Spring*, Pierrot's voices fail to see that vision that rejects a real woman in favor of an imagined ideal reveals that its primary desire is to possess idealized mirror images of itself and that art derived from such vision is imitative and repetitious.

Contrasted to what Pierrot's voices hear as actual but deceptive music is the persona's own memory or impression of music, "soundless rings" or "quiet sound" or a "silence [that] sings" (pp. 37, 36). This kind of music, emanating from the persona's own imagination, can lead to productive vision, vision capable of creating a compelling work of art. *Vision*'s persona does not reject this vision outright, but seems, nonetheless, to fear it. Thus he once more reaffirms and reinstates Pierrot's voices after briefly parodying them (*VIS* IX, pp. 55–64). How Faulkner manipulates vision in this sequence provides a map of his progress toward understanding the forms his own imaginative vision must embrace in order for him to consider his act of translating poetic vision an adequate moral substitute for a life of physical action. While writing as poet Faulkner attempts to live the latter life through his pose as wounded RAF officer. Jill Summers's description of her father's attitude toward war illustrates his continuing ambivalence: "He really did regret not being in action. He loved battles and would often quote Henry V, 'Take me, take a soldier, take a king.' He said all men felt about war the same way, that boys had toy guns to play with while men had war. But he didn't like modern-day war—killing. He liked the panoply. That's why he liked the RAF."[19] As he writes this sequence Faulkner is learning to differentiate between active and passive or fruitful and unfruitful kinds of vision.

He explored variations on this theme in earlier sequences. In *The Marble Faun*, the Faun was an emblem for passive, uncreative vision: he could see but neither speak aloud nor act, so had no power to transform his vision. As this theme's underlying complexity has revealed itself to Faulkner in the course of the past two years, he has required masks of increasing complexity and mobility. Thus his advance from marble statues to marionettes to the disparate human voices in *Vision in Spring*. Each time Faulkner varies his *pierrotique* mask, he adds to its voices, supplying his art with an ever-widening angle of vision. In *The Lilacs* sequence, different characters spoke upon common themes, but never to each other as they do in *Vision in Spring*. The Marble Faun was given only one voice. In *The Marionettes*, Pierrot was both silent and motionless, the Marble Faun's twin. But in dreams, as Pierrot's Shade, he assumed the voice of a secret self, his alter ego, as well as other imagined voices like Marietta and the play's choral figures.

Self-parody is an indicator of self-knowledge. Vision that leads to self-knowledge, that calls upon memory not merely to relive the past but to give the past new meaning, is true vision. The moments of self-parody in *Vision* are brief, and Pierrot's old voices reassert themselves well before *Vision*'s final movement. Nonetheless Pierrot's old voices do not control the sequence's closing statement.

In *Vision*'s conclusion, the impersonal narrator takes over from Pierrot. Speaking in the present tense, asserting a new vision, he claims to bury Pierrot's false voices and visions (poem XIII), especially the "sound" of those visions (p. 85), as he tries to clear the way for a new sound. But he can only provide a series of indefinite suppositions: "Somewhere," along "some ways," the poet will continue his quest for true vision, vision that allows him to use his imagination to give memory new meaning. In writing *Vision in Spring*, Faulkner has begun to accept and put into effect the precept that "all art is a reaction from life, but never, when it is vital and great, an escape."[20]

In "April," *Vision*'s final poem, the time is the present and the season still spring. It is not, however, the spring of the sequence's opening poem, for vision appears to have altered. Rather than a vision of the death of the heart, it is a vision of growth and renewal: of first violets, tender young leaves, and stars that "spring and blossom in the turning sky" (pp. 86, 87, 88). Faulkner retains many of the nature metaphors from the first movement, but by giving vision over to the consciousness of his impersonal narrator he can modulate the tone. For the first time in his poetry, the past is given new meaning, a meaning supplied not by Pierrot or by the narrator but by us as we listen to Faulkner's polyphony and draw upon the voices' combined effect to reach our own conclusions.

CHAPTER IX

"Silent Music": A Poet's Forms, the Novelist's Nascent Vision

With *Vision in Spring* Faulkner introduces a formal structure that permits his own unique style to begin to flourish. In looking at its first three poems in relation to the sequence as a whole, it is apparent that his design is neither simple nor haphazard. Thematic concerns are not as well delineated. Unlike Keats as he wrote the *Endymion*, his "great trial of invention," Faulkner needs not so much to find, as to recognize his subject.[1] Although present in this sequence, it is often confused and indistinct, because the poet's voice, Pierrot, resists his author's novelistic vision, creating a strange, uneasy tension as Pierrot, the would-be poet, vies with his inventor's nascent novelistic intentions.

Pierrot complains tirelessly, but he is a great poseur. He enjoys a solitary life devoted to dreaming about unrequited love and unfulfilled ambitions. Intruding on his solitude is Faulkner's still unacknowledged desire to develop Pierrot's character along narrative lines and give it new dimensions. The glimmerings of plot filter through Pierrot's ambivalent portraits of some of his female protagonists. His imagined loves are childlike "girls," often dancers or musicians, whom he claims to desire but appears to reject. Pierrot's visions or dreams of these girls inject conflict or the "germ" of plot throughout the sequence as they constantly interrupt and disturb his concomitantly professed wish for passivity and noninvolvement. He says they wound "my heart that I so carefully guarded" (*VIS* I, p. 1) and make him think "I should have been a priest" (*VIS* IX, p. 60). Male/female conflict is intertwined with the issue of vision, and together these form a central and recurring motif as they will in Faulkner's novels.

In most of *Vision in Spring* Faulkner approaches these themes obliquely and barely dares to explore them through Pierrot's faintly sexual imagery. Whenever Pierrot's visionary or real women invite him to act as a lover rather than a voyeur, he becomes intensely uncomfortable. His discomfort turns acute in *Vision*'s third movement just after "Love Song" (*VIS* IX), Faulkner's parody of the convention of the *pierrotique* mask. That the poem is a joke, whose object is in part Faulkner's own mask, marks a radical imaginative break-through. With it Faulkner clears a new path through the tangled and thorny underbrush of his dreams and fantasies to create at last an intelligible imaginative cosmos. There, where Pierrot must face the enemy, his poet's mask is no longer adequate.

In the first parts of this sequence, Faulkner is struggling with his novelistic vision, a vision of reality he cannot fully articulate until he discards the voice of Pierrot. When, in its third movement, Faulk-ner transforms his mask's dreams or visions into a joke, he becomes free to touch upon imaginative material that was previously forbid-den.[2] Armed with new insight, Faulkner, in the poems that follow, explores further thematic concerns and moral stances associated with his novels. In most of *Vision in Spring* Faulkner's feelings about the relation of imaginative vision to love and sex are dis-guised. But he was tiring of his mask's pose. In the third movement his decision to unmask through parody gave him an understanding of Pierrot's visions that made them less threatening. Thus in the lat-ter part of *Vision* Faulkner starts to find out what happens once he releases the intense feelings generated by his newly revealed subject.

Pierrot's Lives: Abortive Quests, Sadistic Dancers

The structure and subject of this sequence's title poem serves as a paradigm for many of the poems in *Vision in Spring*.[3] It introduces *Vision*'s central consciousness and its impersonal narrator and fol-lows a pattern of development—moving from external to internal reality—that is repeated in other poems in this sequence. This shift into "the image stream" of Pierrot's mind occurs "as evening fell" in a grove of trees. There, external stimulus—the sound of bells—stirs the poet's memory. His resultant vision of dancers becomes a night-mare that is interrupted as the same bells ring again and transport the poet back to external reality. The poem describes a circle in which there appears to be no progress.

In looking at the language of his vision, there seems to be a great discrepancy between the poet's dream and his reaction to it. The dream seems rather harmless and pleasant: a vaguely erotic fantasy:

Of dancers he had dreamed before him floated,
Calm, unsaddened, in a sea of evening air;—
Lips repeating the melody, sustaining the cooling sunset. (*VIS* I,
    pp. 2–3)

But instead of deriving pleasure from the singing dancers, the dreamer experiences a typical nightmare reaction. He tries to cry out, but no sound comes.

> He raised his hand, and stirred
> And would have cried aloud, but was *dumb* as were the branches
> That tightened to a faint refrain
> Clinging like gossamer about them, that *softly snared* him.
> Then the bells again

> Like falling leaves, rose mirrored up from silence . . . (*VIS* I, pp. 3–4, emphasis added)

Knowing some of the visionary's associations helps to reconcile the disparity between the dream and the dreamer's response. Familiarity with Faulkner's current poetic mentor's poetry, Faulkner's dream-play, and his other poem sequences, combined with clues in the text of this new poem, provides this knowledge.

Women have "snared" Pierrot-like figures before, as in Faulkner's *Lilacs* poem, "After Fifty Years" (see pp. 73–76). Dancers and dancing figured negatively in earlier Faulkner poems. In *The Lilacs* they were associated with sex, betrayal, and death (see discussion of "A Dead Dancer," pp. 90–101). Faulkner first connects seduction and betrayal with dancing in *The Marionettes*. There, the dreaming Pierrot, "weaving his song like a net about her," lures the virgin Marietta from her walled garden: "Come sweet maid, with me and dance" (*TM*, pp. 24, 23). Her aunts have warned her about accepting such invitations, but Pierrot's artistic powers are great and Marietta "in a trance" obeys. They make love, and then Pierrot abandons her. Art always seems to initiate humiliating and dangerous experiences in love. But we are never quite sure why.

Vision's Pierrot also dreams of a series of dancers. But, although he dreams of them, Pierrot does not love women. Rather, his love seems reserved for an idealized and illusory vision of himself—his mirror image. By composing "Vision in Spring" out of a series of literary echoes Faulkner highlights the emotional and aesthetic perils of such idealizing and self-reflexive vision and love. Despite its remarkably proselike verse (it has a loose rhyme scheme but no discernible meter and its verbs operate sequentially as they would in a narrative account), its liquid labials and anthropomorphic trees recall the sounds and metaphors of Swinburne's "A Vision of Spring in Winter." The poem also echoes lines from Aiken's *Forslin* and *The House of Dust*, lines from Faulkner's own sequences *The Lilacs* and

The Marble Faun, and from his adaptation of Mallarmé's "L'Après-midi d'un faune."[4] In short, Faulkner has composed a poem of multiple echoes. *Vision in Spring* is like a hall of mirrors and echoes filled with reflections of the poems Faulkner imitated, adapted, and wrote before the summer of 1921.

Aware of these reverberations, it is not difficult to guess what gives the dreamer nightmares in the first poem. He is afraid and paralyzed because his vision—striving so hard to be imaginative and poetic—is only mirror vision: an imitation of himself imitating other poets. With this poem, then, Faulkner introduces a central concern of *Vision in Spring*: Can Pierrot use his imagination to escape the voices of the past and can he free it enough to see beyond his own mirror image? This is the dilemma he portrays so accurately both in his poignant drawing of Pierrot and the dead Marietta that concludes the text of *The Marionettes* and in his poem about Pierrot, Colombine, death, and a mirror (Figure 2, and chapter II, note 8, pp. 231–232).

Images central to this poem—the broken heart; echoing bells; mirroring visions; the visionary standing alone, cold and mute, fearful of and yet yearning for the "dancers moving to an ancient music"—recur throughout the sequence. We will watch them as we have been trained to watch recurring image patterns and emblematic scenes in Faulkner's novels in order to determine the meaning of the aggregate of all our differing perceptions of these images.

As the title poem ends, its persona stands alone like the Marble Faun in that sequence's concluding eclogue. Spring rises about him

> . . . like a wall
> Beneath which he stood and watched, growing colder and colder,
> A star immaculately fall. (*VIS* I, p. 5)

Like Faulkner's earlier personas—the Marble Faun or the drunken or mourning Pierrot—this lonely dreamer is a passive watcher. He recalls the past only to remember and repeat. Sounds are "mirrored" as are images as his dream dancers float by him, "lips repeating the melody." His visions of past time, a series of literary echoes, offer neither solace nor illumination.

Faulkner forges formal and thematic connections between his sequence's first and second poems by varying and repeating specific phrases. In "Interlude's" opening lines, he combines and compresses elements from the opening and concluding lines of "Vision in Spring" to blend the atmosphere of the two poems (see *VIS* I, pp. 1, 5):

Once more a soft starred evening falls
Upon these empty streets and walls;
Once more the world sinks into dark, he said. (*VIS* II, p. 6)

"Interlude" is just that.[5] Its "vision" elaborates on the one experienced in the first poem, suggesting that "Interlude" serves as a resting point and transition between the more dramatic first and third poems of the symphony's first movement. Like "Vision in Spring," "Interlude" progresses from concrete (the setting) to abstract (the vision), from external to internal reality. The vision, "vagrant music" and dancers "With lifted throats, and hair that floats / With scarce moved knees, and soft breasts bare" (p. 7), is interrupted as in the first poem by noises of the apparently real world of literary allusion. Eliot's "horned gates swing to, and clang" (p. 9) and "Interlude" concludes by returning its voice to external reality.[6]

While more elaborately imaged, Pierrot's vision in "Interlude" does not change significantly. Real music and imaginary dancers figure prominently. An intricate series of correspondences extend to the poems that precede and follow "Interlude" and to the sequence's other movements. Their purpose is to establish and identify the all-encompassing world of Pierrot and his visions and to show that the movement of the sequence is indeed a journey through Pierrot's consciousness. Like Pierrot in "Nocturne" (pp. 22, 26), *Vision*'s third poem, the visionary states that "some day he, too, must die" (p. 6), and his mind is cluttered with some of the same images of death: ". . . calm gusts of stars swept overhead / Like candle flames across a coffin blown" (p. 6). Faulkner also includes phrases and images that he returns to and elaborates on in the second poems of *Vision*'s second and third movements. The image in "Interlude" of a woman,

Raise your face, grown calm and sad; your eyes,
Raise your mouth that seeks and sighs
In simple need of some untasted bliss
To bless in quiet pain, and kiss . . . (*VIS* II, p. 9)

expands and becomes the controlling image in "Portrait," the second poem in *Vision*'s second movement, while a description of dancers,

Quietly the dancing feet
Tread a measure full and strange,
A motion mazed with change oh hushed change (*VIS* II, p. 8)

anticipates both Colombine in *Vision*'s third poem and the dancing girl in a later poem, "The Dancer" (third movement, second poem, p. 65) who, responding to Pierrot's "dark and simple need" (p. 8),

[142]

haunts and tempts him and claims she has "mazed your life against your will" (p. 65). Like all Pierrot's nymphs, the dancer is "swift, so white and slim" (p. 65). In the third movement, as she argues with and pursues Pierrot, he rejects her, as he has other "girls," for disturbing his "silence." Finally, parts of "Interlude" presage phrases from "April," the sequence's concluding poem.

Silence, especially "silent music," is one of Pierrot's visionary images that is generally associated with his ambivalent feelings about women. In Faulkner's novels, men who seek this kind of "silence" are terrified of sexual and emotional entanglements with women. Januarius Jones, Gordon the sculptor, and the Reverend Hightower are three very different but equally threatened examples. When they ask for silence from their women, they do so because only when women are silent (read not real or absent) are they safe to "love." Gordon says of his breastless, legless, armless, headless sculpture, "She is my feminine ideal: a virgin with no legs to leave me, no arms to hold me, no head to talk to me" (*Mosquitoes*, p. 26). Like Pierrot's, his virgin is also "dark, darker than fire" (p. 329). Gordon's artwork is Pierrot's nympholeptic vision brought to perfection. She is accessible yet inaccessible, infinitely virginal and paralyzed. Best of all, she poses no threat. And, unlike Hightower's wife in similar conditions, she will let Gordon attend to his "silent music." This ideal woman permits the dreamer to find his "peace" in solitary dreams.

Vision concludes its first movement with "The World and Pierrot. A Nocturne" (Figure 10).[7] Like all the poems in *Vision in Spring*, and like some of the longer episodes in Faulkner's novels (for example, the "Wash" section in *Absalom, Absalom!*), it is complete in itself but it gains dimension when we discern how Faulkner integrates it into the larger fiction. Repeating the synthesizing device used in "Interlude" (*VIS* II), "Nocturne's" opening lines condense the setting and voice of *Vision*'s first two poems. The visionary now has a name:

Here, where the sound of worlds sinks down the sea
Mountainously echoed, wave by wave,
Pierrot would stand beside a night like a column of blue and silver.
　(*VIS* III, p. 10)

Pierrot continues with his visions, shifting once again from external to internal reality. But this time, as the poem concludes, we remain in Pierrot's consciousness. To emphasize Pierrot's lack of interest in external reality, Faulkner delegates its description to the poem's impersonal narrator as in *Vision*'s first and second poems. Verbal ech-

NOCTURNE.

Colombine leans above the taper flame:
Colombine flings a rose.
She flings a severed hand at Pierrot's feet.

Behind, a perpendicular wall of stars,
Below, a gleam of snows.
Pierrot spins and whirls, Pierrot is fleet;
He whirls his hands like birds upon the moon.

Pierrot spins and whirls . . . .
His eyes are filled with facets of many worlds
Of silver and blue and green,
And he would hide his head, yet the keen
    blue darkness
Cuts his arms away from his face.

Listen! A violin
Freezes into a blade, so bright and thin
It pierces through his brain, into his heart,
And he is spitted by a pin of music on the dark.

Swift the wisps of motion blown across the moon;
Colombine flings a paper rose, —
Pierrot flits like a white moth on blue dark.

Black the taper, sharp their mouths in starlight,
The sky with icy rootless flowers gauntly glows.
They are stiffly frozen, bright and stark.

FIGURE 10. Faulkner's drawing for section two of "Nocturne" (lines 29–50), which he illustrated and published in his university's yearbook (*Ole Miss*, 1920–21, vol. 25, pp. 214–215). Courtesy of Jill Faulkner Summers and the University of Mississippi Library.

oes in the first four lines of "Nocturne"—echoes resonating in part from the first lines of *Vision*'s two earlier poems—identify Pierrot as the unnamed voice of *Vision in Spring* I and II.

That Pierrot is moving ever more deeply into his visionary cosmos and losing touch in the process is apparent from the poem's third line. As "Nocturne" begins, he has divorced himself from the finite universe: he stands *beside* the night, not *in* it, and from this vantage point—like "a column," immobile and mirrorlike—he reflects not external reality but his world of visions: "The column is dusty with facets of worlds that he has seen" (p. 10). Pierrot's proselike verse—

he uses "to be" four times in the next seven lines plus a series of
verbs that signals sequential narrative development—continues and
expands the tone of "Vision in Spring" (*VIS* I). Pierrot appears less
somnambulistic—compare the verbs "spins and whirls . . . swiftly
runs . . . whirls . . ." (*VIS* III, pp. 10–11) with "having followed . . .
he stood . . . and awoke . . . he said . . . had dreamed" (*VIS* I, p. 1).
But because he remains chained to his dreams, his frantic circular motions lead him only deeper into his private and frightening
visions.

"Pierrot the Victim" might be an appropriate subtitle for Faulkner's "Nocturne," for in his visions nature, women, and music combine to try and destroy Pierrot. Building upon an earlier image of the
Marble Faun's moon-mad mother, Faulkner creates another deadly
female, a "spider" moon who becomes Pierrot's "cage," "weaving
her icy silver across his heart" (p. 11). As his dancing partner Colombine flings first a "paper rose" and next a "severed hand at Pierrot's
feet" (p. 12), "blue darkness / Cuts his arms away from his face"
(p. 13). To portray Pierrot's torture, Faulkner steals two misogynous
images from Eliot's "Rhapsody on a Windy Night." While Pierrot's
"mother," the moon, imprisons him, Colombine, his would-be dancing partner, flinging a paper rose, acts like Eliot's old whore, the
moon, whose "hand twists a paper rose, / That smells of dust and
eau de Cologne." Then actual music attacks him like the eyes of
Eliot's real prostitute: " 'And you see the corner of her eye / Twists
like a crooked pin.' "[8]

> Listen! A violin
> Freezes into a blade so bright and thin,
> It pierces through his brain, into his heart,
> And he is spitted by a pin of music on the dark. (*VIS* III, p. 13)

This attack of musical blades and pins is Pierrot's second nightmare
vision: he continues to flit "like a white moth on the dark" (p. 13).
These primitive, sadistic images of mutilation cannot be explained
away by noting Faulkner's interest in commedia dell'arte conventions and Baudelaire's poetry. Even the tapers beside which Pierrot
and Colombine perform their macabre dance are portrayed as monstrous beings who simultaneously penetrate and envelop: "Black the
tapers, sharp their mouths in starlight" (p. 14). Faulkner uses alliteration and assonance to intensify nature's implacable cruelty: "The
sky desert with icy rootless flowers gauntly glows. / They are stiffly
frozen, white and stark" (p. 14). Rapacious nature continues to
dominate Pierrot's vision in this poem's third section. The ocean too

is a cannibalistic creature. Its "starlit waters leap and burn / And freeze like serrated teeth tearing the darkness" (p. 15). Despite Faulkner's inclusion of many conventional poetic devices, the tone of Pierrot's lines remains insistently unpoetic. Even so, the incipient narrative drama present in Faulkner's descriptions of Pierrot's and Colombine's strange coupling remains incipient and its purpose unclear. The novelist's vision, merely hinted at here, creates an uneasy tension. The sequence pulls tentatively in two directions. Neither one satisfies.

Faulkner will enrich and clarify Pierrot's sadomasochistic fantasy (begun in "O Atthis") in *Sanctuary* (1931). At the Old Frenchman place Temple Drake has spent the night flitting about like "a moth in the dark." Finally, "caged," she fantasizes about protecting her virginity with a spiked chastity belt.

> . . . if I just had that French thing. I was thinking maybe it would have long sharp spikes on it and he wouldn't know it until too late and I'd jab it into him. I'd jab it all the way through him and I'd think about the blood running on me and how I'd say I guess that'll teach you!

In the novel's actual world Temple's fantasy is reversed: Popeye does the jabbing and Temple the bleeding.[9]

As Pierrot's vision expands, he transforms himself into the poet-musician he wishes he were, but when he attempts to play his harp the notes he plucks recall the earlier image of Colombine's fake rose:

> . . . the notes fall slowly through his fingers
> Like drops of blood, crimson and sharp:
> He shatters a crimson rose of sound on a carpet of upturned faces.
>   (*VIS* III, p. 19)

Pierrot plays visual and tactile rather than melodic notes, making clear that his "notes" are really weapons transparently disguised as notes. Such is Pierrot's "silent music."[10]

Pierrot's sadistic act, even though perpetrated in the name of art, is quickly punished. He becomes "numb" and cold and his visions "swiftly depart!"

> Pierrot watches the last note fall
> Then finds he cannot see or hear at all. (*VIS* III, p. 20)

Echoing his lament from *Vision*'s first poem, Pierrot claims:

> That . . . was my heart
> That broke and fell away from me

And shattered itself to pieces on the night,
Leaving me frozen, bare of sound and sight. (*VIS* III, p. 20)

Pierrot, his face frozen "into a mask of calmness," approaches his
art with such trepidation because he fears impotence and a kind of
living death in which he can no longer fly, nor can he see or hear.
Pierrot perceives both the spider moon and Colombine as forces acting to prohibit and punish his attempts to be creative. When he tries
to combat either, he becomes impotent. Not so clear is why Pierrot
thinks that women in any form are his enemies.

Faulkner's introductory image in "Nocturne," which identifies another of Pierrot's enemies, suggests an answer. It relates to Pierrot's
nightmare in *Vision in Spring* I. At the beginning of "Nocturne"
Pierrot stands as a reflector, a repository for others' ideas and images: "blue and silver . . . orange and green, / The column is dusty
with facets of worlds that he has seen" (p. 10). The aural similarity
between "column" and "Colombine" suggests that Colombine, a
product of his solipsistic imaginings, is Pierrot's twin, his loved and
hated ideal self. Near this poem's conclusion, despite his frenetic
spinning and whirling, Pierrot fails to escape his overwhelming feelings of circularity, isolation, and impotence:

It is dark . . . now that night has come
Rising like an iron wall about me, I am dumb;
I am dumb and huge in starlight,
I am a cliff breaking above a sea in darkness,
I am bound with chains of blue and green;
I am alone. . . . (*VIS* III, p. 27, emphasis added)

The second line's simile, a variant of the concluding image of Pierrot's imprisonment in *Vision*'s first poem, intensifies our sense of
Pierrot's being trapped and cut off. He identifies his chains of bond-
age not as women but as the voices of the past, both literary and personal, which isolate him "in a forest of sound . . . / Woven with all
beauty that I have felt and seen" (p. 27). The paradox and ambivalence in this metaphor portray Faulkner's own private dilemma: his
difficulty in giving up the "painful" pleasure of this "known beauty"
(other poets' music). Faulkner also uses "bound" to describe his *pierrotique* voices' relations with all women (e.g., *The Marble Faun*,
"After Fifty Years," or "The Dancer"), suggesting that the other
"known beauty" binding him is the mother/child bond, which, as
will become apparent, he is loathe to relinquish. "Weaving," used to
describe the nature of Pierrot's ties first to the spider moon and then
to the beauty created by older poets' voices, suggests a significant

progression from Faulkner's earlier poetry; he could not have written these lines had he not known that he, like Pierrot, would have to abandon the familiar "forest of sound" in order to formulate new and untried visions.

Other hints about what prevents Pierrot from singing effectively and why he feels threatened appear in the third and fourth sections of "Nocturne." Pierrot imagines a dialogue between himself and the stars. The stars imply that because Pierrot is "mortal" his dreams of achieving immortality will be "overblown" (*VIS* III, p. 16): "Look well, Pierrot; there before you are portals / You cannot breach, nor ever hope to climb" (p. 17). The Marble Faun's explanation for failure was that he was a mere piece of sculpture. Pierrot's explanation—that he is human—is more transparent. But, since at this point in the sequence Faulkner has not indicated that he, as the poem's author, is separate from his *pierrotique* mask, Pierrot's predicament cannot be viewed as it will be later, ironically.

The fourth section of "Nocturne" reveals that it is not Pierrot's humanness but his perfectionism coupled with his great fear of failure that make him so vulnerable. The voices liken Pierrot to

> You, the silver bow on which the arrow of your life is set.
> The shaft is tipped with jade desire, and feathered with your illusions,
> *The bow is drawn, yet unreleased*
> *For you are not sure, you are still afraid*
> *That you will miss the mark on which the dart is laid.* (*VIS* III,
>   pp. 17–18, emphasis added)

And so the would-be poet, terrified that he will not achieve greatness, "stiffly bowed / Lest he knock his head against the stars" (p. 18), and remains frozen, isolated from the warm pleasure of success in either love or art. Like Faulkner's earlier mask, the Marble Faun, he stands alone in "carven starlight" (p. 18). This episode's significance is revealed retrospectively, much as the significance of a seemingly unrelated episode in a Faulkner novel becomes clear only when the whole novel is finished. Such a structure makes us participants in the making of the poem sequence's or the novel's meaning as we sort out our own version of the truth from the differing truths told us by the poem's or novel's many voices.

"Nocturne" ends twice, to conclude Pierrot's "Nocturne" and to signal the completion of the sequence's first movement. Taunted and physically and spiritually mutilated by nature, Colombine, and the music he tries so hard to play, Pierrot stands "alone," "frosty" (p. 18), and "chill" (p. 25). He "shivers" because his soul is a flimsy "paper lantern." As he did at the end of *Vision*'s first poem, Pierrot "rises stiffly, the stone has cramped his knees" (p. 23). He dares to ask "Who am I?" But his answer is unsatisfactory, for it is an echo: the Eliot image he has already used (pp. 12–13), which he now transfers into an image of himself doubled and split once more by a mirror:

> Shall I stay alone to watch a dead man pass,
> Gibbering at the moon and twisting a paper rose petal by petal
>   apart,—
> Or do I see my own face in a glass?
>
> Rather I will watch . . .
> .   .   .   .
> While I grow faint upon a wall
> Waiting to fall. (*VIS* III, pp. 26–27)

Unable to escape the "chains" of echoes, Pierrot can only daydream: "Pierrot stirs, and wakes into a dream" (p. 28). In a variation on his initial vision (*VIS* I) he sees dancers again. But here they are fragmented, reflecting Pierrot's own mutilated condition. Pierrot sees their hands "severed" from their arms as his own have been (pp. 11, 12, 28) and he

> Sees shadows and lights and faces before his eyes;
> Flitting feet, and hands in a forest of music;
> And echoes and perfumes are woven about him
> With a silver thread among them, which is pain;—
> Pierrot stares into the dark, and sighs,
> And enters his dream again. (*VIS* III, pp. 28–29)

Pierrot's Mutilation Fantasy and Donald Mahon's Fatal Wounding: From Poetry to the Prose of *Soldiers' Pay*

The further relevance of "Nocturne" to Faulkner's artistic development is that it contains a fantasy that Faulkner will skillfully replay through Donald Mahon in *Soldiers' Pay*, through Bayard Sartoris in *Flags in the Dust* (see especially pp. 278–281), and through Quentin Compson in *The Sound and the Fury*. This fantasy, central to these novels, is one of failure, mutilation, and death. Such punishment, mythical in origin, is, like Icarus's, the price of trying to fly: Pierrot "whirls his hands like birds before the moon" (p. 12) and "flits like a white moth on the dark" (p. 13) while his "winged eyes fly ever before" him (p. 16). Donald and Bayard, both World War I pilots, make Pierrot's fantasy their reality. While Donald's physical war wounds transform him into a vegetable, Bayard's wounds are psychological. They lead him to commit suicide by flight: the action he had originally used to seek fame and glory. And, of course, Quentin's "flight" from the bridge into the Charles River begins in these images from *Vision in Spring*.

Donald's recollection of his last and fatal mission echoes his *pierrotique* progenitor:

> Donald Mahon lay quietly conscious of unseen forgotten spring, of greenness neither recalled nor forgot. After a time the nothingness in which he lived took him wholly again, but restlessly. It was like a sea into which he could neither completely pass nor completely go away from. (*SP*, p. 292; for comparison see *VIS* VIII, pp. 47–54)

Enlarging upon Pierrot's bird image, Faulkner describes Donald as "lonely and remote as a gull." "Then, suddenly, it was as if a cold wind had blown upon him. What is it? he thought. It was that the sun had suddenly been blotted from him. The empty world, the sky . . ." (*SP*, p. 294). Blotting out the sun are German planes. When they attack, Donald tries to defend himself with his symbol of masculinity and power. But just as Pierrot, trapped in his cold, empty world, was punished for trying to fly and to make his own music, so Donald is paralyzed and blinded, his hand and head mutilated for flying and for trying to kill the enemy:

> . . . he felt two distinct shocks at the base of his skull and vision was reft from him as if a button somewhere had been pressed. . . .
> Sight flickered on again, like a poorly made electrical contact, he watched holes pitting into the fabric near him like a miraculous small-pox and as he hung poised firing into the sky a dial on his instrument board exploded with a small sound. Then he felt his hand, saw his glove burst, saw his bared bones. Then sight flashed off again and he felt himself lurch, falling until his belt caught him sharply across the abdomen, and he heard something gnawing through his frontal bone like mice. (*SP*, p. 294)

Donald, like Pierrot, is wounded in sensory organs: his head, hands, and eyes. Like Pierrot, he will never sing or fly, nor can he control his actions. He has become a marionette, a point emphasized by the puppet imagery in this passage.

Despite these similarities, which identify Faulkner as the author of both works, an immense imaginative gap separates Donald Mahon from Pierrot. Donald is believable. Pierrot is not. The reason has a lot to do with voice. Donald, a *pierrotique* figure, is not, as is Pierrot, Faulkner's mask. With appropriate distance put between himself and his fictional characters Faulkner can begin to explore the implications of his early, powerful, private fantasy.[11]

This fantasy continued to figure largely in Faulkner's imagination where it appeared as a nightmare vision of failure. In this nightmare Faulkner transformed to a combination of the tortured Pierrot and his wounded pilot pose. Meta Wilde reports Faulkner's hallucination in the midst of a drinking bout:

> . . . I saw Bill *huddled on one corner of the bed, hands stretched out, palms foremost, as if to ward off something menacing. His head was bent,* eyes mercifully turned away from whatever it was that threatened him, and he moved as I observed him into a *crouched position— knees up, shoulders sagging. . . .*
>
> He looked up, no recognition whatever in his face, and screamed, "They're going to get me! Oh, Lordy, oh, Jesus!" He covered his head with hands that alternately flailed and supplicated, shouting over and over in a litany of dread, "They're coming down at me! Help me! Don't let them! They're coming at me! No! No!"
>
> . . . when I tried to touch him, he recoiled from me convulsively.
>
> "Who?" I asked him. "Who's trying to hurt you?"
>
> *"They're diving down at me. Swooping.* Oh, Lordy!"
>
> "Faulkner, what are you talking about? Who's after you?"
>
> He turned a face as white as library paste toward me. "The Jerries! Can't you see them?" Suddenly *he was doubled over, trying to crawl into himself. "Here they come again! They're after me! They're trying to shoot me out of the sky. . . . they're out to kill me."* (emphasis added)[12]

Wilde never read *Vision in Spring*. Even if she had, the remarkable parallels between her description of Faulkner here and Faulkner's description of Pierrot in "Nocturne" would still be uncanny. The parallels suggest that Pierrot was, throughout Faulkner's career, his nemesis. When he could take this nemesis out of the realm of private dream and fantasy and transform him to a fictional figure of either comic or tragic stature, he gained momentary mastery over him. Otherwise Pierrot remained for Faulkner—especially when he drank—a figure of dread and fear, the embodiment of failure in art and life, his other self, the dark double who in fiction he so triumphantly re-created and vanquished.[13]

Vision's Second Movement: Enter the Human Lover's Voice

Pierrot is a prisoner of echoes and false music. Perhaps another kind of music is the solution to his isolation, impotence, anger, fear, and pain. It is the solution Pierrot tries in a slightly altered voice in the second movement of *Vision in Spring*.

In contrast to the interior monologues and dialogues of the first movement, Pierrot's poems here are addressed to a person who is *not* himself (poems IV–VI, pp. 30–39). As he begins to share his visions, his world gains more texture and complexity. Until the end of the third poem, Pierrot's real and dreamworlds held only himself and his memories of imaginary or dream girls. Though he admitted another living figure to his world—cruel Colombine flinging severed hands and paper roses—still, "The World of Pierrot" remains strictly limited, a stage where stock figures from commedia dell'arte perform highly stylized acts dictated by a mixture of commedia dell'arte and Symbolist dream-play conventions. Even as "Nocturne" begins, Pierrot stands outside reality; he is an actor, a kind of impostor.

The first three poems of *Vision*'s second movement are love lyrics. Addressed to a real "girl," they move beyond the first movement's solitary voices. But Pierrot fails to sustain his new pose, and the countertheme, carried by his earlier voices, reasserts itself. First in "A Symphony" (*VIS* VII) and then in an untitled poem, the sounds of real music herald the return of the golden bells of false vision, which in turn "echo" Pierrot's "life away" (*VIS* VIII, p. 47). In this movement the polyphony initiated in *Vision*'s first movement becomes more complicated. One *pierrotique* voice, claiming he hears "hidden music" (p. 32) and can therefore speak of "we" as opposed to "I," competes with another *pierrotique* voice whose vision is still bound by the poetry of the nineteenth century. Faulkner's concept of "abstract three dimensional polyphonic verse" advocated in his Aiken review appears to dictate the nature of the connections between these poems.

Substantively as well as stylistically these poems are related to Faulkner's fiction; they contain a poetic interior monologue, which he uses as the basis for a climactic moment in *Soldiers' Pay*. Faulkner transfers language from poems in *Vision*'s second movement to write a grotesquely comic love scene between Cecily Saunders and Januarius Jones. The scene, centering upon Jones's interior monologue of desire, reveals why his nympholepsy makes it impossible for him to love a real woman. Jones's comic failings are played off against the tragic or potentially tragic failings of *pierrotique* characters like Margaret Powers and Donald Mahon. Thus Pierrot's multiple-voiced visions in *Vision in Spring* foreshadow both formal and thematic concerns of *Soldiers' Pay*.

Vision's Love Poems: What Is "Hidden Music"? Can It Be Shared?

Throughout the first three poems of Vision's second movement, Pierrot attempts to articulate and share his visions arising from music "that haunts us as we go, / Yet which we cannot grasp, and dare not try" (p. 30). Although he is still fearful, he no longer seems angry. In "After the Concert" (VIS IV), as in "Portrait" (VIS V) and untitled (VIS VI), the setting is emphatically realistic and contemporary.[14] Both setting and title of "After the Concert" are borrowed from Aiken's symphony The Jig of Forslin.[15] As in earlier poems, the speaker's internal reality quickly replaces external setting: a scene of people rising, putting on their coats, and leaving a concert hall fades out as Pierrot's imaginative reconstruction of the concert's music supersedes it. As Pierrot and his lover walk "arm in arm" to "a haunting dim refrain," the concert music transforms to a "thin elusive phantom in our brain / Which we cannot remember, or forget" (p. 31). But for Pierrot, such "hidden music" stirs up deep, overwhelming, and contradictory emotions: "We rise, to a hidden music, out of night, / We laugh and weep, and then to night we yield" (p. 32).

Although Pierrot describes his conversation with his lover as "intimate talk," he also refers to it as a "haze of trivialities" (p. 32). He repeats the latter phrase in the next poem, "Portrait," in which his lover's portrait becomes less and less distinct. Like "Concert," "Portrait" borrows liberally from Aiken's poetry. Faulkner's girl resembles all the innocent and betrayed wives and girl friends in Aiken's symphonies. In "Portrait" Pierrot exhorts his lover to talk with him of "careful trivialities," urging her into a conversation that will reveal her unique personality (p. 33). He then depersonalizes her, sketching her as a shadow figure, describing her "tiny scrap of mouth / So lightly mobile on your dim white face" (pp. 33–34). She, like the nymphs in Pierrot's earlier visions, is "young and white and strange," and her face "scarce-seen" (p. 34). Pierrot makes her speech no more interesting than her looks.

In Vision's sixth poem, the last of the second movement's three love poems, the pierrotique figure, still walking with his lover "in a silence pale with violins," once again asks her to try to share his vision:

> Listen, how once more the silence sings
> Between your hands that you so lightly raise
> And lay upon me, clear and slim with beauty
> Of your nights and days.

Listen . . . Once more this music together we hear . . . (*VIS* VI,
    p. 36)[16]

But since Pierrot's vision is of "silent music" ("the silence sings"),
a vision he fails to articulate, his lover cannot possibly share it. Instead of raising her face as she did in "Portrait" she now raises her
hands. A line Faulkner took from Aiken's "Discordants" reappears
here in a slightly altered form (cf. *VIS* V, p. 33, line 8; see also chapter VII, note 3, pp. 247–248). Instead of her voice (p. 35), it is the silent music that is filled with "faint surprise" (p. 36), rising in his vision "in perfect soundless rings." Pierrot succumbs to this soundless
music, his fantasy world, and yet he exhorts the girl beside him to
embrace him, to touch him: "Place your hand in mine, and lay /
Your formless flower face upon the dusk" (p. 37). But her face *has* no
form. Pierrot has transformed it into a "flower face" in his imagination. He thus reduces her to something emotionally manageable: a
safely unattainable nympholeptic vision in which "I see your face
through the twilight in my brain, / A dusk of forgotten things, remembered things" (p. 37).[17] In Pierrot's new vision, her trivial talk
ceases and she becomes "clothed in quiet sound for my delight"
(p. 37). He continues, as the poem reaches its conclusion, to dwell
upon the importance of her muteness in permitting the flowering of
his vision. He exhorts her to "be silent, do not speak at all. / . . . look
at me, and raise your mouth, and form / The silence in the image of a
word" (pp. 38–39).

It is hard to characterize the quality of the feeling that pervades
the second movement because the *pierrotique* persona is trying to
evoke feelings that he cannot, himself, feel. Pierrot knows what the
feelings should be, but he cannot trust himself to feel them. What
are these "troubling" emotions? His wish to be able to love the
woman to whom he addresses these poems is in conflict with his
belief that only when his love is "clothed in silence," that is, unacknowledged or rejected, can he hear "hidden music." Characterizing
the nature of Pierrot's vision in these poems is also difficult and for a
similar reason. We have a sense that Pierrot knows that true imaginative vision must flow from himself—from "hidden, silent" music
rather than real or others' music—but although he knows this he
has as yet no subject upon which he dares to speak directly. He also
seems to know that to love a real woman he must relinquish his
nympholeptic fantasies, but he dares not do so.

From *Vision* to *Soldiers' Pay*: A Partial Resolution

The powerful hold nympholepsy exercises on a man's imaginative life and the ways it impairs his creative vision are manifested in Faulkner's novelistic renderings of these poems and of "The Dancer," the corresponding poem of "Portrait" (third movement, second poem). In *Soldiers' Pay*, as we have seen, Faulkner portions out Pierrot's different voices and visions to several characters. Most illuminating for purposes of discovering authorial intention are the *pierrotique* elements in the nympholept, Januarius Jones, and in Donald Mahon. One scene in which Faulkner uses a great deal of *Vision in Spring* occurs when Jones, an incurable skirt chaser, has finally cornered one of his "nymphs," Cecily Saunders. Jones thinks he has her where he wants her: alone on a couch in a dimly lit room. But his attendant fantasy makes it abundantly clear that the possibility of actually making love to Cecily gives him no pleasure at all. He claims, "I intend to have your body." Like Gordon in *Mosquitoes*, what he really wants to experience is what he calls "bodyless lust," not the real thing (*SP*, p. 224). As he slouches beside Cecily, he forms the following surreal, grotesque image derived from these poems in *Vision in Spring*: ". . . her lax hand between them grew again like a flower: it was as if her whole body became her hand. The symbol of a delicate, bodyless lust. . . . her body created for all men to dream after" (*SP*, p. 224; see *VIS* III, pp. 12–13). Then, slightly altering the *Vision* image, "And watch the trees step naked from the shadow / Like women shrugging upward from their gowns" (*VIS* VI, p. 38), he sees her body as "a poplar, vain and pliant, trying attitude after attitude, gesture after gesture—'a girl trying gown after gown, perplexed but in pleasure.' Her unseen face nimbused with light and her body, which was no body, crumpling a dress that had been dreamed. Not for maternity, *not even for love: a thing for the eye and the mind. Epicene*, he thought . . ." (*SP*, p. 224, emphasis added).

Over and over, throughout his apprenticeship to poetry, Faulkner uses such fragmented, disassociated language to ward off and deny his mask's desire for sexual expression. Jones's fantasy reveals the paradox of the nympholept's existence, a paradox only hinted at in *Vision in Spring*, but one upon which much of the sequence's meaning depends. Jones/Pierrot wants neither to feel nor to hear the "trivial" talk of any real woman. Jones tells Cecily three times to shut up because her talk is interfering with his vision: "'Hush,' he told her, 'you'll spoil it'" (p. 225). And then, exasperated, he bursts out cruelly, "'What makes you so beautiful and disturbing and so goddamned dull?'" (p. 227). When he does embrace Cecily, "he refused to hear her breath as he refused to feel a bodily substance in his arms" (p. 225). He simply cannot bear either her sexuality or his own: "this is the heart's desire purged of flesh. 'Be quiet,' he told himself as much as her, 'don't spoil it'" (p. 225). Jones's speech and behavior here bear a marked resemblance to Quentin's in his fantasy of committing incest with his sister (*TSATF*, pp. 185–198, especially pp. 194–196).[18] The important distinction between Quentin and Pierrot as Faulkner characters is that Faulkner *is* Pierrot. He is not Quentin. And it was only through experiencing himself as Pierrot and the Faun that he could then go on to create Quentin.

Transposing the image of *Vision*'s Pierrot, wrapped in his sterile vision, hearing "bells echo his life away," Faulkner then portrays Jones, paraphrasing Tennyson, in a state of preorgasmic ecstasy:

> The trumpets in his blood, the symphony of living, died away. . . . Jones felt the slow black sand of time marking his life away. "Hush," he said, "don't spoil it."
> . . . Jones a fat Mirandola in a chaste Platonic nympholepsy, a religio-sentimental orgy in gray tweed, shaping an insincere, fleeting articulation of damp clay to an old imperishable desire, building himself a papier-mâché Virgin . . . (*SP*, p. 225)

Faulkner's parody of Pierrot in Jones draws here on *Vision*'s Pierrot, who kneels prayerfully during his visions, calls the stars "pilgrims," and (in the ninth poem, Faulkner's first self-parody) laments, "I should have been a priest in floorless halls" (pp. 55–64 passim).

That Jones should choose the women he does seems paradoxical, for neither Cecily nor Emmy are virgins. Furthermore, Jones knows of Cecily's "lack," for Faulkner draws our attention to the paradox with Jones's flower image of Cecily and the phrase describing Jones's fantasy of Cecily as a "papier-mâché Virgin."[19]

Cecily, unlike most of Pierrot's women, is exasperatingly real: she talks and moves and even *feels* real and is, therefore, like the girl in "The Dancer," capable of destroying Jones's vision:

> No, no, he thought, with awakened despair, don't spoil it. But she had moved and her hair brushed his face. Hair. Everyone, anyone, has hair. (To hold it, to hold it.) But it was hair and here was a body in his arms, fragile and delicate it might be, but still a body, a woman: something to answer the call of his flesh. *Impalpable and dominating.* He removed his arm.
> "You little fool, don't you know you had me?" (*SP*, p. 226, emphasis added)

Just as Pierrot fears and repulses the dancer because he thinks she will destroy his visions, Jones repulses Cecily. He fears she will destroy him literally with her body. That Faulkner recognized and identified with Pierrot and Jones seems to be the point of his having Jones call Cecily "Atthis," then recite lines from "O Atthis" (*The Lilacs*) and allude to a poem Faulkner included in his 1926 sonnet sequence, *Helen: A Courtship* (XIII, datelined "Lago Maggiore—August-1925").[20] Both of these poems are, as Jones's gloss on the latter makes clear, yet more nympholeptic fantasies in which Jones's disgust with human sexuality verges on the pathological:

> . . . "Do you know how falcons make love? They embrace at an enormous height and fall locked, beak to beak, plunging: an unbearable ecstasy. While we have got to assume all sorts of ludicrous postures, knowing our own sweat. The falcon breaks his clasp and swoops away swift and proud and lonely, while a man must rise and take his hat and walk out." (*SP*, p. 227)

Faulkner's reference to these poems was a purely private joke about his less admirable, less creative younger self—his *pierrotique* mask. His readers could not know that before he had lent them to Jones he had been their real author. "O Atthis" (written in 1919) was not published until 1933 (*A Green Bough* XVII, p. 39), while the sonnet was never published in his lifetime. Jones's attitude reflects one of Faulkner's. According to Wilde, Faulkner was a "fervent" lover

> who suppressed a raging sexuality, wrestling with it constantly, man against savage angel, . . . glancing up suddenly from his writing to see the fearful intruder advancing across the room to take him from his holy work. . . . a man whose carnality would have destroyed him as a writer had he permitted it, had he not for long periods by sheer exercise of will purged himself of the tickle of physical passion and constantly used the accruing power to feed his genius.[21]

Although he was, she says, a great "sensualist" he was also "obsessed with keeping from me the grossness of his physical self, running the water in the bathroom to cover the evidence of his animality, bathing each time we made love" (p. 279). Wilde's accounts of Faulkner sound like more graphic descriptions of Faulkner's *pierrotistes'* sexual behavior.

Vision's Second Movement Concluded

In the last of his three love poems in *Vision*'s second movement, Pierrot began five out of seven strophes with orders to his lover:

"Listen . . . Place your hand . . . Let us go . . . No, be silent, do not speak at all . . . Lift your hand and touch your hair . . ." (pp. 36–39). Despite his ability to exercise control over her, to direct her physical positioning as one would a dancer, an actor, or a marionette, Pierrot, like Januarius Jones, fails to sustain any visions that attend "hidden music."

"A Symphony," the poem that follows (*VIS* VII, pp. 40–46), signals Pierrot's exhaustion. In 115 lines of octosyllabic couplets Faulkner imitates the form and some of the contents of one of Aiken's earliest symphonies, *Earth Triumphant, Part II*. This symphony had been published in *Turns and Movies*.[22] Both in sound and sense Faulkner's imitation is as monotonous as Aiken's original, but the formal connections he forges between this poem and the rest of his sequence tell more about Faulkner's growing talent.[23] The links reveal the means by which Faulkner, hiding behind Aiken's *pierrotique* mask, is evolving his own distinctive narrative style.

He employs his fictional technique of giving his characters a chance to tell different versions of the same story to cement connections between the first and second parts of *Vision*'s second movement, poems VI (untitled) and VII ("A Symphony"). In its repetitiousness, "A Symphony" echoes Pierrot's attempt to render a verbal translation of real music. Its tone—its regular rhyme scheme and monotonous meter—separates it from the earlier part of *Vision*'s second movement. However, the similarity between *Vision in Spring* VI and *Vision in Spring* VII's first five lines (Figure 11)—the same image seen from different perspectives—suggests to the reader a continuity that depends *not* on traditional narrative structures but on the *composite* image the reader constructs from reading the sixth and seventh poems in succession, connecting their visions to each other and to other poems in *Vision*. When we have done this, we realize that Faulkner introduced this new rhyme scheme in *Vision in Spring* VII to indicate that he was using a different voice and an altered perspective. The verbal repetition, coupled with metrical dissimilarities of the opening strophes of VI and VII, highlight the poems' similarities and the differences and create a sense of VI simultaneously dissolving into but separate from VII. This is because between VI and VII Faulkner has shifted from the first person to the voice of *Vision*'s impersonal narrator. The voice is the same and yet different as Faulkner preserves the liquid sounds in lines 2–4 but expands the meaning of the metaphor. In line three in both poems the adverb, though different ("vaguely" to "softly"), is somewhat synonymous and retains the same position and same form when used in

VI	VII
The dark ascends	The dark ascends
Lightly on pale wings of falling light.	On golden wings of violins
Vague dim walls before us vaguely rise	And lights, on music softly played
And then recline again upon faint	As if the shadow fingers strayed
greenish skies.	Upon the soft moon's silver
Slowly, in a silence pale with	strings.
violins,	Then, as all silence smoothly sings,
Let us walk where lilacs on the wall	Rise the quickening silver chimes,
Agitate their hands, and lean and fall,	And in pursuit there swiftly climbs
As the darkness deepens, from our	A slender flute, a clarinet;
sight. (p. 36)	A graceful scented faint regret
	As muted violins rise again,
	Threading with thin silver pain
	A golden weave of solemn horn. (p. 40)

FIGURE 11. Comparison of opening strophes of poems VI and VII in *Vision in Spring*. Courtesy of Jill Faulkner Summers.

VII. Alliteration of the same letter is maintained in the fifth line of both poems. The subject shifts in both poems in the sixth line, which is where VI and VII also depart from each other as VII attempts to imitate the sounds of a symphony. At the beginning of the third strophe of "A Symphony" Pierrot takes over from the impersonal narrator and reintroduces lines spoken in previous poems. He also introduces lines he will return to in later poems. Reiterating the image of fruitless quest he adds that although he has heard music he "Distinguished not a single word; / A 'why' and 'whence' we never knew / As violins rose and fell and flew" (p. 41). Pierrot describes a dream of dancing with his lover to the music of the symphony. The dance is reminiscent of Pierrot and Colombine's dance in *Vision*'s third poem, but now Pierrot and his lover are both transformed to moths who "whirl" on silver wings. Pierrot characterizes his "dance of life" (p. 43, line 4) as a "breathless heartless game / Of hunter and quarry" (p. 44). He continues evoking his dreamworld of "Nocturne": a forest of "hungry stone" where "so many dreams are blown" (p. 44). A deceptively gay singsong meter masks the Swinburnian Pierrot of *Vision*'s first movement.

The bells of *Vision*'s title poem chime again in the eighth and concluding poem of the second movement (pp. 47–54) when Pierrot characterizes his life as a "futile, thwarted dream" (p. 53), not a "passing" but an "endless repeating" (p. 48), as he lies at the edge of the sea listening "while the bells / Echo his life away" (p. 47).[24] Repeating a phrase from "Vision in Spring" and coupling it with slight variation on a refrain from "A Symphony," Pierrot says, "Remember, remember . . . / As dust you rose, as dust you someday fall" (p. 48). All these echoes suggest that Pierrot's earlier self has been resurrected for the concluding poem of *Vision*'s second movement. Faulkner has brought his sequence to a slow halt and has deliberately robbed his unwary readers of any warning signs about the intent or content of the next movement.

From Pierrot to George Farr to Quentin Compson: 1919 to 1928 [25]

This concluding poem of *Vision*'s second movement bears directly on *Soldiers' Pay*. As he had used an earlier poem to help characterize Januarius Jones, so here Faulkner transformed *Vision in Spring* VIII into an emblematic scene portraying the essence of George Farr's connection with Cecily Saunders. Like the poem from which it is derived, this scene is an interior monologue. George Farr describes his feelings as he waits vainly for an assignation with Cecily. Farr, a comic version of Pierrot, lies not on the Swinburnian seashore, but in a damp flower bed where he's getting cold, wet, and muddy. Nonetheless, hypnotized by his vision of Cecily, "her body, like a little silver water sweetly dividing" (*SP*, p. 238), he falls asleep. Like Pierrot's, Farr's vision causes him great pain. But Faulkner, parodying Farr's decadent romanticism, makes it clear that Farr's pain comes from his sleep-cramped limbs rather than a broken heart. His pain, like Pierrot's, also paralyzes him, but rather than discouraging him from living or from pursuing his "quest," as it does Pierrot, Farr's pain just makes him momentarily unable to chase after Cecily: "He could not even take out his watch, he was afraid he would not be able to climb the fence" (*SP*, p. 237). Faulkner, by parodying his poetic mask, has turned a dull romantic lyric into a fine piece of humor. George Farr is Pierrot ridiculed.

> George Farr, lurking along a street, climbed a fence swiftly when the exodus from the picture show came along. . . .
> George Farr stole across a deserted lawn to a magnolia tree. . . . he found a water tap. Water gushed, filling his incautious shoe, and a mocking bird flew darkly and suddenly out. . . .

> Solemnly the clock on the courthouse . . . dropped eleven measured
> *golden bells of sound. Silence carried them away, silence and dark.*
> *. . . The street, the town, the world, was empty* for him.
> *He lay on his back in a slow consciousness of relaxing muscles,*
> *feeling his back and thighs and legs luxuriously. . . .*
> He lay back again cradling his head in his clasped arms . . . *it was*
> *as if he lay on the bottom of the sea while sea-weed, clotting blackly,*
> *lifted surfaceward unshaken by any current, motionless; it was as if*
> *he lay on his stomach, staring downward into water into which his*
> *gorgon's hair, clotting blackly, hung motionless.* Eleven-thirty.
> *He had lost his body. He could not feel it at all. It was as though*
> *vision were a bodiless Eye suspended* in dark-blue space, an Eye with-
> out Thought, regarding without surprise an antic world *where wan-*
> *ton stars galloped neighing like unicorns. . . . After a while, the Eye*
> *. . . ceased to see, and he waked, thinking he was being tortured, that*
> *his arms were being crushed and wrung from his body.* (*SP*, pp. 233,
> 235, 236, emphasis added)

Unlike Pierrot, who soothes himself into numbness with his sea
vision, Farr feels the exquisite "torture" of cramped limbs and damp
ground. Like Pierrot, Farr is obsessed with actual time (those "golden
bells" that "echo his life away," but here used for a very different reason: Farr doesn't want to miss his tryst). Thinking about seducing
Cecily, he echoes lines from "After the Concert": "How can breasts
be as small as yours, and yet be breasts. . . . her arms rising like two
sweet wings of a dream. . . . Her body like" (*SP*, p. 238).

What Faulkner has learned about Pierrot's meaning for him between writing *Vision in Spring* (1921), *Soldiers' Pay* (1925), and *The
Sound and the Fury* (1928) and how it has altered his own vision—
his style and authorial intentions—becomes apparent when the
transformations on a series of images that figure prominently in all
three works are examined. Embedded in George Farr's scene is an
image cluster that echoes and reechoes through Quentin's section,
beginning with his fantasy of killing Caddy and himself as she tells
him of her love for Dalton Ames. Quentin's fantasy, like Pierrot's
(*VIS* VIII), takes place at the water's edge (*TSATF*, pp. 203, 204).

> . . . I was leaning on my other arm it began to jerk and jump . . . when
> I lifted my hand I could still feel crisscrossed twigs and grass burning
> into the palm . . . water gurgling among the willows in the dark and
> waves of honeysuckle coming up the air my arm and shoulder were
> twisted under me . . . (*TSATF*, pp. 188, 189)

Like Pierrot, Quentin and Farr structure their lives by "false music." While apparently obsessed with actual time, they constantly

try to obliterate it by drowning in the "false music" of their fantasies. Simultaneously they use time or fate as an excuse to abdicate responsibility for their actions.

But the moral implications of Farr's and Quentin's misapplication of time are infinitely enriched when we know their genesis. In *Vision in Spring* where this image first appeared, Faulkner forged the initial connections between real music—bells, horns, etc.—and false vision. Knowing this we can then see that Farr's and Quentin's abuse and misunderstanding of the meaning of time is, in the deepest sense, a moral flaw that is rooted in their hopelessly unrealizable and childlike perceptions of the meaning of love. Farr, or Pierrot, the *ridicule*, is doomed to fail with Cecily because his vision of her is false. It is false because it derives from what he wants her to be rather than from what she is. Therefore Farr continually misreads her. Quentin, or Pierrot as tragic figure, kills himself because his nympholepsy makes him deaf to the real Caddy's needs and her love and drives him to desire only his idealized and forbidden image of her. The theme of forbidden love is veiled in *Vision in Spring* where relations with women are imaged as dangerous but not incestuous. In *The Sound and the Fury* the theme is more explicit: Quentin substitutes Caddy for his mother, the original and unconscious object of his incestuous desires: "*Father I have committed* what a pity you had no brother or sister No sister no sister . . . *My little sister had no. If I could say Mother. Mother*" (*TSATF*, p. 117).

Faulkner also connects Quentin and Pierrot of *Vision* explicitly (see *VIS* III, p. 17) by transforming Pierrot's arrow "tipped with jade desire, and feathered with your illusions," into Quentin's vision of merging with Caddy. This merging is imagined, as is Pierrot's first with Marietta and later with his dancer in *Vision*'s tenth poem (*VIS* X, p. 66) as "*the clean flame the two of us more than dead. Then you will have only me then only me then the two of us amid the pointing and the horror beyond the clean flame* The arrow increased without motion, then in a quick swirl the trout lipped a fly beneath the surface. . . . *Only you and me then amid the pointing and the horror walled by the clean flame*" (*TSATF*, p. 144).[26] Faulkner had originally used this metaphor in his dedication to Estelle Franklin written on her daughter's copy of his 1920 play. Faulkner in love seems to have made little distinction between the women in his life and the women in his books and poems.

The trout Quentin sees, "a shadow hanging like a fat arrow stemming into the current" (*TSATF*, p. 144), becomes for him a vision of his dark shadow self, the shadow he has tried all day to "blot out," to "drown," and to "trample" (*TSATF*, pp. 111, 118, 119, 149). The trout, like Quentin's shadow, is the idealized, adored, and hated quest symbol. As the fishermen say, "They've been trying to catch that trout for twenty-five years" (p. 145) but it always escapes. The fishermen are sane: they don't need to catch the trout. But Quentin is not. Rather than give up listening to false music or living in false visions, he will kill himself to "blot out" his shadow, the loved and hated double his shadow represents.[27]

Vision in Spring, particularly "A Symphony," offers other clues about the meaning of Quentin's "wall of clean flame." In "A Symphony," Faulkner states that a wall of flame separates his characters from reality and keeps them locked in their private and self-consuming visions. As Pierrot describes himself and his lover dancing he says, "our shadows merge." Their merging generates a vision, which Pierrot describes as a feverish and circular escape into a dreamworld:

> . . . a febrile whirl
> Above the dark where lurks the world;
> Within these safe walls we have raised
> And beyond which we have never gazed. (*VIS* VII, p. 44)

In terms of voice alone, there are immense stylistic differences between the Faulkner of *Vision in Spring* and the Faulkner of either *Soldiers' Pay* or *The Sound and the Fury*. Faulkner's point of view becomes more varied. For example, Quentin engages simultaneously in present dialogue, past dialogue, and interior monologue in the present and in the past. He also carries on imagined dialogues with numerous characters. His is truly an "abstract three dimensional polyphonic prose." But Faulkner's style, his language, his images of Quentin's and Farr's obsessions and preoccupying fantasies, all have their genesis in the persona of Pierrot, the would-be poet of *Vision in Spring*. With his novelist's voice and vision Faulkner uses these poetic images as irony and parody to transform his maudlin, self-pitying Pierrot mask into a laughable Jelly Bean, or a tragic adolescent. And, when he does so, the impostor of the poetry becomes the artist of fiction.

CHAPTER X

The Mask Unmasked:
Pierrot Meets Prufrock

Faulkner purposely does not prepare his reader for the surprises awaiting discovery in the third movement of *Vision in Spring*. As the second movement reaches its languid conclusion, Pierrot's voices are locked into "futile thwarted" dreams of circular motions and echoing "golden bells" (*VIS* VIII, p. 53). "Walls of blind despair" enclose the mask for whom "life is not a passing: it is an endless repeating" (*VIS* VIII, p. 48). Pierrot's final solution, in the sequence's eighth poem, is to attempt an erotic drowning. For him, as later for Quentin Compson, sex is twinned with death by water, the "fair white mother," the "perfect lover" whose "large embraces are keen like pain": [1]

> Dark drew slowly nearer on the sand
> And, as he slept, it filled his eyes;
> And the sea approached and ran its hand
> Lightly along his limbs and back and thighs. (*VIS* VIII, p. 54)

Pierrot's suicide seems a logical end for this sequence but the problem with which the cycle began has not yet been resolved. While the poet has abandoned Swinburne's rhythms, he has not relinquished Swinburne's death-embracing visions. A more radical change of voice, one involving sense as well as sound, is required. So Faulkner, with an abrupt shift in tone, begins *Vision*'s third movement, which has four parts. They are "Love Song" (*VIS* IX), "The Dancer" (*VIS* X), untitled (*VIS* XI), and "Orpheus" (*VIS* XII). "Love Song" is a double parody in which the poet ridicules his own and other early Modernists' *pierrotique* masks, [2] proposing as he does so a new solution to Eliot's question, "Where do we go from Swinburne?" The targets of Faulkner's satire are formidable figures: J. Alfred Prufrock and his own Pierrot.

Parody was a logical but daring form to choose for coming to terms with Swinburne and for continuing his dialogue with the Modernists, especially T. S. Eliot, himself a master of self-parody. Satirizing Prufrock, an infinitely superior model of the mask he himself had adopted, Faulkner wrote his first sustained piece of humor.[3] Faulkner's discovery of his capacity for comedy was essential: like his tragic vision, his humor—especially his satire—is basic to his fictional voice. Writing "Love Song" taught him the power of humor and opened up a totally new range of invention.

Mocking Prufrock's moral weakness—his failure of will—and showing through satire why such a solipsistic mask, one so inward turning and so concentrated on self, is unsatisfactory for a writer who wants to communicate revealed to Faulkner the rhetorical and moral weakness of his own *pierrotique* voices. Having written "Love Song" Faulkner, in the following poems, can make Pierrot confront his deepest fears and give them a communicable, imaginative form. The fears are (1) that if he acts upon his love for and desire to possess a mortal woman ("The Dancer") he will destroy his own ability to hear and re-create "silent music" and (2) that if he loves a player of real music ("Marriage") he will lose his sanity.

Parody can be seen as an imitation that is funny because it unmasks the object imitated.[4] Explaining its unmasking properties Freud wrote, "Parody and travesty achieve the degradation of something exalted . . . by destroying the unity between peoples' characters as we know them and their speeches and actions."[5] In "Love Song" Faulkner parodies or unmasks Pierrot, the persona he has used ever since he began writing poetry. The meaning of this parody is, on one level, intensely personal: it is a way of questioning the authority and validity of a voice he adopted and the task it has performed for the past five years. In this sequence, Faulkner defines Pierrot as the sum of his visions or dreams. Thus, by analogy and extension, parodying Pierrot serves to unmask his dreams. Faulkner uses the terms "dream" and "vision" interchangeably, but the more accurate term would be "dream," as vision suggests illumination and Pierrot's dreams are remarkably deficient in this respect. "Love Song" is Faulkner's attempt to interpret, and thus destroy, the defensive, creatively inhibiting function that Pierrot's dreams have hitherto served.[6] Parody and dreaming are similar in that they are both methods of coming to terms with troubling or threatening aspects of reality: "Dreams serve predominantly for the avoidance of unpleasure, jokes for the attainment of pleasure; but all our mental activities converge in these two aims." But since parody is a means of unmasking and dreams are a kind of "masquerade," their effects are opposite and require antithetical mental activity and social behavior: whereas a joke's purpose is to communicate, a dream's purpose is to *fail* to do so.[7] Faulkner's parody serves both to explain or unmask Pierrot's dreams and, as he said of his first Yoknapatawpha novel, to "control the stuff and fix it on something like rational truth."[8]

"Love Song" is the pivotal poem of *Vision in Spring*. In it Faulkner the poet, the subjective passive dreamer, becomes momentarily the novelist, Faulkner the distanced observer, as, through parody, he repudiates his *pierrotique* mask. "Love Song" is Faulkner's first successful attempt to interpret Pierrot's visions in spring.

Substantive, Linguistic, and Metrical Parodic Devices in Faulkner's "Love Song"

Critics have noted Eliot's obtrusive presence in "Love Song." Blotner calls Faulkner's poem an "imitation" and a paraphrase,[9] while Brooks writes that "Love Song" is a "patent imitation" and says it "apparently follows Eliot's 'Love Song' almost obsequiously."[10] Neither suggests that Faulkner might be using Eliot's poem for humorous or parodic purposes, nor do they consider the poem in its context. Had they done so, they would have noted that Faulkner's poem, which uses Eliot's ironically lyrical metaphors for a deliberately alyrical, often ludicrous effect, is considerably more ambitious than an "imitation" or "obsequious paraphrase."

To argue that "Love Song" parodies "Prufrock" is a delicate task, not least because Eliot himself uses Prufrock to satirize Prufrock at a number of points. But clues to Faulkner's parodic intent appear in the first few lines of "Love Song" (Figure 12). "My mental hair" is placed very early in the poem (line 4); considered alone or compared to the original—"With a bald spot in the middle of my hair"—it is hard to interpret in any way except a comic one. Furthermore, the phrase, in revealing just how muddled Pierrot's thinking is, provides an amusing gloss on his earlier overblown "corridor of profundities" (line 1). As a play upon Eliot, Faulkner's phrase is a condensed and exaggerated rendition of Prufrock's intensely narcissistic reference to his appearance. Thus the phrase both comments on his own mask and gives new meaning to Eliot's. The intentional awkwardness of his phrase also makes clear that these *pierrotique* masks' "mental hair" really needs smoothing. For it is their obsessive self-scrutiny rather than their physical attributes that makes them so painfully self-conscious. Were their "mental hair" in place, they would not, like Quentin Compson, be so preoccupied with their outward appearance.[11]

Throughout "Love Song," Faulkner aims his parody at three targets: Eliot's Prufrock, his own *pierrotique* persona, and, occasionally, himself.[12] As Faulkner does not proceed with a line-by-line take-off of Eliot's poem, it is important to clarify what he chooses to parody, because his parodic thrusts represent the voice of the novelist asserting itself against the vision of the poet. In the first line of "Love Song," Faulkner undercuts Eliot's first line both substantively and metrically. Eliot's hortatory "Let us . . ." invites the reader into Prufrock's timeless world by offering a metaphorical vision of the interior journey that is about to begin. He leads the reader into Prufrock's mind with imagery that accumulates in large syntactical units (see especially lines 2, 3, 5–7). The compound words, the couplets joining run-on lines, catch us up in the seductive rhymes and rhythms of his mask's voice. The tone is deceptively inviting and easy, suggesting always, as Smith has observed, that iambic pentameter will be the lyric's underlying metrical pattern. In contrast Faulkner's opening line waddles in: "Shall I walk, then, through a corridor of profundities," deliberately and clumsily breaking up Eliot's lyrical tones. This is achieved by means of a series of small syntactical units that bump against one another as they describe Pierrot acting out Prufrock's thought processes, his "tedious argument." The often choppy sentence structure and pedantic diction of "Love Song" are meant to imitate the hesitating, halting quality of Prufrock/Pierrot's actions.

Faulkner underscores the parody of Prufrock by using intentionally disruptive syntax—"as to brow . . . as to knee"—and some of Eliot's phrases and metrical devices (e.g., couplets and caesuras) in ways that impede rather than encourage the flow of his poem's thought. Faulkner's lines, like Eliot's, reflect the state of his persona's mind. But this mind, hesitating, balking abruptly at the sound of its own verbiage, is a bold caricature rather than an imitation of Prufrock. In breaking up Eliot's lines as he does, Faulkner seems to ask, "How can such a stifled mind write such flowing verse?" Here, as in many other places throughout "Love Song," he takes conventional devices for metrical tension to an extreme and uses meter to disrupt the lines' normal rhythmical flow. Thus he constantly disappoints any expectations of Prufrockian rhythmic regularity. Faulkner's favorite devices are excessive use of caesura and the inclusion of superfluous words in an otherwise Prufrockian line ("then" in line 1, "a" in line 10). In the first example, the parody is obvious, because "then" is *not* a superfluous word in the first line of "Pru-

Love Song

Your face . . . is a corridor, dark and cool
with music,
Too dim for sight (VIS VI, p. 37)

Shall I walk, then, through a corridor of   *Shall I say, I have gone at dusk*
    profundities

Not Eliot   Carefully erect (I am taller that [*sic*] I look)
To a certain door—and shall I dare ↑
To open it? I smoothe my mental hair   *With a bald spot in the middle*
[5] With an oft changed phrase that I revise again   *of my hair*
Until I have forgotten what it was at first;   *There will be time to murd*
and create
Verb initial lines in   *settling a pillow by her head*   *And time for all the works*
descriptive passages   Settle my tie with: I have brought a book,   *and days of hands*
Then seat myself with: We have passed the   *That lift and drop a questi*
    worst.   *on your plate.*
Then how should I begin
Then I shall sit among careful cups of tea,
[10] Aware of a slight perspiring as to brow,
(The smell of scented cigarettes will always
    trouble me); ←   *parenthetical insertion*
I shall sit, so patently at ease,   *and ices*
Not Eliot   Stiffly erect, decorous as to knees   *its crisis*
Among toy balloons of dignity on threads of talk.

[15] And do I dare
(I once more stroke my hand across my hair)
But the window of my mind flies shut, I am in a
    room
Of surcharged conversation, and of jewelled   *Of restless nights . . .*
    hands;   *If one, settling a pillow or throwi.*
—Here one slowly strips a flower stalk.   *off a shawl*
[20] It is too close in here, I rise and walk,   *It is impossible to say just what I*
mean
Not Eliot   Firmly take my self-possession by the hand.   *My self-possession flares u*
for a second:
She has a bowl of lilacs in her room   *This is as I had reckoned .*
And twists one in her fingers while she talks. ("Portrait")   *("Portrait",*
Now, do I dare,
Who sees the light gleam on her intricate hair?   *But in the lamplight,*
Shall I assume a studied pose, or shall I stand—   *downed with light*
distills Prufrockian indecision into Eliotic syntax   *brown hair*

FIGURE 12. Text of Faulkner's "Love Song" (*Vision in Spring* IX, pp. 55–64). In the margins are relevant lines from Eliot's "Love Song of J. Alfred Prufrock" and from other poems in *Prufrock and Other Observations*.

[25] Oh, Mr. . . . ? You are so kind . . . .
Again the door slams inward on my mind.

Not at all . . . . *That is not it at all*

Replace a cup, *. . . a shawl*
Return and pick a napkin up. *. . . at all.*

[30] My tongue, a bulwark where a last faint self-
possession hides, *My self-possession gutters; we are really in the dark*
Fails me: I withdraw, retreat, *I mount the stairs and turn the handle*
Conscious of the glances on my feet, *of the door*
And feel as if I trod in sand. *And feel as if I had mounted on my hands and knees.*
("Portrait")

Yet I may raise my head a little while.
[35] The world revolves behind a painted smile. *The worlds revolve like ancient*
women
And now, while evening lies embalmed upon the *Gathering fuel in vacant lots*
west *When the evening is spread out against the sky* *("Preludes" IV)*
And a last faint pulse of life fades down the sky,
We will go alone, my soul and I, *Let us go then, you and I*
To a hollow cadence down this neutral street; *. . . certain half-deserted streets,*
[40] To a rythm [*sic*] of feet *The muttering retreats*
Commoner in Faulkner by far than in Eliot
Now stilled and fallen. I will walk alone,
The uninvited one who dares not go
Whither the feast is spread to friend and foe,
Whose courage balks the last indifferent gate, } *Not Prufrockian*
[45] Who dares not join the beggars at the arch of
stone.

Change and change: the world revolves to worlds,
To minute whorls
And particles of soil on careless thumbs.
Now I shall go alone,
[50] I shall echo streets of stone, while evening comes
Treading space and beat, space and beat. *My heart that I so carefully guarded,*
empty
The last left seed of beauty in my heart } *Of plant of seed, the acts of day by*
day
That I so carefully tended, leaf and bloom, } *Which would have made of it a*
Falls in darkness. *garden or age to nod in,*
Has broken and fallen away.
(VIS I, pp. 1–2)

[55] But enough. What is all beauty? What, that I
    Should raise my hands palm upward to the sky,   *Not Prufrockian*
    That I should weakly tremble and fall dumb
    At some cryptic promise or pale gleam;—
    A sudden wing, a word, a cry?   *Where the evening is spread*
[60] Evening dies, and now that night has come   *out against the sky*
    Walking still streets, monk-like, grey and dumb; *Like a patient etherized*
    Then softly clad in grey, lies down again;   *upon a table*
    I also rise and walk, and die in dream,
    For dream is death, and death but fathomed dream.

Not Eliot [65] <u>And shall I walk</u> these streets while passing
        time   *They will say, "How his hair is growing*
    Softly ticks my face, <u>my thinning hair</u>? *thin!"*
    I should have been a priest in floorless halls *I should have been a pair*
    Wearing his eyes thin on a faded manuscript. *of ragged claws*
                           Scuttling across the floors
                           of silent seas.

    The world revolves. High heels and <u>scented</u>
        <u>shawls</u>, . . . *perfume from a dress* . . . *wrap about a shawl*
[70] Painted masks, and kisses mouth and mouth:
    Gesture of a senile pantaloon
    To make us laugh.

    I have measured time, I measured time *I have measured out my life*
    With span of thumb and finger   *with coffee spoons*
                           . . .
[75] As one who seeks a bargain: sound enough *For I have known them all*
    I think, but a slightly worn;   *already, known them all—*
    There's still enough to cover me from cold, *. . .*
    Momentous indecisions, change   *And I have known the eyes*
    And loneliness. Does not each fold *already, known them all—*
[80] Repeat—the while I measure time, I measure *. . .*
        time—   *And I have known the arms*
    The word, the thought, the soundless empty *already, known them all—*
        gesture   *. . .*
    Of him that it so bravely once arrayed? *Inversion not Eliot*

    Spring . . . shadowed walls, and kissing in the dark.
    I, too; was young upon a time, I too; have felt
[85] All life, at one small word, within me melt;
    And strange slow swooning wings I could
        not see   *Not Eliot*
    Stirring the beautiful silence over me.

I grow old, I grow old.   *I grow old . . . I grow old . . .*
Could I walk within my garden while the night
[90] Comes gently down,
And see the garden maidens dancing, white   *Nonphrasal break not Eliot*
And dim, across the flower beds?

I would take cold: I dare not try,
Nor watch the stars again born in the sky
[95] Eternally young.

I grow old, I grow old.
Submerged in the firelight's solemn gold   *(VIS XI)*
I sit, watching the restless shadows, red and
    brown, *By sea-girls wreathed with sea weed red and brown*
Float there till I disturb them, then they drown.
           Till human voices wake us, and we drown.
[100] I measure time, I measure time.
I see my soul, disturbed, awake and climb
A sudden dream, and fall
And whimpering, crowd near me in the dark.

                 To wonder, "Do I dare?" and,
And do I dare, who steadily builds a wall   *"Do I dare?"*
[105] Of hour on hour, and day, then lifts a year
That heavily falls in place, while time   *With a bald spot in the middle of*
Ticks my face, my thinning hair, my heart   *my hair*
In which a faint last long remembered beauty *(They will say: "How his hair is*
    hides?   *growing thin!")*

I should have been a priest in floorless halls ⎤
[110] Whose hand, worn thin by turning endless | *Evocative of the impotent cleric,*
    pages, | *Gail Hightower*
Lifts, and strokes his face, and falls ⎦
And stirs a dust of time heaped grain on grain,
Then gropes the book, and turns it through
    again;

           The yellow smoke that rubs its muzzle on the
Who turns the pages through, who turns again, *window-panes*
[115] While darkness lays soft fingers on his eyes *Licked its tongue into the corners*
And strokes the lamplight from his brow,   *of the evening,*
    to wake him, and he dies.
    Till human voices wake us, and we drown.

frock." The extra words deliberately destroy what would otherwise be an approximation of an iambic pentameter line.[13]

There are two couplets in Faulkner's first fourteen lines, in contrast to Eliot's six, and even these are overridden by enjambment (lines 3, 4) and medial caesuras or by contextual contradictions (lines 12, 13), so that there is a perpetual jolting sensation. Pierrot holds his jerky sentences together with conjunctions and adverbs rather than prepositional phrases: ". . . I rise and walk, / Firmly take my self-possession by the hand" (lines 20–21). Faulkner seems to have included them to give an impression of comic verbosity and to further destroy any lyrical tendencies in a line. Often he adds extra words to Eliot's phrases (see the first, third, and fourth lines), making a joke of Eliot's irony.

A rhetorical question in the opening lines of "Love Song" draws attention to the speaker's precious subjectivity. It is meant to undercut Prufrock's unanswerable question, "Shall I dare . . . ?" Here Pierrot answers himself in deliberately ametaphorical language that is associated by its syntax to narrative chronological sequence and by its context to the explicit present:

> Shall I walk, then, through a corridor of profundities
> Carefully erect (I am taller than I look)
> To a certain door—and shall I dare
> To open it?

Prufrock's fear of disturbing the universe is for Pierrot an issue of whether or not to open a literal door, just as Prufrock's great existential question is reduced to a practical matter of which polite phrase of greeting Pierrot will choose to utter at the tea party he is about to join.

Pierrot refers to being erect twice in the first fourteen lines of "Love Song." "Carefully" and "stiffly" are the adverbs Faulkner selects to connote the quality of Pierrot's erect(ion). The placement of this joke makes it clear that Pierrot is excited more by his fantasies than by any actual women, as these have not yet appeared on the scene. He attempts to disguise his emotional and physical state by being "decorous as to knees"—that is, crossing his legs. Had Faulkner meant "Love Song" as an imitation rather than a parody, he would not have slipped in this allusion to Pierrot's sexual preoccupations (lines 2, 13). Furthermore, such broad sexual humor is hardly Eliot's style.

Faulkner elaborates this pun later in "Love Song," once in a mocking echo that comments upon his own Pierrot's lament and behavior in *Vision in Spring*'s first poem and once in reference to Pierrot's grandiose fantasies of fame in *Vision*'s third poem, "The World and Pierrot. A Nocturne."[14] In mocking Pierrot's earlier claim that his quest for love has led only to old age and a broken heart, Faulkner in "Love Song" can question just what kind of love Pierrot sought. As he once more walks "alone" down "streets of stone" he laments,

> The last left seed of beauty in my heart
> That I so carefully tended, leaf and bloom,
> Falls in darkness. (*VIS* IX, lines 52–54)

A sympathetic or serious reading of Pierrot's earlier "that was my heart that broke" is no longer possible. For now it is clear that Pierrot has spent his seed in empty streets rather than in lovemaking, as he claimed earlier. Faulkner alludes to this image later when he condenses Eliot's lines, "and indeed there will be time" and "I have measured out my life in coffee spoons." In his condensation Pierrot appears to be describing either impotence or a wet dream:

> I measure time, I measure time.
> I see my soul, disturbed, awake and climb
> A sudden dream, and fall
> And whimpering, crowd near me in the dark. (*VIS* IX, lines 100–104)

"Prufrock" has been characterized as a poem "about a man who cannot love women."[15] Faulkner's parody shows how attuned he is to this quality in Eliot's lyric as he simultaneously deflates Prufrock's own self-mockery and questions Pierrot's claims to quest for artistic fame and women's love. Such humor anticipates Faulkner's fictional voice; his novels contain many amusing sexual allusions and puns. In contrast, his poetry before "Love Song" is notable for its lack of jokes.

Faulkner plays with Eliot's language in many ways throughout his poem, invoking the original through verbal and phrasal echoes and near-echoes. Examples of this are the title; the two occurrences of "do I dare" (lines 15, 104); "settle" (line 8; cf. "If one settling a pillow . . ."); "Shall I walk then . . ." (line 1; cf. "Let us go then, . . ."); "We will go alone, my soul and I" (line 38; cf. "Let us go then, you and I . . ."); the two occurrences of "I grow old, I grow old" (lines 88, 96); the successive lines ending "red and brown," "drown," like the last two lines of "Prufrock" (lines 98, 99); and "the lamplight" (line 116). Faulkner echoes Eliot not merely to imitate but to question the validity of Eliot's ironic self-deprecatory mask. For example, by making explicit what was vague but implicit in Eliot's "Let us go then,

you and I," Faulkner specifies the source of Pierrot/Prufrock's malaise: that "you and I" is really only "I."

Faulkner focuses his parody on several Eliotic habits of phrase: (1)
phrasal repetitions of a rhetorical self-dramatizing kind, (2) line-final
rhyme series, (3) disposition of syntactical units within irregular
line units, and (4) choice of vocabulary. He is sufficiently imitative to
set up the desired resonances, but on the whole he is freewheeling.
Examples of phrasal repetition are picking up on (1) Eliot's "For I
have known them all already, known them all . . . / And I have
known the eyes already, known them all . . . / And I have known the
arms already, known them all . . ." in his own lines 73, 84, and 100,
and (2) Eliot's "do I dare" series (lines 15 and 104). Perhaps Faulkner's
best effect in this vein occurs in line 24, where Prufrockian indecision and self-absorption are distilled into Eliotic syntax: "Shall I assume a studied pose, or shall I stand . . ."

Faulkner has recurrent success with his line-final rhyme series,
which evokes the insistent, irregularly patterned rhymes of "Prufrock" from end to end of "Love Song." His best effects in this cate-
gory are lines 12 and 13 (cf. Eliot's "and ices/its crisis") and lines 28
and 29. Here Faulkner outdoes the ices/crisis effect by using it
twice: "at ease/to knees," "a cup/napkin up." He carries out his parody by exaggeration and repetition in several ways. Dogged elaboration is a favorite. His lines taking off on Eliot's measuring (lines
75–82, 101–103) and his lament, "I should have been a priest in
floorless halls," glancing at Eliot's "pair of ragged claws," are examples. By imitating Eliot's syntax and rhyme but grossly altering its
meaning, Faulkner accentuates and thus reveals the absurdity of the
self-pitying melodramatic rhetoric of Prufrock's assertion.[16] Faulkner's imitation of line-final and, to some extent, line-internal rhymes
is his closest formal approach to Eliot.

The evidence is mixed concerning Faulkner's disposition of syn-
tactic units within his irregular line units. "Prufrock" ends every
line at a phrase boundary; so does "Love Song," except at lines 79
and 80 and at 91 and 92, where Faulkner enjambs across compound
phrases. Even this enjambment, though, is handled conservatively;
the lines are not, for example, broken after the *and*s. As for syntax
and line beginnings, Faulkner is most Eliotic in his sentence-initial
*And*s, in his "I + verb" combinations and other parallel constructions ("Shall I," "Do I," etc.), and in his use of time adverbials (Faulkner's *until, now, yet,* for Eliot's *after*s). Faulkner, however, uses
prepositional phrases to start lines more frequently than Eliot does.
Faulkner begins lines in ways that "Prufrock" does not, most nota-

bly with adverb + verb phrases (see lines 2, 13, 21, 66, 95). He also uses main verbs to start lines of self-description by the character (see lines 5, 31, 32, 97); in Eliot such lines are reserved for description of observed objects or persons external to the speaker (the evening "stretched on the floor," the fog passage, etc.).

Metrically, Faulkner is spectacularly unlike Eliot. "Prufrock" is generally iambic; the rhythms of "Love Song" are jagged and irregular. Faulkner is also more diverse in his lyric modality; the calculated civilities and understatements of "Prufrock" give way to Aikenesque and Swinburnian swish and palpitation (see lines 55–64, 83–87) and to a pontificating voice that generalizes at a level of abstraction and transcendence that appears, for example, in *Vision in Spring* III but not in "Prufrock" (see lines 35, 41–45, 69–72, 81–82, 94–95).

Another indicator that Faulkner parodies rather than imitates "Prufrock" is the presence of humorous devices that Eliot eschews. Faulkner uses the grotesque here for comic effect by condensing Eliot's first simile into a metaphor, substituting "embalmed" for "etherized" and having the embalming occur *before* "death":

> And now, while evening lies embalmed upon the west
> And a last faint pulse of life fades down the sky,
> We will go alone, my soul and I,
> To a hollow cadence down this neutral street . . . (*VIS* IX,
>   lines 36–39)

Faulkner also subverts Eliot's meaning to create a grotesque effect. For example, he gives a literal, concrete, specific meaning to a phrase that Eliot has used abstractly and metaphorically: "And time yet for a hundred indecisions, / And for a hundred visions and revisions . . ." (see lines 4–6). As a result, the voice we hear is absurd rather than ironic or gently self-deprecating. Prufrock has been transformed into a pretentious clown. Or, by using it for antithetical purposes, Faulkner may satirize a particularly lyrical and evocative phrase like, "Is it perfume from a dress / That makes me so digress?" Then, rather than seeming sensitive and whimsical beneath his ironic mask, Faulkner's *pierrotique* voice sounds prissy and pedantic: "Aware of a slight perspiring as to brow, / (The smell of scented cigarettes will always trouble me) . . ." (*VIS* IX, lines 10–11).

In later lines, mocking both his own earlier personas (especially *VIS* I and II) and Prufrock (and anticipating the hapless George Farr), his Pierrot combines Swinburnian breathiness with Prufrockian phrases as he moans:

I grow old, I grow old.
Could I walk within my garden while the night
Comes gently down,
And see the garden maidens dancing, white
And dim, across the flower beds?

I would take cold: I dare not try,
Nor watch the stars again born in the sky
Eternally young.

I grow old, I grow old.
Submerged in the firelight's solemn gold
I sit, watching the restless shadows, red and brown,
Float there till I disturb them, then they drown. (*VIS* IX, lines 88–99)

In mocking Prufrock's fantasy life, Faulkner also mocks one of Pierrot's most obsessive nympholeptic visions, "the garden maidens dancing, white / And dim" of this sequence's first two poems. He also makes fun of Prufrock's solipsism by taking to a logical extreme what remains unstated in Eliot's lines:

I grow old . . . I grow old . . .
I shall wear the bottoms of my trousers rolled.
Shall I part my hair behind? Do I dare to eat a peach?

Faulkner's addition "I would take cold: I dare not try" reveals Prufrock as the quintessential narcissist.

It might be argued that Faulkner's parody is unintentional and that it arises from his incompetence as a poet rather than from any conscious purpose. But his demonstrated metrical skill, not only here in his play upon Eliot but in his earlier poetic imitations and adaptations, suggests otherwise. Furthermore, there are too many instances in "Love Song" where Faulkner skewers Prufrock and Pierrot for the parodic effect to be unintentional. Line 14, where Faulkner employs metaphor to transform both Prufrock and Pierrot into comic-strip characters, is visually and linguistically artful. As Pierrot sits sweating "among toy balloons of dignity on threads of talk," his little balloonlike alliterative phrases are set off so insistently by caesuras that they can only be read as a mimicry of the *pierrotique* voice and approach to life. Finally, in these opening lines, Faulkner mocks his own and Eliot's *pierrotique* voices by making a joke of an image Pierrot had used to describe his lover's face. Thus, "a corridor soft and cool with music" becomes "a corridor of profundities." Pierrot's image of romance has transformed into a mixed metaphor that mirrors Pierrot/Prufrock's jumbled mind. The refrain of "Love

Song," "I should have been a priest in floorless halls," mocks Prufrock's self-parodic allusion to *Hamlet*. It also makes fun of Pierrot's prayerful pose in *Vision*'s title poem, where he rose "from stiffened knees" after a hard night's visions (*VIS* I, p. 5). The line also undermines the sincerity of Pierrot's vision in "Nocturne" (*VIS* III, pp. 15–16), where he had engaged in soul-searching dialogue with the "pilgrim" stars. Throughout "Love Song" Faulkner deflates metaphors used seriously in previous poems to provide a comic commentary on his own poetic language.

Faulkner pokes fun at one of Eliot's favorite devices for closure: the unrhetorical questions in his early dramatic monologues.[17] He can do so because he has understood what Eliot was trying to achieve with these kinds of unanswerable questions. Parody is more than mere comic unmasking. It can also imply admiration and appreciation. Faulkner parodies the deliberate anticlosure of "Prufrock" because he recognizes it, as he does compatible formal and thematic elements in Aiken's and other poets' works, as something he wants to develop even further or in a slightly different way. As Smith points out in her discussion of this effect, "a lingering suspension so typical of modern closure" results in a situation where, "although Prufrock himself has reached no point of stability, the poet has allowed the reader to do so."[18] This same situation is repeated in this poem sequence and in Faulkner's novels.

As an indicator of Faulkner's growth as a writer, the personal parody in "Love Song" is perhaps less important than his parodies of *pierrotique* masks. But it is worth noting, since in *Soldiers' Pay*, *Mosquitoes*, and *The Sound and the Fury* he continues to make fun of his own poetry by inventing as its fictional authors rather less than admirable characters. Furthermore, it touches on two areas that concerned him: his appearance and his ability to write. Unlike Pierrot in "Love Song," "(I am taller than I look)," in photographs Faulkner looked taller than he was. Perhaps this was why during his life he arranged for the portraits in which he is portrayed as tall and physically daring.[19] In fact Faulkner was only 5'5". He and his mother, who was less than five feet tall, contrasted sharply with his father and his brother Jack, who stood over six feet in height. His mother, as if to call more attention to Faulkner's deficiency, made him wear a back brace so that he, like Pierrot in this poem, would stand "carefully erect."[20] As a result, Faulkner's posture was almost a caricature of military correctness. Pierrot's reference to his "oft changed phrase that I revise again / Until I have forgotten what it was at first" probably refers to Faulkner's characteristic method of composition. As we know, Faulkner the poet sometimes drafted as many as nine or ten versions of the same twenty lines.

There is language in "Love Song" that is markedly not like Eliot's. The breathy Swinburnian lines, portentous generalizations ("the word, the thought, the soundless empty gesture" [lines 70–72, 81–82, 84–85]), and banal self-dramatizations in equally banal verse (lines 40–45, 52–54, 57, 58, 84–88, 101–103) combine the worst of both Swinburne and Aiken. Do such lines indicate that Faulkner is unable to sustain his parody for 116 lines and so regresses occasionally to his earlier voices? Or are these lines inserted deliberately for a different kind of parodic effect?

I suggest that the tactic of modulating from passages that sound like Eliot's persona to these much more mawkish and maudlin tones without perceptibly changing the speaker effectively saddles Eliot's mask with a dual sensibility. By giving Eliot's mask the opportunity to speak less circumspectly and formally, Faulkner allows us a look behind the scenes. The huge rhythmic dissimilarities between Faulkner's poem and Eliot's may now be satisfactorily explained. Eliot's iambic Prufrock comes across as veneered, carefully selected, and groomed, readied by himself and his creator for public presentation. In contrast, Faulkner's persona allows himself and is allowed by his creator more self-exposure through his shifting, irregular speech patterns. Hence parodic imitation modulates into exposé beyond the effects of parody. We find out from Faulkner, as we were not able to find out from Eliot, what a dead end in melodramatic preciosity and sentimental self-absorption this lyric mask produces.

In "Prufrock" the young Eliot pretended to give us the lowdown, but didn't really. Faulkner's parody does deliver, and the low turns out to be down indeed. Moreover, it is the seamy Swinburnian underlay of the *pierrotique* mask that now calls forth Faulkner's strongest moral indictment. In "Love Song," Faulkner does not say where he will go from Swinburne, but he does say where he will not go.

Novelistic Implications of "Love Song"

The language of "Love Song" figures significantly in much of Faulkner's fiction but is of particular interest in *Light in August*, where Faulkner uses it to illuminate the nature of both Joe Christmas's tragic quest and Lena Grove's comic one, transforming an originally poetic image into a synecdoche for a major novel's central theme.

This extended image was a hybrid traceable to a triad composed of Eliot, Aiken, and Faulkner. The strongest influence in "Love Song" was Eliot. As Faulkner worked closely with Eliot's language, stripping it of metaphor as a way of parodying it and condensing it to give different meanings or to make his own jokes, he also gained a greater understanding of how metaphor can work. The metaphor that surfaces continually in Faulkner's parody, one of several to which he returns in *Light in August*, characterizes the nature of Prufrock's inner life. It encompasses the deserted streets to which he constantly retreats, the rooms he dares not enter, the windows into which he peers, all of which represent the question he cannot ask. Since the quest theme is traditionally associated with this metaphor ("So I find words I never thought to speak / In streets I never thought I should revisit"), Eliot's use of it as a metaphor for Prufrock's antiquest is all the more powerful as Prufrock is fated to go nowhere. Since Prufrock's fate mirrored to some extent that of Faulkner's Pierrot, it is no wonder Faulkner was attracted to the poem and that he chose to play with this metaphor in his own "Love Song."

The playing proved exceedingly productive, particularly in *Light in August* and *As I Lay Dying*, where images of "the road" and forbidden "rooms" and "windows" dominate the interior and exterior landscape. In *Light in August* the metaphor achieves both a comic and a tragic effect as it weaves formal and thematic relationships between Lena Grove and Joe Christmas, two characters who never meet. Both Lena and Joe literally travel many roads. Joe's journey lasts thirty-three years while Lena's lasts only a few months. Joe's ends in death, Lena's in giving birth and in courtship. Lena's comic quest provides the novel's frame, beginning: "although I have not been quite a month on the road I am already in Mississippi" (*LIA*, p. 1) and concluding: "'Here we aint been coming from Alabama but two months, and now it's already Tennessee'" (*LIA*, p. 480). The story of a "young, strapping," unwed country girl crawling in and out of windows in quest of love and then riding the southern roads in search of her baby's shiftless father provides a way into and out of Joe's tragic journey.

Faulkner's use of the road/house metaphor as a thematic motif in *Light in August* is very different from but reminiscent of Eliot's use of it in "Prufrock." Faulkner extends the metaphor to portray Joe's twisted, tortured, and self-torturing behavior, transferring devices normally associated with poetry into prose fiction. Especially important are accretion of imagery through repetition and variation of specific phrases, assonance, alliteration, and metrical regularity. (Anyone who has heard recordings of Faulkner reading his fiction will note that he stresses this regularity.) Roads, corridors, doors, and windows control Joe's thoughts and actions. A "quiet empty corridor" literally leads Joe to loss of innocence as he wanders down it through a "door" into the orphanage dietician's room. There, "sweating" and "watching himself," like the self-conscious narrator of "Love Song," Joe watches the dietician and her lover have intercourse (*LIA*, pp. 111–114). That "corridor, quiet and empty," and other doors and windows appear and reappear throughout chapter 7, just as images of streets and roads echo throughout chapter 10 and on through chapter 19, where Joe is castrated and killed. Joe's quest leads through "a thousand savage and lonely streets. They run from that night when he lay and heard the final footfall and then the final door . . ." (*LIA*, p. 207).

Joe Christmas, like Prufrock and Pierrot, is looking for himself. But each time he walks through a door or looks through a window and thinks he has found a love in which he can participate rather than just observe, he destroys and allows himself to be destroyed by it. Joe's tragedy is, in part, that he, like Prufrock and Pierrot, cannot love.[21] And so although he drinks himself into senselessness, or beats his lovers mercilessly, or kills them to try to eradicate his own fear and pain, his streets, like those of his predecessors, run on and on (*LIA*, pp. 210, 211):

> He thought that it was loneliness which he was trying to escape and not himself. But the street ran on: catlike, one place was the same as another to him. But in none of them could he be quiet. But the street ran on in its moods and phases, always empty: he might have seen himself as in numberless avatars, in silence, doomed with motion, driven by the courage of flagged and spurred despair; by the despair of courage whose opportunities had to be flagged and spurred. (*LIA*, p. 213)

In making streets a metaphor for the "image stream" of Joe's mind and by evoking Eliot's sense of emptiness and doom through phrasal variants like those concluding the final sentence above, Faulkner utilizes what he learned eleven years earlier in parodying Eliot:

> He did not know that he had even wondered or tasted until his jaw stopped suddenly in midchewing and thinking fled for twentyfive years back down the street, past all the imperceptible corners of bitter defeats and more bitter victories, and five miles even beyond a corner where he used to wait in the terrible early time of love, for someone whose name he had forgot; five miles even beyond that it went *I'll*

know it in a minute. I have eaten it before, somewhere. In a minute I
will memory clicking knowing I see I see I more than see hear I hear
I see my head bent I hear the monotonous dogmatic voice which I
believe will never cease. . . . (LIA, p. 217)

The stylist here could be no one but Faulkner, but Joe's thoughts, his forbidden rooms and beckoning streets, the strange and wonderful intersections of language and tone and rhythm begin in Faulkner's parody of "The Love Song of J. Alfred Prufrock."

Roads, rooms, windows, and doors also permeate the metaphorical and literal atmosphere of Lena Grove's amorous escapades and subsequent journey. Lena's story, its ludicrous parallels to Joe's heightened through this controlling metaphor, serves as emotional counterpoint, presenting the tragic as humorous. Her alternative way of life holds out both the possibility and the moral validity of another, less deterministic perception of reality. The humor with which Faulkner surrounds and encloses Lena Grove and *Light in August* is infinitely more sophisticated than his 1921 parody of Prufrock/Pierrot. But the presence of the metaphor in this novel and others suggests that, for Faulkner, it was one of many in *Vision in Spring* that continued to serve as vast storehouses of emotional and imaginative power.

Like Pierrot and Joe Christmas, Lena Grove quests for love by going in and out of parts of houses. But in contrast to her progenitor Pierrot—"The window of my mind flies shut"—Lena has no qualms about daring to open doors and windows leading to her sexual and emotional growth. Nor, once she opens them and slips through, does she ever look back to blame or regret. Like Joe, she too is an impoverished orphan. But, unlike Joe, she's at peace with her history. She lives with her grown brother and his family where she, like Joe at the MacEachern's, is an unpaid servant:

> She slept in a leanto room at the back of the house. It had a window
> which she learned to open and close again in the dark without mak-
> ing a sound, . . . She had lived there eight years before she opened the
> window for the first time. She had not opened it a dozen times hardly
> before she discovered that she should not have opened it at all. She
> said to herself, 'That's just my luck.' (*LIA*, p. 3)

In reversing the line from "Love Song"—"the window of my mind flies shut"—to portray Lena's first recorded action, Faulkner captures that quality in her that makes her the reverse and comic counterpart of Joe Christmas. For Joe's attitude toward sex and women is life denying, onanistic, sadistic, and prurient. He is, in short, Pierrot/Prufrock taken to an extreme.

Lena makes a joke of a potentially serious situation, indicating that she can master her circumstances. Unlike Joe, she does not consider sexuality an unmitigated disaster. Faulkner plays up the dichotomy between Joe's and Lena's attitudes about sex and self by encompassing both characters within similar metaphorical structures.

The meaning of this metaphor is revealed in the furniture dealer's account of his experience with Lena, who, with new baby and faithful suitor in tow, had hitched a ride in the back of the dealer's truck. On his return home to his own marriage bed where he and his wife have just made love and are now resting, talking, and joking, the dealer begins to describe Byron's feverish attempts to make love with Lena. He says,

> " . . . he was desperated up to something. But even then I didn't know what it was."
>
> *What was it?* the wife says
> *I just showed you once. You aint ready to be showed again, are you?*
> *I reckon I dont mind if you dont.* (*LIA*, p. 472)

The furniture dealer and his wife enjoy being in bed together, and because they do, they accept and take pleasure in Lena and Byron's courtship. The dealer goes on to tell his wife about Byron's last-ditch effort to make Lena let him come where she and the baby are spending the night. His account is bursting with metaphorical echoes from Joe's tortured and torturing affairs with Bobbie and Joanna Burden, echoes themselves that can be traced to "Love Song" and "Prufrock":

> I heard him come up, quiet as a cat, and stand over me, looking down at me, listening. . . .
>
> I just watched him climb slow and easy into the truck and disappear. . . . (*LIA*, pp. 476–477)

This description of Byron mirrors an earlier, threatening scene where Joe stands over Lucas Burch/Joe Brown, deciding whether to murder him:

> He stood in the darkness above the prone body, with Brown's breath alternately hot and cold on his fingers, thinking quietly *Something is going to happen to me. I am going to do something* . . . But he did not do it. Perhaps thinking . . . *This is not the right one* Anyway he did not reach for the razor. (*LIA*, p. 97)

The way Faulkner joins and juxtaposes these two scenes in his fiction shows him making use of a structural and metaphoric technique he learned from writing poem sequences. The language that weaves the two scenes together is one of repetition and amplification, with polyphony supplied by the reversal of intent. That is, although both Byron and Joe are "catlike" (*LIA*, p. 216), Byron is bent on love while Joe is bent on death. Faulkner's purpose in both poetry and prose is the same: to create through polyphony a sustained but elliptical narrative.

Lena refuses Byron that night but he persists, and the next day she does let him in "the back door of the truck." In talking about Lena, the furniture dealer's language echoes the language of Joe's empty and destructive quest, but his humorous perception of Lena's quest transforms its meaning:

> . . . do you know what I think? I think she was just traveling. I dont think she had any idea of finding whoever it was she was following. I dont think she had ever aimed to, only she hadn't told him yet. . . . I think she had just made up her mind to travel a little further and see as much as she could, since I reckon she knew that when she settled down this time, it would likely be for the rest of her life. (*LIA*, p. 480)[22]

Lena's quest succeeds, and Joe's fails tragically, because Joe remains committed to a dream he refuses to interpret while Lena becomes an increasingly accomplished joker. It has been noted that dreams are a passive means of avoiding "unpleasure" while jokes are an active and creative technique for conquering pain by transforming it to pleasure. Although both dreaming and joking are ways of coping with psychic distress or anxiety, they remain vastly "dissimilar mental functions" that occur in "quite different regions of mental life . . . A dream still remains a wish, even though one that has been made unrecognizable; a joke is developed play." While dreaming is a solitary activity, joking requires the presence and participation of other people: "a dream is a completely asocial mental product; it has nothing to communicate to anyone else; . . . A joke, on the other hand, is the most social of all mental functions that aims at a yield of pleasure."[23] One would be hard put to deny that Pierrot and Joe Christmas, locked into their wishes or dreams, are asocial creatures who have serious difficulty communicating. In contrast, Lena Grove aims from the beginning to the end of her journey in *Light in August* for the greatest possible pleasure and communication.

Parody performs another function in spurring Faulkner's creativity: it is a means of comic unmasking directed primarily against "people and objects which lay claim to authority and respect." By turning from a more passive to an active and aggressive form of creative expression, Faulkner reveals the poverty and emotional bankruptcy of a mask like Prufrock or Pierrot. "The discovery that one has it in one's power to make someone else comic opens the way to an un-dreamt-of yield of comic pleasure and is the origin of a highly developed technique."[24] Freud's pun here vividly illustrates his point.

"Love Song" is the first poem in *Vision* that is not a dream. Rather it is dream's opposite, a joke on *Vision*'s dreamer. Unmasking his own persona gave Faulkner access to new, more imaginatively productive ways of thinking about men, women, and sex. Having ridiculed his poet's mask and transformed his dreams or visions into a joke, he could then explore imaginative material that was previously forbidden. It is difficult to laugh about something threatening unless you understand why you feel threatened. Faulkner could not have dared to imagine either Lena or Joe until he understood and dropped his *pierrotique* mask. The next poems in *Vision* illustrate what happened after Faulkner took his first step toward unmasking.

"The Dancer" and "Marriage": Pierrot Confronts the Enemy

Until this point in *Vision in Spring* Pierrot talks only to the voices in his visions, extensions of himself. "The Dancer" and "Marriage," the poems that follow "Love Song," enlarge Pierrot's voices. Here Faulkner uses methods more commonly associated with fiction than with poetry: dramatic dialogue between two different characters and a counterpoint of two interior monologues interspersed with exterior dialogue. He can now look more honestly and objectively at the sources of Pierrot's malaise and bring his mask face to face with the fantasies whose meanings were obscured by the protective screen of his dreams. Thus these next two poems manifest Pierrot's great fear: that pursuit of women and artistic excellence, or "silent music," will end in failure, impotence, and even death. In "The Dancer" and "Marriage" Faulkner clarifies his perception of the vital connections between imaginative vision, "silent music," real music, and adult sexuality.

To strengthen the formal structure of his sequence, Faulkner includes two poems rather than one so that Pierrot can speak in the voice of both *Vision*'s first and second movements. For once these voices state their problem clearly. Faulkner resorts to his by now familiar technique of borrowing the form and language of another poet's poem for his own intentions as he costumes "The Dancer" as Conrad Aiken's "Dancing Adairs."[25] Similarities between the two poems—both dramatic dialogues—are so pronounced that it is easy to miss the striking differences between Aiken's loving couple and Faulkner's warring one (Figure 13). In both poems the dancer is an elusive figure who "haunts" Pierrot. But in Aiken's poem Dancing Adairs pursues the dancer: "I follow you as remorselessly as darkness." His intent is to embrace and merge with her; his feelings of anticipation are joyful: "I surround and love you . . . take you into my heart's great void of silence." Adairs welcomes the dancer, for she banishes empty silence and fills him with love.

In contrast, Faulkner's Pierrot resists the dancer. She is a familiar Lamia figure "so swift, so white and slim, / Who haunts you, tempts you," a Colombine who says "I will hurt you . . . [because] I have mazed your life against your will." He resists in vain: the dancer succeeds in entering him (final strophe). Her forced entry, almost a rape, instead of filling Pierrot's silence, creates a mute and heavy pall reminiscent of Pierrot's experience in "Nocturne" (VIS III): she replaces Pierrot's "silent music" with real silence. "And your heart, like lips where my clear lips were laid, / Parts, and silence lays its hand on them" (VIS X, p. 66).[26]

Besides borrowing from Aiken's plot, structure, and characters, Faulkner also adapts Aiken's metaphors, but for quite different purposes. For example, Aiken's Adairs calls his dancer "Firefly" and says, "You are flame"; Faulkner's flame image describes only his imaginative representation of her, a representation that bears little resemblance to its real counterpart. In answer to the dancer's claim that she is Youth, Faulkner's Pierrot says:

You are Youth? Yet you cannot appease
This flame that, like a music from your hair,
Sheds through me as though I were but air;
That strips me bare, my sudden life reveals. (VIS X, p. 65)

Pierrot, like Januarius Jones, is attracted to his image of the dancer, not her reality, which repels and threatens him, for it reveals his emptiness. He also loves the image because it is his own creation or impression and as such is more compelling than reality. The real dancer cannot, like her image the flame, appease Pierrot's intense desire for "a chaste Platonic" nympholeptic vision (see pp. 156–157).

Aiken's version:

XV. DANCING ADAIRS

Behold me, in my chiffon, gauze, and tinsel,
Flitting out of the shadow into the spotlight,
And into the shadow again, without a whisper!—
Firefly's my name. I am evanescent.

Firefly's your name. You are evanescent.
But I follow you as remorselessly as darkness,
And shut you in and enclose you, at last, and always,
Till you are lost,—as a voice is lost in silence.

Till I am lost, as a voice is lost in silence. . . .
Are you the one who would close so cool about me?
My fire sheds into and through you and beyond you:
How can your fingers hold me? I am elusive.

How can my fingers hold you? You are elusive?
Yes, you are flame; but I surround and love you,
Always extend beyond you, cool, eternal,
To take you into my heart's great void of silence.

You shut me into your heart's great void of silence. . . .
O sweet and soothing end for a life of whirling!
Now I am still, whose life was mazed with motion.
Now I sink into you, for love of sleep.

Until this point in *Vision in Spring* the meaning of Pierrot's recurrent visions of dancers has been ambiguous. Although he seemed to welcome the visions, they have not given him much pleasure, particularly in the sequence's first and third poems. In the second and seventh poems, his vision of dancers led Pierrot in circles and trapped him within "empty streets and walls" (*VIS* II, p. 6). In the fourth strophe of "The Dancer," as Faulkner moves both the poem and his sequence toward resolution, Pierrot suggests for the first time that even his mind's image of the dancer fails to stir him. He also suggests why: "That you have flown like music, and my mind / Like water, wrinkles back where your face mirrored was" (*VIS* X, p. 66). Imitative and ephemeral, this mirror vision has, unlike true art, no immortality.

Faulkner's version:

X. THE DANCER

I am Youth, so swift, so white and slim,
Who haunts you, tempts you, bids you fly
Across this floor of polished porphyry,
To raise your arms, to try and clasp my knees.

You are Youth? Yet you cannot appease
This flame that, like a music from your hair,
Sheds through me as though I were but air;
That strips me bare, my sudden life reveals.

Yes, I will hurt you, as my tiny heels
—That you could cup in your two hands, and still—
Have mazed your life against your will
With restless little flames, like mercury, like [gold?]

You have mazed my life with swiftness, for I hold
The phantom that I thought was you, and find
That you have flown like music, and my mind
Like water, wrinkles back where your face mirrored was.

I am Youth. White sprays of stars
Crowned me, shattering fell, while my slight music played;
And your heart, like lips where my clear lips were laid,
Parts, and silence lays its hand on them.

FIGURE 13. Aiken's poem "Dancing Adairs" from *Turns and Movies* and Faulkner's poem "The Dancer" from *Vision in Spring*. Themes and phrasing Faulkner borrowed and reworked are underlined in both poems. Bracketed word in line 12 is erased in the photocopy of *Vision in Spring*. Inserted substitute appears in another version of "The Dancer."

Speaking last, as she does to conclude Aiken's poem on a very different note, the dancer further articulates the meaning of Pierrot's recurrent vision. A mirrored image of a woman dancing to music provokes a vision that can only repeat the past. It is retrospective, not innovative. In contrast to old memories, the real woman imprisons, rapes, and forces the poet's voices of vision—imitative, ephemeral, and reflexive though they are—into a deadly silence: "silence lays its hand." The threat of sexual union endangers the very existence of the poet's imagination.

Pierrot's "Silent Music" Wars with Temptation's Real Music

Faulkner composed "The Dancer" as a simple counterpoint dialogue. The structure of *Vision*'s next poem, untitled in this sequence but referred to here as "Marriage," its title in a later draft, is more complex.[27] Faulkner orchestrates two counterpointed interior monologues, connecting narrative, and several lines of direct address as he probes further into the meaning of "silent music." The poem's structure, thematic content, and the relation of both to the sequence as a whole and to Faulkner's fiction provide more information about how *Vision in Spring* aided Faulkner in his quest for a voice of his own. The role of "Marriage" in Faulkner's imaginative life extends well beyond this sequence, as he returns to it when writing *Flags in the Dust* and *Light in August.*

Faulkner later published "Marriage" in his 1933 collection *A Green Bough.* Cleanth Brooks considers it one of the young poet's best efforts. His comments are helpful in pointing to some of the poem's strengths but they also exemplify the kind of misreading that occurs when Faulkner's poems are analyzed out of the context of his life and work.[28] Faulkner borrowed the poem's dramatic elements as well as several key lines from poems in two of Aiken's symphonies, *Turns and Movies* and *Earth Triumphant, Part II.* (The latter was published in the edition of *Turns and Movies* that Faulkner reviewed.) As Brooks says, "Marriage" is indeed well conceptualized; but it is so in part through a complex interweaving of its themes. One important aspect of the poem that is overlooked in his reading is its counterpoint theme:

> . . . music played by the woman stirs in the man an emotion that finally becomes an overwhelming desire to possess her. . . . At the end, the woman has risen from her piano and begins to mount the stair. She stops at the turning of the stair, "and trembles there, / Nor watches him as he steadily mounts the stair."

In an earlier version the concluding lines read: "At the turn she stops, and shivers there, / And hates him as he steadily mounts the stair." The man in the poem is not depicted as an unfeeling brute. The poem has aimed at and succeeds in rendering with psychological realism some of the tensions of married life. Such an interpretation is rather confirmed by the fact that in the earlier version the poem is entitled "Marriage."[29]

In "Marriage's" opening lines the poet states clearly that the woman is *not* playing the piano. Thus the speaker's sexual fantasies emphatically do *not* arise from hearing the woman's music. Before the woman begins to play, Pierrot already has an overwhelming sense that her "music" will somehow damage him. His fear of her competes with his desire for her—a desire arising from his own "silent music"—and, as the poem reveals, the resulting tension drives him mad. The woman's music is not really her piano playing, to which Pierrot is deaf, but her sexuality to which he is exquisitely attuned. The poem's title is dispensable. In fact, Faulkner included it untitled in both *Vision in Spring* and *A Green Bough*. The critic's belief that Faulkner's poetry for the most part lacks "controlling metaphor and concentrated symbolism" may explain why he misinterprets the symbolism of the woman's piano playing and disregards the multiple meanings of music in this poem.[30] Much of the poem's power is lost when it is read out of its original context: the metaphoric structure of "Marriage" is derived from and linked to the poems that precede and follow it in *Vision in Spring*. Such formal similarities between Faulkner's poem (and poem sequence) and his fiction illustrate ways in which Faulkner's poetry evolved into prose.

When "Marriage" is read in the context of *Vision in Spring*, Pierrot's violent reaction to the woman in this poem becomes more understandable. For "Marriage" articulates fully the connections between vision, music, and sexuality that Faulkner has been driving toward throughout this sequence. These concern what kind of music really stirs Pierrot's senses and how his visions are affected by the disturbance. By contrasting Pierrot's and the woman musician's reactions to real music Faulkner illuminates the emotional distance separating his two characters.

An alternative reading can clarify what actually happens in this poem. Most important to note are (1) when and why the woman begins to play her piano and (2) real music's effect on the poem's characters. In the opening strophes Pierrot experiences only "silent music," his own imaginative constructions triggered by visual images of the rhythmical patterns of firelight playing over the woman. In the first three of "Marriage's" seven strophes Pierrot, sitting in a room, watches a woman at her piano:

> Laxly reclining, he sees her sitting there
> With the firelight like a hand laid on her hair,
> With the firelight like a hand upon the keys
> Playing a music of lustrous muted gold.
> *Bathed in gold she sits, upon her knees*
> *Her languid hands, palm upward, lie at ease,*
> *Filling with gold at each flame's spurting rise,*
> *Spilling gold as each flame sinks and dies . . .*
> (*VIS* XI, p. 67, emphasis added)

His unarticulated response to an image—the motion of the firelight playing upon her and the piano keys "in cumulate waves"—is what drives him mad: "Until his brain, stretched and tautened, suddenly cracks." This is "silent music," which Pierrot describes as "muted gold." As usual, Pierrot responds to rhythm and sight, *not* heard melody. Borrowing from Aiken to dispel this disturbing vision, the poet commands the woman to play some *real* music: "Play something else" (*VIS* XI, p. 69).[31] Still his brain continues to "fragment." Again he says,

> Play something else.
> > He tries to keep his tone
> Lightly natural, watching the shadows thrown,
> Watching the timid shadows near her throat
> Link like hands about her from the dark.
> His eyes like hurried fingers fumble and fly
> About the narrow bands with which her dress is caught
> And lightly trace the line of back and thigh.
> He sees his brain disintegrate, spark by spark.
>
> Play something else, he says.
> (*VIS* XI, pp. 69–70)

The woman's real music fails to banish Pierrot's disturbing fantasy, for he has been "snared" in the sensuous rhythms of his waking dream. But this snaring is unlike any that has occurred before, because in "Marriage" Pierrot has begun to interpret his dreams. They are no longer disguised as disturbing "dancers dancing to an ancient music" or as the senselessly cruel Colombine flinging a severed hand at Pierrot's feet. Undisguised, unmasked, these dreams reveal previously obscured aspects of Pierrot's wishes. In "Marriage," as he plays "silent music," he imagines undressing and ravishing the woman. Concurrently he sees and feels his brain disintegrate (*VIS*

XI, p. 69). It is now clear that Pierrot believes that sexual activity, masked or unmasked, will destroy his imagination—his brain. He tries to banish his terrifying vision by closing his eyes, but fails: his mind-rape continues to the rhythmical but not melodic accompaniment of "silent music" (*VIS* XI, p. 70).

In contrast, the woman's vision, in the fourth and fifth strophes, derives from the melodic quality of the music she is now actually playing at the man's command. Furthermore, her vision's sources are her memories. The sources of Pierrot's visions are tactile (the "palpable gloom"), visible (the firelight), or olfactory (a bowl of lilacs), but hers are only aural. The woman's real music makes her remember an old and disappointing love affair: "a certain spring . . . a shattered spring that, softly playing, / She sought to build into a whole again. / . . . She saw again ["sought" in *A Green Bough*], with pain dark eyes, a face . . ." (pp. 72, 73). Her vision here is a mere memory, like Pierrot's spring vision in the sequence's title poem (stirred there, like hers, by real music: the bells). In remembering, she looks to a rejecting lover and to time for solace and fulfillment: "to build into a whole again." Like Pierrot in earlier poems she only wants a lover she cannot have. She fails to use her memory imaginatively, and thus quests in vain. Yet, unlike Pierrot, who hears "silent music," she does not risk death.

In creating this kind of woman and contrasting her in this way to Pierrot, Faulkner has begun the process of transferring his *pierrotique* mask to a character that is clearly not himself. In creating a more honest and direct voice for Pierrot, he has begun the equally necessary process of finding out what happens when he allows his most troubling fantasies an artistic rather than a dream shape.

In the sixth strophe of "Marriage," Faulkner moves back into Pierrot's fantasy as "Laxly reclining, he feels the firelight beating / A clamor of endless waves against the dark" (*VIS* XI, pp. 73–74). Like the sea's swell, Pierrot's fantasy is rhythmic and repetitive; it proceeds outside of chronological time. Once more he sees "his brain disintegrate" as he visualizes touching the woman and continues to undress her.

In the seventh and final strophe, Pierrot transmutes his fantasy to action for the first time in *Vision in Spring*. But, in a dramatic reversal borrowed from the last lines of another Aiken poem (in *Turns and Movies*),

He stands and watches her mount the stair
Step by step, with her subtle suppleness,

This nervous strength that was ever his surprise;
The lifted throat the thin crisp swirl of dress
Like a ripple of naked muscles before his eyes.
A bursting moon: wheels spin in his brain,
Shrieking against sharp walls of sanity,
And whirl in a vortex of sparks together again.
At the turn she stops, and shivers there,
And hates him as he steadily mounts the stair. (*VIS* XI, pp. 74–75)[32]

Despite the fairly numerous end rhymes, insistent meter, and closing couplet, these lines, like the rest of the poem, can easily be read
as prose. Faulkner contains his dramatic narrative in a superfluous
casing of verse conventions that distracts and hinders rather than en-
courages the flow of the meaning. The novelist's voice is trying to
escape from earlier well-loved poetic conventions and visions that
seem here like the remnants of Pierrot's old masks.[33]

Although Pierrot may fail to realize his fantasy (the woman hates
him) he does convey to us that for him real music is irrevocably
linked to women and sex. This is why he cannot hear it. He also
clarifies the meaning of silent music. It is the music of the intensely
private vision Pierrot experiences (the rhythms of the firelight, of
the woman's movements) as he watches the woman engaged in her
real music, or just sitting, or, in other poems, dancing. In short, his
experience is imagined only.

Concluding the Third Movement: "Orpheus," Return and Ramification

Walter Jackson Bate emphasizes that the progress of Keats's genius
was not strictly linear: "Keats's development naturally circles and
eddies. He constantly goes back, even in his short life, to premises
and values, or to the challenges or impressions, of a year before—or
two or three years before—and then reconsiders, ramifies, and begins
again, as indeed we all do, though often in a slower progression."[34]

"Orpheus," the poem that ends the third movement of *Vision in
Spring*, is an instance of just such a moment of circling and eddying.[35] The structure of "Orpheus," so similar to the two poems preceding it, hints that its function in the sequence as a whole will resemble that of "The Dancer" and "Marriage." Like them it appears
to be a dramatic dialogue between two lovers. But "Orpheus," rather
than extending and elaborating on the two previous poems, returns
instead to the stance Pierrot held before "Love Song." Instead of

another dialogue with a real woman, Pierrot (now calling himself Orpheus, the ideal poet) holds a dialogue with a vision or dream of Eurydice. The poem occurs after Orpheus has lost Eurydice to the Underworld. Once more Orpheus/Pierrot steeps himself in his lonely, isolated world of vision and dream, where his "dialogue" with his lover turns out to be a dialogue with himself. The thwarted, mirroring quality of such a dialogue manifests itself in the poem's language and content (Eurydice's few lines mimic Orpheus's). Even the analogy drawn between Pierrot and the mythical poet fails to override this sense of stasis and failure, and it is thoroughly undermined by Orpheus/Pierrot's song. Thus on two counts—its form and the myth it invokes—"Orpheus" is not what it at first appears to be: a dramatic dialogue between two distinct characters or a free and fearless Orphic cry. Rather, it is Pierrot's ultimate nympholeptic fantasy and, as such, it is a summarizing vision or re-vision of Pierrot's primary thematic concerns in this sequence: Can he love anything but idealized mirrors of himself and, concomitantly, can he know who he is?

Recalling the language, setting, time frame, and formal organization of the sequence's opening poem, the impersonal narrator once more introduces us to *Vision*'s persona:

> Here he stands, while eternal evening falls
> And it is like a dream between grey walls
> Dimly falling, dimly falling
> Between two walls of shrunken topless stone,
> Between two walls with silence on them grown.
> Here he stands, in a litter of leaves upon the floor;
> In a solemn silver of scattered springs,
> Among the smooth green buds before the door
> He stands and sings. (*VIS* XII, p. 76)

Pierrot's key words are all here: evening, dream, grey walls, silence, spring, and the door to love that he can never, it seems, permit himself to penetrate. Faulkner returns to these images to conclude "Orpheus" in order to make the shape of Orpheus's song imitate the encircling wall the dreamer has built for himself with his visions.

Orpheus's only action has been to deprive himself of the possibility of love by *looking* at Eurydice. Both what Orpheus says about love and what he imagines Eurydice to answer are closely related to his concern about who he is; seven of his song's nine short strophes contain the phrase "I am." Besides recalling Pierrot's question in *Vision*'s first movement ("Who am I?"), Orpheus's answers echo Pierrot's nonanswers in the beginning of *Vision*. But they also show that Orpheus defines himself and Eurydice in terms of his dreams about their lost love. Because this definition derives from a dream, and a "shattered" one at that, it is tenuous and unconvincing. The more Orpheus piles up his series of *I am*s, striving harder and harder toward definition, the more fragile his dream appears. Images of fragmentation and disassociation accumulate: Orpheus describes his body as pieces of unconnected matter like Pierrot's images of himself in *Vision*'s third poem, "Nocturne" (*VIS* III, pp. 10–29). Reviving other images from that poem, from "Love Song," and from "The Dancer" and "Marriage," Orpheus/Pierrot portrays the scene of his dream: a twilight "severed with waters always falling" (p. 76), spring herself "sowing silver seeds of pain in frozen places" (p. 77) and across "wrinkled streams" (p. 78).

For Orpheus, as for Pierrot in "Nocturne," this dream terrain reflects his preoccupation with looking and watching rather than with acting:

> I am he who, ringed about with faces,
> Stared on a spectral darkness stiff with eyes.
> . . . .
> I am the brain that, lying on the ground,
> Flowered in tenebrous wisps upon the dark.
> . . . .
> I am the hands in which this gold was caught;
> . . . .
> I am he who, sleepless, staring down,
> Saw shadows crossing marbled walls of sound:
> A sea in which I sink, yet cannot drown. (*VIS* XII, pp. 78, 79, 80, 81)

Only ghosts stir this fragmented insomniac from the passive state he has assumed since the moment he banished Eurydice.

> And I, raised by shadow hands,
> Go softly where together we walked and dreamed
> To a music on our joined flesh calmly played. (*VIS* XII, p. 79)

Apparently Orpheus/Pierrot has no trouble fantasizing about joined flesh as long as the actuality remains an impossibility. Since Orpheus defines himself as an actor in a dream whose only movement in the poem is into more dreams, and since his answers to Pierrot's "Who am I?" all echo Pierrot's earlier nonanswers to the same question, he blocks the progress of the sequence, showing why the poet must abandon this kind of persona in order to have *Vision in Spring* reach a resolution.

What is the function, then, of "Orpheus" in this sequence? Is it merely a series of formal and thematic repetitions of earlier sections of the sequence? "Orpheus" is an instance of circling and eddying, but it is also a poem in which Faulkner appears to be retreating, shoring up, perhaps almost fumbling as he prepares for the last great imaginative leap he will make in *Vision in Spring*—his daring introduction, in its concluding movement, of an *unreliable* impersonal narrator. In "Orpheus," having reconsidered and ramified the voices of his Pierrot persona and once more found them wanting, he can, in concluding the sequence, take his next step toward "authentic and fluent speech."

CHAPTER XI

The Novelist's Voice:
Closure in *Vision in Spring*

In *Vision in Spring*'s two concluding poems, "Philosophy" (*VIS* XIII) and "April" (*VIS* XIV), the impersonal narrator, who so far has played a minor role, appears to take command.[1] Pierrot's disappearance, the narrator's sudden assumption of Pierrot's position, and the subjects of these poems indicate that Pierrot has chosen to die rather than to continue to pursue and come to terms with the meaning of his visions in spring. (Under similar circumstances, two of Pierrot's fictional successors, Bayard Sartoris and Quentin Compson, also kill themselves.)

The final poems in *Vision* comment on Pierrot's choice; they represent the narrator's "philosophy" or point of view. But because this narrator is not omniscient, he does not finally control the meaning of *Vision in Spring*. Thus he presages the functions of a series of final speakers in Faulkner's novels. *Vision*'s concluding voice prefigures Miss Jenny philosophizing at Bayard's grave, Benjy riding to the Compson graveyard, and Gavin Stevens and the furniture dealer explaining Joe Christmas and Lena Grove. None of these final speakers control the meaning of their novels. That knowledge and that control first belong in *Vision in Spring* (as it previously did not in either *The Marble Faun*, *The Lilacs*, or *The Marionettes*) to William Faulkner, who now makes us, his readers, reach our own conclusions. In *Vision in Spring*, by gradually removing himself as a character in his poetic drama and substituting an impersonal, unreliable narrator, Faulkner succeeds in freeing himself to act as an effective writer.

The voice shift in *Vision*'s final movement, though very noticeable, has been prepared for by the three preceding movements. In *Vision*'s first and second parts, Pierrot's dreams or visions chained him to passivity and impotence; in short, they mastered him. In the third movement Pierrot achieved momentary mastery of his visions by parodying them. Parody proved to Pierrot that he could use his imagination to transform fearful visions into funny ones. His success in turning his dreams into jokes signaled his first imaginatively active step. In the poems following "Love Song," Pierrot introduced new fictional structures to tease out the meanings of his dreams. But when he began to explore the meanings his parody had unmasked, his mastery slipped from his grasp. Such slippage showed that as long as the Pierrot mask was the dominant voice of *Vision in Spring*, his creator, Faulkner, could not effectively structure his own imaginative material. To overcome this difficulty, Faulkner replaces Pierrot with an impersonal yet unreliable narrator in *Vision*'s final movement and at last claims ultimate control of his art. This may seem paradoxical: that by gradually removing himself as a character in his fictional drama he becomes its most active participant. Freud points out that "as the child passes over from the passivity of the [unpleasant] experience to the activity of the game, he hands on the disagreeable experience to one of his playmates and in this way revenges himself on a substitute."[2]

By extension of that analogy, the author (player) achieves greatest mastery when he no longer plays roles in his drama, even in disguise. He has moved from participant and then participant-observer to become the originator as well as director of his drama. By absenting himself from his art Faulkner had learned, as he said a successful writer must, "that to be a writer, one has first got to be what he is, what he was born. . . . you had only to remember what you were."[3] Faulkner illustrated his complete sense of ownership and control when, on the map of Yoknapatawpha county he drew for *Absalom, Absalom!*, he wrote, "William Faulkner, / Sole Owner & Proprietor." How much this is his sole right and how jealously he guards it are shown by the device he uses so often of having his fictional narrators make concluding statements based on their possessing only a fraction of the information (some of it blatantly false) that both we and other voices in the novel are privy to. The device appears so often as to beg us to attend to the moral implications of this kind of closure. Kinney notes that at the conclusion of a Faulkner novel

> the final focus is never on source as it is never on fact, but is rather on the perception of fact or the alternative ways of seeing facts. This is where truth finally lies for Faulkner, in fiction as in life, and it must be made sufficiently available within his novel so as to be embodied as perceptions not only in the characters but in us, his readers, as well.[4]

The conclusion of *Vision in Spring* anticipates similar narrative feats Faulkner performs on a much larger and more complex scale in *Flags in the Dust, The Sound and the Fury, Light in August, Sanctuary*, and *Absalom, Absalom!*

By renouncing his Pierrot mask and by substituting one or more fallible narrators in his stead, Faulkner gives up the notion that a single human being, real or imagined, can ever know the whole truth. In making the concluding character's voice often the least knowledgeable of all, Faulkner underscores the importance of this point. Furthermore, in doing so, he questions the necessity, relevance, even the goodness or ethical rightness of an absolute definition of truth in life or art and by extension of people who insist on such a definition. Rather, he suggests that what is most valuable is being able to *listen* to the many different versions of truth his imaginative voices have spoken, and then interpret for ourselves their meaning.

As his choice and handling of voice and structure in *Vision in Spring* prefigure the novels, so does the language and content of its final movement. Put simplistically, both *Flags in the Dust* and *The Sound and the Fury* end in or on the way to graveyards. In both novels the ceremonial act of visiting the dead symbolizes a character's vain attempt—Miss Jenny's in *Flags* and Benjy's in *The Sound and the Fury*—to insist in the face of overwhelming evidence to the contrary on some kind of order and rationale for living. The irony of both characters' acts, an irony alluded to in *Vision*'s final movement and elaborated on in these novels, is that such order is not intrinsic. It is man-made and operates when imposed through formalized ceremonies, like mourning. Such attempts at imposing order are external; mere rubber stamps on irrational acts like Bayard's or Quentin's suicides, which the survivors could not order, comprehend, or prevent. The surface quality of this order and its uselessness as a means for interpreting the past are symbolized in *Vision*'s concluding poems: by the pat "Philosophy" of the impersonal narrator and by his description in "April" of a conventional pastoral scene. Formal closure, a return to the landscape of the sequence's opening scene, is thus pasted on to what appears to be a thematically open-ended sequence that seems to have been moving on a treadmill: vision in spring has proceeded no further than "April."

Because the most striking formal element in this final movement is Faulkner's shift from Pierrot's voice to that of the impersonal narrator, the different vocal qualities must be noted. The narrator speaks only in the present tense. The past does not interest him. He commands attention by his highly rhetorical mode of address: a series of negative factual statements. The poem's opening lines set its breathy, meretricious tone:

There is no shortening breasted nymph to shake
The thickets that stem up the lidless blaze
Of sunlight stiffening the shadowed ways,
Nor does the haunted silence ever wake
　　Nor ever stir.

No footfall trembles in the smoky brush . . . (*VIS* XIII, p. 83)

In thirty lines, the word "no" or its equivalent appears seven times. Other semantically negative words like "empty," "bare," and "silence" appear eight times. But the speaker, in grandly proclaiming the death of Pierrot's visions (nymphs, ornate compound phrases like "shortening breasted" and "lidless blaze" borrowed from Swinburne and Mallarmé) and his own inventions ("wheeling gold" or "peopled / Stillness"), borrows Pierrot's language. He uses Pierrot's vocabulary while denying its referential function. He tells us that Pierrot's world doesn't exist, yet every descriptive statement he makes invokes it. In this dark, still, cold, empty graveyard, the silence even works

. . . to still the pulsing thrush
　　And frighten her

With the contact of its chilly hands
Until she falls, and melts into the night
Among the cedars splashing on the light
That crowd the folded darkness as it stands
　　About each grave,

Whose headstone glimmers dimly in the gloom,
Threaded by the doves' unquiet calls,
Like memories that swim between the walls
And dim the peopled stillness of a room . . . (*VIS* XIII, pp. 83–84)

In "Philosophy," continuing the process he initiated in "Marriage," Faulkner transfers Pierrot's painful subjectivity onto the impersonal narrator who uses rhetorical flourishes to project a voice that is as stridently subjective as any of the voices Pierrot adopted:

Here the sunset paints its wheeling gold
Where there is no breast to still in strife
Of joy and sadness, nor does any life
Flame the hills and vales grown thin and cold
　　And bare of sound. (*VIS* XIII, p. 85)

Although he claims that Pierrot's false voices and visions are dead—especially dead as to "sound"—the narrator's own language belies this assertion. We leave the poem wondering what, indeed, is going on. For Faulkner has confronted us with a totally unreliable impersonal narrator, who enters, like *Light in August*'s furniture dealer, at the very last moment.

From "Philosophy" and "Marriage" to *Flags in the Dust*

The narrator of "Philosophy" makes an assertion that contains some truth: Pierrot, as mask, is dead. The lie is that Pierrot's visions have also perished. Such ambiguity allows Faulkner to suggest that what matters is not so much Pierrot's life or death but how Faulkner interprets his character's visions. Do they remain untranslated dreams or will he divine their meaning and, in doing so, transform them into art?

Miss Jenny, the narrator of the final graveyard scene in *Flags in the Dust*, inherits the impersonal narrator's world.[5] And she uses his images—a cedar-shadowed graveyard, doves, the contrast between the bright noon sunlight and the tree-shadowed gloom—to create a pattern of language that describes the lives and deaths of four generations of Sartoris men, all in some way *pierrotique* figures. The scene's tension derives from and centers in Miss Jenny's consciousness where two antithetical responses to these men are constantly at war. One minute she claims they are fools, the next she speaks the same bombastic, romantic language that we have come to identify with Pierrot, the Sartorises, and the Compsons. This second language, reiterated throughout the scene like a choral refrain, is constructed of images from "Philosophy":

> They went on and into the white folks' section and passed now between marble shapes bearing names that she knew well, and dates in a stark and peaceful simplicity in the impervious stone. Now and then they were surmounted by symbolical urns and doves and surrounded by clipped tended sward green against the blanched marble and the blue, dappled sky and the black cedars from among which doves crooned endlessly reiterant. (*FITD*, pp. 425–426)

When she arrives at the newest grave, her tone shifts to her other language, which is colloquial, ironic, and tart. The contrast is almost shocking. Halfway through she shifts again into bombast:

> The masons were just beginning to lay the curbing around it, and the headstone itself sat nearby beneath a canvas cover. She lifted the cover and read the clean, new lettering: Bayard Sartoris. March 16, 1893–June 5, 1920. That was better. Simple: no Sartoris man to in-

vent bombast to put on it. Cant lie dead in the ground without strut-
ting and swaggering. Beside the grave was a second headstone; like
the other save for the inscription. But the Sartoris touch was there,
despite the fact that there was no grave to accompany it, and the
whole thing was like a boastful voice in an empty church. Yet withal
there was something else, as though the merry wild spirit of him who
had laughed away so much of his heritage of humorless and fustian
vainglory, managed somehow even yet to soften the arrogant gesture
with which they had said farewell:

LIEUT. JOHN SARTORIS, R.A.F.
Killed in action, July 19, 1918.

'I bare him on eagles' wings
and brought him unto Me'

A faint breeze soughed in the cedars like a long sigh, and the
branches moved gravely in it. Across the spaced tranquility of the
marble shapes the doves crooned their endless rising inflections.
(*FITD*, pp. 426–427)[6]

Bayard's baroque language, engraved on his twin brother's headstone, language that belonged first to Pierrot in *Vision in Spring*, seduces Miss Jenny and transforms her from a tough, pragmatic little
old lady into a mouthpiece for the Sartoris vision of "fatality and
doom."

Old Bayard's headstone was simple too, having been born, as he
had, too late for one war and too soon for the next one, and she
thought what a joke They had played on him: denying him opportuni-
ties for swashbuckling and then denying him the privilege of being
buried by men who would have invented vainglory for him. The
cedars had almost overgrown his son John's and John's wife's graves.
Sunlight reached them only in fitful splashes, dappling the weathered
stone with brief stipplings. . . . (p. 427)

She sees how absurd these men are, yet she continues to succumb to
their vision, "their vainglory and the carven gestures of it in enduring stone" (p. 429).[7] But it is much clearer here than it is in *Vision in
Spring* that Faulkner himself has not succumbed. This point is made
when Miss Jenny describes the statue that stands upon the grave
of the eldest Sartoris. Like Faulkner's own great-grandfather's, the
statue dominates the scene: like Colonel Falkner, Colonel Sartoris
stands "in his frock coat and bareheaded, one leg slightly advanced
and one hand resting lightly on the stone pylon beside him." He also
bears such an uncanny resemblance to the Marble Faun that it

seems logical to suggest that Faulkner, for the same reasons as Freud's child at play, has here transferred his old Pierrot mask to his familial ideal, the famous and powerful Colonel Falkner:

> He stood on a stone pedestal, . . . his back to the world and his carven eyes gazing out across the valley where his railroad ran and beyond it to the blue changeless hills, and beyond that. The pedestal and effigy were mottled with sessions of rain and sun and with drippings from the cedar branches. . . .
>
> The wind drew among the cedars in long sighs, and steadily as pulses the sad hopeless reiteration of the doves came along the sunny air. (*FITD*, pp. 427–428)

Because Faulkner has made the tension between Miss Jenny's two kinds of thinking one of the novel's central organizing themes, there is an honest and explicable correlation between her two voices and the perceptions she registers. Miss Jenny constantly struggles between the hypnotic, reiterative, or echoing realm of "vainglorious" dream and ordinary existence. The polyphony of her shifting language records and mirrors that struggle.

Miss Jenny reacts to burying the last adult Sartoris male with the same tone of finality heard in "Philosophy": "Well it was the last one, at least . . ." But because she is ambivalent, her sense of relief is tainted with uncertainty. The same uncertainty was present in "Philosophy" in the contradiction between what the narrator claimed was not and the language he used to claim it. However, there is an essential difference: in *Flags* the reason for that contradiction has been given. Thus what appeared as an aesthetic flaw in *Vision in Spring* has, by being clarified, become a strength instead.

Her uncertainty registers upon us as a change in tone. From the straightforward "Well it was the last one . . . ," Jenny slips once more into her high rhetorical mode as she recalls the words of her niece Narcissa, who lives entirely in a world of passive dreamscapes: "she remembered something Narcissa had said once, about a world without men, and wondered if therein lay peaceful avenues and dwellings thatched with quiet; and she didn't know" (p. 429).[8] Miss Jenny returns home to Narcissa's piano playing. When she first enters, Miss Jenny speaks brusquely, "It always does me good to see those fool pompous men lying there with their marble mottoes and things . . ." (p. 432). But as she talks on, remembering the pain these men have caused her, she loses her grasp on reality. Trying desperately not to succumb to the world of false vision, the Sartoris world, Miss Jenny, like Pierrot in "Marriage" says,

> ". . . Play something." Narcissa obeyed, playing softly, and Miss Jenny
> sat listening for awhile. . . . Narcissa played quietly on, her white
> dress with its black ribbon at the waist vaguely luminous in the
> gloom. Jasmine drifted steadily in, . . . Narcissa played with rapt inat-
> tention, as though she were not listening. (*FITD*, p. 432)

But Miss Jenny loses the battle and starts calling Narcissa's infant by
one of the dead twin's names—shades of Joe Christmas's grandmother.[9] When Narcissa corrects her, Miss Jenny retorts with a hard
question: "Do you think that because his name is Benbow, he'll be
any less a Sartoris and a scoundrel and a fool?" Narcissa ignores her
aunt's question. Born a Benbow, then wife to and mother of Sartorises, she apparently will continue to support and encourage their
self-destructive, *pierrotique* dreams and visions:

> Narcissa played on as though she were not listening. Then she
> turned her head and without ceasing her hands, she smiled at Miss
> Jenny quietly, a little dreamily, with serene fond detachment. Beyond
> Miss Jenny's trim fading head the window curtains hung motionless
> without any wind; beyond the window evening was a windless lilac
> dream, foster-dam of quietude and peace. (*FITD*, p. 433)

This dreamlike, static landscape reflects the characters it encloses. Miss Jenny is fading and will soon die. Then Narcissa, no
longer questioned by her aunt, can reside peacefully in her *pierrotique* "windless lilac dream." But Miss Jenny's question hangs there,
in Narcissa's motionless air. And her question, juxtaposed with the
landscape and with Narcissa's vision, carries the moral implications
and central concerns of *Flags in the Dust*. Miss Jenny's ambivalence
is effective because it has been revealed to us through the phrases
she thinks and speaks in. Throughout *Flags*, then, Faulkner has
demonstrated what he has only been able to tell us in concluding
Vision in Spring.

There the impersonal narrator had, as we have seen, used Pierrot's
language to assert that he and his false visions are dead. Then, in the
sequence's final poem, he tries to say what new visions or sounds
will take their place. In linking the rhetorical problem of "April" to
that of "Philosophy," Faulkner maintains a similar rhetorical organization. This time the narrator's strident, declaratory statements are
positive rather than negative. But Faulkner undercuts the affirma-
tion by introducing three out of four strophes with the indefinite adverb "somewhere."[10] The narrator's language, supposed to embody a
new vision, is Pierrot's, but it undercuts and questions Pierrot's. Al-

though Faulkner has continued to use the same rhetorical device, he extends it here to achieve strong closural force. Thus, while in "Philosophy" we were not sure Pierrot's visions were dead, we are sure, as we finish reading "April," that in their present form they are not imaginatively useful. And the narrator here is no longer Pierrot. His description of the emotion evoked by the season is antithetical to Pierrot's. Rather than "the cruelest month" he gives us an April of rebirth: "here the hidden violets first appear," "here the young leaves shy appear," and "birches in a hood / Of tender green" (*VIS* XIV, pp. 86–87). Even the stars "spring and blossom in the turning sky" of his happy pastoral:

> Somewhere a girl goes, slender white,
> While sunset swims in her eyes' pool
> To meet her shepherd ere the night
> Descends on clear dark wings to lull and cool
> And dim the world in brooding fold on fold. (*VIS* XIV, pp. 87–88)

But "somewhere" coupled with past associations evoked by these lines leads us to distrust the sequence's concluding voice. For these are visions that earlier poems in *Vision* have taught us to doubt.[11] We now know that for Pierrot slender white girls spell danger; that night not only cools, it freezes and paralyzes the will; that "April's" final line echoes the quintessential *pierrotiste*, the Marble Faun. What purpose do the contradictions in this concluding poem serve? Do they amplify the range of the impersonal narrator's voice or "philosophy"? If not, what is the poet's intention?

What is here in skeletal form is a typical Faulknerian ending. Such ambiguity and contradiction draw the reader into the questioning process to participate in solving the issues of interpretation raised in *Vision in Spring*. What we may once have thought was the authorial voice—Faulkner's mask, Pierrot—has been replaced by an untrustworthy narrator. The narrator's closing description suggests that, although he has tried, he has failed to bury Pierrot: Pierrot cannot be killed. But, as Pierrot's own voice suggested in his self-parody, he can be transformed by his author in ways that force the reader to question Pierrot's perception or vision.

By making us participate in solving issues of interpretation and by introducing in its final movement an unreliable, impersonal narrator, Faulkner appears to be abdicating control of his fictional material. In fact, the truth is precisely the opposite. For at the end of *Vision* no voice is safely identifiable as the real authorial voice. Faulkner has succeeded in standing outside his fiction, and from that vantage point he appears to champion or identify with none of the voices while directing them all. Having succeeded by this narrative device in divorcing himself from his old persona, Pierrot, he can, in this last movement, give us a momentary view of the totality of his own imaginative vision. Now that he has glimpsed the whole picture, he can begin, in his fiction that follows, to show us how to see it, too.

CHAPTER XII

A New Beginning: "The Thunder and the Music of the Prose" (1921 to 1925)

Vision in Spring was a pivotal apprenticeship work, the one in which we sense the greatest tension as the poet's faulty vision pits itself against the novelist's increasingly assertive voice. The meanings of synecdochic scenes in some of Faulkner's finest novels have their genesis in the "silent music" of all his poetic sequences, but particularly in this one, his verbal symphony. That his poetry and fiction are thus connected suggests that the former continually fed and sustained his imagination. To understand its symbolic meaning and thus how it encouraged and shaped Faulkner's mature creative vision we turn, finally, to his life to see what role actual music and poetry played there.

Throughout his life Faulkner closely associated actual music and poetry with women he loved. But, oddly, Faulkner, like his mother, Maud, was more than indifferent to music. He often claimed to actively dislike it. Jill Faulkner Summers says, "He liked to listen to Gershwin and the Negroes' singing but otherwise I never heard him listen to any music. He had no ear for it. It was not part of life as far as he was concerned."

In contrast Estelle Faulkner and her daughter loved music. Summers says,

> My mother's family was extremely musical—literally they *all* played musical instruments. But my Grandmother [Faulkner's mother] hated music. There was never any question of having records to play at her house or at ours. When I was 14 or 15 my brother-in-law [her stepsister's husband] gave me a record player. But I was only allowed to play it when Pappy wasn't there. I was not allowed to play the piano when he was around either. I had to go to my other Grandmother's to have my music lessons and to practice. My mother couldn't play the piano when Pappy was home but when he was away she'd play for hours. She was very good.[1]

Faulkner was no more tolerant of his friends' love for music than he was of his wife's and daughter's. In *A Loving Gentleman*, Meta Wilde writes at some length on this subject. Like his wife and daughter she also loved to listen to and play music. Had she had the talent and money she would, she says, have aspired to be a concert pianist. Instead she worked as Howard Hawks's secretary and "script girl." But she maintained close friendships with many musicians, eventually marrying one. She also played the piano and went to concerts regularly. This is her account of Faulkner's reaction the first time she played for him:

> Glancing his way, I was startled to see that he was squirming in his chair. He had written in *A Green Bough* of "music of lustrous silent gold." Why was he restless? Later, "You didn't like my playing"—the accusation offhand, lightly admonitory.
>
> "You play very well, m'honey."
>
> "But it didn't do anything for you."
>
> "I don't appreciate music as much as I ought to," Bill apologized. "It's one of my flaws I reckon. . . . Language is my music," he said. "All I'll ever need."[2]

Wilde concludes, "Faulkner didn't think I played very well."[3] He refused to attend concerts with her and once when he interrupted her as she listened to a love duet from *Tristan und Isolde* the following occurred:

> . . . I waved Bill away as he approached calling my name. For a moment he gazed at me in absolute disbelief, the impact of my impatient gesture drawing the blood to his face, then slammed out of the room.[4]

She apologized profusely, explaining, "'When I hear music like that, I get lost in it. . . . Nothing else seems to exist for me. . . . Can't you see that music is to me what books are to you?'" His response, "'I just don't know ma'm.'"[5] She then elaborates:

> But the realization that music possessed me, that I was bonded to it as I could never be to a lover, troubled him. . . . Estelle, who "played piano right well," according to Bill, had never been passionate about music; hers was an accomplishment to be shown off in the front parlor. . . . Bill began to think of music as a rival and more than once asked how I could be under vassalage to something that he considered "white and opaque and distant." He could no more follow me into my world of symphony, chamber music, recital, and opera than I could enter his innermost domain, where he sat hunched over paper making tiny bird's-feet tracks with his pen.[6]

Since she was not living with Faulkner, Wilde had considerably more leverage with him on this issue, but her leverage seems to have afforded her little insight. Ironically, the metaphor in the lines she quotes from *A Green Bough*, "music of lustrous silent gold," partly explains Faulkner's antipathy. The word "music" was a private, symbolic metaphor whose meaning altered with its context. It stood, apparently, for many things that Faulkner felt were forbidden. But when music was also "silent" it referred to his creative imaginings.[7] Faulkner characterized real music to Wilde as "white and opaque and distant." Music, when it comes from the outside, seems to represent the Pierrot mask's most paralyzing fantasy. Faulkner describes such music with the same adjectives as he uses for the "white woman," the temptress who lures Pierrot and destroys his own "silent music." Wilde further illuminates this issue when she says, "I can be tremendously moved by music. When I'm involved in listening to something fine, tears come. This is just conjecture—it may sound far-fetched—but I wonder if perhaps he didn't feel a little bit left out." Her conjecture, while true, is not the whole story, as her next remark makes clear. She says Faulkner appeared to enjoy her husband's playing: "Wolfgang was different. He was in the presence of an artist."[8] Wolfgang may have been an artist but, more important for Faulkner, he was a man. Thus his "music" did not have the power to threaten Faulkner's imagination. In this sense Wolfgang's music affected Faulkner no more or less than his black servants' singing did.

Since, like his mother, Faulkner disliked or claimed to dislike actual music so much, it seems odd that he chose both a wife and a lover who were accomplished musicians. It seems equally odd that he should, in 1921, write a poetic sequence modeled upon Aiken's verbal symphonies and containing poems with musical titles and/or more poems whose subjects are music, musicians, and dancers. (Wilde describes Faulkner as the world's worst dancer. In adolescence he also refused to dance although Estelle loved dancing.)[9] To understand this apparent paradox and its role in shaping Faulkner's art we need to know more about the circumstances under which Faulkner wrote his musical poem sequence.

During the summer of 1921, Faulkner continued, as he had since he returned from the RAF in December 1918, to live at home with his parents. But he gave *Vision in Spring*, a sequence brimming with musical allusions and unfulfilled desires, to a married woman, a musician, and a person for whom his mother had little affection. Jill Faulkner Summers describes these women's relationship:

> Granny was not happy with any of her sons' marriages. There weren't
> a lot of people she liked besides her grandchildren. She disliked
> women in general, as a breed I think. She was an extremely down-to-

earth, pragmatic little lady and I think she thought my mother was flighty—a sort of butterfly. There was very little interaction between Granny and my mother. Granny always wished that Pappy had not married Mama.[10]

Summers observed that although they shared physical characteristics, her mother and Maud Falkner appeared to have little in common. But together they supplied his antithetical but concomitant desires for what a woman should be:

My grandmother was very small, less than five feet tall. She was very tough and independent. She had painted above her stove "DON'T COMPLAIN DON'T EXPLAIN" and she would not answer to anyone for anything she did. She was stubborn with a very quiet wit. Sometimes she would say something and it wasn't until two or three minutes later that you realized how funny it was, or that perhaps you'd been had.

Now one of the qualities about my mother that my father claimed distressed him was her *lack* of independence. In part I think this was because for him, she was the idealized female figure in his poetry, and he saw everything about her through a romantic haze. There were always these two kinds of women in his mind and he needed both. The fact that my mother was physically frail appealed to him. The times he was most caring was when she was not well. He didn't appear to like toughness in her and flatly refused to see the strengths she did have. My mother was very Southern in that she could make any man believe that he was superman. She was also very manipulative for she was, like most Southern women, taught to obey implicitly, "so far as he is wise and she is able."[11]

Faulkner's dual standard for women placed special demands upon his daughter:

He seemed to feel that frailty was a virtue and liked the idea of little girls in pinafores. I was a terrible Tom-boy and he encouraged it generally—I think because he wished I were a boy. But that wasn't all of it. He wanted women to be self-sufficient and resilient like my Grandmother but he wanted them to *appear* frail and weak. He abhorred women who gave outward and ostentatious signs of proficiency but he also liked the idea of my spending the day on a horse in pants. He just didn't want me around him otherwise in pants. When I was out riding he liked it because then, for him, I was "Bill" not "Jill."

But there was a dividing point and it took me awhile to understand. It was very easy for him to be many people but it was very difficult for me. Although he encouraged me to be independent he still wanted me to go through the motions of being helpless and female.

To teach her the importance of adhering to his Janus-faced feminine ideal Faulkner did the following:

> I can tell you exactly when it was that I at last completely understood where the dividing point lay. It was in the early '50's. I was downtown in Oxford in my blue jeans and Malcolm's [her step-brother's] shirt and I saw Pappy coming from the post office. I saw him from far away and I waved. When he came up to me he walked right by me as if I didn't exist. When I got home I was in a lot of trouble. I never went to town in jeans again.[12]

In 1924 Faulkner dedicated his one published sequence, *The Marble Faun*, to his mother (remember the Faun was truly impotent). In 1925 and 1926 he repeated himself as he gave other handmade books—a fable, and his sonnet sequence of love poems, *Helen: A Courtship*—to another unattainable woman, the artist Helen Baird. In the late 1930s he wrote and recited poetry to Meta Wilde. These women resembled each other in several ways: they were independent, they were not available to Faulkner as marriage partners, and their interest was in art forms other than language (Faulkner's mother was also a painter).

Possibly Faulkner chose musical forms and subjects for *Vision in Spring* to please Estelle. It might also be argued that, like other Modernists, he was interested in working within the convention of borrowing musical language and musical analogies for writing poetry. But neither of these explanations addresses the issue of why the language and themes of this sequence permeate so many emblematic scenes in Faulkner's novels. Such continuous usage suggests that this sequence served as a touchstone for his imagination, one that continued to inspire him throughout his career.

The subjects of *Vision in Spring*—sex, love, power, impotence, death, and the powers of the imagination—are universal. Faulkner had written of them in earlier sequences but always literarily and obliquely. In *Vision* he comes closer than he ever has to breaking through that "white, opaque, distanced" language: other poets' music. Dimly through this music—to borrow his metaphor—we hear an original author's voice. In *Vision*, particularly in the three poems of its third movement, we begin to hear some life in Faulkner's voices and a hint of genuine emotion. Our reading experience becomes enriched as we see vague outlines of a "story" forming in the intricate formal and thematic connections Faulkner has worked out between the poems in his sequence.

What then is the nature of Faulkner's "poetic" touchstone? Of what is it composed that makes it so rich with invention? The kinds of metaphorical connections Faulkner worked out here between music and vision served as a means for expressing imaginatively a series of conflicts and issues that figured prominently in his real life and in his fantasy life. It seems fair at this point to suggest that these conflicts center on Faulkner's attitudes toward his art and toward women. To say that Faulkner is Pierrot is too simple, but there is enough evidence from Faulkner's art and life to note certain resemblances.

More precisely, Faulkner's conflicts, like those of Pierrot, concern his desire for yet fear of loving a real woman (Estelle and, later, other women who were not his mother). Could he simultaneously love and be loyal to his mother and another woman when his mother had made it quite clear that she disliked and placed no value on either music or other women? (Faulkner maintained his primary allegiance, visiting his mother every day he was in Oxford throughout his married life.)[13] And could he, unlike his fictional would-be artist Elmer, be successful in both art and love? Faulkner's apparent solution in life was to live with other women but to deny that he could take pleasure in or hear their music—real or metaphorical. But even punishing himself and his lovers in this way was not sufficient pay for experiencing the double thrill of artistic creativity and adult sexuality, no matter how surreptitiously. Thus, for much of his adult life he apparently did not sleep with the woman with whom he lived nor did he live with the woman with whom he slept. Faulkner told Wilde he had not had sexual relations with Estelle since Jill's birth in 1933.[14] Whether or not he told the truth is impossible to know. They did have separate bedrooms. Despite this living arrangement, according to Wilde, Faulkner refused either to separate from or divorce his wife. In different ways and degrees Faulkner seems to have withheld sexually and emotionally from both Wilde and his wife.

In 1921, when he wrote *Vision in Spring*, his temporary solution to this conflict was a compromise. In the sequence, real music performed by other artists who also happen to be women—Colombine the actress, the dancers, the musicians—suggests and signifies Pierrot's fear that he will fail as a poet or artist of words. Meanwhile, the sequence itself, love poetry drawing on music for its metaphorical structure and formal organization and addressed to a woman who is not his mother—a woman who loves music—is, in itself, Faulkner's bid for independence from his mother's exclusive love and her values.

Writing "Love Song," a poem whose only music is the "cadence" of Pierrot's feet, allowed Faulkner to make a further bid for independence. There he simultaneously unmasked both Eliot, a recognized poet, and that fearer of women, eternal adolescent, and mother's boy, the would-be poet-actor Pierrot. Parody enabled Faulkner to be more explicit in stating the previously hidden import of his fantasy material. In "The Dancer" and "Marriage" Pierrot confronts a real woman with whom he actually converses. She is no longer the silent dream image of earlier poems like "Portrait." Furthermore, Pierrot begins to express an overt interest in and desire for adult sexual experiences. He no longer dwells exclusively in the isolated world of memory and dreams.

As Pierrot confronts these real women, the symbolic meaning of real music and dance (art forms these women initiate to charm him) is revealed to be death or failure. When he denies women's power over his fantasy life—the dancer is nothing compared to his imaginative impression of her and the piano player cannot banish his sexual fantasy of her—he makes an emotional compromise. This denial permits him to demonstrate his continuing primary love for and attachment to his mother. Faulkner represents her in his poetry as the Marble Faun's and later Pierrot's "moon mother" as well as the Miss Havisham figure in "After Fifty Years" (*The Lilacs*). She always "snares" her young male victim making him impotent, even as he is simultaneously obsessed with and repelled by a desire to experience an adult love relationship.

In Faulkner's novels such male victims persist. Their actual mothers are either malevolent, ineffectual, or dead. Popeye and Joe Christmas are examples.[15] A contemporary critical description of the close relation between Laforgue, the supreme and influential Pierrot poet, and his masks applies, in some ways, to Faulkner's with Popeye and Joe Christmas:

> And yet his poses *pierrotiques* seem to have affected profoundly, and disturbingly, what we can only call his consciousness of self. . . . In one of the most recent studies of the poet, Reboul writes that "*sexuality in Laforgue seems, indeed, to have been abnormal (as one says) —rather weak, irritated by an over-subtle intellect, complicated by a deliberately unchecked imagination, satisfied especially by sight and thought, dulled—notwithstanding its very real presence—by the notion of imperfection and sin.*" (emphasis added)[16]

That Faulkner, like Laforgue, may still have not entirely separated his Pierrot pose from his "consciousness of self" is suggested by Meta Wilde's comments and confirmed by one of his few available personal letters, written to his mother from Paris (22 September

1925). It is of interest not only because of what Faulkner writes in it but also because of how he orders his thoughts.

Went to the Moulin Rouge last night. Anyone in America will tell you it is the last word in sin and iniquity. It is a music hall, a vaudeville, where ladies come out clothed principally in lip stick. Lots of bare beef, but that is only secondary. Their songs and dances are set to real music—there was one with not a rag on except a coat of gold paint who danced a ballet of Rimsky-Korsakoff's, a Persian thing; and two others, a man stained brown like a faun and a lady who had on at least 20 beads, I'll bet money, performed a short tone poem of the Scandinavian composer Sibelius. It was beautiful. Every one goes there—often you have to stand up.

They have plays here just for Americans. The suggestive lewd, where it is indicated that the heroine has on nothing except a bath robe, say. Then at the proper time the lights are all turned off and you are led to believe that the worst has happened. Nasty things. But Americans eat it up, stand in line for hours to get tickets. The French of course dont go to them at all. After having observed Americans in Europe I believe more than ever that sex with us has become a national disease. The way we get it into our politics and religion, where it does not belong anymore than digestion belongs there. All our paintings, our novels, our music, is concerned with it, sort of leering and winking and rubbing hands on it. But Latin people keep it where it belongs, in a secondary place. Their painting and music and literature has nothing to do with sex. Far more healthy than our way.

I can tell you about paintings when I get home. I have spent afternoon after afternoon in the Louvre—(that Carnegie was a hot sport) and in the Luxembourg; I have seen Rodin's museum, and 2 private collections of Matisse and Picasso (who are yet alive and painting) as well as numberless young and struggling moderns. And Cezanne! That man dipped his brush in light like Tobe Caruthers would dip his in red lead to paint a lamp-post. . . .

I did this from a mirror my landlady loaned me. Didnt notice until later that I was drawing on a used sheet. This [is] part of 'Elmer.' I have him a half done, and I have put him away temporarily to begin a new one. Elmer is quite a boy. He is tall and almost handsome and he wants to paint pictures. He gets everything a man could want— money, a European title, marries the girl he wants—and she gives away his paint box. So Elmer never gets to paint at all.

My beard is getting along quite well. Vannye laughed at it, because she could see right through it to the little boy I used to be. Both the french language and the French people are incomprehensible to Vannye. She cant even get what she wants to eat. So the other day I took her to lunch and got her a steak, well done, fried potatoes and sliced tomatoes and a cup of coffee. . . .[17]

These righteous remarks to his mother about Paris night life, the art scene, American lewdness, his own writing, his self-portrait, and his Jamesian female relative were written less than a month after he arrived in Paris. They may be, in part, another mask. But if we follow Faulkner's thoughts in this letter as he moves from his observations and judgments about reality to his comments on the novel he is trying to write, the turns his mind takes suggest a very strong moral connection between his life and his art. After commenting on his faunlike self-portrait (am I a man or little boy?) drawn upon a page of his own fiction, Faulkner summarizes his novel (Figure 14).[18] Its hero, a would-be artist (am I a writer or artist?), fails because he succumbs to the prurient leer of gross American female sexuality: "pure beef," "lewd . . . nasty things." Sex for Elmer, as for the Marble Faun or the Americans Faulkner denigrates in his letter, is a "disease." Although Faulkner gives Elmer everything he needs for artistic success, Elmer, whose mother has died, chooses a wife who "gives away his paint box. So Elmer never gets to paint at all."

Faulkner's earlier sequences, *Vision in Spring*, and finally the unfinished *Elmer* manuscripts themselves make one wonder who really gave away Elmer's paint box (the manuscripts indicate it was Elmer himself), an object whose erotic significance Faulkner describes with loving detail. As the novel begins in what appears to be its earliest version, Elmer lies on the deck of an ocean liner fantasizing:

> . . . to think of nothing consciously: of his comfortable body, of girls
> without emphasis, of somewhere within him tickling his entrails
> pleasantly, loneliness.
> Then he would rise, and in his cabin draw forth his new unstained
> box of paints. To finger lasciviously smooth dull silver tubes virgin
> yet at the same time pregnant, comfortably heavy to the palm———
> such an immaculate mating of bulk and weight that it were a shame
> to violate them, innocent clean brushes slender and bristled to all
> sizes and interesting chubby bottles of oil . . . Elmer hovered over
> them with a brooding maternity, taking up [the cylinders (deleted)]
> one at a time those fat portentous tubes in which was yet wombed his
> heart's desire, the world itself—thick-bodied and female and at the
> same time phallic: hermaphroditic. He closed his eyes the better to
> savour its feel. . . .[19]

For Elmer, to paint, to create, is to violate the inviolate, whom he imagines as the supreme maternal image—the "phallic" pregnant virgin.[20] By analogy this fantasy suggests Elmer sees himself as God. Thus his aspirations resemble the Marble Faun's.

Just as he had given up his poetry Faulkner abandoned *Elmer* when it had served his purposes. But he kept Elmer's much-fondled tubes of paint, transforming them in *Light in August* to the tube of toothpaste that both fascinates and repels the child Joe Christmas (*LIA*, pp. 112–114). Elmer's original paints, "eight colored wax crayons," were given him by his second passionate love, "Jo with whom he slept."[21] This epicene elder sister is androgynously named Jo-Addie (Elmer's nickname is "Ellie"). Elmer's first love is, of course, his mother.[22] He describes his sister and mother as mirror images: Jo has "a bitter beauty," his mother a "stark bitter face." The adjective he chooses also characterizes the quality of his love for them—bitter, because never consummated.

Elmer's mother despises her husband, a useless drunk: "about all Elmer's father had ever given his children was lightish hair, and he hadn't been able to do this for Jo." And Elmer clearly is confused about and questions whether indeed the father is, anatomically, a man, as he calls him "an inverted Io with hookworm."[23]

Consistently in Faulkner's novels, strong, outwardly sexless, man-like women treat all males like fools and children, but few (Addie Bundren excepted) seem to dislike their husbands as much as Elmer's and Faulkner's mothers did. According to Faulkner, the following exchange occurred shortly before his mother died:

> . . . I created a fairy tale for her. I would tell her about Heaven, and what it was going to be like, how nice it was going to be and how she would like it.
> She said, "Will I have to see your father there?"
> "No," I said, "Not if you don't want to."
> "That's good," she said, "I never did like him."[24]

Whether Faulkner actually had this conversation with his mother is irrelevant. What is important is that Faulkner said he did, and therefore it reflects his perception of his parents' relationship. In the story Faulkner tells here, it is he who still, at sixty-three, is his mother's lover, and he who with his art—a "tale"—banishes his father, the husband she claims to hate. As *Vision in Spring* and his other poetry indicate, Faulkner's imaginative powers were not always this potent.

Although Faulkner often referred to himself as a "failed poet" he continued throughout his life to write poetry for the women he loved: Estelle Faulkner, his daughter Jill, Helen Baird, Meta Wilde, and later Joan Williams. Since poetry was the mode in which Faulkner communicated least effectively, it seems paradoxical that he

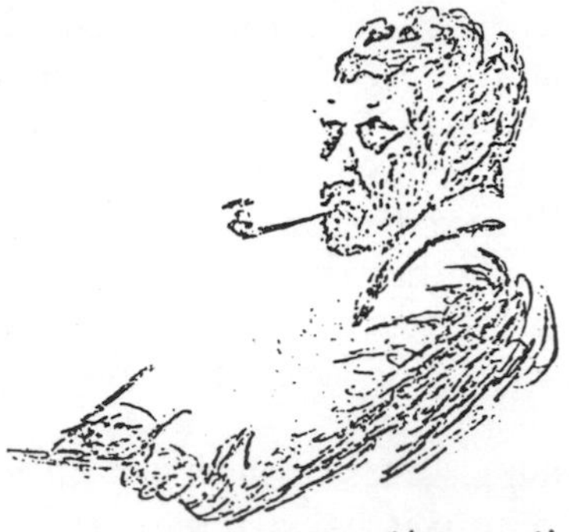

I did this from a mirror my landlady loaned me. Didn't notice until later that I was drawing on a used sheet. This part of "Elmer." I have him a half done, and I have put him away temporarily to begin a new one. Elmer is quite a boy. He is tall and blond and almost handsome and he wants to paint pictures. He gets everything a man could want — money, a European title, marries the girl he wants —— and she gives away his paint box. So Elmer never gets to paint at all.

My beard is getting along quite well. Vannye laughed at it, because she could see right through it to the little boy I used to be. Both the French language and the French people are incomprehensible to Vannye. She cant even get what she wants to eat. So the other day I took her to lunch and got her a steak, well done, fried potatoes and sliced tomatoes and a cup of coffee. In a restaurant where they specialize in paté and snails and such, and where every dish is a work of art. They looked at Vannye and me in amazement. In France you eat things one at a time. You have meat, then potatoes, then tomatoes, then coffee. But to have them all at one time, and all fried! Vannye doesn't even drink wine. I think that was the first time they ever saw anyone drink coffee with a meal. The waitress said to me, "What will madam drink?" I say, coffee. She says "Pardon me?" I say coffee. She says "But — coffee?" "Of a truth," I say, "but certainly. Is it not so?" "But yes," she says, "It is so. But — coffee. It is perhaps the wine of Anjou to which mister refers?" "No no one thousand," I say himself. "Madam does not admire the wine. Madam would but of the coffee. This makes itself is it not so?" "Yes yes," she says, "of the coffee makes himself here always. But — coffee." "Yes yes," I say. "Let to arrange himself for Madam the coffee." "Madam would that the coffee arrange himself during the march of the meal?" "Yes yes, if one permits him." "Yes yes, mister. One permits him. But —— coffee. It is perhaps ________" So Vannye got her coffee. Coffee here is a general term which means nothing: Something black in a glass which authorizes you to sit in a cafe for an hour and watch the people pass. For breakfast you can get it, but most people take either a cup of chocolate or a glass of white wine. I join the chocolate. I was caught too late to drink wine before 12:00. And 1:00 o'clock is thirteen o'clock here. 10:00 P.M. is 22 o'clock.

FIGURE 14. Faulkner's self-portraits drawn in letters to his mother and his great-aunt Bama (both written in September 1925) and in the four-page booklet he gave to Estelle Franklin (ca. 1918, see Blotner, *Faulkner*, pp. 194–195). A photocopy of this booklet was found in the same envelope as the photocopy of *Vision in Spring*. The location of the original is unknown. Courtesy of Jill Faulkner Summers, William Faulkner Collections (Acc. No. 6271-ak), University of Virginia Library, and Joseph Blotner.

A SONG

It is all in vain to implore me,
    To let not her image bequile,
For her face is ever before me —
    And her smile.

Even though she choose to ignore me,
    And all love of me to deny,
There is nought then behind or before me —
    I can die.

should use it for the language of intimacy. But perhaps that is pre-cisely the point. For Faulkner, love was always "opaque": symbolic of failure or anticipated failure. Thus he reserved his "failed" voice for it.[25] Also he could use poetry—the language he so clearly associ-ated with a dream state—to anesthetize his feelings in a "romantic haze" of false music: other poets' sounds and rhythms. Poetry con-tinued, for Faulkner, to remain the language of his most impossible dreams:

> 'Perhaps they were right in putting love into books,' he thought
> quietly. 'Perhaps it could not live anywhere else.' (Gail Hightower,
> *Light in August*, p. 456)

Epilogue

Three and a half years passed between the time Faulkner wrote *Vi-sion in Spring* (1921) and the January day he fired off a jubilant tele-gram to Phil Stone announcing that he was well into his first novel, *Soldiers' Pay*.[26] Blotner's account of those years, the most complete we have, is sparse: a mere sixty-four pages in contrast to the eighty-six he devotes to the first six months of 1925. But both it and extant manuscripts and typescripts indicate that these were the years Faulk-ner spent laboriously reworking and revising both his 1921 sequence and *The Marble Faun* in hopes that one or the other would even-tually be accepted for publication.[27] By the summer of 1921, al-though he did not yet know it, he had learned all he could from his apprenticeship to poetry. Now, through extensive reworking, he had to consolidate that knowledge in order to cut himself loose from his Pierrot mask. Years later he explained that process to another young would-be writer:

> I learned to write from other writers. Why should you refuse to?
> You could even do this: when I think you need help, take the help
> from me. Then, if your conscience troubles you because the story is,
> as you feel, not completely yours, just remember what you learned
> from that one and burn the story itself up, until you can use what you
> have learned, without needing to turn to me. The putting of a story
> down on paper, the telling it, is a craft. How else can a young carpen-
> ter learn to build a house, except by helping an experienced carpenter
> build one? He cant learn it just by looking at finished houses. If that
> were so, anyone could be a carpenter, a writer.[28]

What is known of these years suggests that the strain of being so apparently unproductive was considerable. Faulkner maintained and embroidered upon his various impostures at home, during a brief trip to New York in the fall of 1921, and during frequent short trips to Memphis and New Orleans.[29] He also drank more and more heavily, a factor that contributed to his eventually being fired both from his detested post-office job and his volunteer position as Boy Scout master.[30]

But by June of 1923 he had apparently revised *Vision in Spring* so that to him it seemed good enough to send off to Conrad Aiken's publishers, the Four Seas Company.[31] Unfortunately this typescript seems to have disappeared. We know its title from Faulkner's letters: *Orpheus, and Other Poems*.[32] The publishers wrote Faulkner that they would publish *Orpheus* if he would pay the publishing costs.[33]

Although he would accept a similar offer in November of 1923, less than six months later, for publishing *The Marble Faun*, Faulkner seemed insulted by their proposal. He wrote, "As I have no money I cannot very well guarantee the initial cost of publishing this mss.; besides, on re-reading some of the things, I see they aren't particularly significant and one may obtain no end of poor verse at a dollar and twenty-five cents per volume."[34] To a friend he said, "Its not what they're reading. Dammit, I'll write a book they'll read. If they want a book to remember, by God I'll write it."[35] It was the latter response, a good, healthy, aggressive, and positive anger rather than the self-pitying sarcasm of his first hurt, that shortly prompted him (in May 1924) to tender, through his mentor Phil Stone, the same offer the Four Seas had proposed originally, but for *The Marble Faun*, not *Orpheus*.[36]

Now Faulkner knew and accepted that he had to have something tangible to show for what amounted to at least six years of work. His autobiographical note in *The Marble Faun* suggests as much, making clear that the man who wrote the poetry in this volume in 1919 is not the same man as the one offering it for publication in 1924. In disowning that poetry, he appears also to be discarding the mask of the man who wrote it. For he made the mask itself into a published fiction:

Born in Mississippi in 1897. Great-grandson of Col. W. C. Faulkner, C.S.A., author of "The White Rose of Memphis," "Rapid Ramblings in Europe," etc. Boyhood and youth were spent in Mississippi, since then has been (1) undergraduate (2) house painter (3) tramp, day laborer, dishwasher in various New England cities (4) Clerk in Lord and Taylor's bookshop in New York City (5) bank- and postal clerk. Served during the war in the British Royal Air Force. . . . Present temporary

FIGURE 15. William Faulkner the novelist (Paris, 1925). For other portraits taken by Odiorne during this period, see Blotner, *Faulkner*, pp. 384, 482, and Cofield, *The Cofield Collection*, p. 71. Photograph courtesy of Jill Faulkner Summers.

address, Oxford, Miss. "The Marble Faun" was written in the spring of 1919.[37]

No sooner was publication of *The Marble Faun* assured than Faulkner was dismissed from both the post office and the scouts. On his post office resignation he signed himself, appropriately, "W. C. Falkner."[38] His ties to Oxford, which he had stated in his autobiographical sketch was only his "temporary address," were fast disappearing. Although Estelle Franklin returned in December to Oxford, Faulkner, as if accepting the impossibility of enjoying her presence under current circumstances, left shortly to begin what, with few interruptions, became a seven-month stay in New Orleans.[39] In January, having apparently heard nothing from Faulkner, Phil Stone wired, "What's the matter? Do you have a mistress?" Faulkner's cocky answer, "Yes, and shes 30,000 words long,"[40] signaled the birth of his fictional voice. Between January and July 1925, when he sailed from New Orleans for Europe, Faulkner published fourteen sketches and short stories in the New Orleans *Times-Picayune* and *The Double Dealer*.[41] Before leaving, he sent *Soldiers' Pay* off to his new mentor Sherwood Anderson's publisher, Boni and Liveright. Faulkner did not need to wait for their acceptance letter; he knew he was good. When the letter arrived in October in Paris he had already begun both *Mosquitoes* and *Elmer* and may even have started on *Sanctuary*, beginning with its closing scene.[42] In letters to his mother and his Aunt Bama, he asserts his new and final commitment:

> I have just written such a beautiful thing that I am about to bust— 2000 words about the Luxembourg Gardens and death. It has a thin thread of plot, about a young woman, and it is poetry though written in prose form. I have worked on it for two whole days and every word is perfect. I havent slept hardly for two nights, thinking about it, comparing words, accepting and rejecting them, then changing again. But now it is perfect—a jewel. I am going to put it away for a week, then show it to someone for an opinion. So tomorrow I will wake up feeling rotten, I expect. Reaction. But its worth it, to have done a thing like this.[43]

It is all here as it was in the beginning: a formal garden, love, death, and a maiden. But Faulkner's conception is entirely new. Instead of a lyric cry he has written two thousand words of "poetry . . . in prose form." Instead of a single moment in time there is "a thin thread of plot." It is indeed a new beginning.

Notes

Introduction

1. Butterworth, "Census." (For complete publication data for this and most other references in the notes, see the bibliography.) Before its publication, the average reader—unfamiliar with the contents of the Faulkner manuscript collections at the University of Virginia and at the Humanities Research Center, the University of Texas, Austin—had no idea of the sheer magnitude of Faulkner's poetic experiments. The "Census" first suggested to me the importance of Faulkner's poetry to his imaginative growth.

2. Bibliographical information on *The Lilacs* (thirty-six pages of burnt, handwritten fragments) and one other incomplete sequence (seven poems) is listed in Hamblin and Brodsky, *Selections*, pp. 23–24. Nine of *The Lilacs*'s thirteen poems have been published separately, but the sequential arrangement Faulkner works out for them both enlarges their individual meaning and creates a work of considerable stylistic interest. The Hamblin/ Brodsky catalog also lists other poem fragments, but since the catalog represents only a "selection" it is not as helpful as it might be. Faulkner published separately five of the fourteen poems in his most ambitious sequence, *Vision in Spring*. (The entire sequence has now been published. See bibliography.) As with his two other early complete sequences and with *Helen: A Courtship*, it is the sequential arrangement of the poems that reveals the burgeoning novelist. For titles of the sixteen sonnets (nine previously published) in *Helen: A Courtship* see Bonner, *William Faulkner*, pp. 36–37. The Wisdom Collection (Tulane University) also contains several other poem manuscripts. *Helen* is excluded from my study as Faulkner wrote and bound it after he wrote *Soldiers' Pay*. This sequence and Brodsky's incomplete sequence and five individual poems ("Mississippi Poems") are now in print. See Faulkner, *Helen: A Courtship and Mississippi Poems*.

3. Notable exceptions, besides Collins's and Blotner's introductions to *Helen: A Courtship and Mississippi Poems*, are James B. Meriwether's numerous bibliographical publications, articles by Martin Kreiswirth, Gail Moore Morrison, Noel Polk (see Faulkner, *The Marionettes*), Margaret Yonce, and parts of Linda W. Wagner's *Hemingway and Faulkner*. Invaluable to a student of Faulkner's poetry is Butterworth's census. Since its publication we have learned of more poetry, so this bibliography needs updating. At the moment it is the most complete and accurate listing we have of Faulk-

ner's poetry. All poems I discuss are supplied with an updated bibliography that in most cases originates from the data in Butterworth's census. Brodsky has thus far published two bibliographies of his private collection of Faulkner materials (see Hamblin and Brodsky, *Selections* and *The Biobibliography*). Earlier general articles by George P. Garrett (1957), Richard P. Adams (1962), and Lewis P. Simpson (1975) are also useful.

4. Brooks, *Toward Yoknapatawpha*, p. ix.

5. Housman's *A Shropshire Lad* is the other major modern poem sequence that influenced the shape and content of some of Faulkner's poetry. What may be his earliest sequences (incomplete; seven of the "Aunt Bama Poems" and the first seven of the "Mississippi Poems") are primarily reworked Housman and Swinburne. (For a listing of the "Aunt Bama Poems" see Hamblin and Brodsky, *Selections*, pp. 23–28.) Faulkner eventually published many of these in his 1933 collection *A Green Bough*. Doubtless Housman's ironic stance, and what has often been described as his adolescent tone, appealed to Faulkner, but his poetry's relevance to Faulkner's prose style is tangential. Partially this is because Faulkner's response to Housman was to imitate rather than to initiate a dialogue. Thus, while he learned much about versification, he never really made Housman's "tiny" lyrics his own and they did not therefore contribute in any significant way to his growth as a novelist.

6. ". . . Pierrot's theatrical and literary history is the record of his vacillations between two dramatic and psychological types. At one pole stands . . . Pedrolino . . . a creature of insouciance and activity, a character of almost no psychological depth, a symbol of comic irrepressibility and unselfconscious verve. He inhabits a dense social world, but, curiously, rarely suffers pangs of social conscience. At the other pole stands Hamlet—a figure of melancholy indolence, a character of inscrutable depth and complexity, a symbol of human vulnerability and mortality, a moralist tortured by conscience—but, just as curiously, an egoist who is profoundly asocial and solipsistic. These two types of humanity . . . live in a universe in which time is conspicuous either by its relentless advance or by its momentary suspension" (Storey, *Pierrot: A Critical History*, pp. xiv–xv).

7. I have adopted the terms *pierrotique* and *pierrotiste* from Storey as the clearest and simplest references to the Pierrot mask.

Accurate dating of Faulkner's poetry is impossible. Faulkner dated few of his manuscripts and typescripts and some that he did date (for example, *The Marble Faun*, April, May, June 1919) may indicate the moment of conception rather than completion. Since my focus is upon tracing Faulkner's imaginative development and growth rather than on compiling a strictly accurate chronology of his artistic productions, I discuss Faulkner's work here in the order that best illuminates that progress.

8. Storey, *Pierrot: A Critical History*, p. 14.

9. For intrinsic evidence that Faulkner read Symons see Kreiswirth, "Faulkner as Translator," pp. 429, 433.

10. Lines and images from Eliot's 1917 volume reverberate in Faulkner's 1921 sequence (see part III) and appear earlier, as Margaret Yonce has noted, in his first completed sequence, *The Lilacs*. See Yonce, "'Shot Down Last Spring.'" Besides his sequential structures, Faulkner also lifts numerous phrases, images, and tonal qualities from Conrad Aiken's symphonic sequences written between 1916 and 1921. These borrowings appear in both *The Lilacs* and *Vision in Spring* (see chapters V–XI).

11. Storey, *Pierrot: A Critical History*, pp. 159, 151, 136, 151, 147, 122.

12. An earlier typescript version of *The Marble Faun* bound with green construction-paper covers and grommets (at the Humanities Research Center, University of Texas at Austin) has the titles "Prologue," "Spring," "Summer," "Noon," "Autumn," "Winter," and "Epilogue" marking its major divisions. Several pages are dated "1920." This typescript is number 39.a under "Published Poetry" in Butterworth's census.

13. Smith, *Poetic Closure*, p. 3.

14. These novels are *Soldiers' Pay, Mosquitoes, Flags in the Dust, The Sound and the Fury, Sanctuary, As I Lay Dying, Light in August,* and *Absalom, Absalom!* Hereafter I will sometimes refer to them in text and notes as *SP, M, FITD, TSATF, S, AILD, LIA,* and *AA*.

15. Rosenthal has written a short essay that asserts in general terms the genre's existence but defines it at once too inclusively and exclusively. While he claims that the "modern sequence is the outstanding development in our period for over a century" he also asserts that "every successful long work of the past, is, after all a sequence beneath its surface continuity and uniformity" (Rosenthal, "Poetic Sequences," p. 416). His new book will no doubt expand and clarify his argument. Such an assertion negates any distinctions one must make between the traditional narrative poem and a poem sequence—a necessary distinction if one is trying to establish the existence of the poem sequences. According to Rosenthal, "any volume of poems, if it somehow involves a single impulse of realization, may be a sequence." He also says that the modern poem sequence always "conflates the political and the personal." Faulkner's sequences are profoundly apolitical. Thus by Rosenthal's definition neither he nor Aiken writes sequences.

More helpful are articles and books on specific sequences, or references in larger critical studies. The most useful are as follows: Frances C. Ferguson, "The Lucy Poems: Wordsworth's Quest for a Poetic Object," *ELH* 40, no. 4 (Winter 1973): 532–549; Robert F. Gleckner, "Keats's Odes: The Problem of the Limited Canon," *Studies in English Literature* 5 (1965): 577–585; idem, "Blake's Songs"; Helen Gardner, *The Art of T. S. Eliot* (London/Boston: Faber and Faber Ltd., 1949); idem, *The Composition of Four Quartets*; Golden, "'The Game of Sentiment'"; Langbaum, "Dynamic Unity"; idem, "Browning," pp. 76–120; Edward Mendelson, *Early Auden*, chaps. 7 and 15 on the "Cantos" and Auden's sonnet sequence "In Time of War" and his references throughout to "Horae Canonicae"; Sperry, *Keats the Poet*; and Williamson, "Allen Tate." Smith's *Poetic Closure* proved especially relevant, and I have applied, in a general way, her criteria for closure within a single poem to Faulkner's poem sequences, taking into account certain obvious differences. Her discussion of closure and anticlosure in modern poetry (pp. 234–260) is most useful.

16. In his authorized biography of Faulkner Joseph Blotner, the only scholar who has apparently seen the original volume of *Vision in Spring*, gives it five pages. See Blotner, *Faulkner*, pp. 307–312. Owned by Estelle Faulkner and in her possession when Blotner saw it, the book seems to have disappeared. I recovered a photocopy of it among letters, documents, and other Faulkner manuscripts in Jill Faulkner Summers's attic during the fall of 1979. Jill Summers lent it to me until I had completed my book (this photocopy is part of Summers's private collection).

17. Stevens, *Letters*, p. 231.

Chapter I. Apollonian Vision

1. Colonel William Clark Falkner, for whom William was named, had changed his name from "Faulkner" to "Falkner" supposedly to distinguish his family from a poorer family of Faulkners who lived nearby (Joseph Blotner, telephone conversation, 18 May 1983). So William, in returning the name to its original spelling, was not only separating himself from his immediate family but also tracing his genealogy directly to his great-grandfather, as he would do in 1924 when his publishers asked for some biographical material for the jacket cover of *The Marble Faun*. Here he changed the spelling of the Colonel's name back to its original and listed him as his only relation. The sketch reads "Born in Mississippi in 1897. Great-grandson of Col. W. C. Faulkner, C.S.A., author of 'The White Rose of Memphis,' 'Rapid Ramblings in Europe,' etc. . . ." (Blotner, *Faulkner*, p. 361). Blotner's two-volume biography remains the most inclusive source of factual data on the Faulkner family. His revised and condensed one-volume edition, to be published in 1984, corrects unavoidable errors in such an inclusive and quickly assembled work and provides as well much new information.

2. Ibid., pp. 229, 226.

3. Ibid., pp. 229–232.

4. Access to these papers courtesy of Jill Faulkner Summers.

5. Blotner, *Faulkner*, p. 232. Fifteen months after his discharge Faulkner was "gazetted an honorary second lieutenant."

6. "Lowe, Julian, number——, late a Flying Cadet, . . . regarded the world with a yellow and disgruntled eye. He suffered the same jaundice that many a more booted one than he did; . . . they had stopped the war on him.

So he sat in a smoldering of disgusted sorrow, not even enjoying his Pullman prerogatives, spinning on his thumb his hat with its accursed white band" (*SP*, p. 7).

7. Faulkner creates at least two caricatures of a would-be war hero. The first is Isom, the sixteen-year-old son of a black servant who has just re-

turned from World War I. He is described in his father's borrowed uniform:

> His lean sixteen-year-old neck rose from the slovenly collar's limp, overlarge embrace, and an astonishing amount of his wrists was visible beneath the cuffs. The breeches bagged hopelessly into the unskillful wrapping of the putties which, with either a fine sense for the unique or a bland disregard of military usage, he had donned prior to his shoes, *and the soiled overseas cap came down most regrettably on his bullet head.* (*FITD*, p. 53, emphasis added)

The second is a blind negro beggar who plays a guitar and mouth organ, another bard:

> . . . he too wore filthy khaki with a corporal's stripes on one sleeve and a crookedly sewn Boy Scout emblem on the other, and on his breast a button commemorating the fourth Liberty Loan and a small metal brooch bearing two gold stars, obviously intended for female adornment. *His weathered derby was encircled by an officer's hat cord*, and on the pavement between his feet sat a tin cup containing a dime and three pennies. (*FITD*, pp. 127–128, emphasis added)

8. Adams, Brooks, Collins, Garrett, Kenner (*A Homemade World*), Millgate, and Richardson have noted Faulkner's debt to the Symbolist movement (see bibliography). See also Noel Polk's introduction to *The Marionettes*, p. xi.

9. Faulkner stopped attending school in the eleventh grade. He entered the university by a special decree admitting all returning servicemen (Blotner, *Faulkner*, p. 248). Here is an example of Faulkner imposturing as a wounded soldier to gain an approved status in the eyes of his community. He retained this status only from September 1919 to June 1920 and September to November 1920, when he withdrew.

10. While many critics have examined various aspects of Faulkner's attitude toward his male ancestors, few have noticed the equal if not greater importance of the women in his life. While he had, as a child, an ineffectual father and an alcoholic grandfather coupled with his dead mythical great-grandfather, he also had two, some would argue three, physically small but intellectually and emotionally strong mothers (see chapter IV). For some discussions of Faulkner's paternal relations see Blotner, *Faulkner*; Irwin, *Doubling and Incest*; Minter, *William Faulkner*; Guerard, *Triumph of the Novel*; Wittenberg, *The Transfiguration of Biography*; and Wyatt, *Prodigal Sons*.

11. Blotner, *Faulkner*, p. 105.

12. The earliest articles on Faulkner's poetry are still among the best: Adams, "The Apprenticeship of William Faulkner," and Garrett, "An Examination of the Poetry." Both are reprinted in Wagner, *Four Decades of Criticism*. Brooks catalogs literary influences in his notes on "Literary Borrowings and Echoes in Faulkner," pp. 345–354 in *Toward Yoknapatawpha*. The most extensive treatment is Richardson, *The Journey to Self-*

Discovery. For his detailed metrical analysis of *The Marble Faun* see pp. 52–53.

13. See Bate's discussion of this concept in Bate, *John Keats*, pp. 169–170. See also Bate, *Burden of the Past*, and Harold Bloom's later elaboration and "misprison" in *The Anxiety of Influence* and *The Breaking of the Vessels*.

14. Quoted in Bate, *John Keats*, p. 170.

15. Garrett, "An Examination of the Poetry." Garrett was the first critic to take a close look at any of Faulkner's poetry. He observed that *The Marble Faun*'s formal connecting structure was guided by "the cycle of the four seasons and the hours of the day." Martin Kreiswirth has recently disagreed, saying that the poems in *The Marble Faun* "remain fundamentally separate units" and that *The Marble Faun* has no "internally related, temporally consistent structure." In fact he says, "sequential development of the time-scheme is repeatedly undermined" (p. 338) and claims "there remain but the bare outlines of the seasonal superstructure of the poems' more temporally consistent prototype, a twenty-seven page typescript, which is divided into 'Prologue, Spring, Summer, Noon, Autumn, Winter, and Epilogue'" (p. 338 [he refers here to Faulkner's 1920 typescript version of *The Marble Faun*]).

I disagree with Kreiswirth. (1) In *The Marble Faun* (1924) the time in poem IV is noon on a spring day: "Through a valley white with may . . . / While a blackbird calls and knocks / At noon across the dusty downs" (poem IV, p. 20). In *The Marble Faun* (1920 typescript) poem IV is a night scene: "Mists as soft and thick as hair / Rise silver to the moon." The difference shows that Faulkner has revised in order to strengthen temporal sequentiality, because the next poem, poem V (poem VI in 1920 typescript), is called "Noon" in the 1920 typescript. (2) In the 1920 typescript the order is "Summer" (V), "Noon" (VI). (3) In the 1924 version what was poem IX in the 1920 typescript has been moved toward the end of the sequence, becoming poem XVI, again strengthening temporal movement of the later version: nightmares often come just before break of day as they do in the subsequent eclogue in the 1924 version. See Kreiswirth, "Faulkner's *The Marble Faun*."

16. See Bate, *John Keats*, and also Erik Erikson on George Bernard Shaw in "The Problem of Ego Identity," *Psychological Issues* 1, no. 2 (1959): 104–105.

17. Bate quoting Douglas Bush's analysis of *Endymion* in *John Keats*, p. 179.

18. *The Marble Faun*, prologue, p. 12, hereafter *TMF*.

19. Phil Stone, Faulkner's first mentor who wrote the introduction to *The Marble Faun*, claimed he supplied the poem's title. Previous scholars (Collins, Meriwether, and Blotner) have found Stone's statements notoriously inaccurate. Even if he were correct, it is nonetheless true that Faulkner, always very careful about the finished appearance of his books, had the right, the self-confidence, and the obligation to have changed the title had he thought it inappropriate. Instead, he denied having ever heard of Hawthorne's novel (Blotner, *Faulkner*, p. 379), much as he would deny Eliot's

influence and claim he had never read Joyce or Freud. Finally, intrinsic evidence from the poem itself only reinforces the title's suggested identification (see the discussion comparing thematic similarities). Toward the end of his career Faulkner could be much less defensive about his borrowings. When asked if *As I Lay Dying* consciously or unconsciously "paralleled" *The Scarlet Letter*, Faulkner answered: "No, a writer don't have to consciously parallel because he robs and steals from everything he ever wrote or read or saw. . . . I took whatever I needed wherever I could find it, without any compunction and with no sense of violating any ethics or hurting anyone's feelings because any writer feels that anyone after him is perfectly welcome to take any trick he has learned or any plot that he has used. Of course we don't know just who Hawthorne took his from. Which he probably did because there are so few plots to write about" (May 16, 1957, Gwynn and Blotner, *Faulkner in the University*, p. 115).

20. Part of Hawthorne's fascination (personal as opposed to aesthetic) for Faulkner may have been that he too was an outcast and renegade. See Matthiessen, *American Renaissance*, p. 200.

21. Hawthorne, *The Marble Faun*, pp. 106–107.

22. Ibid., pp. 306–307.

23. Ibid., pp. 39, 40, 54, 352. She also claims, "It will be a fresher and better world, when it flings off this great burden of stony memories, which the ages have deemed it a piety to heap upon its back" (p. 97).

24. Lewis, *The American Adam*, p. 125. Lewis does not see that it is a *double* imitation.

25. Hawthorne, *The Marble Faun*, pp. 262, 352. Miriam's self-imposed penalty for aspiring to be an artist and for expressing her sexuality is to deny herself all creative outlets. As a penitent—spiritually but never sexually joined to her lover—she may neither paint nor experience carnal passion (p. 262, see also Matthiessen, *American Renaissance*, p. 312). This was the last novel Hawthorne completed, a fact that makes it tempting to read Miriam's punishment as at the very least an unconscious autobiographical statement. Hawthorne's daughters became living Miriams: "Una accepted the Anglican faith after a long struggle, and devoted herself to works of charity until she died while on a visit to a Protestant convent. Rose married . . . converted to Catholicism . . . became a nun . . . founded . . . a sisterhood for the relief of victims of incurable cancer" (Matthiessen, *American Renaissance*, p. 362).

26. Hawthorne, *The Marble Faun*, pp. 9–10.

27. Donatello's name incorporates another possibly ironic mirror image: the Renaissance Florentine sculptor (1386–1466), an innovator who abandoned the earlier Gothic style for realism.

28. "The poet and the dreamer are distinct, / Diverse, sheer opposite, antipodes. / The one pours out a balm upon the World, / The other vexes it" (Keats, "The Fall of Hyperion: A Dream," lines 199–202, p. 408 in *The Poems*).

29. Faulkner, *The Marble Faun and A Green Bough*, prologue, p. 12. I have used the 1924 published version throughout both because it is readily available and because, other than the changes noted in note 15, the substantive revisions from the earlier Texas typescript to the published version do not affect my argument.

30. Tennyson, *The Princess, a Medley*, in *The Poetical Works of Tennyson*, p. 134.

31. Faulkner, *Light in August*, p. 459. Faulkner returns again to Tennyson in 1936 to characterize Wash's blind hero worship of Sutpen in *Absalom, Absalom!* Wash's "dream" leads to three murders and a suicide. See *Absalom, Absalom!*, pp. 282, 287, 288. Paying his ultimate tribute to Tennyson's poem he once more "makes it truly his own." For more discussion see Lawrence Lipking's distinction between borrowing or imitating and farming and cultivating. The mature poet generally performs the latter, which indicates that he has passed beyond the imitative phase of his development and can now return to the works he once merely borrowed from and use them as a means for creating something that is truly his own—something new (Lipking, *The Life of the Poet*, p. 78).

32. *Light in August*, pp. 441, 458–459. For Faulkner's views on Tennyson, Hightower, and his attitudes toward both in 1957 see Gwynn and Blotner, *Faulkner in the University*, p. 93, where he simultaneously rejects and embraces identification with Hightower.

33. The Prince in Tennyson's poem, like Hightower, is possessed by a fantasy. The dreamlike state it induces springs, like Hightower's, from his familial past. The Prince's curse is inherited. Unlike Hightower, the Prince wants to escape his shadow world. He describes his cursed condition variously as "Oh Death in Life, the days that are no more!" (IV, line 40) and "I seem'd to move among a world of ghosts" (IV, line 542). This description is remarkably similar to the narrator's description of Hightower.

34. For a historical and psychoanalytical description of this phenomenon, see Erikson, "Ego Development." Erikson cites Southerners as being particularly prone to this form of ego identity crisis (see pp. 35–36).

Chapter II. Virginity's Burden

1. See Simpson, "Southern Symbolism of Pastoral."

2. Faulkner, *The Marionettes*, p. xxv. Faulkner made at least four copies of *The Marionettes*. He gave one to Estelle Franklin, dedicating it to "Cho-Cho," her first child by Cornell Franklin. According to Ben Wasson, a fellow classmate at "Ole Miss," Faulkner gave him an inscribed copy "near the end of 1920" (Blotner, *Faulkner*, p. 295). For a detailed bibliographical discussion see Noel Polk's excellent introduction.

3. Faulkner, *Sanctuary*, p. 3.

4. Faulkner, *Sanctuary*, p. 13. The Faun's mother is the mad moon whose "white feet mirrored in my eyes / Weave a snare about my brain" (*TMF* IX,

p. 33). See also Noel Polk's afterword to Faulkner, *Sanctuary: The Original Text*, p. 298.

5. Faulkner, *Sanctuary: The Original Text*, p. 300.

6. Pierrot, the generator of the Marionettes, sprawls "in a drunken sleep, . . . He does not change his position during the play" (*TM*, pp. 2–3).

7. Polk has noted these influences (*TM*, pp. xxvi–xxviii). Wilde's *Salomé* and Mallarmé's *Hérodiade* seem especially relevant.

8. I include the poem here courtesy of Professor James B. Meriwether, to whom Robert W. Daniel gave a photocopy. It has two bibliographical entries, one in Butterworth, "Census," and the other in Hamblin and Brodsky, *Selections*. It has recently been published in the *Mississippi Quarterly*. See "Pierrot, Sitting Beside The Body of Colombine, suddenly Sees Himself in a Mirror," *Mississippi Quarterly* 35, no. 3 (Summer 1982): 306–308. Copyright © 1982 Jill Faulkner Summers.

Pierrot, cramped from sitting so long, felt darkness
Coldly descending like water upon him, and saw his hands
Dissolve from his knees and the crumpled wrists of his jacket:
Pierrot saw his face in the mirror before him
Slowly extinguished like a match, then washed into darkness
By a wind which stirred the curtains there at the window,
Leaving the mirror empty, inscrutable, smooth.

And he dropped his eyes to the couch between him and the mirror
Like two worn pennies, and his memory dived behind them
Like[?] a lithe boy, down through a long blue wave of darkness
To grope in the opaque lambent silence, to waver and pause
Where Colombine lay, so young, and dead and timeless
Between her thin arms, straight in the dusk, and lustrous
And poignantly quiet beside her, beneath her hair.

He turned his head to stare between the restless curtains
Above his garden of roses, across a silence
Murmurous with the slumber of a fountain, above a darkness
Laced with exhalations of dreams woven in slumber.
Below him were houses, and hills beyond: a bland wall somber in
    starlight,
Beyond the hills, cities: a cumulous flickering of fireflies;
Then once more a room and a window, and aimless curtains
And a face like an extinguished flame staring between them at
    nothing,
At cumulate cities and hills, and stars and the long grey sound of rain.

Steadily gazing across the dark, he raised his hand
And he lightly touched her hair, faintly expecting
To find that it had no substance, was but a shadow
Shaken across her small breasts, tightly confined, that under
His fingers had trembled like captured birds, and that now
Were curiously relaxed and fallen. Yet surely it could not be a shadow
Which had once been so shrill with motion, that once had snared him
And intricately bound his heart with threads of fire.

Quietly he withdrew his hand, while silence
Flowed into the room on the wind, to a stirring of curtains,
While the scent of flowers came up on the wind
And blossomed about him in impalpable haunting fragrance;
Quietly he sat, cramped with long sitting, and saw
A slender bough reach down and pluck the moon
Out of the east, and roundly hold it up to him.

And he thought how all his life, his youth so bright and beautiful,
That had mazed him, had raised him beyond his world of hills and
  cities
And dust, and the remote long sound of rain, in a net of blue and
  silver,
Had parted beneath him. Timidly he touched her hair again
And thought that he, in his turn, lay finally quiet, and lifeless
Among the shattered petals of his youth, that another
Lightly touched a hand to his hair, staring beyond him
At a world of hills and cities and rain and dust
In a motionless silence and the immaculate chiming of stars.

. . . . He stirred, expecting to see—What had he thought to see there?
Had he thought, perhaps, to feel the life that was in him
Swirl once more to the heart breaking swirl of her skirts
That once had seemed to enclose them, to knit
The strings of his heart and her heart together?
But there was no movement to tighten his heart in the darkness,
No sharp slender turn of a palm, nor flick of a skirt
About her childish legs which had mazed his life with their swiftness,
And which now were quiet at last, eternal, more childish than ever.

Pierrot, grown cramped from sitting so long, stirred at last
And, turning to the mirror, saw, in its mutable shadow,
His face like a dead match held there before him
Beyond the body of Colombine, so young, and dead and timeless
Whose skirts, which had drawn them and whirled them together
Until they were wearied of a motion sustained and swift and
  meaningless,
Now lying crushed and lifeless and infinitely pitiful, seemed to him
The symbol of his own life: a broken gesture in tinsel.

9. For one of many fictional renderings of this image see Hightower just before his final illumination, in which he recognizes that all he is is an antic "showman, . . . a charlatan preaching worse than heresy"; in short, an impostor (*LIA*, p. 462). "His bandagedistorted head has no depth, no solidity; immobile, it seems to hang suspended above the twin pale blobs which are his hands lying upon the ledge of the open window" (*LIA*, p. 460).

10. See also Hamblin and Brodsky, "Faulkner's 'L'Apres-Midi d'un Faune.'"

11. Blotner, *Faulkner*, p. 243. She was born 8 February 1919.

12. Ibid., p. 247, and Sensibar, "Pierrot and the Marble Faun," pp. 473–476.

13. Faulkner, *The Marionettes*, appendix, p. 82.

14. Faulkner, *Mosquitoes*, p. 20. In fiction men will destroy the metaphorical flames of real women by torching them (e.g., Joe Christmas—or Joe Brown?—to Miss Burden in *LIA* and Darl to his mother in *AILD*). "The Dancer" (*VIS* X) is perhaps the best poetic rendering of this image (see pp. 184–188).

Chapter III. Women and Language

1. For the best and worst examples see *TMF* VI, pp. 25, 27.
2. Faulkner, *Soldiers' Pay*, pp. 173–212.
3. A good fictional analogue is Temple Drake's flight to the orderly Luxembourg Gardens at the end of *Sanctuary*.
4. Blotner, *Faulkner*, passim.

Chapter IV. Ancestral Echoes

1. See Storey, *Pierrot: A Critical History*, and Blotner, *Faulkner*, pp. 238, 292, 313.
2. Although Jill Summers says she doesn't remember her father mentioning the Colonel and although Maud's attitude toward him was ambivalent, Faulkner heard plenty of praise for the Colonel at reunions of Civil War veterans held at his grandfather's (see Blotner, *Faulkner*, pp. 102–103) and from the Colonel's only surviving child, Faulkner's much-loved great-aunt Alabama McLean. (See Broach, *Grande Dame*. This monograph was privately printed in October 1976. A copy is in the Faulkner Collection at the University of Mississippi Library, Oxford, Mississippi.) Since Faulkner's mother disliked Aunt Bama intensely (see chapter XII, note 10), this would have enhanced the Colonel's appeal to Faulkner who, like most of us, was not adverse to playing off the various rivals for his affections (see pp. 53–54).
3. "I would furthermore emphasize that successful imposture involves also a social element—in the cooperation of its victims. Consequently, a large-scale imposture is most successful in times of disturbed or near-revolutionary social conditions, when people are looking for panaceas and a savior, and are uncritical and overly ready to believe" (Greenacre, "The Relation of the Impostor," p. 526).
4. Dates on the Library of Congress copies of Colonel Falkner's poem and first novel suggest that Falkner wrote the novel first (Thomas C. Moser, letter to author, 31 May 1983).
5. "I write not for renown or praise,— / Great men are too common in modern days, / Neither do I scribble for infernal pelf, / But I write only to amuse myself" (Colonel William Falkner, *The Siege of Monterey* [Cincinnati: n.p., 1851], I.v).
6. ". . . sustained imposture . . . is the living out of an oedipal conflict through revival of the earliest definite image of the father. In so far as *the*

imposture is accomplished, *it is the killing of the father through the complete displacement of him. It further serves to give a temporary feeling of completion of identity* (sense of self) . . ." (Greenacre, "The Impostor," p. 371, emphasis added). "It is conspicuous that *the imposture itself is most often the assumption of the identity of a father or an older brother, on the scale of the family romance: a distinguished noble or famous person, who is symbolically killed by the imposture and robbed of his greatest treasures—his fame, his wealth, his achievements*" (Greenacre, "The Relation of the Impostor," p. 525, emphasis added).

7. Phyllis Greenacre mentions Goethe, Fritz Kreisler, and Thomas Chatterton (Greenacre, "The Relation of the Impostor," p. 525).

8. Bate, *John Keats*, pp. 137–140.

9. "The impostor is a person who assumes a false name or identity for the purpose of deceiving others; he is a type of pathological liar who hopes to gain some advantage from his deception. Unlike the show-off or poseur who fails to deceive people and leaves them chiefly impressed with his pretentiousness, the impostor succeeds at least for awhile in charming his audience into believing his deceptions. His role playing differs from more normal forms of pretending and acting a part, which are forms of mastery or play, because it involves driven, repetitive behavior that stems from unresolved pathological inner conflicts" (Finkelstein, "The Impostor," p. 85).

10. See Quentin Compson in *The Sound and the Fury*, who, like his father, lives in the shadow of his grandfather's exploits and can only confirm his being by suicide. Quentin's father drinks himself to death (Faulkner, *The Sound and the Fury*, especially pp. 211, 216, 218). Horace Benbow in *Sanctuary*, Joe Christmas in *Light in August*, Addie in *As I Lay Dying*, and Rosa Coldfield and Judith Sutpen in *Absalom, Absalom!* are a few of the major characters who come to mind.

11. What psychoanalysts call "defective super-ego functioning" or what we would call lack of conscience or amorality directs the behavior of all impostors described in medical literature. Finkelstein quotes his patient Teddy, explaining that

> he lived out his role, using particular defense mechanisms to prevent the intrusion of unpleasant realities. Among these were *denial*: "When I imagine I will do something, like paint a picture, I really can't believe that I couldn't be another Picasso"; *rationalization*: "It doesn't matter if I'm pretending; everyone is a bit of a phony"; and *splitting*: "If I tell someone that I'm a lawyer, I forget about what I really am and I have no feeling of guilt at the time." These defenses allowed unconscious self-representations to re-emerge and to be acted out without any conflict with reality-oriented ego functions. (Finkelstein, "The Impostor," pp. 91–92)

12. Helene Deutsch quotes her patient: "Jimmy, while firmly pretending that he *was* what he pretended to be, asked me again and again, sometimes in despair: 'Who am I? Can you tell me that?'" (Deutsch, "The Impostor,"

pp. 24, 497). Many of Faulkner's characters, like those mentioned in note 10, ask precisely this question.

13. Whenever Faulkner places himself in a new situation or strange surroundings he either elaborates on his current imposture or assumes a new one. Additions occur when he enrolls at the University of Mississippi, where he alternates between the wounded hero, the impeccably dressed aesthete, and the ragged poet. He was also, according to Blotner, drinking fairly heavily, even for a Southerner during this and the next stages of his imposture—in New York in the fall of 1921 and during his first extended trip to New Orleans. There, where he adopted a new mentor, Sherwood Anderson, and wrote his first novel, *Soldiers' Pay*, he further exaggerated his limp, claimed he also had a metal plate in his head, and drank to ease the pain of his war wounds.

14. Faulkner in a letter to his publisher Horace Liveright (late July 1927), quoted in Blotner, *Selected Letters*, p. 37.

15. Faulkner brings in the ghost in the first chapter:

As usual old man Falls had brought John Sartoris into the room with him. Freed as he was of time, he was a far more definite presence in the room than the two of them cemented by deafness to a dead time and drawn thin by the slow attenuation of days. He seemed to stand above them, all around them, with his bearded, hawklike face and the bold glamor of his dream. (*FITD*, p. 5)

The black servants also feel the spell of his unseen presence:

Quite often these days Isom could hear his grandfather talking to John Sartoris . . . mumbling away to that arrogant ghost which dominated the house and its occupants and the whole scene itself across which the railroad he had built ran punily with distance but distinct, as though it were a stage set for the diversion of him whose stubborn dream, flouting him so deviously and cunningly while the dream was impure, had shaped itself fine and clear now that the dreamer was purged of the grossness of pride with that of flesh. (*FITD*, p. 120)

16. Greenacre, "The Relation of the Impostor," p. 525.

17. *The Pontotoc True Democrat*, May 1886, quoted in Blotner, *Faulkner*, p. 11.

18. Ibid., p. 14.

19. Ibid., pp. 15–19.

20. Interview with William's cousin Sallie Murry Williams, 1965, quoted in ibid., p. 17.

21. Ibid., p. 19.

22. Ibid., p. 37.

23. Ibid., p. 36.

24. Ibid., p. 67.

25. Ibid., p. 68.

26. Erikson, "Ego Development," pp. 33–34.

27. Blotner, *Faulkner*, p. 80. In *Elmer*, the unfinished novel Faulkner

worked on sporadically between 1925 and 1929, Faulkner returns to this family argument. But in his fictional re-creation Elmer's mother, not his shiftless father, is the parent who insists on moving to Texas. There she is punished for her rash and willful action: she loses her house to fire, her daughter to the streets, and dies an early death. But worst of all, her son Elmer, unlike the real Faulkner, fails to become an artist.

28. This nickname served also as a veiled attack on Maud Falkner as it referred to the shape of William's mouth, which resembled his mother's. For the inarticulate Murry Falkner (on an unconscious level), mother and son with their "snake lips" were inextricably allied against him.

29. See Karl Abraham, "The History of an Impostor in the Light of Psychoanalytical Knowledge," *Psychoanalytic Quarterly* 4 (1935): 570–587; Deutsch, "The Impostor"; Otto Rank, *The Double*, trans. and ed. Harry Tucker, Jr. (Chapel Hill: University of North Carolina Press, 1971); Finkelstein, "The Impostor"; Greenacre, "The Relation of the Impostor." For an illuminating analysis of Faulkner's fictional rendition of this year see Wittenberg, *The Transfiguration of Biography*, p. 20.

30. Blotner, *Faulkner*, pp. 140, 157. Faulkner later linked the need to drink to salving another wound, this one real. On a sustained binge in New York, he fell in his hotel room against a radiator pipe where he lay undiscovered for several hours. The burn on his back was severe enough to require several skin grafts. From that time he suffered fairly continual back pain that he exacerbated by continuing to ride horseback. Looked at together, these disparate details spanning Faulkner's lifetime describe a pattern of identity conflict. Relief was ultimately sought by returning to the physical site where conflict was first experienced, i.e., in Faulkner's back. For it was in his back that he first felt the pain and punishment for not measuring up to one of his ideals, the stiff-backed Civil War hero with military bearing, Colonel William Clark Falkner.

31. Ibid., p. 494.

32. Blotner, *Selected Letters*, p. 20. Jay Martin, in a recent article on Faulkner's early life, says he will treat "the history of Faulkner's imagination." He then uses two biographical incidents as the basis for his thesis. The first of these concerns Faulkner's infant feeding habits as reported by his younger brother John. The second is this screen memory. Martin offers an interpretation but in doing so he mixes up key adjectives:

> . . . Maud is represented in his cousins. The love-object is split in two. Each woman is divided into good and bad. On the one hand is the idealized "good" mother, the *warm, glowing, approving* and sensuous mother—with hair like honey, suggestive of both light and food. On the other is the "bad" mother: *aloof, impersonal, quick,* and *dark*— associated with images of distant coldness and harshness. . . . There is no reciprocity: "she was touching me." That is how, in his wordless loneliness and sorrow, he was carried home, jostled in the dark yet dreaming of a honey-haired mother. (Martin, "The Early Life of William Faulkner," p. 613, emphasis added)

33. See chapters XI and XII.

34. "The women he most loved and admired were Aunt Bama, his mother, and Mammy Callie. . . . Mammy Callie meant the most to him. She was independent, positive, and self-sufficient" (Jill Faulkner Summers, interview, 20 August 1980). Although John Falkner and Blotner quoting him say Caroline Barr began working for the Falkners in 1907 after they moved to Oxford, the contents of Faulkner's screen memory (it occurs in Ripley where the Falkners lived until September 1902 when William was five) suggest that Malcolm Franklin's assertion that Barr was employed by the Falkners *before* William's birth is accurate (Franklin, *Bitterweeds*, p. 110). Jill Faulkner Summers concurs: "Mammy used to tell me about coming to Oxford with Pappy. She'd also often talk about 'When we lived in Ripley. . . .' She had been a house-servant of my grandfather's before Pappy was born" (Jill Faulkner Summers, interview, 16 May 1983). If Summers and Franklin are correct—and Faulkner's dark and light, sensual and cold mothers in this memory support them—then what we see here is that Faulkner *really* had two antithetical mothers, hence the ease with which he and his characters constantly see their "mothers" as antithetical doubles.

35. In less than half a page Faulkner mentions the light of the candle four times. Joe's obsessively repetitive and violent acceptance and rejection of the food various women in his life offer mirror the violence of his feelings of love and hate toward the women themselves and suggest the origins of his feelings are preoedipal. See Sensibar and Strauss articles in *Creative Biography*.

36. Summers went with her father when she was little "but Granny didn't really care for either of us [her two granddaughters Jill and Dean] when we became full-grown. I stopped going with Pappy or staying overnight with Granny—which I used to do on a regular basis—when I began to feel that the empathy which was there before had been lost" (Jill Faulkner Summers, interview, 16 March 1982).

37. Letter from William Faulkner to Maud Butler Falkner dated "Easter 1943." Faulkner Collection, University of Virginia Library, number 10443. Courtesy of the University of Virginia Library.

38. See chapter XII for its survival as a private identity.

39. William Faulkner, unfinished essay. Beinecke Library, Yale University. See Joseph Blotner, "William Faulkner's Essay on the Composition of Sartoris," *The Yale University Library Gazette* 47 (January 1973): 121–124. Lawrence Lipking notes an analogous work in Yeats's canon. When Yeats completed *Per Amica Silentia Lunae*, his initiation, though delayed, "was complete. Time stopped for him, and he began to write with all the energy of a young man or a convert. Almost every paragraph of *Per Amica*, on re-reading, turned out to contain material for a new poem. He would never again exhaust his stock. Nor would he ever again lose faith in his power to renew creation. Against all odds, weary, aging, self-doubting, confused, the poet actually did begin another life. And poems began to come" (Lipking, *The Life of the Poet*, p. 61).

40. "I think that was his [Joe Christmas's] tragedy—he didn't know what he was, and so he was nothing. . . . that to me was the tragic, central idea of the story—that he didn't know what he was. . . . Which to me is the most tragic condition a man could find himself in—not to know what he is and to know that he will never know" (Gwynn and Blotner, *Faulkner in the University*, p. 72, 13 April 1957).

Chapter V. Lyric or Narrative?

1. Gwynn and Blotner, *Faulkner in the University*, pp. 202, 207, 5 June 1957.

2. Golden, "'The Game of Sentiment,'" p. 267.

3. Aiken's review of his "symphony" *The Charnel Rose* (*Poetry*, June 1919) is his clearest statement of what he means by "symphonic form" and why he chose to write poem sequences.

4. When Faulkner wanted to write sequences using stricter formal structures he imitated the author of *The Shropshire Lad*. Although extant typescripts of Housman-like quatrains indicate that Faulkner intended to make them into sequences, he did not, as far as I know, ever make any of these incomplete typescript sequences into separate booklets (see Hamblin and Brodsky, *Selections*, and University of Virginia Faulkner Collection). These sequences are all incomplete. Thus they are not germane to my discussion as they cannot contribute to our understanding of how Faulkner developed from a poet to a novelist. Faulkner did eventually publish some of his Housman-like lyrics in his much later collection of poems, *A Green Bough* (1933). But the circumstances under which this volume was published, the fact that it is a collection of poems rather than a poem sequence, and the date of its publication all serve to exclude it here. Faulkner wrote his publisher in January 1932:

> . . . the stuff [*A Green Bough*] does not seem so bad, on rereading. I wish you would let the blank pages remain in, as they supply some demarcation between separate and distinct moods and methods [they were not included in the published version]—*provided such terms can be used in respect to 2nd class poetry, which this is.* . . .
>
> *Also, I will need money soon*[er] *than I thot.* Can I have that (or part of) advance on the novel now? (Blotner, *Selected Letters*, p. 54, emphasis added)

5. Blotner, *Faulkner*, p. 15, notes.

6. The original copy of *The Lilacs* is owned by L. D. Brodsky, a private collector. I have not had access to it. However, I have seen a photocopy of it at the University of South Carolina. I have quoted from this photocopy where necessary with the written permission of Jill Faulkner Summers, who holds the copyright to all unpublished Faulkner materials.

Between 1918 and 1926 Faulkner completed several other poem sequences that he also made into books. These are *The Lilacs*, *Vision in Spring* (summer 1921), *Orpheus, and Other Poems* (1923), *The Marble Faun* (begun perhaps as early as 1918, essentially complete by the spring of 1920, revised and published commercially in 1924), and the sonnet sequence *Helen: A Courtship* (summer 1926). Besides these there are several incomplete sequences, parts of which were later incorporated into his 1933 collection of poems, *A Green Bough*. Copies of many of these poems (from the "Aunt Bama Poems" and the "Mississippi Poems") may be found in the Faulkner Collection at the Alderman Library, University of Virginia. The originals are owned by L. D. Brodsky (see Introduction, note 2). More sequence fragments are owned by other private collectors. Two books Faulkner wrote, bound, and illustrated during these years are not poem sequences: *The Marionettes* (winter 1920) and a fable, *Mayday* (1926). Since my intent here is to trace Faulkner's development as a writer, I discuss those sequences and poems that best illustrate growth and change.

7. Faulkner claims that he picked up some literary tricks from Thomas Beer, the author of *The Mauve Decade, American Life at the End of the Nineteenth Century* (New York: Knopf, 1926). His remarks about Beer give insight into his own thoughts about literary borrowing: "I got quite a lot of words, approach to incident. I think a writer is completely amoral. He takes whatever he needs, wherever he needs, and he does that openly and honestly because he himself hopes that what he does will be good enough so that after him people will take from him, and they are welcome to take from him as he feels he would be welcome by the best of his predecessors to take what they've done. . . . When I was a young man . . . Thomas Beer . . . influenced me a lot" (Gwynn and Blotner, *Faulkner in the University*, pp. 20, 24).

8. See Hamblin and Brodsky, *Selections*, number 17, and Brodsky, "Additional Manuscripts."

9. Words remaining of the fourth poem are "dusk . . . grey . . . whispering candles," of the sixth, titled "Living," "beseeching hands . . . her hair . . . her breasts . . . as young . . . and now bear kisses . . . nor sighs nor any tears . . . she only hears," and the ninth, "Bathing," is about a "sprite." Visible rhymes are "moon/June" "gleams/dreams," and "eyes/thighs." In the thirteenth and last poem, titled ". . . Storm," visible phrases are "whipping hair," "thin garments to the sun," and "Chicago." Courtesy of Louis Daniel Brodsky, who supplied me with a photocopy of the typescript of his bibliographical entry for "The Lilacs" (letter, 4 March 1979).

10. See Cleanth Brooks, Joseph Blotner (*Faulkner*), and Margaret Yonce. It seems to be the most written about Faulkner poem. Because of the plethora of other criticism, I have limited my own discussion of it.

11. A bibliographical description of each poem is included to give an idea of how hard Faulkner worked on revisions. An asterisk indicates where my additions to Butterworth's census begin:

a. "The Lilacs," *Double Dealer* 7 (June 1925): 185–187. This is *A Green Bough* I.

b. Untitled [canceled title: "The Lilacs"], 1 p. typescript, incomplete, University of Mississippi (Rowanoak Papers). Added in Faulkner's hand is "Pub. 'Double Dealer,' 1924."

c. "The Lilacs," 1 p. typescript: burned fragment, Humanities Research Center, University of Texas, Austin (UT). This is a separate title page for a draft of the poem.

d. Untitled, 1 p. typescript: burned fragment, 25 lines visible, 19 complete, UT.

e. Untitled, 1 p. typescript: burned fragment, 30 lines visible, 18 complete, UT.

f. Untitled, 1 p. typescript: burned fragment, 25 lines visible, 22 complete, UT.

g. Untitled, 1 p. typescript: burned fragment, last 11 lines of poem complete, UT.

h. Untitled, 1 p. typescript carbon: burned fragment, 23 lines visible, 8 complete, UT.

i. Untitled, 1 p. typescript carbon: burned fragment, 23 lines visible, 12 complete, UT.

j. Untitled, 1 p. typescript carbon: burned fragment, 10 lines visible, 3 complete, UT.

k. Untitled, 1 p. typescript carbon: burned fragment, 14 lines visible, 13 complete, UT.

*l. "The Lilacs," 5 pp. carbon typescript: 99 lines; dedication at top reads "To A . . . and H . . . , Royal Air Force / August 1925," at end is typed "William Faulkner 1925," University of Virginia (UVa).

m. "The Lilacs," 1 p. manuscript: lines on recto and on verso, UVa.

n. "We sit drinking tea," first line of untitled 2 pp. manuscript: lines on recto and on verso of p. 1, on recto and on verso of p. 2, UVa.

o. "It was a morning in late May," 1 p. manuscript fragment: lines on recto and on verso, UVa.

p. "The Lilacs," 10 pp. manuscript fragments: parts of lines visible. This is *The Lilacs* I (1 January 1920), owned by L. D. Brodsky.

The publishing history of "The Lilacs" recorded in this bibliographical entry indicates that Faulkner liked it despite its rather obvious weaknesses. He made only slight changes in "The Lilacs" when he published it as the first poem in *A Green Bough* (1933).

12. Yonce, "'Shot Down Last Spring.'"

13. See ibid. I have quoted from the version of "The Lilacs" in this booklet, but I have used other variants and the published version in *A Green Bough* to complete fragmented lines.

14. a. "Cathay," *The Mississippian* (12 November 1919), p. 8.

b. "Cathay," Collins, *Early Prose and Poetry*, p. 4.

c. "Cathay," 1 p. typescript, UVa. This typescript is reproduced in Meriwether, *Bibliographical Study*, Figure 3.

d. "Cathay," 1 p. typescript carbon: burned fragment, 20 lines visible, 17 complete, UT.

*e. "Cathay," 2 pp. manuscript fragments: 20 lines visible, none complete. This is *The Lilacs* II.

15. a. "To a Co-ed," *Ole Miss* (Yearbook) 24 (1919–1920): 174.

b. "To a Co-ed," Collins, *Early Prose and Poetry*, p. 70.

*c. "To a Co-ed." This is *The Lilacs* III.

16. a. "On Seeing the Winged Victory for the First Time," 1 p. typescript, UVa. This is *A Green Bough* XVII.

b. Untitled, 1 p. typescript: 7 lines, incomplete, UT.

c. Untitled, 1 p. typescript: burned fragment, 8 lines visible, 7 complete, UT.

d. ". . . the First Time," 1 p. typescript: burned fragment, parts of 7 lines and title visible, UT.

e. Untitled, 1 p. typescript: burned fragment, parts of 8 lines visible, UT.

f. Untitled, 1 p. typescript: burned fragment, parts of 8 lines visible, UT.

g. Untitled, 1 p. typescript carbon: burned fragment, parts of 8 lines visible, UT.

h. ". . .y for the First Time," 1 p. typescript carbon: burned fragment, parts of 7 lines and title visible (*d* is ribbon copy), UT.

*i. "O Atthis," 1 p. manuscript: burned fragment, 8 lines visible, 6 complete. This is *The Lilacs* V.

17. Pound's poem reads: Faulkner's poem in *The Lilacs* reads:

O Atthis	O Atthis
Thy soul	For a moment, an eon
Grown delicate with satieties,	I pause, blind
Atthis.	Drawn down
O Atthis,	Consumed
I long for thy lips.	In the blaze of the son[g(?)]
	That burns on thy [lips(?)]
I long for thy narrow breasts,	
Thou restless, ungathered.	O Atthis

Pound's poem first appeared in *Poetry* 8, no. 6 (September 1916): 276. Both versions also suggest Pierrot in *TM*.

18. "As with Mallarmé, Swinburne's ideal poetry is impersonal, toneless, even (in a sense) without meaning. Swinburne never tires of excoriating [didactic] poets . . . and he never stops saying that poetry's gifts are such things as light, and fire, and song. . . . Such terms do not have a meaning, they have a context; they do not explain what the world is, they reveal how and in what way it is. Thus his poetry is fundamentally anti-rationalistic but also extremely ordered and highly wrought. He is against meanings, not order, precepts, not law. . . .

Swinburne and Mallarmé have differences enough, particularly in their poetic styles; it remains nonetheless true that their aesthetics are remarkably similar and grow out of common assumptions about the nature of poetry and its language" (McGann, *Swinburne*, pp. 65, 79).

19. a. "L'Apres-Midi d'un Faune," *New Republic* 20 (6 August 1919): 24 (40 lines). In Collins, *Early Prose and Poetry*, pp. 39–40.

b. "L'Apres-Midi d'un Faune," *The Mississippian* (29 October 1919), p. 4 (40 lines). In Collins, *Early Prose and Poetry*, pp. 123–125.

*c. "L'Apres-Midi d'un Faune," 1 p. typescript: n.d., 32 lines, 2 verses, first line "I peep through the slender trees" typed on back of J. W. T. Falkner's First National Bank stationery. Below typed poem 13 autograph lines also from this poem. UVa.

d. Holograph manuscript: 3 partially canceled lines, 2 strophes, second strophe begins "I have a sudden wish to go" (41 lines), UVa.

e. Holograph manuscript: 7 partially canceled lines, 2 strophes, second strophe begins "Ah, the dancers whirling past" (40 lines), UVa.

f. 1 p. fragment on torn piece of lined paper, first line "Shakes down her blown and vagrant hair," on recto is fragment from "A Dead Dancer" beginning

[(?)g]irl she   is dead
  [(?)]o a short yesterday
  [(?)]. felt dawn and night and day [UVa]

g. 3 pp. manuscript: burned fragments. This is *The Lilacs* VI, owned by L. D. Brodsky.

h. Hamblin and Brodsky, "Faulkner's 'L'Apres-Midi d'un Faune.'"

i. This is also listed in Hamblin and Brodsky, *Selections*, as number 15, where it is described as "L'Apres-Midi d'un Faune." Holograph fragment, 15 lines, in pencil on torn half-cover (7 x 11 inches) of the *Saturday Evening Post*, 31 August 1918.

j. Holograph penciled fragment: 14 lines written in Faulkner's copy of Ralph Hodgson's *Poems* (New York, 1917), Jill Faulkner Summers private collection.

k. *K* is published in Sensibar, "Pierrot and the Marble Faun."

20. My comparison of the two poems draws on Weinberg's gloss of Mallarmé's poem in *The Limits of Symbolism*, pp. 127–170.

21. The importance Faulkner placed on the typographical indicators is evidenced in the annoyed and anguished letters he wrote to his editor, Ben Wasson, in response to Wasson's tinkering with them when he edited the manuscript of *The Sound and the Fury*. See letters in Blotner, *Selected Letters*, pp. 44–45.

22. a. "Une Ballade des Femmes Perdues, Mais où sont les nieges d'antan," *The Mississippian* (28 January 1920), p. 3.

b. "Une Ballade des Femmes Perdues," Collins, *Early Prose and Poetry*, p. 54.

*c. ["Une Ballade des Femmes Perdues"(?)], holograph poem VIII in *The Lilacs*, 2 pages, parts of 19 lines visible, none complete.

23. Faulkner knew "Felise" for it also was included in his Modern Library edition of Swinburne's *Poems*, p. 125. Unless otherwise noted, all Swinburne quotations are from this edition, which was the one Faulkner owned from 1918 until his death.

24. Quoted in Weinberg, *The Limits of Symbolism*, p. 135.

25. Collins, *Early Prose and Poetry*, p. 54.

26. Faulkner responded with gusto. See Blotner, *Faulkner*, pp. 264–270.

27. Arthur Symons's worshipful accounts of the lives of poets like these would have done little to discourage such behavior. He praised Rimbaud as the *"enfant terrible* of literature, playing pranks . . . , knocking down barriers for the mere amusement of the thing, getting all the possible advantage of his barbarisms in mind and conduct. And so, in life, he is first of all conspicuous as a disorderly liver, a revolter against morals as against prosody" (Symons, *The Symbolist Movement*, p. 37). Sanctioning Verlaine's "forbidden passions" he says, "The artist, it cannot be too clearly understood, has no more part in society than a monk in domestic life: he cannot be judged by its rules. . . . It is the poet against society, society against the poet, a direct antagonism" (Symons, *The Symbolist Movement*, pp. 44, 45).

28. Note bathing scenes from *Mayday* (1926), "Adolescence" (1922), *Soldiers' Pay*, *Mosquitoes*, and *The Sound and the Fury* for just a few.

29. a. "After Fifty Years," *The Mississippian* (10 December 1919), p. 4.

b. "After Fifty Years," Collins, *Early Prose and Poetry*, p. 43.

*c. "After Fifty Years." This is *The Lilacs* X.

30. Collins, *Early Prose and Poetry*, p. 53.

31. Ibid.

Chapter VI. Sex and Death in *The Lilacs*

1. Russo, "A Study in Influence," p. 684. This article also suggested the lines from Wordsworth's "Prelude" as an epigraph for these chapters.

2. William Faulkner, "Verse Old and Nascent: A Pilgrimage," *Double Dealer* 7 (April 1925): 129–131. Reprinted in Collins, *Early Prose and Poetry*, pp. 114–118.

3. Textual evidence will be cited in the course of this chapter. Biographical information was supplied by Jill Faulkner Summers in a series of interviews conducted between 1979 and 1983, by Meta Wilde in a 1982 interview, and by Joan Williams in a 1983 interview.

4. Jill Faulkner Summers, interview, 10 May 1979.

5. a. "Sapphics," *The Mississippian* (26 November 1919), p. 3.

b. "Sapphics," Collins, *Early Prose and Poetry*, pp. 51–52.

*c. ["Sapphics"(?)], 3 page holograph poem, *The Lilacs* XI, parts of 21 lines visible, none complete.

6. Brooks, *Toward Yoknapatawpha*, pp. 2–3. Brooks's comments on this poem illustrate how reading a poem out of its sequential context can result in misinterpreting the poet's intention. Here Brooks is hardly at fault because when he wrote about "Sapphics" I do not believe he knew of its part in *The Lilacs*. For a discussion of the Decadents' effect on Faulkner's early work see Bleikasten, "Pan et Pierrot."

7. McGann, *Swinburne*, p. 112.

8. Swinburne, *Poems*, p. 139.

9. McGann, *Swinburne*, p. 114.

10. Swinburne, *Poems*, pp. 139, 140.

11. Weinberg, *The Limits of Symbolism*, pp. 168–169.

12. "Anactoria," in Swinburne, *Poems*, pp. 153–154.

13. Blotner, *Faulkner*, pp. 400–416, passim. Faulkner published his first essay on Sherwood Anderson in the *Dallas Morning News*, 26 April 1925. James B. Meriwether provides a detailed account of this and Faulkner's 1953 Anderson essay in his article "Faulkner's Essays on Anderson."

14. Collins, *Early Prose and Poetry*, pp. 114–118.

15. Ibid., pp. 114–116.

16. Jill Faulkner Summers, interviews, May and November 1979.

17. See McGann's discussions of "A Match" and *Atalanta in Calydon* in *Swinburne*, pp. 41–44, 95–107.

18. Swinburne, *Poems*, p. 82.

19. McGann, *Swinburne*, p. 171.

20. Swinburne, *Poems*, p. 152. McGann explains that such pairing results in a poetry that "is remarkably rich in boundaries—in images, poetic forms, and prosodic devices which can suggest a point of limits. . . . Once this peculiarly Swinburnian place is noticed, its prevalence may seem surprising. It not only pervades *Poems and Ballads*, First Series; it probably locates the most important aspect of the entire volume" (McGann, *Swinburne*, p. 171).

21. Gwynn and Blotner, *Faulkner in the University*, p. 84, 15 April 1957.

22. Faulkner, *Absalom, Absalom!*, p. 142.

23. Faulkner, *As I Lay Dying*, p. 54.

24. Swinburne, *Poems*, p. 137.

25. See McGann, *Swinburne*, pp. 181–182.

26. Ibid., p. 182.

27. Ibid., p. 181.

28. Both "A Dead Dancer" and fragments of "Storm" (the short poem that concludes *The Lilacs*) are in free verse. In her discussion of closural devices in free verse poems Barbara Herrnstein Smith notes "the formal resources of closure decrease as the form of the poem is increasingly undetermined" (*Poetic Closure*, p. 84) and that in free verse, closural properties are contained primarily in a poem's theme or themes rather than in its formal structure (pp. 78–79).

29. Crane and Freudenberg in *Man Collecting* (pp. 131–133) have collated the three versions of "A Dead Dancer" in the Alderman Faulkner Collection. L. D. Brodsky has reconstructed and collated *The Lilacs* version of this poem to the Crane/Freudenberg collation and published it and three fragments of other versions, all from his Faulkner collection. See below, *h*. Readers may refer to both articles.

a. "A Dead Dancer," Crane and Freudenberg, *Man Collecting*, pp. 131–133. A collation of 3 autograph manuscript versions at the Alderman Library that are listed below (*b–d*).

b. Number 1: recto of autograph manuscript in ink, legal-size paper, 4 strophes, 40 lines, 4½ lines canceled.

c. Number 2: verso of autograph manuscript in pencil, legal-size paper, 5 strophes, 43 lines, 4+ lines canceled.

d. Number 3: 1 p. autograph manuscript in ink on 8½ x 11-inch paper on recto of M. C. Falkner Hardware Store stationery, 3 strophes, 26 lines, 2 words canceled.

e. "A Dead Dancer," 3 pp. manuscript fragment. This is *The Lilacs* XII. Parts of 27 lines visible. Owned by L. D. Brodsky and listed as number 17 in Hamblin and Brodsky, *Selections*.

f. Autograph manuscript fragment: 2 strophes, 22 lines, 2 lines canceled. Number 14a in Hamblin and Brodsky, *Selections*.

g. Autograph manuscript: 3 variants of last strophe of "A Dead Dancer," 14 lines. Number 14d in Hamblin and Brodsky, *Selections*.

h. Letters *e*, *f*, and *g* are owned by L. D. Brodsky and are published in *Studies in Bibliography*, vol. 34 (Charlottesville: The Bibliographical Society of the University of Virginia, 1981), pp. 267–270.

Butterworth, "Census," lists the following versions of "A Dead Dancer" under Unidentified Fragments, number 58:

a. "While each one murmurs: Pray for me," first complete line 1 p. typescript carbon: burned fragment, 23 lines visible, 13 complete, Humanities Research Center, University of Texas, Austin (UT).

b. Untitled, 1 p. typescript carbon: burned fragment, parts of 16 lines visible, 3 holograph arrows in margin, UT.

c. Untitled, 1 p. typescript: burned fragment, parts of 16 lines visible, UT.

d. Untitled, 1 p. typescript: burned fragment, 20 lines visible, 13 complete, UT.

e. Untitled, 1 p. typescript: burned fragment, 22 lines visible, 16 complete, UT.

30. Faulkner, *Sanctuary*, p. 277. Her hair is "a black sprawl" (p. 146).

31. Wilde and Borsten, *A Loving Gentleman*, pp. 91, 133, 77–78.

32. Aiken, *Nocturne of Remembered Spring* (see note 37 below, "Episode in Grey").

33. Faulkner refers to *Forslin* in his 1921 review of Aiken's *Turns and Movies*: "The most interesting phase of Mr. Aiken's work is his experiments with an abstract three dimensional verse patterned on polyphonic music form: The Jig of Forslin and The House of Dust. This is interesting because of the utterly unlimited possibilities of it, he has the whole world before him; for as yet no one has made a successful attempt to synthesize musical reactions with abstract documentary reactions" (quoted in Collins, *Early Prose and Poetry*, p. 76).

34. Aiken, *The Jig of Forslin*, preface, p. 8.

35. Ibid., p. 9.

36. See, for example, Conrad Aiken, "The Deterioration of Poets," *The Dial* 64, no. 765 (January–June 1918): 404.

37. From Aiken, *Nocturne of Remembered Spring*:

We have deceived ourselves, but not each other:
Pretending love for what we could not love,
Now in a love of ghosts we are bound together
And struggle and cry and rage, and cannot move. ("Episode in Grey"
    III, p. 68)

You are not she I passionately made love to,
Nor am I he you cunningly adored. ("Episode in Grey" IV, p. 70)

This hand that touches me is not the hand
Of the silver queen I dreamed of, nor these lips
The lips of the cool white-hearted nereid. ("Episode in Grey" V, p. 71)

Compare these Aiken lines to those of the lovers' section in "A Dead Dancer," numbers 1 or 2. I will quote from number 2 as it is the one that otherwise most closely resembles number 4:

An arc light spills. Two lovers in shadows down below
That life has cruelly made of one being
Cling to each other in the aftermath of love
And kiss the awkward after kisses in the glow
They were god and goddess then, but now
Are slightly wearied of each other, yet they cannot part
Because of something vague and thin as air
Intangible yet strong as steel that binds them heart to heart.

The two final lines of "A Dead Dancer" number 1 are identical to two of Aiken's lines in "Episode in Grey." Faulkner's lines are "The interlacing of the threads of life / They know too much." Aiken's lines read:

The interlacing of the threads of life
They know too much.
And now, you say, we cannot move apart . . .
The minutes, the hours, the days we wove together
In a mesh of pain have bound us, heart to heart. ("Episode in Grey" III,
    p. 67)

38. Forslin, like the mourners in "A Dead Dancer," sits in the dusk meditating, following the myriad paths of his own streams of consciousness:

In the mute evening, as the music sounded,
Each voice of it, weaving gold or silver,
Seemed to open a separate door for him . . .
. . . .
Which way to choose, in all this labyrinth?
Did all lead in to the self-same chamber? (Aiken, *The Jig of Forslin*,
    p. 14)

Later Forslin asks himself, "Was it I who heard one night the rain / Weaving in silver an intricate pattern of pain?" (p. 25). Faulkner's arc light spilling over the disaffected lovers "slightly wearied of each other" but still pretending passion seems drawn from the arc light that shines on Forslin as he pursues his own deceitful past on his journey inward to the self:

And we walk, as we have walked a thousand times,
Past trees and curbs and gutters
Mark how the arc-lamp dims and starts and sputters,
Muse bewitching scandals, ponder crimes,
Laugh with a friend, concealing what we think,
Or sit, to chat and drink. (Aiken, *The Jig of Forslin*, p. 39)

39. Aiken, *The House of Dust*, p. 74.

40. Aiken, *Senlin: A Biography*, p. 15.

41. This adjective and its associated metaphor recur in the context of Wash's final illumination in *Absalom, Absalom!* At one level Wash's innocence is comparable to Lena's. See *AA*, pp. 283, 290.

42. From Crane and Freudenberg, *Man Collecting*, with number 4 added by the author.

43. Smith says, "Although a lyric may be dramatic or narrative in certain respects, what distinguishes it from a versified play or novel is the fact that it is the representation, not of an action or the chronicle of an action, but of an utterance" (*Poetic Closure*, p. 122).

44. Faulkner transforms these drawings into language in his initial descriptions of another virgin dancer, Temple Drake. Peeping at her through a window "Tommy could hear the faint chatter of the shucks inside the mattress where Temple lay, her hands crossed on her breast and her legs straight and close and decorous, like an effigy on an ancient tomb" (*Sanctuary*, p. 69).

Chapter VII. Aiken and Freud

1. Meanwhile, like his contemporaries in London and Paris, he was reading Symons very carefully. See Kreiswirth, "Faulkner as Translator." Faulkner's Verlaine poems were "Fantouches," "Clair de Lune," "Streets," and "A Clymene." All are reprinted in Collins, *Early Prose and Poetry*. Kreiswirth suggests it is no coincidence that translations of all four poems appear in an appendix to the 1919 edition of Symons's book (*The Symbolist Movement*, p. 430).

2. Review of W. A. Percy's *In April Once* in *The Mississippian* (10 November 1920), p. 5. This, the five other reviews, and published poetry Faulkner wrote between November 1920 and December 1922 are reprinted in Collins, *Early Prose and Poetry*.

3. William Faulkner, "Books and Things: *Turns and Movies*," in Collins, *Early Prose and Poetry*, pp. 74–76. In answer to his query, Aiken wrote Blotner that he and Faulkner had met only once, when they had the following dialogue concerning the poem Faulkner quoted in his 1921 review. Aiken wrote him the following about this meeting:

Brewster, Mass.
May 16 64

Dear Mr. Blotner:

Thanks for your letter. Indeed I admired Faulkner, as you will know from my essay on him, and I knew *about* him through various close friends for thirty years or more, and saw him, but not to speak to—he so obviously didn't want to be spoken to—at the National Institute on sundry occasions. But I never actually met him until he came up to receive the Institute's Gold Medal for fiction, such a short time ago. And thereby hangs a tale, which I hope isn't a tale out of school. For it happened that I was on the committee for the Gold Medal, had missed an earlier meeting, and when I attended the second was astounded to find that in a list of a dozen or more names proposed for the award there was no Faulkner. On my querying this, there was some dismay, for apparently there was a notion that it should go to K. A. Porter. Anyway, I nominated him, with the inevitable result that when it came to a vote by the members at large he won it easily. And so, when he came up for the occasion *I* seized the occasion to introduce myself. And here follows the only conversation I ever had with him. Faulkner: Music I heard with you was more than music, and bread I broke with you was more than bread. Aiken: No, Mr. Faulkner, I've changed the second line—it's *bed* I broke with you was more than bed. Faulkner: Bread I broke with you was more than bread. Aiken: *Bed* I broke with you was more than bed. Faulkner: Bread I broke with you was more than bread. Aiken: Bed I broke with you was more than bed. Faulkner: Bread—— And looking each other steadily in the eye, we tacitly decided that it was a dead heat, and broke off. My only conversation, and there was never any correspondence. I do know that my early poetry influenced him—I have somewhere a New Orleans magazine with a poem of his, beside which my friend R. N. Linscott had written, If Faulkner hasn't been reading Aiken, I'm a horse-thief. It was in the style of Senlin or Festus. And that is all. If you want to see me, I'll be at the above address till late fall, but I'm not sure there's much that I can say.

Yours sincerely,
Conrad Aiken

See also Blotner, *Faulkner*, p. 1823 and notes. This letter is printed here courtesy of Joseph Blotner, who supplied me with a photocopy of the original, and with the permission of Mary Hoover Aiken, Conrad Aiken's executor. According to Joseph Killorin, who is now writing a biography of Aiken, although Aiken and Faulkner did not correspond, Faulkner did enclose notes to Aiken in advance copies of his own books that he sent to the poet (Joseph Killorin, letter to author, 25 August 1983).

4. T. S. Eliot, "Ezra Pound," *Poetry* 68 (1946): 326–327.

5. Although Eliot in this essay (ibid.) does not acknowledge Aiken's much earlier enthusiastic reading of "Prufrock" or say that it was Aiken who first showed it to Pound, he does say that "in 1915 (and through Aiken) I met Pound" (ibid., p. 327). Aiken writes Harriet Monroe in 1915 to defend his

articles attacking the Imagist platform. In doing so he says he objects not to radicalism or experimentation, but to "formlessness."

> If proof is needed that I am not so provincial a Victorian as you say, I may add that I was indirectly, and largely, responsible for the publication of Eliot's "Love Song of J. Alfred Prufrock" in your June issue, 1915. That poem was written, if I remember rightly, nearly four years ago, and I had a copy of it from the first; and as Eliot himself was heartlessly indifferent to its fate, it was I who sought publication for it. Four years ago! So you see, if I am suffering from a "culture" of radicalism—and I am sure you did not consider Eliot's poem precisely old-fashioned—I have been suffering from it rather longer than most of the Imagists. Yours sincerely, Conrad Aiken. (Killorin, *Selected Letters*, p. 42)

6. Faulkner, "Verse Old and Nascent: A Pilgrimage," *The Double Dealer* 7 (April 1925): 129–131. Reprinted in Collins, *Early Prose and Poetry*, pp. 114–118. An extant typescript of this essay dated "October 1924" is in the Faulkner Collection at the University of Virginia.

7. Storey, *Pierrot: A Critical History*, p. xiii. This book provides an excellent account of the literary history of Pierrot as it relates to "the poetry of Laforgue and . . . the most prominent American poets of this century, T. S. Eliot and Wallace Stevens."

8. The last three chapters of Storey's book discuss the role of the *pierrotique* narrator in Eliot's and Stevens's development. Frederick Hoffman says of Aiken, "He was, of course, fascinated by the mixture of comic irony, dramatic assertion, and essential sadness, of the Laforguian Pierrot and the gestures of comical contempt in the clown's and the puppet's occasional defiance of 'the truth'" (Hoffman, *Conrad Aiken*, p. 88). A well-argued critique of Aiken's total work is Martin, *Conrad Aiken*.

9. Booth, *The Rhetoric of Fiction*, p. 229.

10. Blotner, *Faulkner*, pp. 292, 324.

11. Ibid., p. 232.

12. Ibid., p. 233.

13. Ibid., p. 255.

14. Ibid., p. 251. Blotner quotes a Louis Cochran interview in *William Faulkner of Oxford*, ed. James W. Webb and A. Wigfall Green (Baton Rouge: Louisiana State University Press, 1965), p. 102.

15. Blotner, *Faulkner*, p. 264.

16. Ibid., pp. 282–283.

17. Ibid., p. 287.

18. Ibid., p. 344.

19. Reprinted in Collins, *Early Prose and Poetry*, pp. 74–76.

20. It is possible that these verses are drafts for yet another sequence called *Michael*, fragments of which belong to at least one private collector. The *Michael* fragments I have seen are redolent of Aiken. Thus, whether the verses belong with *Vision, Orpheus, Michael*, or even another unidentified and now lost cycle does not affect my argument, for both technically and

thematically the poetry is of a piece with much of *Vision in Spring*.

21. Excluding numerous screenplays he wrote in Hollywood between 1932 and 1954, the only other play Faulkner wrote was *Requiem for a Nun* (1951). For a complete discussion of Faulkner's film work see Bruce F. Kawin, *Faulkner and Film* (New York: Frederick Ungar Publishing Co., 1977), and idem, *Faulkner's MGM Screenplays* (Knoxville: University of Tennessee Press, 1982).

22. Faulkner dates the bound typescript of *Vision in Spring* "1921." Thus my dating is only approximate and determined by the drafts of *Vision in Spring* done on Faulkner's Aiken review, typescript fragments of *Vision in Spring* poems dated "1920" at the Humanities Research Center, University of Texas at Austin, and the fact that Faulkner was already experimenting with Aiken in his 1920 poem sequence *The Lilacs*. For further evidence of Faulkner's deep interest in Aiken and the time at which it occurred, see Ben Wasson's account of Faulkner reading all of *Turns and Movies* aloud to him at one sitting (Wasson, *Count No 'Count*, pp. 32–33). On Faulkner's awareness of plagiarism, see ibid., p. 41.

23. Blotner, *Faulkner*, pp. 307–312.

24. "The World and Pierrot. A Nocturne," *Vision in Spring* III (1921), pp. 25–26.

25. Storey quoting T. S. Eliot on himself in *Pierrot: A Critical History*, p. 160. Faulkner steals phrases from these poems to ornament *The Marble Faun*, *The Lilacs*, and *Vision in Spring*. They are "Conversation Galante," "Portrait of a Lady," and "The Love Song of J. Alfred Prufrock." Faulkner parodies "Prufrock" in the climactic poem in *Vision*.

26. According to Joseph Blotner and Jill Faulkner Summers, both sets of parents disapproved of Faulkner's marrying Estelle Oldham. While this may not be the whole truth it was certainly the public perception. See Blotner, *Faulkner*, passim. Summers says, "The relationship between the Oldhams and the Faulkners was difficult. Neither approved of the other. They married her to Franklin originally because they thought the Faulkners were beneath them" (Jill Faulkner Summers, interview, 20 August 1980).

27. Faulkner's interest in unattainable women obtained in life as well. To express it he chose an appropriate spokesman. Blotner notes Faulkner's early identification with Cyrano de Bergerac's love language. Faulkner quotes fragments of Cyrano's love speeches to Estelle Oldham Franklin, Helen Baird, Meta Wilde, and Joan Williams (Blotner, *Faulkner*, notes p. 77; Wilde, and Williams, interviews). Acknowledging his persistent identification with Cyrano and his persistent interest in unavailable women, Jill Faulkner Summers says that *Cyrano de Bergerac* was "a key work." Faulkner often quoted Cyrano's "plume speech" to her:

The concept of the white plume was very important to Pappy although he may have taken frequent liberties with it. It stood, I think, for how he would have *liked* to have been. Cyrano himself was in many ways how Pappy really did see himself. More often than not in the course of his romantic excursions when the person he *thought* was unavailable became suddenly attainable, he was shocked—sort of like those poems of Provence and courtly love. In his heart of hearts Pappy preferred, I think, to think of all women as unattainable. He even seemed extremely surprised when I showed up with my first baby. (Jill Faulkner Summers, interview, 21 July 1980)

Thomas Sutpen, Faulkner's fictional hero most disastrously beaten in his quests for fame and an ideal mate, wears a broken plume as does Joe Christmas's vanquished grandmother. "The Knight of the Black Plume" was the Colonel's honorary Civil War title (Blotner, *Faulkner*, p. 23). Faulkner must have delighted in the irony.

28. Storey, *Pierrot: A Critical History*, pp. 140, 150.

29. Adolphe Willete, *Feu Pierrot, 1857–19?* (Paris, 1919), p. 128. Quoted in ibid., pp. 121–122.

30. In January 1921 Phil Stone gave Faulkner William Stanley Braithwaite's *Anthology of Magazine Verse for 1920* (Blotner, *Faulkner*, p. 299).

31. According to Blotner, Estelle's first visit home after her marriage to Franklin and move to Honolulu occurred June 1919 to 29 September 1919. Her baby daughter was then four months old. Estelle's second visit occurred in May 1920 and her third in May 1921.

32. Previous critics (Brooks, Blotner, Yonce, and Polk [in Faulkner, *Marionettes*, and *Sanctuary: The Original Text*]) have noted Eliotic echoes in Faulkner's early poetry and prose. Blotner (the only critic who has written on *Vision in Spring*) in *Faulkner*, pp. 307–312, calls the sequence's ninth poem ("Love Song") Faulkner's "Prufrock" poem. In 118 lines "Faulkner had seemingly set himself the task of paraphrasing Eliot's 131 line poem" (p. 309). Blotner also notes echoes of "The Preludes" and "Sweeny among the Nightingales" in other poems in the sequence. However, none of these critics seem aware that a close personal and poetic relationship existed between Eliot and Aiken from 1908 when they first met and began to exchange ideas and poems in the offices of the *Harvard Advocate* through 1922 when Eliot published *The Waste Land*. Joseph Warren Beach has commented on the cross-influence and parallels in the poetry of these two men. His article concludes "not merely that so interesting and ingenious a poet as the Conrad Aiken of 1914–24 could find in Eliot hints for making his work still more interesting . . . but also that the incomparable Eliot may have taken from Aiken hints for images as imaginatively provocative as the Tarot cards and the voices out of the empty cisterns" ("Echoes and Overtones," p. 762). Beach based his article on the then available published evidence in both poets' poems: borrowings in Aiken's *Nocturne of Remembered Spring* from Eliot and borrowings in Eliot's *Waste Land* from Aiken's *Jig of Forslin*. Writing in 1954, Beach had not seen Aiken's letters (in Killorin, *Selected Letters*), especially his letters to Eliot and the letter to Houston Peterson (pp. 142, 145–146). Aiken's undergraduate poem *The Clerk's Journal* (written 1910, published 1971) also adds further evidence and support to Beach's

contention. *The Clerk's Journal* suggests in many regards, specifically in its theme and texture, a Prufrock in embryo. Its *pierrotique* persona is a shy little clerk, "the romantic and prosaic are juxtaposed to produce ironic effect, lyric musings are interrupted by voiced comments," and the poetry, as Aiken also notes, contains "a prophetically modern vocabulary of images: written in 1910, several years before Prufrock, it is already talking of lunch counters, plates of beans, the moon among the telephone wires, and life being paved with cobblestones." He then adds, implicitly making the point that tracing of influences is a tricky business, that Robinson "maybe the earliest of the modernizers had already written these kinds of lines phrased in this range of vocabulary" (Aiken, *The Clerk's Journal*, pp. 4–5). Between 1908 and 1913, when Aiken left Harvard, the question, What was poetry? "was their constant concern. They exchanged poems and discussed them. How to find a new poetic language. We were feeling our way towards it, something less *poetic*, more inclusive, more quotidian, admitting even the vernacular, and lower in pitch: a new poetic voice, one in which one could *think*."

The whole story of the mutual debt between Aiken and Eliot is yet to be told. The teller, taking evidence from the complete published letters of both poets and noting the history of significant manuscripts' publication (for example, it was Aiken who took Eliot's "Prufrock" to Ezra Pound), will be hard put at times not to confuse "what is derivative in either with what is similar or parallel" (Russo, "A Study in Influence," p. 687). Aiken's poetry has not received the attention it merits. Looked at merely from the viewpoint of its seminal influence on two of the twentieth century's most original writers (Eliot and Faulkner), it provides a vital clue for tracing the development of Modernism. Aiken's poetry and criticism played a pivotal role in developing the voices of our greatest Modernist writers—one a poet's, the other a novelist's. Faulkner's *Vision in Spring* contains Eliotic lines but its overall tone and texture and, most important, its shape derive from Aiken's "symphonies."

33. Aiken, *The Jig of Forslin*.

34. In "American Drama: Inhibitions," *The Mississippian* (17 March 1922), p. 5 and (24 March 1922), p. 5, reprinted in Collins, *Early Prose and Poetry*, pp. 93–97, Faulkner writes, "Writing people are all so pathetically torn between a desire to make a figure in the world and a morbid interest in their personal egos—the deadly fruit of the grafting of Sigmund Freud" (p. 93). Along with socialism Faulkner here cites "psycho-analysis" as one of the greatest obstacles the writer in America "must combat." Characters who take Freud seriously are ridiculed in *Mosquitoes* (1926). In 1958 Faulkner answers a psychiatrist's question "You don't have any idea of [where you learned psychology]?" "No sir, I don't . . . What little of psychology I know the characters I have invented and playing poker have taught me. Freud I'm not familiar with" (Gwynn and Blotner, *Faulkner in the University*, p. 268).

35. *The New York Independent* (1916–1917), quoted in an advertisement

on the end pages of Conrad Aiken's *Nocturne of Remembered Spring*.

36. Aiken read *The Interpretation of Dreams* in 1913 when it was first translated into English.

37. Aiken, *The Jig of Forslin*, pp. 8–9.

38. Ibid., p. 9.

39. Aiken, preface to *The Charnel Rose* (1915), pp. 91–92.

40. Ibid., p. 92.

41. Bowra, *The Heritage of Symbolism*, p. 3.

42. Stéphane Mallarmé, "Sainte," *Poésies* (1877).

43. Conrad Aiken, "Counterpoint and Implication," *Poetry* (June 1919), reprinted in Aiken, *The Divine Pilgrim*, p. 286.

44. Ibid., p. 287.

45. From a letter Aiken wrote Frederick J. Hoffman. See Hoffman, *The Twenties, American Writing in the Post-War Decade* (New York: Collier Books, 1962), p. 97, note.

Aiken described Freud's early influence on his work in a letter to Houston Peterson, 8 June 1928:

> *Freud had been influencing me since my last two years in college;* his shadow (and Ellis's, too, whose six volumes of sex studies I had read) *was on the Charnel Rose; and it furnished the starting-point and main theme of Forslin.* Rumours of Le Bon [Gustave Le Bon (1841– 1931), *The Crowd: A Study of the Popular Mind* (1897), a translation of *Psychologie des foules* (1895), is the book Aiken had seen in 1915.] and crowd psychology crossed me while I was in the midst of Forslin, and the House of Dust took off from that . . . *The whole problem of the nature of mind fascinated me* and was the constant subject of our talks. (Killorin, *Selected Letters*, p. 144, emphasis added)

46. Conrad Aiken, *New Verse*, 1937.

47. In 1923, discussing Freud's theory about relationship of the pleasure principle to the creative impulse, Aiken wrote:

> Let us rashly posit, that the pleasurable feeling we know as "beauty" is simply in essence, the profound satisfaction we feel when, through the medium (of poetry, art, music, etc.) we escape from imposed limitations into an aggrandized personality and harmonized universe. The very essence of beauty is "illusion" . . . Freud is not, by two thousand two hundred years, the first to see art as primarily a process of wish-fulfillment. Let us recall Aristotle's theory of Katharsis, and rub our eyes. ("A Basis for Criticism," *The New Republic* 34 [April 1923]: 1–6)

48. Conrad Aiken, "The Mechanism of Poetic Inspiration," *Scepticisms, Notes on Contemporary Poetry* (New York: Alfred A. Knopf, 1919), p. 47. "Faulkner had access through Phil Stone to current literary journals including *Poetry*, *The Dial*, and *The Little Review*" (Richard P. Adams, "The Apprenticeship of William Faulkner," *Tulane Studies in English* 12 [1962], p. 114). Aiken's essays also appeared in these periodicals.

49. Advertisement in the *Poetry Journal*, vol. 6, no. 2 (December 1916). Owned, published, and edited by the Four Seas Company, Boston. Doubtless Aiken read and approved this copy. He may even have written it. Another ad said, "Psychologically *The Jig of Forslin* is highly interesting. It reproduces . . . in rich variation, the amoral impulses and desires of adolescence . . . the author escapes the dicta of the moral censors" (*The Poetry Journal* [March 1917]).

50. Many of these fragments are in the Faulkner Collection at the Humanities Research Center, University of Texas at Austin. The content and the phrasing of Faulkner's comments on Aiken's craft show his familiarity with Aiken's criticism and poetry. Most of the essays Faulkner draws from were reprinted in *Scepticisms* (1919). For a full discussion see Sensibar, "William Faulkner, Poet," pp. 251–260. *Scepticisms* does not appear in Blotner's catalog of the books Faulkner owned when he died. But neither do many of the books Faulkner read, like *The Limits of Symbolism* or Aiken's *Turns and Movies, The Jig of Forslin*, and *The House of Dust*.

51. Collins, *Early Prose and Poetry*, p. 74.

52. Ibid., p. 75.

53. Aiken, "The Impersonal Poet." Also see T. S. Eliot, "Tradition and the Individual Talent" (1919) in *The Sacred Wood*, p. 58. Hugh Kenner argues convincingly that "Tradition and the Individual Talent" had its genesis in Eliot's 1916 dissertation on F. H. Bradley (Kenner, *The Invisible Poet*, p. 49). He is probably correct but I think Aiken's essay certainly influenced Eliot's thoughts.

54. Aiken, "The Impersonal Poet," p. 65.

55. Ibid., p. 63. He differs here from Eliot, who asserts that although art may develop and become increasingly complex, it does not necessarily improve.

56. Ibid., pp. 64, 66. Eliot's differentiation between an immature and a mature poet and the relation of the poem to its author build from the sentence in Aiken's "The Impersonal Poet" that I have underlined. According to Eliot, the poem of a mature poet is "a more finely perfected medium in which special, or very varied, *feelings are at liberty* to enter into new combinations . . . the poet has, not a 'personality' to express, but a particular medium, which is only a medium and not a personality, *in which impressions and experiences combine in peculiar and unexpected ways . . . The business of the poet is not to find new emotions, but to use the ordinary ones and, in working them up into poetry, to express feelings which* are not in actual emotions at all" (Eliot, "Tradition and the Individual Talent," in *The Sacred Wood*, pp. 56, 58, emphasis added).

57. Collins, *Early Prose and Poetry*, p. 75.

58. Aiken, "Counterpoint and Implication," in *Scepticisms*, p. 155.

59. William Faulkner, "Interviews in Japan, 1955," in Meriwether and Millgate, *Lion in the Garden*, pp. 146–147.

60. Cowley, *Writers at Work*, p. 133.

61. Gwynn and Blotner, *Faulkner in the University*, p. 122. Was Faulkner with these answers stealing once again from Conrad Aiken? If not, there is an uncanny similarity between Faulkner's remarks here and Aiken's 1939 written comments on the form of *The Wild Palms*. In this ground-breaking essay, one of the first and still one of the best on the structure of Faulkner's narrative poetics, Aiken says of *The Sound and the Fury, The Wild Palms, Absalom, Absalom!,* and *As I Lay Dying,* "the richness and complexity is chiefly obtained by a very skillful fugue-like alternation of viewpoint." He also speaks here of *The Sound and the Fury*'s "massive four-part symphonic structure" (Conrad Aiken, "William Faulkner: The Novel as Form," *Atlantic Monthly* [November 1939]: 650–654). When he wrote this essay Aiken of course had no idea that the symphonic forms of his early poem sequences had influenced Faulkner's fictional structures.

62. Collins, *Early Prose and Poetry*, p. 76.

Chapter VIII. Sequence and Mask as Guiding Formal Principles

1. Kartiganer, *The Fragile Thread*, p. xvii.

2. Ibid., p. xiii.

3. Kinney, *Faulkner's Narrative Poetics*, p. 9.

4. Kinney points out stylistic similarities in these novels' endings, specifically the functions of Aunt Jenny in *Flags*, the furniture dealer in *Light in August*, and the impersonal narrator who records *Sanctuary*'s final vision in the Luxembourg Gardens.

5. Kinney, *Faulkner's Narrative Poetics*, p. xiii.

6. Ibid., p. xiii.

7. Kinney observes that Faulkner's fictional voices alternate these modes.

8. This image anticipates Faulkner's recurrent trope for Temple Drake's self-imprisonment in *Sanctuary*. From the moment she appears ("her long legs blonde with running . . . a final squatting swirl of knickers . . . as she sprang in to the car . . .") to her stay at Goodwin's ("she whirled and sat up, her mouth open upon a soundless wail. . . . she half spun, poised with running") to Miss Reba's, Temple too, perpetually spins and whirls (pp. 28, 38, 41).

9. See also *TMF* XVII, p. 48.

10. Faulkner's unfortunate adaptation of Swinburne's line from a chorus of *Atalanta in Calydon*, "Her bright breast shortening into sighs" (Swinburne, *Poems*, p. 151).

11. Because the original booklet has disappeared, I have worked from a photocopy (see my introduction, Faulkner, *Vision in Spring*). Blotner describes the original as a carbon typescript (see chapter XII, note 32, p. 268). Faulkner rebound *Vision in Spring* in 1926 and noted the date of rebinding on the typescript's final page, "REBOUND 26 JANUARY 1926. OXFORD, MISSISSIPPI." According to Blotner's description the cover was a mottled watercolor gouache of browns and greens (Blotner, *Faulkner*, p. 307); thus it

would have matched the covers he had made for his sonnet sequence *Helen: A Courtship*, dated Oxford, Mississippi, June 1926, and his fable *Mayday*, dated Oxford, Mississippi, 27 January 1926.

12. If so, then Faulkner would be imitating Aiken's conception of the interrelationship of the five symphonies that he ultimately published under the title *The Divine Pilgrim* and spoke of as his "own complete(?) view of the world" (Killorin, *Selected Letters*, p. 144). And he would be anticipating his own remarks concerning his invented "apocrypha." Unpublished preface to *The Sound and the Fury*, Berg Collection, New York Public Library.

13. Letters of Pound to Eliot, in *A.B.C. of Reading* (New York: New Directions Press, 1960 [new edition]), p. 36.

14. In Eliot's *Four Quartets* where he reaches for a more expansive poetic form (see Gardner, *The Composition of Four Quartets*, pp. 14–17), his formal intentions are in one respect, despite his own disavowals, remarkably similar to those Aiken was striving toward in his symphonic sequences. Writing to Hayward concerning his sequence's title Eliot says:

> How great is the resistance to "quartets"? I am aware of general objections to these musical analogies: there was a period when people were writing long poems and calling them, with no excuse, "symphonies" (J. Gould Fletcher even did a "Symphony in Blue" I think, thus achieving a greater *confusion des genres*). But I should like to indicate that these poems are all in a particular set form which I have elaborated, and the word "quartet" does seem to me to start people on the right tack for understanding them ("sonata" in any case is *too* musical). It suggests to me the notion of making a poem by weaving in together three or four superficially unrelated themes: the "poem" being the degree of success in making a new whole out of them. (Eliot to Hayward, 2 September 1942, quoted in Gardner, *The Composition of Four Quartets*, p. 26)

15. Killorin, *Selected Letters*, p. 143.

16. Aaron Copland, *What to Listen for in Music*, p. 127. Copland calls the creation of the symphonic poem "one of the few new forms of the nineteenth century" (p. 130). Of Strauss's contributions he says, they "astonished the musical world by their freedom and daring. . . . The earlier symphonic poem (invented by Liszt) was analogous with a single movement of a symphony, but the Straussian tone poem is more the equivalent of a full-sized symphony" (p. 131).

17. See Kermode's discussion of Yeats's poetry in *The Romantic Image*.

18. This novel's Marble Faun is the blind, almost mute, and finally motionless Donald Mahon, identified previously by Margaret Yonce and other critics writing on early Faulkner.

19. Jill Faulkner Summers, interview, 16 March 1982.

20. Kermode, *The Romantic Image*, pp. 83, 25.

Chapter IX. "Silent Music"

1. Bate, *John Keats*, p. 170.

2. Freud, *Jokes*, pp. 159–180.

3. a. "Vision in Spring," 5 pp. photocopy of carbon typescript, 52 lines. This is *Vision in Spring* I, pp. 1–5. For prior listing of *b* and *d*, see Butterworth, "Census," Published Poetry, number 69.

b. "Visions in Spring," *Contempo* 1 (1 February 1932): 1 (52 lines).

c. "Vision in Spring," 3 pp. typescript with two holograph corrections, stanzas 2–5 repeated and stanzas 8–11 repeated but canceled. Final stanza varies from *b*, University of Virginia (UVa).

d. "Vision in Spring," 3 pp. typescript, Humanities Research Center, University of Texas, Austin (UT). Has one holograph correction in ink.

4. See Swinburne, "A Vision of Spring in Winter," in *Poems*, pp. 187–190, passim. Some Aiken lines or phrases are:

In the mute evening, as the music sounded,
Each voice of it, weaving gold or silver,
Seemed to open a separate door for him . . . (*The Jig of Forslin* I, i,
   p. 14)

While the dancers whirled and danced. (ibid. I, i, p. 15)

Well, I am frustrate; life has beaten me,
The thing I strongly seized has turned to darkness,
And darkness rides my heart. . . . (*The House of Dust* IV, iii, p. 127)

It is noon; the bells let fall soft flowers of sound. . . .
. . . .
Do not disturb my memories, heartless music!
I stand once more by a vine-dark moonlit wall,
The sound of my footsteps dies in a void of moonlight,
I watch white roses softly fall.
Is it my heart that falls? (*Senlin: A Biography* II, v, pp. 29, 30)

The similarity between Aiken's Forslin and Faulkner's Pierrot is especially apparent when we compare Forslin's definition of peace. Compare the concluding lines of the first movement of Aiken's symphony, *The Jig of Forslin*, to Pierrot's in *Vision in Spring*'s first movement:

But this was peace, this darkness!—like old music,
Music heard in a dream; or hid in a wall;
Like a slow music, moving under a sea,
A waveless music, seethed and frothed in starlight,
Desireless; cold; and dead . . . (*The Jig of Forslin* I, v, p. 29)

This kind of borrowing from Aiken occurs throughout *Vision in Spring*. For specific borrowings in each poem see Sensibar, "William Faulkner, Poet," chaps. 10–12.

5. a. "Interlude," 4 pp. photocopy of carbon typescript, 49 lines. This is *Vision in Spring* II, pp. 6–9. For prior listing of *b* and *c*, see Butterworth, "Census," Unpublished Poetry, number 18.

b. "Interlude," 3 pp. typescript identical to *Vision in Spring* version other than some changes in punctuation, UT.

c. "Interlude," 2 pp. typescript fragment, 46 lines visible, 28 lines complete, has "5." in black ink over title, UT. This fragment is reproduced in Faulkner, *Vision in Spring*, Appendix B.

6. Still surrounded by the ghosts of his visions, Pierrot walked "along the phantomed street / And rang the hollow pavement with his feet" (p. 9). This line echoes Aiken's concluding image for the first movement of *Forslin*: "He saw himself limp down the windy street, / Bending his face against the relentless cold" (*The Jig of Forslin* I, iv, p. 26).

7. a. "The World and Pierrot. A Nocturne," 18 pp. photocopy of carbon typescript, 224 lines. This is *Vision in Spring* III, pp. 10–29. See Butterworth, "Census," Published Poetry, number 45 for prior listing of *b* and *c*.

b. "Nocturne," *The Ole Miss, 1920–1921*, no. XXV, pp. 214–215, lines 29–50 of *a* with 11 variants. Reproduced in Meriwether, *Bibliographical Study*, Figure 2.

c. "Nocturne," Collins, *Early Prose and Poetry*, pp. 82–83. Both *b* and *c*, which are listed in Butterworth, "Census," are part 2 of this 8-part poem (pp. 12–14 in *Vision in Spring*).

8. Eliot, *Collected Poems*, pp. 29, 27.

9. Faulkner, *Sanctuary*, pp. 210–211.

10. Some Aiken lines Faulkner draws upon for "Nocturne" are "Death, among violins and paper roses, / Leering upon a waltz, in evening dress . . ." (*The Jig of Forslin* I, vi, p. 30) and "And the cold blood drips from the rose . . ." (*The Jig of Forslin* III, iv, p. 69). Identity is Forslin's problem too and is posed similarly:

I walked by the river, once, and heard the waves
Slapping the sunlit stones . . . But was that I?
Or was it I who saw a pigeon falling. . . .
Or was it I who heard one night the rain
Weaving in silver an intricate pattern of pain? (*The Jig of Forslin* I, iv,
   p. 25)

The concluding lines of "Nocturne" (see p. 149) echo Aiken's: "We open our eyes and stare at the coiling darkness, / And enter our dreams again" (*House of Dust* III, xii, p. 113).

11. Faulkner elaborates on this fantasy with Bayard Sartoris in *Flags in the Dust* (1927), Quentin Compson in *The Sound and the Fury* (1929), and in his much more subtle and powerful portrayal of Temple Drake's "flight" in *Sanctuary* (1931).

12. Wilde and Borsten, *A Loving Gentleman*, pp. 142, 143. Both Faulkner's attachment to and fear of this fantasy are illustrated in a similar but less dramatic incident that Ben Wasson describes (see Wasson, *Count No 'Count*, pp. 124–125). In this instance Faulkner achieves mastery by creating "Turnabout."

13. For a complete listing of other Faulkner pilot stories see Brooks, *To-*

ward Yoknapatawpha, pp. 403–406. Also his remarks on Faulkner's novel *Pylon* (1935), pp. 395–406. The tone and language of Rider's drunk scenes in "Pantaloon in Black" (1940) derive explicitly from "Nocturne" too.

14. a. "After the Concert," 3 pp. photocopy of carbon typescript, 39 lines. This is *Vision in Spring* IV, pp. 30–32.

b. "So we walk and dumbly raise our eyes," first line, 1 p. typescript: burned fragment, 12 lines complete, UT (Butterworth, "Census," Unidentified Fragments, number 50).

c. "After the Concert," 1 p. black ribbon typescript fragment, a version of *Vision in Spring* IV, lines 1–21, has "4." in black ink above title, 21 lines visible, 14 complete, UT (Butterworth, "Census," Unpublished Poetry, number 3). This fragment is reproduced in Faulkner, *Vision in Spring*, Appendix B.

a. "Portrait," 3 pp. photocopy of carbon typescript, 24 lines. This is *Vision in Spring* V, pp. 33–35. For prior listing of *b–d*, see Butterworth, "Census," Published Poetry, number 52.

b. "Portrait," *Double Dealer* 3 (June 1922): 337, 24 lines, 14 variants.

c. "Portrait," Collins, *Early Prose and Poetry* (identical to *b*), pp. 99–100.

d. "Portrait," 1 p. typescript: burned fragment, 19 lines visible, 13 complete, "3." in ink above title, UT.

15. Aiken borrowings here are the setting and title "The Concert: Harmonics" from *The Jig of Forslin* V, iv, p. 112 and phrases from it and from *The Jig of Forslin* I, vii, p. 35.

The lamps are turned out on the music racks,
The concert ends, the people rise,
The applause behind us roars like rain on a roof,
The great doors close. We shrink beneath blue skies.

16. a. Untitled, 4 pp. photocopy of carbon typescript, 47 lines. This is *Vision in Spring* VI, pp. 36–39.

b. "The dark ascends," first line, 1 p. typescript: burned fragment, 22 lines visible, 16 complete, UT (Butterworth, "Census," Unidentified Fragments, number 18). Typescript has "6." above poem.

c. "Let us go alone, then, you and I, while evening grows," first line, 1 p. typescript: burned fragment, 19 lines visible, 15 complete, UT.

d. "Your eyes like rain upon two pools," first complete line, 1 p. typescript: burned fragment (variant) of last 2 strophes, 15 lines visible, first 4 incomplete, and "William Faulkner. / July 1920." typed at bottom of poem. This fragment is reproduced in Faulkner, *Vision in Spring*, Appendix B.

17. Relevant Aiken lines:

I would like to sit with you, and hear soft music
. . . .
I would like to hear you talking of simple things,
Of leaves that hang on trees and softly fall:
I would like to have your hands touch mine like wings,

And see your face, so white and young and fragile,
Against the golden darkness of a wall. . . . ("Sonata in Pathos," in
  Nocturne of Remembered Spring, pp. 42–43)

Her brow so placid and so wise,—
He saw the graceful small hand rise
To brush the soft hair from her eyes. . . . ("This Dance of Life," in
  Turns and Movies, p. 54)

18. See Irwin, *Doubling and Incest*. Irwin ascribes the relation of this and other similar scenes in Faulkner's novels to what he calls a character's pathological narcissism. Of Quentin here he says, "The fear of castration fixes Quentin in secondary narcissism, for by making sexual union with a woman synonymous with death, the castration fear prevents the establishment of a love object outside the ego. Quentin's fear of castration is projected onto the figure of his sister, incest with whom would be punished by castration. Thus in her encounters with Quentin, Candace becomes the castrator" (pp. 46–47). Irwin concludes that this theme—confrontation with a double—is one "Faulkner never tires of reiterating: by courageously facing the fear of death, the fear of castration, the fear of one's own worst instincts, one slays the fear; by taking the risk of being feminized, by accepting the feminine elements in the self, one establishes one's masculinity. And it is by allowing the fear of death, of castration, of one's own instincts, of being feminized, to demarcate the ego that one is paralyzed, rendered impotent, unmanned, as in the case of Quentin" (pp. 58–59). I would argue rather that textual evidence indicates that Quentin's fear is of *total annihilation* and therefore of preoedipal origin.

19. Faulkner, like the fictional Jones, seemed especially attracted to "papier-mâché Virgins." In fact, both Estelle Faulkner and Meta Wilde had been divorced prior to their involvement with him, while Joan Williams's marriage at seventeen had been annulled. See Blotner, *Faulkner*; Wilde and Borsten, *A Loving Gentleman*; and Joan Williams, interview, 20 June 1983.

20. Number XIII, "O I have heard the evening trumpeted," in *Helen: A Courtship and Mississippi Poems*, p. 124. The original booklet is in the William B. Wisdom Collection, Howard Tilton Memorial Library, Tulane University. For contents of this collection see Bonner, *William Faulkner*.

21. Wilde and Borsten, *A Loving Gentleman*, pp. 126–127.

22. Laughter, rise! Music, come!
  Into the blood bring horn and drum!
  Sweet violins that edge with pain,
  Insidiously, the softest strain!
  Pulse and sing and blow and beat
  Faster for these dancing feet!
  Clanging cymbals be not mute,
  Lift your voices, fife and flute,
  Throb, you harps, cry, clarinets,
  Mad music for life's marionettes!
  . . . .

Let this dance of life called pleasure
Move to an ever-changing measure!
. . . .
A threadlike music, shining thin,
Spun from a single violin. (Aiken, "This Dance of Life," in *Turns and Movies*, p. 81)

Blotner says Estelle Franklin wrote in "A Symphony" (Blotner, *Faulkner*, p. 309). Jill Faulkner Summers says it is "not my mother's handwriting" (Jill Faulkner Summers, interview, 29 July 1980).

23. a. Untitled, 7 pp. photocopy of carbon typescript, 115 lines, line 41 canceled but legible and illegible lines written at bottom of p. 46. This is *Vision in Spring* VII, pp. 40–46. "A Symphony" is penciled at top of p. 40 (not Faulkner's handwriting).

b. "Symphony," 4 pp. typescript: burned fragment, 88 lines visible, 71 complete, UT (Butterworth, "Census," Unpublished Poetry, number 33).

c. Untitled, 1 p. typescript: burned fragment, third and part of fourth strophe visible, 24 lines visible, 16 complete, UT (Butterworth, "Census," Unidentified Fragments, number 41).

d. Untitled, 1 p. typescript: burned fragment, 25 lines visible, 22 complete, UT.

e. "Like leaves, like stars along the sky," first line, 1 p. typescript: burned fragment, sixth and parts of fifth and seventh strophes, 22 lines visible, 13 complete, UT.

f. "Pulse, you timbrels, flare and knock," first line, second stanza, 1 p. typescript: burned fragment, 23 lines visible, 17 complete, UT (Butterworth, "Census," Unidentified Fragments, number 41).

g. Untitled, 1 p. typescript: burned fragment, 24 lines visible, 22 complete, UT (Butterworth, "Census," Unidentified Fragments, number 41).

24. Untitled, 8 pp. photocopy of carbon typescript, 92 lines. This is *Vision in Spring* VIII, pp. 47–54. It appears to be a unique copy. I found no other versions or variants in any of the Faulkner collections consulted. Lines 30–31 have overstrike and penciled correction "Led" [not Faulkner's handwriting].

25. According to Blotner, Faulkner began writing *TSATF* as a short story entitled "Twilight" in the spring of 1928 and completed it as a book by October 1928 (Blotner, *Faulkner*, pp. 566, 569, 590).

26. In Faulkner's novels fire destroys a series of essentially *pierrotique* relationships and visions. See, for example, *Sanctuary*, *Light in August*, and *Absalom, Absalom!*

27. For a detailed "speculative" reading of this theme throughout Faulkner's major novels see Irwin, *Doubling and Incest*.

Chapter X. The Mask Unmasked

1. Swinburne, "The Triumph of Time," in *Poems*, pp. 36, 35.

2. "Love Song," 9 pp. photocopy of carbon typescript, 116 lines. This is

Vision in Spring IX, pp. 55–64. Butterworth ("Census," Unpublished Poetry, number 28) calls the "Love Song" fragments at the Humanities Research Center, University of Texas (UT), Faulkner's "Prufrock poem." There are 29 pp. of typescript fragments of a poem similar to "Love Song." Twenty-three sheets of these UT "Prufrock" fragments have holograph drafts of "Love Song" (*Vision in Spring* IX) on the verso. One of these holograph pages (*VIS* IX, lines 60–74) is reproduced in Faulkner, *Vision in Spring*, Appendix B.

3. Faulkner had indulged in brief and very broad parody before. See Blotner, *Faulkner*, pp. 263–270. But "Love Song" was not in this league.

4. That Faulkner is beginning to take a harder look at earlier ideals is clear. Until now, by presenting Pierrot sympathetically, Faulkner has indicated that he considers him a "sublime" and "exalted" figure. "Caricature, parody and travesty (as well as their practical counterpart, unmasking) are directed against people and objects which lay claim to authority and respect, which are in some sense 'sublime'" (Freud, *Jokes*, p. 200).

5. Ibid., p. 201.

6. Dreams and jokes are very dissimilar mental functions: "A dream is a completely asocial mental product; it has nothing to communicate to anyone else. . . . Not only does it not need to set any store by intelligibility, it must actually avoid being understood, for otherwise it would be destroyed; it can only exist in masquerade" (ibid., p. 179).

7. Ibid., pp. 180, 179.

8. Blotner, *Selected Letters*, p. 37.

9. Blotner, *Faulkner*, p. 309.

10. Brooks, *Toward Yoknapatawpha*, p. 13.

11. Faulkner, *The Sound and the Fury*, especially pp. 99, 213–214, 222.

12. Indicating great familiarity with Eliot's 1917 volume Faulkner also alludes in "Love Song" to "Portrait of a Lady" (*VIS* IX, p. 56) and "Preludes" (*VIS* IX, p. 59).

13. Smith, *Poetic Closure*, p. 148.

14. "That—he said, and trembled— / Was my heart, my ancient heart that broke" (*VIS* I, p. 1) and "He rose from stiffened knees" (*VIS* I, p. 5). In *VIS* III, Pierrot's "youth hangs like a bright sword at [his] side" (line 78) and his soul, "a paper lantern . . . that he once carried so carefully before him / Now gutters and drips: the flame is nearly gone" (lines 156, 158–159).

15. Miller, *T. S. Eliot's Personal Waste Land*, p. 66.

16. In discussing influence Bloom notes, in this context, that "the poet confronting his Great Original must find the fault that is not there" (Bloom, *Anxiety of Influence*, p. 31).

17. Smith, *Poetic Closure*, pp. 247–248.

18. Ibid., pp. 248, 147.

19. Blotner, *Faulkner*, photographs, passim. Early photos show him in military uniform while in the late portraits he appears in full hunt regalia.

20. See p. 51.

21. "The realization of impotence, of one's own inability to love, in consequence of mental or physical disorder, has an exceedingly lowering effect upon self-regard" (Freud, "On Narcissism," in *History of the Psychoanalytic Movement*, p. 98).

22. Gavin Stevens's explanation of Joe's motive mirrors the furniture dealer's syntax and offers yet another instance of Faulkner's careful structuring of his language to enforce meaning in this novel. This is also another example of a formal technique Faulkner invented in *Vision in Spring* that he then used to great advantage in fiction:

> He began the story as they rode to town and finished it as they sat on the veranda of Stevens' home, and there recapitulated. "I think I know why it was, why he ran into Hightower's house for refuge at the last. I think it was his grandmother. . . . I dont think that the old lady had any hope of saving him when she came, any actual hope. I believe that all she wanted was that he die 'decent,' as she put it. . . . I think she came here just to watch that old man. . . .
> . . . I believe she told him about Hightower, that Hightower could save him, was going to save him.
> "But of course I dont know what she told him. . . .
> "And he believed her. I think that is what gave him not the courage so much as the passive patience to endure and recognise and accept the one opportunity which he had to break in the middle of that crowded square, manacled, and run. But there was too much running with him, stride for stride with him. Not pursuers: but himself: years, acts, deeds omitted and committed, keeping pace with him, stride for stride, breath for breath, thud for thud of the heart, using a single heart." (*LIA*, pp. 421, 423, 424)

23. Freud, *Jokes*, p. 179.

24. Ibid., p. 189.

25. Aiken's poem concludes his circus symphony, *Turns and Movies*.

a. "The Dancer," 2 pp. photocopy of carbon typescript, 20 lines. This is *Vision in Spring* X, pp. 65–66.

b. "The Dancer," 1 p. typescript, 20 lines in quatrains, beneath the title is typed "to V. de G. F." (Faulkner's step-daughter), University of Virginia (UVa).

c. "Your bonds are strong as steel, but soft—," first complete line, 1 p. typescript: burned fragment, 9 lines visible, 8 complete in quatrains, UT (Butterworth, "Census," Unidentified Fragments, number 60).

26. These lines also serve to extend the meaning of Pierrot's "death" in the final lines of "Love Song": "While darkness lays soft fingers on his eyes / And strokes the lamplight from his brow, to wake him, and he dies" (*VIS* IX, p. 64).

27. a. Untitled, 9 pp. photocopy of carbon typescript, 102 lines. This is *Vision in Spring* XI, pp. 67–75. For prior listing of b–f, see Butterworth, "Census," Published Poetry, number 40.

b. "Marriage," 4 pp. typescript with one holograph correction, UVa. This is *A Green Bough* II.

c. "Marriage," 4 pp. typescript, University of Mississippi Library (Rowanoak Papers).

d. Untitled, 1 p. typescript: burned fragment, 16 lines visible, 12 complete, UT.

e. Untitled, 1 p. typescript: burned fragment, 17 lines visible, 11 complete, UT.

f. Untitled, 1 p. typescript: burned fragment, 13 lines visible, 10 complete, UT.

28. Cleanth Brooks says "Marriage" is "remarkably good, in concept and line by line." He then remarks that it reminds him of the opening section of "Peter Quince at the Clavier." In making this analogy he misses a major formal consideration: Stevens's poem is meditative, Faulkner's is dramatic. Furthermore, its literary influence derives from a very different kind of poet (Brooks, *Toward Yoknapatawpha*, pp. 27, 28). Brooks read "Marriage" out of its context because evidently he did not have the opportunity to see it in *Vision in Spring*. Thus he could not have known how "Marriage" gains in meaning when it is read as part of its sequence.

29. Ibid.

30. Brooks, *Toward Yoknapatawpha*, p. 30.

31. And lightly then she turned away.
Ironic music rippled gay,—
Subtle sarcastic flippancies
Disguising speechless ecstacies . . .
"Play something else . . ." He rose to turn
The pages, while the deep nocturne
Struck slow rich chords of plangent pain,
. . . .
All of her body, hidden so
In saffron satin's flush and flow,—
Its white and simple loveliness,—
Came on his heart like giddiness,
Seductive as this music came;
Until her body seemed like flame,—
Intense white flame . . . (Aiken, "This Dance of Life," in *Turns and Movies*, p. 85)

32. "And in the taxi, sitting dark beside him, / She moved, and touched his knee, / And when he kissed her, hated him, but kissed him, passionately" (Aiken, *Turns and Movies* XI, p. 15).

33. Reading these lines one hears the language of both Hightower's and Joe Christmas's climactic scenes. For Hightower, "thinking begins to slow now. It slows like a wheel beginning to run in sand . . ." (*LIA*, p. 462). "The wheel turns on. It spins now, fading, without progress, as though turned by that final flood which had rushed out of him, leaving his body empty and lighter than a forgotten leaf . . ." (*LIA*, p. 466). As his pursuers watch Christ-

mas die, they see his "pent black blood," which seems "to rush out of his pale body like the rush of sparks from a rising rocket; upon that black blast the man seemed to rise soaring into their memories forever and ever" (*LIA*, p. 440).

34. Bate, *John Keats*, p. x.

35. a. "Orpheus," 7 pp. photocopy of carbon typescript, 79 lines. This is *Vision in Spring* XII, pp. 76–82. See Butterworth, "Census," Published Poetry, number 49.

b. "Orpheus," 2 pp. typescript: burned fragments, 43 lines visible, 40 complete, Beinecke Library, Yale University. This fragment is transcribed in Faulkner, *Vision in Spring*, Appendix B.

c. *A Green Bough* XX (1933) is composed of the first 13 lines plus lines 23–26 of *Vision in Spring* XII, "Orpheus."

Chapter XI. The Novelist's Voice

1. a. "Philosophy," 3 pp. photocopy of carbon typescript, 30 lines. This is *Vision in Spring* XIII, pp. 83–85. See Butterworth, "Census," Published Poetry, number 50.

b. "Philosophy," 2 pp. typescript, 30 lines with one pencil correction apparently not in Faulkner's handwriting, University of Virginia (UVa). This is *A Green Bough* V.

c. Untitled, 1 p. typescript: burned fragment, 17 lines visible, 14 complete, Humanities Research Center, University of Texas (UT).

d. Untitled, 1 p. typescript: burned fragment, part of 1 line visible, UT.

e. Untitled, 1 p. typescript: burned fragment, parts of 4 lines visible, UT.

f. Untitled, 1 p. typescript: burned fragment, parts of 5 lines visible, UT.

g. Untitled, 1 p. typescript: burned fragment, parts of 14 lines visible, UT.

h. Untitled, 1 p. typescript carbon: burned fragment, 15 lines visible, 1 complete, UT. Has holograph instructions in the right margin.

i. Untitled holograph manuscript: burned fragment, last 4 lines are also in *a*, UT.

a. "April," 3 pp. photocopy of carbon typescript, 40 lines. This is *Vision in Spring* XIV, pp. 86–88. At bottom of p. 88 is typed "(end)." Also see Butterworth, "Census," Published Poetry, number 6.

b. "April," *Contempo* 1 (1 February 1932): 2.

c. "April," 2 pp. typescript, UVa.

d. Untitled, 1 p. typescript: burned fragment, 22 lines visible, 18 complete, UT.

e. Untitled, 1 p. typescript: burned fragment, 11 lines visible, 9 complete, UT.

f. Untitled, 1 p. typescript: burned fragment, second and fragments of first and third strophes, 20 lines visible, 18 complete, UT.

2. Freud, *Beyond the Pleasure Principle*, p. 17.

3. William Faulkner, "Sherwood Anderson: An Appreciation," in *Essays, Speeches, and Public Letters by William Faulkner*, ed. James B. Meriwether (New York: Random House, 1965), p. 8.

4. Kinney, *Faulkner's Narrative Poetics*, p. 8.

5. Faulkner, *Flags in the Dust*, pp. 425–429. Both Thomas L. McHaney and George F. Hayhoe have shown how and where this edition of *Flags* is "a corrupt text." But I have used it here as it is the only published edition. For their criticism see George F. Hayhoe, "William Faulkner's *Flags in the Dust*," *Mississippi Quarterly* 28 (Summer 1975): 370–386, and Thomas L. McHaney, "The Text of *Flags in the Dust*," *Faulkner Concordance Newsletter*, no. 2 (November 1973): 7–8.

6. Blotner and others have pointed out that Faulkner used this inscription, despite his mother's disapproval, on his youngest brother's gravestone. Dean died in a flying accident in 1935.

7. As these "heroes" are marble fauns, their visions echo the Marble Faun's vision of stasis and numbness: "my carven eyes embrace" (*TMF* X, p. 36) and "My heart is full, yet sheds no tears / To cool my burning carven eyes" (*TMF*, epilogue, p. 51).

8. Narcissa, like several of Faulkner's fictional women, has her origins firmly planted in *Vision's* eleventh poem, "Marriage." She and her counterpart, her brother's mistress Belle, often dream while they play their respective pianos. As Narcissa plays at the end of *Flags*, she thinks of her brief marriage to the most recent Sartoris suicide. She imagines herself as a totally self-sufficient, pregnant virgin:

> All of Narcissa's instincts had been antipathetic to him; his idea was a threat and his presence a violation of the very depths of her nature: in the headlong violence of him she had been like a lilly in a gale which rocked it to its roots in a sort of vacuum, without any laying-on of hands. . . . the bell itself was untarnished save by the friction of its own petals. The gale is gone and though the lilly is sad a little with vibrations of ancient fears, it is not sorry. (p. 431)

Belle and Narcissa are one more set of Faulkner's prostitute/virgin fictional twins. Here Faulkner uses them, as he will later and more blatantly use Caddy and her mother, to indicate that his hero's desire for sexual union is both narcissistic and incestuous. Faulkner's masturbatory imagery here, composed of symbols from his poetry ("a single lilly" [*TMF*] and the bell [*VIS*]), confirms such a reading.

9. Faulkner's favorite relative besides his mother, his great-aunt Alabama, insisted until her death on calling Faulkner's daughter, Jill, by Jill's dead older sister's name, Alabama. She even addressed Jill's wedding present to Alabama (Jill Faulkner Summers, interview, August 1980).

10. Faulkner indulges in some more private self-parody when in *Soldiers' Pay* Januarius Jones, once again in hot pursuit of female flesh he doesn't want, quotes Faulkner poetry: "As autumn and the moon of death draw nigh" and then hearing "a mocking bird somewhere, somewhere . . . Jones

sighed" (*SP*, p. 315). Faulkner next attaches this same refrain to Gilligan's and the Rector's final visions. Their visions originate in music as they hear singing from a black church: "the crooning submerged passion of the dark race. . . . Feed Thy Sheep, O Jesus. All the longing of mankind for a Oneness with Something, somewhere" (*SP*, p. 319). The effect is, of course, to force the reader to equate Jones's vision with the Rector's and Gilligan's and to conclude that none of these characters have a very firm grasp on reality.

11. Also see *The Marble Faun* X, p. 35 and XVII, p. 48.

Chapter XII. A New Beginning

1. Jill Faulkner Summers, interview, 30 July 1980.
2. Wilde and Borsten, *A Loving Gentleman*, p. 65.
3. Meta Wilde, interview, 4 March 1982.
4. Wilde and Borsten, *A Loving Gentleman*, p. 137.
5. Ibid., p. 138.
6. Ibid., p. 140.
7. In 1955, in discussing his writing in an interview, Faulkner stated this quite precisely when he said, "since words are my talent, I must try to express clumsily in words what the pure music would have done better. That is, music would express better and simpler, *but I prefer to use words as I prefer to read rather than listen. I prefer silence to sound, and the image produced by words occurs in silence. That is, the thunder and the music of the prose take place in silence*" (Meriwether and Millgate, *Lion in the Garden*, p. 248, emphasis added).
8. Meta Wilde, interview, 4 March 1982.
9. Blotner, *Faulkner*, pp. 155, 157, 175, 190. In 1964 and 1969 interviews Estelle Faulkner speaks of her continuing love for dancing and music and her new interest in painting. Both interviews occurred prior to openings of exhibits of her works in Charlottesville. Saying she first began painting in Shanghai when she lived there (1921–1927), she added that she had given it up during the years she spent with Faulkner in Oxford: "Bill's mother, Maud, was an artist. She was one of the reasons I didn't paint in Oxford" (interviews with Estelle Faulkner, *Charlottesville Daily Progress*, 3 November 1964 and 26 January 1969).
10. Jill Faulkner Summers, interview, 20 August 1980. Maud Falkner also maintained an adversary relationship with her son's favorite great-aunt Alabama: "They heartily loathed each other. You felt it—even as a child I felt it. She spoke disparagingly of my father's relationship with Aunt Bama—as if it were some lapse of taste" (Jill Faulkner Summers, interview, 16 March 1982).
11. One source of Estelle Faulkner's "strength" manifests itself in a January 1969 newspaper interview. In it she said, "I have never been bored in my life. Lonely, maybe, but never bored. . . . If you don't have any enthusiasm

you might as well dig a hole and crawl in it" (*Charlottesville Daily Progress*, 26 January 1969).

12. Jill Faulkner Summers, interview, 16 March 1982.

13. Blotner, *Faulkner* , p. 631. According to his step-son Malcolm Franklin, Faulkner "adored his mother. He would stop by every morning at the house on South Street. . . . This became an absolute ritual" (Franklin, *Bitterweeds*, p. 97).

14. Wilde and Borsten, *A Loving Gentleman*, pp. 52, 127, and Meta Wilde, interview, 5 March 1982. See also Franklin, *Bitterweeds*, pp. 23, 24, 45.

15. Faulkner doubled this image in both *Sanctuary* and *Light in August*: Popeye's grandmother is malevolent and his mother ineffectual while Joe's grandmother is ineffectual and his mother dead.

16. Storey, *Pierrot: A Critical History*, p. 152. This description could easily be applied to Popeye, Horace Benbow, or Quentin Compson.

17. Blotner, *Selected Letters*, pp. 24–25.

18. Faulkner wrote this letter on a discarded page of *Elmer* (ibid., p. 25).

19. *Elmer*, corrected to UVa, Accession No. 6074, Box No. 7, Book I, chapter 1, pp. 3–4. These and subsequent quotes from *Elmer* are from the typescript originally at the University of Virginia, now at the University of Mississippi. Quotations courtesy of the University of Mississippi Library and Jill Faulkner Summers. For a transcription of this 136-page typescript, see *Mississippi Quarterly* 36 (Summer 1983): 343–460.

20. This is also a fine oedipal fantasy as it does away completely with the need for an earthly father.

21. *Elmer*, op. cit., pp. 5, 18.

22. Elmer describes his mother's rocker as "the low chair in which his mother rocked while he knelt in an impossible excrutiating rapture with his head in her lap . . ." (ibid., p. 6).

23. Ibid., pp. 5, 18.

24. Blotner, *Faulkner*, pp. 1761–1762.

25. Summers further illuminates this issue with her comments on the importance *Cyrano de Bergerac* had for Faulkner: "I think he identified with Cyrano in that he liked the idea of not being physically held responsible for what he said. It's really like being at a masquerade—you're not expected to complete an action—you can just talk a lot and not be responsible for your words: like Cyrano with Roxane" (Jill Faulkner Summers, interview, 16 March 1982).

26. Blotner, *Faulkner*, p. 397.

27. See ibid., p. 356, and Butterworth, "Census."

28. Blotner, *Selected Letters*, p. 350.

29. Blotner, *Faulkner*, pp. 313, 318, 323, 326, 330.

30. Ibid., pp. 357, 363, 366, 369.

31. Ibid., p. 347, and Blotner, *Selected Letters*, p. 5.

32. *Orpheus, and Other Poems* is thought to have been a revision of the 1921 sequence. Blotner thinks that some of the versions and fragments of drafts of poems in *Vision in Spring* that are in the University of Texas Faulk-

ner Collection were written after 1921 and are therefore revisions made in preparation for the *Orpheus* manuscript (Joseph Blotner, letter, 25 April 1979). Blotner also thinks that it is possible that Faulkner "gave Estelle a carbon of the collection of poems, bound it and titled it *Vision in Spring*, asked her for her comments, then used the ribbon copies to make up *Orpheus, and Other Poems*, which he then sent to Four Seas. It's not impossible that when they sent it back he destroyed it, or kept it and cannibalized it. You noticed all the pencil markings on *Vision in Spring* I'm sure. And they clearly aren't his. I'm sure they are Estelle's" (Joseph Blotner, letter, 4 June 1983).

33. Blotner, *Faulkner*, p. 350.

34. Blotner, *Selected Letters*, p. 6.

35. Blotner, *Faulkner*, p. 350.

36. Ibid., p. 355.

37. Blotner, *Selected Letters*, p. 7.

38. Millgate, *The Achievement of William Faulkner*, p. 10. That Faulkner in 1924 had little emotional investment in *TMF* is suggested by a letter he wrote Wasson, saying the Four Seas Company was publishing it only because they were "unperceptive enough to accept it" (Wasson, *Count No 'Count*, pp. 65–66).

39. In October Faulkner drafted another farewell to his poetic persona. This appeared the following spring in *The Double Dealer* (William Faulkner, "Verse Old and Nascent: A Pilgrimage," *The Double Dealer* 7 [April 1925]: 129–131. Reprinted in Collins, *Early Prose and Poetry*, pp. 114–118). An extant typescript of this essay dated "October 1924" is in the Faulkner Collection at the University of Virginia. This typescript is useful because it dates Faulkner's return to New Orleans during the same month that he gave the Four Seas Company the final proofs for *The Marble Faun* (16 October 1924; Blotner, *Faulkner*, p. 373). With this essay Faulkner formally concludes his apprenticeship to poetry. In it he dismisses both Swinburne and Aiken and says he no longer reads much nineteenth- or twentieth-century poetry: "That page is closed to me forever. I read Robinson and Frost with pleasure, and Aldington; Conrad Aiken's minor music still echoes in my heart; but beyond these, that period might never have been" (pp. 116–117).

40. Blotner, *Faulkner*, p. 397.

41. William Faulkner, *New Orleans Sketches*, ed. Carvel Collins (New Brunswick: Rutgers University Press, 1958).

42. Blotner, *Selected Letters*, pp. 13, 17.

43. Ibid., p. 17. See also letter to Bama McLean in which he records his screen memory and draws another self-portrait. See Blotner, *Selected Letters*, pp. 19–20; this volume, p. 52, and Figure 14.

Bibliography

Adams, Richard P. "The Apprenticeship of William Faulkner." *Tulane Studies in English* 12 (1962): 113–156. Reprinted in Wagner, ed., *Four Decades of Criticism.*

Aiken, Conrad. *The Clerk's Journal: Being the Diary of a Queer Man.* New York: Eakins Press, 1971.

———. *The Divine Pilgrim.* Athens: University of Georgia Press, 1949.

———. *The House of Dust.* Boston: The Four Seas Co., 1920.

———. "The Impersonal Poet." *Poetry Journal* 5 (December 1916): 63–66.

———. *The Jig of Forslin.* Boston: The Four Seas Co., 1916.

———. *Nocturne of Remembered Spring.* Boston: The Four Seas Co., 1917.

———. *Scepticisms, Notes on Contemporary Poetry.* New York: Alfred A. Knopf, 1919.

———. *The Charnel Rose, Senlin: A Biography, and Other Poems.* Boston: The Four Seas Co., 1918.

———. *Turns and Movies and Other Tales in Verse.* Boston: Houghton Mifflin Co., 1916.

Bate, Walter Jackson. *The Burden of the Past and the English Poet.* New York: W. W. Norton and Co., Inc., 1972.

———. *John Keats.* London: Chatto and Windus, 1979.

Beach, Joseph Warren. "Conrad Aiken and T. S. Eliot: Echoes and Overtones." *PMLA* 69 (September 1954): 753–762.

Bleikasten, André. "Pan et Pierrot, ou les premiers masques de Faulkner." *Revue de littérature comparée* (July–September 1979).

Bloom, Harold. *The Anxiety of Influence: A Theory of Poetry.* London and New York: Oxford University Press, 1975.

———. *The Breaking of the Vessels.* Chicago: University of Chicago Press, 1982.

Blotner, Joseph. *Faulkner: A Biography.* New York: Random House, 1974.

———, ed. *Selected Letters of William Faulkner.* New York: Random House, 1977.

———. "William Faulkner's Essay on the Composition of *Sartoris*." *Yale Library Gazette* 47 (January 1973): 121–124.

Bonner, Thomas, Jr., comp. *William Faulkner. The William B. Wisdom Collection: A Descriptive Catalogue.* New Orleans: Tulane University Libraries, 1980.

Booth, Stephen. *An Essay on Shakespeare's Sonnets*. New Haven: Yale University Press, 1969.

Booth, Wayne C. *The Rhetoric of Fiction*. Chicago and London: University of Chicago Press, 1961.

Bowra, C. M. *The Heritage of Symbolism*. London: Macmillan and Co., 1947.

Broach, Vance C. *Grande Dame: A Tribute to Bama Falkner McLean*. Privately printed monograph, 1976. Faulkner Collection, University of Mississippi at Oxford.

Brodsky, Louis Daniel. "Additional Manuscripts of Faulkner's 'A Dead Dancer.'" *Studies in Bibliography* 34 (1981): 267–270.

———. "William Faulkner: Poet at Large." *Southern Review* 18 (Fall 1982): 767–775.

Brooks, Cleanth. *William Faulkner: Toward Yoknapatawpha and Beyond*. New Haven and London: Yale University Press, 1978.

Broughton, Panthea Reid. "An Interview with Meta Carpenter Wilde." *Southern Review* 18 (Fall 1982): 776–801.

Butterworth, Keen. "A Census of Manuscripts and Typescripts of William Faulkner's Poetry." *Mississippi Quarterly* 26 (Summer 1973): 333–359. Reprinted in *A Faulkner Miscellany*, ed. James B. Meriwether. Jackson: University Press of Mississippi, 1974.

Cofield, Jack. *William Faulkner, the Cofield Collection*. Oxford, Miss.: Yoknapatawpha Press, 1978.

Collins, Carvel, ed. *William Faulkner: Early Prose and Poetry*. London: Jonathan Cape, 1963.

Copland, Aaron. *What to Listen for in Music*. New York: New American Library, 1967.

Cowley, Malcolm, ed. *The Faulkner-Cowley File: Letters and Memories, 1944–1962*. New York: Viking Press, 1966.

———, ed. *Writers at Work: The Paris Review Interviews*. New York: Viking Press, 1957.

Crane, Joan St. C. and Anne E. H. Freudenberg. *Man Collecting: Manuscripts and Printed Works of William Faulkner in the University of Virginia Library*. Charlottesville: University of Virginia Press, 1975.

Deutsch, Helene, M.D. "The Impostor: Contribution to Ego Psychology of a Type of Psychopath." *Psychoanalytic Quarterly* 24 (1955): 483–505.

Eliot, T. S. *Collected Poems of T. S. Eliot, 1909–1935*. New York: Harcourt Brace and Co., 1934, 1936.

———. *Four Quartets in Collected Poems, 1909–1962*. New York: Harcourt Brace and World, Inc., 1970.

———. *The Sacred Wood*. London: Methuen and Co. Ltd., 1920.

Erikson, Erik H. "Ego Development and Historical Change." *Psychological Issues* 1, no. 1 (1959): 33–38.

Faulkner, William. *Absalom, Absalom!* New York: Modern Library pbk., 1966.

———. *As I Lay Dying*. New York: Random House, Vintage pbk., 1964.

———. *Essays, Speeches and Public Letters by William Faulkner*, ed. James B. Meriwether. New York: Random House, 1966.

———. *Flags in the Dust*, ed. Douglas Day. New York: Random House, Vintage pbk., 1974.

———. *Helen: A Courtship and Mississippi Poems*, with introductions by Carvel Collins and Joseph Blotner. Oxford, Miss.: Yoknapatawpha Press; New Orleans: Tulane University Press, 1981.

———. *Light in August*. New York: Random House, Modern Library pbk., 1967.

———. *The Marble Faun and A Green Bough*. *The Marble Faun*, copyright 1924 by the Four Seas Co., renewed 1952 by William Faulkner; *A Green Bough*, copyright 1933 and renewed 1960 by William Faulkner. Reissued in one volume. New York: Random House, 1965.

———. *The Marionettes: A Play in One Act*, ed. Noel Polk. Charlottesville: University Press of Virginia, 1977.

———. *Mayday*, with introduction by Carvel Collins. Notre Dame: University of Notre Dame Press, 1980.

———. *Mosquitoes*. New York: Dell pbk., 1965.

———. *Sanctuary*. New York: Random House, Vintage pbk., 1958.

———. *Sanctuary: The Original Text*, ed. Noel Polk. New York: Random House, 1981.

———. *Soldiers' Pay*. New York: Horace Liveright pbk., 1910.

———. *The Sound and the Fury*. New York: Random House, Vintage pbk., 1963.

———. *Vision in Spring*, with introduction by Judith L. Sensibar. Austin: University of Texas Press, 1984.

———. *The Wild Palms*. London: Chatto and Windus, 1970.

Ferguson, Frances C. "The Lucy Poems: Wordsworth's Quest for a Poetic Object," *ELH* 40, no. 4 (Winter 1973): 532–549.

Finkelstein, Lionel, M.D. "The Impostor: Aspects of His Development." *Psychoanalytic Quarterly* 43, no. 1 (1974): 85–155.

Franklin, Malcolm A. *Bitterweeds: Life with William Faulkner at Rowan Oak*. Irving, Tex.: The Society for the Study of Traditional Culture, 1977.

Freud, Sigmund. *Beyond the Pleasure Principle, Group Psychology and Other Works*. Vol. 18 of *The Standard Edition of the Complete Psychological Works of Sigmund Freud*, trans. and ed. James Strachey et al. London: Hogarth Press, 1953–1974.

———. "On Narcissism." In *On the History of the Psychoanalytic Movement, Papers on Metapsychology and Other Works*. Vol. 14 of *The Standard Edition of the Complete Psychological Works of Sigmund Freud*, trans. and ed. James Strachey et al. London: Hogarth Press, 1953–1974.

———. *Jokes and Their Relation to the Unconscious*. Vol. 8 of *The Standard Edition of the Complete Psychological Works of Sigmund Freud*, trans. and ed. James Strachey et al. London: Hogarth Press, 1953–1974.

Gardner, Helen. *The Composition of Four Quartets*. London: Faber and Faber, 1978.

Garrett, George P., Jr. "An Examination of the Poetry of William Faulkner." *Princeton University Library Chronicle* 18, no. 3 (Spring 1957): 124–135. Reprinted in Wagner, ed., *Four Decades of Criticism*.

Gleckner, Robert F. "Keats's Odes: The Problem of the Limited Canon." *Studies in English Literature* 5 (1965): 577–585.

———. "Point of View and Context in Blake's Songs." In *William Blake: Songs of Innocence and Experience*, ed. Margaret Bottrall. Nashville and London: Aurora Publishers, Casebook Series, 1970.

Golden, Arline. "'The Game of Sentiment': Traditions and Innovation in Meredith's *Modern Love*." *ELH* 40, no. 2 (Summer 1973): 264–285.

Greenacre, Phyllis, M.D. "The Childhood of the Artist." *Psychoanalytic Studies of the Child* 12 (1957): 47–72.

———. "The Impostor." *Psychoanalytic Quarterly* 27 (1958): 359–382.

———. "The Relation of the Impostor to the Artist." *Psychoanalytic Study of the Child* 13 (1958): 521–540.

Guerard, Albert. *The Triumph of the Novel*. New York: Oxford University Press, 1976.

Gwynn, Frederick L. and Joseph Blotner, eds. *Faulkner in the University: Class Conferences at the University of Virginia, 1957–1958*. Charlottesville: University Press of Virginia, 1959.

Hamblin, Robert W. and Louis Daniel Brodsky. *Faulkner: A Comprehensive Guide to the Brodsky Collection. Volume I: The Biobibliography*. Jackson: University Press of Mississippi, 1982.

———. "Faulkner's 'L'Apres-Midi d'un Faune': The Evolution of a Poem." *Studies in Bibliography* 33 (1980): 254–263.

———. *Selections from the William Faulkner Collection of Louis Daniel Brodsky: A Descriptive Catalogue*. Charlottesville: University Press of Virginia, 1979.

Hawthorne, Nathaniel. *The Marble Faun*. New York: Federal Book Co., n.d.

Hoffman, Frederick. *Conrad Aiken*. New York: Twayne, 1962.

Irwin, John T. *Doubling and Incest/Repetition and Revenge: A Speculative Reading of Faulkner*. Baltimore and London: Johns Hopkins University Press, 1975.

Kartiganer, Donald. *The Fragile Thread: The Meaning of Form in Faulkner's Novels*. Amherst: University of Massachusetts Press, 1979.

Keats, John. *The Poems of John Keats*. London: Oxford University Press, 1960.

Kenner, Hugh. *A Homemade World: The American Modernist Writers*. New York: Alfred A. Knopf, 1974.

———. *The Invisible Poet: T. S. Eliot*. London: W. H. Allen, 1960.

Kermode, Frank. *The Romantic Image*. New York: Random House, 1957.

Killorin, Joseph, ed. *The Selected Letters of Conrad Aiken*. New Haven and London: Yale University Press, 1978.

Kinney, Arthur F. *Faulkner's Narrative Poetics: Style as Vision*. Amherst: University of Massachusetts Press, 1978.

Kreiswirth, Martin. "Faulkner as Translator: His Versions of Verlaine." *Mississippi Quarterly* 30 (Summer 1977): 429–432.

———. "Faulkner's *The Marble Faun*: Dependence and Independence." *English Studies in Canada* 6 (Fall 1980): 333–344.

Langbaum, Robert. "Browning and the Question of Myth." *The Modern Spirit: Essays on the Continuity of Nineteenth and Twentieth Century Literature*. New York: Oxford University Press, 1970.

———. "The Dynamic Unity of *In Memoriam*." *The Modern Spirit: Essays on the Continuity of Nineteenth and Twentieth Century Literature*. New York: Oxford University Press, 1970.

Lewis, R. W. B. *The American Adam: Innocence, Tragedy, and Tradition in the Nineteenth Century*. Chicago: University of Chicago Press, 1955.

Lipking, Lawrence. *The Life of the Poet: Beginning and Ending Poetic Careers*. Chicago and London: University of Chicago Press, 1981.

Mallarmé, Stéphane. *Selected Poems*, trans. F. MacIntyre. Berkeley, Los Angeles, and London: University of California Press, 1971.

Martin, Jay. *Conrad Aiken: A Life of His Art*. Princeton: Princeton University Press, 1962.

———. "'The Whole Burden of Man's History of His Impossible Heart's Desire': The Early Life of William Faulkner." *American Literature* 53, no. 4 (January 1982): 607–629.

Matthiessen, F. O. *American Renaissance: Art and Expression in the Age of Emerson and Whitman*. London: Oxford University Press, 1974.

McGann, Jerome. *Swinburne: An Experiment in Criticism*. Chicago: University of Chicago Press, 1972.

Mendelson, Edward. *Early Auden*. New York: Viking Press, 1981.

Meriwether, James B. "Faulkner's Essays on Anderson." In *Faulkner: Fifty Years after the Marble Faun*, ed. George H. Wolfe. Tuscaloosa: University of Alabama Press, 1976.

———. *The Literary Career of William Faulkner: A Bibliographical Study*. Princeton: Princeton University Library, 1961.

Meriwether, James B. and Michael Millgate, eds. *Lion in the Garden: Interviews with William Faulkner, 1926–1962*. Lincoln and London: University of Nebraska Press, 1968; Bison Book pbk., 1980.

Mermin, Dorothy M. "Poetry as Fiction: Meredith's *Modern Love*." *ELH* 43, no. 1 (Spring 1976): 100–119.

Miller, James E., Jr. *T. S. Eliot's Personal Waste Land: Exorcism of the Demons*. University Park and London: Pennsylvania State University Press, 1977.

Millgate, Michael. *The Achievement of William Faulkner*. Lincoln and London: University of Nebraska Press, 1963; Bison Book pbk., 1978.

Minter, David. *William Faulkner: His Life and Work*. Baltimore: Johns Hopkins University Press, 1980.

Morrison, Gail Moore. "'Time, Tide, and Twilight': *Mayday* and Faulkner's Quest toward *The Sound and the Fury*." *Mississippi Quarterly* 31 (Summer 1978): 337–358.

Richardson, H. Edward. *William Faulkner: A Journey to Self-Discovery*. Columbia: Missouri University Press, 1969.

Rosenthal, M. L. "Modern British and American Poetic Sequences." *Contemporary Literature* 18, no. 3 (Summer 1977): 416–422.

Russo, John Paul. "A Study in Influence: The Moore-Richards Paradigm." *Critical Inquiry* 5 (Summer 1979): 683–712.

Samway, Patrick. "Faulkner's Poetic Vision." In *Faulkner and the Southern Renaissance*, ed. Doreen Fowler and Ann J. Abadie, pp. 204–244. Jackson: University Press of Mississippi, 1982.

Sensibar, Judith L. "Pierrot and the Marble Faun: Another Fragment." *Mississippi Quarterly* 32 (Summer 1979): 473–476.

———. "William Faulkner, Poet: Origins of His Art (1916?–1936)." Ph.D. dissertation, University of Chicago, 1982.

———. "William Faulkner, Poet to Novelist: An Impostor Becomes an Artist." In *Creative Biography: Proceedings of a Conference at the Chicago Institute for Psychoanalysis, 1982*. New York: International University Press, 1984.

Simpson, Lewis P. "Faulkner and the Southern Symbolism of Pastoral." *Mississippi Quarterly* 28 (Fall 1975): 401–416.

Smith, Barbara Herrnstein. *Poetic Closure: A Study of How Poems End*. Chicago and London: University of Chicago Press, 1968.

Sperry, Stuart M. *Keats the Poet*. Princeton: Princeton University Press, 1973.

Stevens, Holly, ed. *Letters of Wallace Stevens*. New York: Alfred A. Knopf, Inc., 1966.

Storey, Robert F. *Pierrot: A Critical History of a Mask*. Princeton: Princeton University Press, 1978.

Strauss, Dr. Harvey. "A Discussion of Judith L. Sensibar's 'William Faulkner, Poet to Novelist: An Impostor Becomes an Artist.'" In *Creative Biography: Proceedings of a Conference at the Chicago Institute for Psychoanalysis, 1982*. New York: International University Press, 1984.

Swinburne, A. C. *Poems of Algernon Charles Swinburne*, ed. Ernest Rhys. New York: Random House, Modern Library, 1919.

Symons, Arthur. *The Symbolist Movement in Literature*, with an introduction by Richard Ellmann. New York: E. P. Dutton and Co., Inc., 1919, 1958.

Tennyson, Alfred, Lord. *The Poetical Works of Tennyson*. Boston: Cambridge Edition, Houghton Mifflin Co., 1974.

Verlaine, Paul. *Fêtes galantes, la bonne chanson, romances sans paroles*. Manchester: Editions de l'Université de Manchester, 1942.

Wagner, Linda W. *Hemingway and Faulkner: Inventors/Masters*. Metuchen, N.J.: Scarecrow Press, 1975.

————, ed. *William Faulkner: Four Decades of Criticism*. East Lansing: Michigan State University Press, 1973.

Wasson, Ben. *Count No 'Count: Flashbacks to Faulkner*. Jackson: University Press of Mississippi, 1983.

Weinberg, Bernard. *The Limits of Symbolism*. Chicago: University of Chicago Press, 1966.

Wilde, Meta Carpenter and Orin Borsten. *A Loving Gentleman: The Love Story of William Faulkner and Meta Carpenter*. New York: Simon and Schuster, 1976.

Williamson, Alan. "Allen Tate and the Personal Epic." *Southern Review* 12 (Autumn 1976): 714–732.

Wittenberg, Judith Bryant. *Faulkner: The Transfiguration of Biography*. Lincoln: University of Nebraska Press, 1979.

Wyatt, David. *Prodigal Sons: A Study in Authorship and Authority*. Baltimore: Johns Hopkins University Press, 1980.

Yonce, Margaret. "'Shot Down Last Spring': The Wounded Aviators of Faulkner's Wasteland." *Mississippi Quarterly* 31 (Summer 1978): 359–368.

Index

Adams, Richard P., 227 n. 12
Aiken, Conrad: and Eliot, mutual
debts, 122–124, 248 n. 5, 251
n. 32, 254 nn. 53, 56, 256 n. 14;
and Freud, 95, 117–121, 253
nn. 45, 47, 254 n. 49; influence of,
in Faulkner's fiction, 94, 97–98,
124–125, 255 n. 61; influence of,
on Faulkner's imaginative development, 105–106, 119, 250 n. 22;
meets Faulkner, 247–248 n. 3; as
source for Faulkner's poetic mask,
xvii–xviii, 107, 109, 114, 115,
247 n. 3; and theory of "impersonal poet," 120, 122–124. *See
also* Faulkner, William, criticism
by: Review of *Turns and Movies*;
Lilacs, The, influences in: Aiken;
Modernism: Aiken's role in development of; Poem sequences:
"symphonies in verse"; *Vision in
Spring*, influence of Aiken in
—poems by, imitated and/or borrowed from by Faulkner
"Dancing Adairs," in *Vision in
Spring*, 184–188
House of Dust, The, in *The
Lilacs*, 97; in *Vision in Spring*,
257 n. 4, 258 n. 10
Jig of Forslin, The, in *The Lilacs*,
96–97, 246 n. 38; in *Vision in
Spring*, 153, 257 n. 4, 258 nn. 6,
10, 259 n. 15
Nocturne of Remembered Spring,
in *The Lilacs*, 92, 94, 96, 245
n. 37; in *Vision in Spring*, 258

n. 10, 259–260 n. 17
Senlin: A Biography, in *The
Lilacs*, 97; in *Vision in Spring*,
257 n. 4
*Turns and Movies and Other
Tales in Verse*, in *The Lilacs*,
96; in *Vision in Spring*, 158,
185–188, 191, 259–260 n. 17,
260–261 n. 22, 264 nn. 31, 32
Alcohol and alcoholism: Faulkner
and, 38, 43, 219, 235 n. 13, 236
n. 30; Murry Falkner and, 48–50,
116; Pierrot and, xvii, xviii, 36,
116; as theme in Faulkner's fiction, 215, 258–259 n. 13
"American Drama: Inhibitions,"
252 n. 34
Anderson, Sherwood, 54, 84, 197,
221, 235 n. 13
As I Lay Dying, 88, 215, 228–229
n. 19
"Aunt Bama Poems, The," 224 n. 5,
238–239 n. 6

Baird, Helen, 210, 223 n. 2, 250–
251 n. 27
Barr, Caroline "Callie," 52–53, 237
n. 34
Bate, Walter Jackson, xv, 8, 18, 42,
138, 192
Beach, Joseph Warren, 251–252
n. 32
Beer, Thomas, 239 n. 7
Bloom, Harold, 262 n. 16
Blotner, Joseph, xvi, 44, 49, 114,
166, 218, 223 n. 3, 226 nn. 1, 16,